Renault 20
Owners
Workshop
Manual

Ian Coomber

Models covered
Renault 20 TL five-door Saloon; 1647 cc ohv
Renault 20 LS and TS five-door Saloons; 1995 cc ohc
Renault 20 TX five-door Saloon; 2165 cc ohc

Covers automatic transmission and four- and five-speed manual gearboxes
Does not cover diesel-engined models

ISBN 1 85010 065 9

ⓒ   Haynes Publishing Group 1980, 1984

ABCDE
FGHIJ
KLM

Printed in England   (477-6K1)

HAYNES PUBLISHING GROUP
SPARKFORD YEOVIL SOMERSET
BA22 7JJ ENGLAND

HAYNES PUBLICATIONS INC
861 LAWRENCE DRIVE
NEWBURY PARK
CALIFORNIA 91320   USA

British Library Cataloguing in Publication Data

Coomber, Ian
   Renault 20 1976–1984 owners workshop manual.–
(Owners Workshop Manual)
1. Renault automobile
I. Title
629.28'722   TL215.R4
ISBN 1–85010–065–9

Acknowledgements

Thanks are due to Régie Renault for the supply of technical information and certain illustrations, to Castol Limited who supplied lubrication data, and to the Champion Sparking Plug Company who supplied the illustrations showing the various spark plug conditions.

Special thanks are due to all the people at Sparkford who helped in the production of this manual.

About this manual

Its aim

The aim of this manual is to help you get the best value from your car. It can do so in several ways. It can help you decide what work must be done (even should you choose to get it done by a garage), provide information on routine maintenance and servicing, and give a logical course of action and diagnosis when random faults occur. However, it is hoped that you will use the manual by tackling the work yourself. On simpler jobs it may even be quicker than booking the car into a garage, and going there twice to leave and collect it. Perhaps most important, a lot of money can be saved by avoiding the costs the garage must charge to cover its labour and overheads.

The manual has drawings and descriptions to show the function of the various components so that their layout can be understood. Then the tasks are described and photographed in a step-by-step sequence so that even a novice can do the work.

Its arrangement

The manual is divided into thirteen Chapters, each covering a logical sub-division of the vehicle. The Chapters are divided into Sections, numbered with single figures, eg 5; and the Sections into paragraphs (or sub-sections), with decimal numbers following on from the Section they are in, eg 5.1, 5.2, 5.3 etc.

It is freely illustrated, especially in those parts where there is a detailed sequence of operations to be carried out. There are two forms of illustration; figures and photographs. The figures are numbered in sequence with decimal numbers according to their position in the Chapter: eg Fig. 6.4 is the 4th drawing/illustration in Chapter 6. Photographs are numbered (either individually or in related groups) the same as the Section or sub-section of the test where the operation they show is described.

There is an alphabetical index at the back of the manual as well as a contents list at the front.

References to the 'left' or 'right' of the vehicle are in the sense of a person in the driver's seat facing forwards.

Unless otherwise stated, nuts and bolts are removed by turning anti-clockwise, and tightened by turning clockwise.

Vehicle manufacturers continually make changes to specifications and recommendations, and these, when notified, are incorporated into our manuals at the earliest opportunity.

Whilst every care is taken to ensure that the information in this manual is correct, no liability can be accepted by the authors or publishers for loss, damage or injury caused by any errors in, or omissions from, the information given.

Introduction to the Renault 20

The Renault 20 was first introduced to the French market in November 1975 and became available in the United Kingdom in October 1976. The R20 filled the gap in the ranks of the Renault range between the R16 and R30 models. The TL version uses the TX engine of the R16, the bodyshell of the R30 and retains the principal advantages of each. It offers spacious, comfortable transport readily adaptable to the needs of the family motorist, combined with a reliable and economical power unit. The TS version of the R20 became available in November 1977, powered by a newly designed two litre, single overhead camshaft engine. As with the TL, the TS version retains the R30 type body and fittings. In July 1979 an LS version was added to the range, this being intended mainly for fleet use. This model is technically similar to the TS, but without some of the latter's refinements such as central door locking, electric window winders, etc.

A four-speed or five-speed manual transmission is standard fitting dependent on year and model, and automatic transmission is available as an option. The transmission is mounted in-line behind the engine, the transmission casing also housing the differential unit which transmits drive to the front wheels.

The suspension system is independent, front and rear. The braking system comprises disc type brakes at the front with drum type brakes at the rear, operated by a dual circuit incorporating a pressure regulator to the rear wheels. The handbrake is cable operated from a centrally located lever.

Rack and pinion steering is utilised, power assisted steering being a standard fitting on TS models. Also a standard fitting on TS models are the electrically operated front windows. A centralised door locking system is fitted on both models.

Both models are pleasant to look at, and have proved to be reliable, comfortable and generally appealing.

Contents

Renault 20

Dimensions and weights

For LS and TX versions refer to the specifications given for TS models for approximate values

Dimensions
Overall length
TL . . . . 4520 mm (178·0 in)
TS . . . . 4520 mm (178·0 in)

Overall width
TL . . . . 1726 mm (68·0 in)
TS . . . . 1726 mm (68·0 in)

Overall height
TL . . . . 1435 mm (56·5 in)
TS . . . . 1438 mm (56·6 in)

Wheelbase
TL (without power assisted steering) . . . . 2659 mm (104·7 in)
TL (with power assisted steering) . . . . 2665 mm (104·9 in)
TS (with power assisted steering) . . . . 2671 mm (105·1 in)

Front track
TL . . . . 1450 mm (57·0 in)
TS . . . . 1444 mm (56·8 in)

Rear track
TL . . . . 1458 mm (57.4 in)
TS . . . . 1436 mm (56·5 in)

Ground clearance (all models) . . . . 120mm (4·7 in)

Turning circle (between walls)
TL (without power assisted steering) . . . . 11·20 m (441 in)
TL (with power assisted steering) . . . . 11·60 m (446·5 in)
TS (with power assisted steering) . . . . 11·40 m (419·5 in)

Weights
Kerb weights
TL (manual transmission) . . . . 2590 lb (1175 kg)
TL (automatic transmission) . . . . 2678 lb (1215 kg)
TS (manual transmission) . . . . 2778 lb (1260 kg)
TS (automatic transmission) . . . . 2822 lb (1280 kg)

Maximum payload
TL (manual and automatic transmission) . . . . 3560 lb (1615 kg)
TS (manual transmission) . . . . 3726 lb (1690 kg)
TS (automatic transmission) . . . . 3770 lb (1710 kg)

Maximum trailer weight
TL . . . . 2249 lb (1020 kg)
TS . . . . 2866 lb (1300 kg)

Buying spare parts
and vehicle identification numbers

For modifications, and information applicable to later models, see Supplement at end of manual

Buying spare parts

Spare parts are available from many sources, for example: Renault dealers, other garages and accessory shops, and motor factors. Our advice regarding spare part sources is as follows:

Officially appointed Renault garages – This is the best source of parts which are peculiar to your car and are otherwise not generally available (eg complete cylinder heads, internal gearbox components, badges, interior trim etc). It is also the only place at which you should have repairs carried out if your car is still under warranty – non-Renault components may invalidate the warranty. To be sure of obtaining the correct parts it will always be necessary to give the storeman your car's vehicle identification number, and if possible, to take the old part along for positive identification. It obviously makes good sense to go straight to the specialists on your car for this type of part for they are best equipped to supply you.

Other garages and accessory shops – These are often very good places to buy materials and components needed for the maintenance of your car (eg spark plugs, bulbs, fan belts, oils and greases, filler paste etc). They also sell general accessories, usually have convenient opening hours, charge reasonable prices and can often be found not far from home.

Motor factors – Good factors will stock all the more important components which wear out relatively quickly (eg clutch components, pistons, valves, exhaust systems, brake cylinders/pipes/hoses/seals/ shoes and pads etc). Motor factors will often provide new or reconditioned components on a part exchange basis – this can save a considerable amount of money.

Vehicle identification numbers

Modifications are a continuous and unpublicised process carried out by the vehicle manufacturers, so accept the advice of the parts storeman when purchasing a component. Spare parts lists and manuals are compiled upon a numerical basis and individual vehicle numbers are essential to the supply of the correct component.

The vehicle identification plate and *body serial number plate* are located on the top right-hand side of the engine compartment above the headlights.

The body serial number is stamped onto the right-hand side of the engine compartment toward the rear. This should be quoted when ordering body parts.

The engine number plate is located on the cylinder block, positioned as shown on the illustrations. This should be quoted when ordering engine parts.

These identification plates are shown in the accompanying illustrations. The main identification for both vehicle types is as follows:

R20 TL model — *vehicle type R1271*
R20 TS model — *vehicle type R1272*

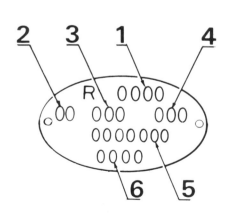

The oval plate gives the following information

1	Factory symbol	4	Optional equipment
2	Vehicle details		originally fitted
3	Equipment number	5	Fabrication number
		6	Model year

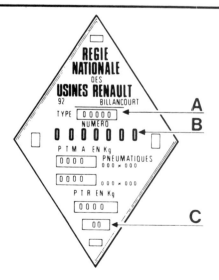

The lozenge plate gives the following information

A	Vehicle type	C	Model year
B	Chassis number		

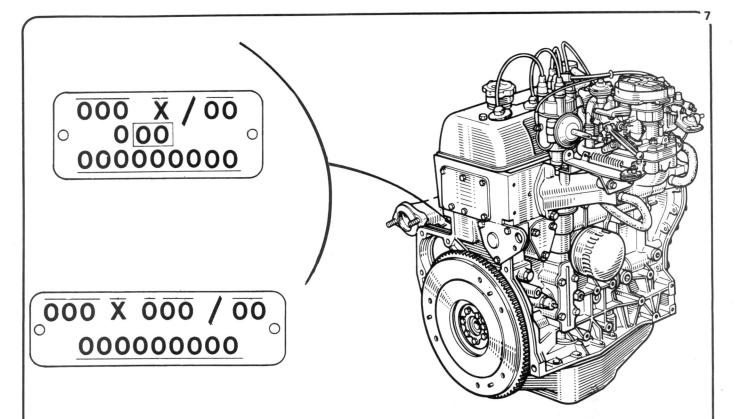

The engine identification plate position on the TL engine — either of the two plate types shown will be fitted

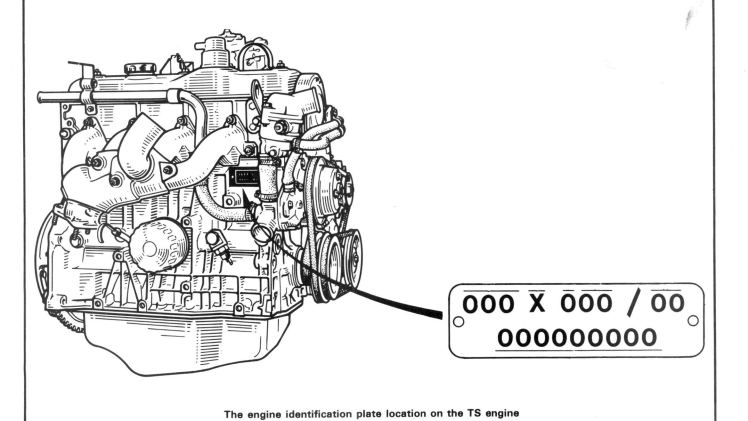

The engine identification plate location on the TS engine

Tools and working facilities

Introduction

A selection of good tools is a fundamental requirement for anyone contemplating the maintenance and repair of a motor vehicle. For the owner who does not possess any, their purchase will prove a considerable expense, offsetting some of the savings made by doing-it-yourself. However, provided that the tools purchased are of good quality, they will last for many years and prove an extremely worthwhile investment.

To help the average owner to decide which tools are needed to carry out the various tasks detailed in this manual, we have compiled three lists of tools under the following headings: *Maintenance and minor repair, Repair and overhaul,* and *Special.* The newcomer to practical mechanics should start off with the *Maintenance and minor repair* tool kit and confine himself to the simpler jobs around the vehicle. Then, as his confidence and experience grows, he can undertake more difficult tasks, buying extra tools as, and when, they are needed. In this way, a *Maintenance and minor repair* tool kit can be built-up into a *Repair and overhaul* tool kit over a considerable period of time without any major cash outlays. The experienced do-it-yourselfer will have a tool kit good enough for most repair and overhaul procedures and will add tools from the *Special* category when he feels the expense is justified by the amount of use to which these tools will be put.

It is obviously not possible to cover the subject of tools fully here. For those who wish to learn more about tools and their use there is a book entitled *How to Choose and Use Car Tools* available from the publishers of this manual.

Maintenance and minor repair tool kit

The tools given in this list should be considered as a minimum requirement if routine maintenance, servicing and minor repair operations are to be undertaken. We recommend the purchase of combination spanners (ring one end, open-ended the other); although more expensive than open-ended ones, they do give the advantages of both types of spanner.

Combination spanners - 9, 10, 11, 12, 13, 14, & 17 mm
Adjustable spanner - 9 inch
Engine sump/gearbox drain plug key (where applicable)
Spark plug spanner (with rubber insert)
Spark plug gap adjustment tool
Set of feeler gauges
Brake adjuster spanner (where applicable)
Brake bleed nipple spanner
Screwdriver - 4 in long x $\frac{1}{4}$ in dia (flat blade)
Screwdriver - 4 in long x $\frac{1}{4}$ in dia (cross blade)
Combination pliers - 6 inch
Hacksaw, junior
Tyre pump

Tyre pressure gauge
Oil can
Fine emery cloth (1 sheet)
Wire brush (small)
Funnel (medium size)

Repair and overhaul tool kit

These tools are virtually essential for anyone undertaking any major repairs to a motor vehicle, and are additional to those given in the *Maintenance and minor repair* list. Included in this list is a comprehensive set of sockets. Although these are expensive they will be found invaluable as they are so versatile - particularly if various drives are included in the set. We recommend the $\frac{1}{2}$ in square-drive type, as this can be used with most proprietary torque wrenches. If you cannot afford a socket set, even bought piecemeal, then inexpensive tubular box spanners are a useful alternative.

The tools in this list will occasionally need to be supplemented by tools from the *Special* list.

Sockets (or box spanners) to cover range in previous list
Reversible ratchet drive (for use with sockets)
Extension piece, 10 inch (for use with sockets)
Universal joint (for use with sockets)
Torque wrench (for use with sockets)
'Mole' wrench - 8 inch
Ball pein hammer
Soft-faced hammer, plastic or rubber
Screwdriver - 6 in long x $\frac{5}{16}$ in dia (flat blade)
Screwdriver - 2 in long x $\frac{5}{16}$ in square (flat blade)
Screwdriver - 1$\frac{1}{2}$ in long x $\frac{1}{4}$ in dia (cross blade)
Screwdriver - 3 in long x $\frac{1}{8}$ in dia (electricians)
Pliers - electricians side cutters
Pliers - needle nosed
Pliers - circlip (internal and external)
Cold chisel - $\frac{1}{2}$ inch
Scriber (this can be made by grinding the end of a broken hacksaw blade)
Scraper (this can be made by flattening and sharpening one end of a piece of copper pipe)
Centre punch
Pin punch
Hacksaw
Valve grinding tool
Steel rule/straight edge
Allen keys
Selection of files
Wire brush (large)
Axle-stands
Jack (strong scissor or hydraulic type)

Special tools

The tools in this list are those which are not used regularly, are expensive to buy, or which need to be used in accordance with their manufacturers' instructions. Unless relatively difficult mechanical jobs are undertaken frequently, it will not be economic to buy many of these tools. Where this is the case, you could consider clubbing together with friends (or a motorists' club) to make a joint purchase, or borrowing the tools against a deposit from a local garage or tool hire specialist.

The following list contains only those tools and instruments freely available to the public, and not those special tools produced by the vehicle manufacturer specifically for its dealer network. You will find occasional references to these manufacturers' special tools in the text of this manual. Generally, an alternative method of doing the job without the vehicle manufacturer's special tool is given. However, sometimes, there is no alternative to using them. Where this is the case and the relevant tool cannot be bought or borrowed you will have to entrust the work to a franchised garage.

Valve spring compressor
Piston ring compressor
Balljoint separator
Universal hub/bearing puller
Impact screwdriver
Micrometer and/or vernier gauge
Dial gauge
Stroboscopic timing light
Dwell angle meter/tachometer
Universal electrical multi-meter
Cylinder compression gauge
Lifting tackle
Trolley jack
Light with extension lead

Buying tools

For practically all tools, a tool factor is the best source since he will have a very comprehensive range compared with the average garage or accessory shop. Having said that, accessory shops often offer excellent quality tools at discount prices, so it pays to shop around.

Remember, you don't have to buy the most expensive items on the shelf, but it is always advisable to steer clear of the very cheap tools. There are plenty of good tools around at reasonable prices, so ask the proprietor or manager of the shop for advice before making a purchase.

Care and maintenance of tools

Having purchased a reasonable tool kit, it is necessary to keep the tools in a clean serviceable condition. After use, always wipe off any dirt, grease and metal particles using a clean, dry cloth, before putting the tools away. Never leave them lying around after they have been used. A simple tool rack on the garage or workshop wall, for items such as screwdrivers and pliers is a good idea. Store all normal spanners and sockets in a metal box. Any measuring instruments, gauges, meters, etc, must be carefully stored where they cannot be damaged or become rusty.

Take a little care when tools are used. Hammer heads inevitably become marked and screwdrivers lose the keen edge on their blades from time to time. A little timely attention with emery cloth or a file will soon restore items like this to a good serviceable finish.

Working facilities

Not to be forgotten when discussing tools, is the workshop itself. If anything more than routine maintenance is to be carried out, some form of suitable working area becomes essential.

It is appreciated that many an owner mechanic is forced by circumstances to remove an engine or similar item, without the benefit of a garage or workshop. Having done this, any repairs should always be done under the cover of a roof.

Wherever possible, any dismantling should be done on a clean flat workbench or table at a suitable working height.

Any workbench needs a vice: one with a jaw opening of 4 in (100 mm) is suitable for most jobs. As mentioned previously, some clean dry storage space is also required for tools, as well as the lubricants, cleaning fluids, touch-up paints and so on which become necessary.

Another item which may be required, and which has a much more general usage, is an electric drill with a chuck capacity of at least $\frac{5}{16}$ in

(8 mm). This, together with a good range of twist drills, is virtually essential for fitting accessories such as wing mirrors and reversing lights.

Last, but not least, always keep a supply of old newspapers and clean, lint-free rags available, and try to keep any working area as clean as possible.

Spanner jaw gap comparison table

Jaw gap (in)	Spanner size
0·250	$\frac{1}{4}$ in AF
0·276	7 mm
0·313	$\frac{5}{16}$ in AF
0·315	8 mm
0·344	$\frac{11}{32}$ in AF; $\frac{1}{8}$ in Whitworth
0·354	9 mm
0·375	$\frac{3}{8}$ in AF
0·394	10 mm
0·433	11 mm
0·438	$\frac{7}{16}$ in AF
0·445	$\frac{3}{16}$ in Whitworth; $\frac{1}{4}$ in BSF
0·472	12 mm
0·500	$\frac{1}{2}$ in AF
0·512	13 mm
0·525	$\frac{1}{4}$ in Whitworth; $\frac{5}{16}$ in BSF
0·551	14 mm
0·563	$\frac{9}{16}$ in AF
0·591	15 mm
0·600	$\frac{5}{16}$ in Whitworth; $\frac{3}{8}$ in BSF
0·625	$\frac{5}{8}$ in AF
0·630	16 mm
0·669	17 mm
0·686	$\frac{11}{16}$ in AF
0·709	18 mm
0·710	$\frac{3}{8}$ in Whitworth; $\frac{7}{16}$ in BSF
0·748	19 mm
0·750	$\frac{3}{4}$ in AF
0·813	$\frac{13}{16}$ in AF
0·820	$\frac{7}{16}$ in Whitworth; $\frac{1}{2}$ in BSF
0·866	22 mm
0·875	$\frac{7}{8}$ in AF
0·920	$\frac{1}{2}$ in Whitworth; $\frac{9}{16}$ in BSF
0·938	$\frac{15}{16}$ in AF
0·945	24 mm
1·000	1 in AF
1·010	$\frac{9}{16}$ in Whitworth; $\frac{5}{8}$ in BSF
1·024	26 mm
1·063	$1\frac{1}{16}$ in AF; 27 mm
1·100	$\frac{5}{8}$ in Whitworth; $\frac{11}{16}$ in BSF
1·125	$1\frac{1}{8}$ in AF
1·181	30 mm
1·200	$\frac{11}{16}$ in Whitworth; $\frac{3}{4}$ in BSF
1·250	$1\frac{1}{4}$ in AF
1·260	32 mm
1·300	$\frac{3}{4}$ in Whitworth; $\frac{7}{8}$ in BSF
1·313	$1\frac{5}{16}$ in AF
1·390	$\frac{13}{16}$ in Whitworth; $\frac{15}{16}$ in BSF
1·417	36 mm
1·438	$1\frac{7}{16}$ in AF
1·480	$\frac{7}{8}$ in Whitworth; 1 in BSF
1·500	$1\frac{1}{2}$ in AF
1·575	40 mm; $\frac{15}{16}$ in Whitworth
1·614	41 mm
1·625	$1\frac{5}{8}$ in AF
1·670	1 in Whitworth; $1\frac{1}{8}$ in BSF
1·688	$1\frac{11}{16}$ in AF
1·811	46 mm
1·813	$1\frac{13}{16}$ in AF
1·860	$1\frac{1}{8}$ in Whitworth; $1\frac{1}{4}$ in BSF
1·875	$1\frac{7}{8}$ in AF
1·969	50 mm
2·000	2 in AF
2·050	$1\frac{1}{4}$ in Whitworth; $1\frac{3}{8}$ in BSF
2·165	55 mm
2·362	60 mm

Jacking and towing

Jacking

The jack supplied with the vehicle is not designed for service or repair operations, but purely for changing a wheel in the event of a puncture. A strong pillar or trolley type jack should be employed for maintenance and repair tasks requiring the vehicle to be raised.

The jack point location is of particular importance on a vehicle of this type. Always locate a wood block between the jack and chassis to protect the metal from deforming.

At the front, position the jack directly underneath the sidemembers and in line with the suspension arm centres. At the rear, position the jack under the triangular suspension arms so that the wood block straddles the two, locating in the holes as shown in the accompanying illustrations. At the side, position the jack and block as shown directly under the body valance under the front door.

Note: *Never lift the vehicle with the jack under the steering or suspension components or under the towing hooks.*

Towing

Should you have the misfortune to require the vehicle to be towed home or to a garage, it is essential that the correct procedure is adhered to.

Where possible, use a tow rope (in preference to chains) and ensure that it is of sufficient length. Towing hooks are provided at the front and rear of the vehicle as shown in the illustrations, and only these should be used for towing or when being towed. Never attach the tow rope to suspension or body parts.

When towing a vehicle equipped with automatic transmission, it must be remembered that the transmission fluid pump is driven directly by the engine. The front wheels must therefore be raised clear of the ground when towing.

Under circumstances in which the maximum distance to be towed does not exceed 30 miles (50 km), the vehicle may be towed normally at a speed of 18 mph (30 km/h) or less, but an extra 4 pints (2 litres) of transmission fluid must be added to the transmission before commencing the journey. This additional oil must then be drained off on arrival at your destination.

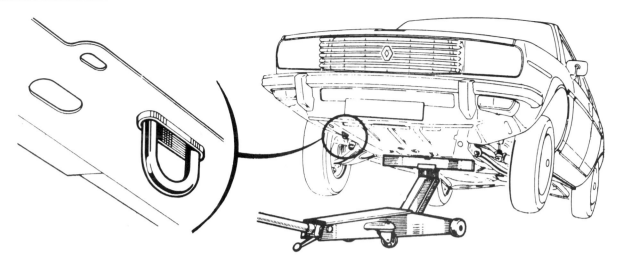

The towing eye location at the front of the vehicle – note jacking position

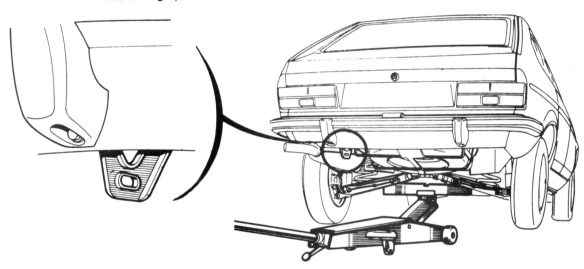

The towing eye location at the rear of the vehicle – note jacking position

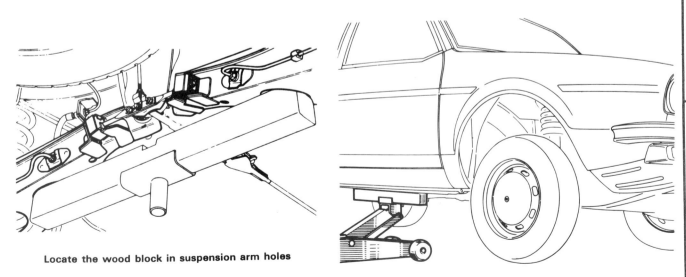

Locate the wood block in suspension arm holes

Jack location for side lifting

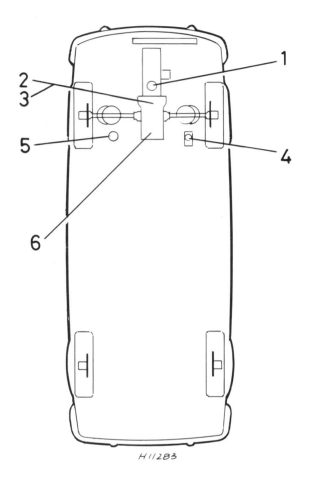

H11283

Recommended lubricants and fluids

Component or system	Lubricant type or specifications
Engine (1)	20W/50 multigrade engine oil
Manual transmission (2)	SAE 80W hypoid gear oil to API GL4 or API GL5
Automatic transmission (3)	Automatic transmission fluid (Dexron type)
Brake fluid reservoir (4)	SAE J1703 hydraulic fluid
Power assisted steering (5)	Automatic transmission fluid (Dexron type)
Final drive (6)	SAE 80W hypoid gear oil to API GL5

Safety First!

Professional motor mechanics are trained in safe working procedures. However enthusiastic you may be about getting on with the job in hand, do take the time to ensure that your safety is not put at risk. A moment's lack of attention can result in an accident, as can failure to observe certain elementary precautions.

There will always be new ways of having accidents, and the following points do not pretend to be a comprehensive list of all dangers; they are intended rather to make you aware of the risks and to encourage a safety-conscious approach to all work you carry out on your vehicle.

Essential DOs and DON'Ts

DON'T rely on a single jack when working underneath the vehicle. Always use reliable additional means of support, such as axle stands, securely placed under a part of the vehicle that you know will not give way.

DON'T attempt to loosen or tighten high-torque nuts (e.g. wheel hub nuts) while the vehicle is on a jack; it may be pulled off.

DON'T start the engine without first ascertaining that the transmission is in neutral (or 'Park' where applicable) and the parking brake applied.

DON'T suddenly remove the filler cap from a hot cooling system — cover it with a cloth and release the pressure gradually first, or you may get scalded by escaping coolant.

DON'T attempt to drain oil until you are sure it has cooled sufficiently to avoid scalding you.

DON'T grasp any part of the engine, exhaust or catalytic converter without first ascertaining that it is sufficiently cool to avoid burning you.

DON'T syphon toxic liquids such as fuel, brake fluid or antifreeze by mouth, or allow them to remain on your skin.

DON'T inhale brake lining dust — it is injurious to health

DON'T allow any spilt oil or grease to remain on the floor — wipe it up straight away, before someone slips on it.

DON'T use ill-fitting spanners or other tools which may slip and cause injury.

DON'T attempt to lift a heavy component which may be beyond your capability — get assistance.

DON'T rush to finish a job, or take unverified short cuts.

DON'T allow children or animals in or around an unattended vehicle.

DO wear eye protection when using power tools such as drill, sander, bench grinder etc, and when working under the vehicle.

DO use a barrier cream on your hands prior to undertaking dirty jobs — it will protect your skin from infection as well as making the dirt easier to remove afterwards; but make sure your hands aren't left slippery.

DO keep loose clothing (cuffs, tie etc) and long hair well out of the way of moving mechanical parts.

DO remove rings, wristwatch etc, before working on the vehicle — especially the electrical system.

DO ensure that any lifting tackle used has a safe working load rating adequate for the job.

DO keep your work area tidy — it is only too easy to fall over articles left lying around.

DO get someone to check periodically that all is well, when working alone on the vehicle.

DO carry out work in a logical sequence and check that everything is correctly assembled and tightened afterwards.

DO remember that your vehicle's safety affects that of yourself and others. If in doubt on any point, get specialist advice.

IF, in spite of following these precautions, you are unfortunate enough to injure yourself, seek medical attention as soon as possible.

Fire

Remember at all times that petrol (gasoline) is highly flammable. Never smoke, or have any kind of naked flame around, when working on the vehicle. But the risk does not end there — a spark caused by an electrical short-circuit, by two metal surfaces contacting each other, or even by static electricity built up in your body under certain conditions, can ignite petrol vapour, which in a confined space is highly explosive.

Always disconnect the battery earth (ground) terminal before working on any part of the fuel system, and never risk spilling fuel on to a hot engine or exhaust.

It is recommended that a fire extinguisher of a type suitable for fuel and electrical fires is kept handy in the garage or workplace at all times. Never try to extinguish a fuel or electrical fire with water.

Fumes

Certain fumes are highly toxic and can quickly cause unconsciousness and even death if inhaled to any extent. Petrol (gasoline) vapour comes into this category, as do the vapours from certain solvents such as trichloroethylene. Any draining or pouring of such volatile fluids should be done in a well ventilated area.

When using cleaning fluids and solvents, read the instructions carefully. Never use materials from unmarked containers — they may give off poisonous vapours.

Never run the engine of a motor vehicle in an enclosed space such as a garage. Exhaust fumes contain carbon monoxide which is extremely poisonous; if you need to run the engine, always do so in the open air or at least have the rear of the vehicle outside the workplace.

If you are fortunate enough to have the use of an inspection pit, never drain or pour petrol, and never run the engine, while the vehicle is standing over it; the fumes, being heavier than air, will concentrate in the pit with possibly lethal results.

The battery

Never cause a spark, or allow a naked light, near the vehicle's battery. It will normally be giving off a certain amount of hydrogen gas, which is highly explosive.

Always disconnect the battery earth (ground) terminal before working on the fuel or electrical systems.

If possible, loosen the filler plugs or cover when charging the battery from an external source. Do not charge at an excessive rate or the battery may burst.

Take care when topping up and when carrying the battery. The acid electrolyte, even when diluted, is very corrosive and should not be allowed to contact the eyes or skin.

If you ever need to prepare electrolyte yourself, always add the acid slowly to the water, and never the other way round. Protect against splashes by wearing rubber gloves and goggles.

When jump starting a car using a booster battery, for negative earth (ground) vehicles, connect the jump leads in the following sequence: First connect one jump lead between the positive (+) terminals of the two batteries. Then connect the other jump lead first to the negative (−) terminal of the booster battery, and then to a good earthing (ground) point on the vehicle to be started, at least 18 in (45 cm) from the battery if possible. Ensure that hands and jump leads are clear of any moving parts, and that the two vehicles do not touch. Disconnect the leads in the reverse order.

Mains electricity

When using an electric power tool, inspection light etc which works from the mains, always ensure that the appliance is correctly connected to its plug and that, where necessary, it is properly earthed (grounded). Do not use such appliances in damp conditions and, again, beware of creating a spark or applying excessive heat in the vicinity of fuel or fuel vapour.

Ignition HT voltage

A severe electric shock can result from touching certain parts of the ignition system, such as the HT leads, when the engine is running or being cranked, particularly if components are damp or the insulation is defective. Where an electronic ignition system is fitted, the HT voltage is much higher and could prove fatal.

Routine maintenance

For modifications, and information applicable to later models, see Supplement at end of manual

Maintenance is essential for ensuring safety and desirable for the purpose of getting the best in terms of performance and economy from your car. Over the years the need for periodic lubrication – oiling, greasing and so on – has been drastically reduced if not totally eliminated. This has unfortunately tended to lead some owners to think that because no such action is required, components either no longer exist, or will last forever. This is a serious delusion. It follows therefore that the largest initial element of maintenance is visual examination. This may lead to repairs or renewals.

The summary below gives a schedule of routine maintenance operations. More detailed information on the respective items is given in the Chapter concerned. Before starting on any maintenance procedures, make a list and obtain any items or parts that may be required. Make sure you have the necessary tools to complete the servicing requirements. Where the vehicle has to be raised clear of the ground pay particular attention to safety and ensure that chassis stands and/or blocks supplement the jack. Do not rely on the jack supplied with the car – it was designed purely to raise the car for changing a wheel in the event of a puncture.

Every 250 miles (400 km) or weekly – whichever comes first

Check the oil level in the sump and top-up with the correct grade of oil, if required (photos)
Check the coolant level in the expansion bottle and top-up as detailed in Chapter 2, if necessary
Check the windscreen washer bottle fluid level and top-up, if necessary (photo)
Check the battery electrolyte level (see Chapter 10) (photo)
Make a general inspection for oil, water or petrol leaks and repair as necessary
Check tyre pressures (photo)
Examine tyres for wear

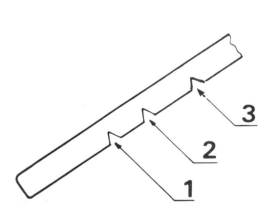

Automatic transmission oil level dipstick markers. With transmission cold 1 is minimum mark and 2 is maximum. With transmission hot 2 is minimum mark and 3 is maximum

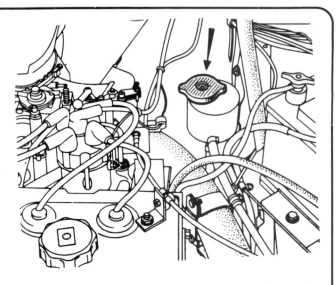

Check the power steering oil level in reservoir (arrowed)

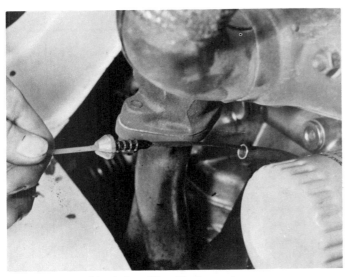

Check the oil level in the engine ...

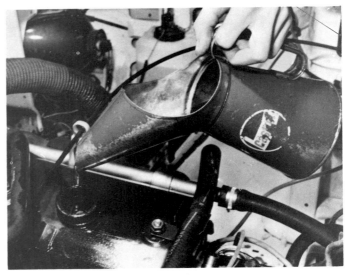

... and top-up if necessary

Check windscreen washer bottle and top-up if necessary

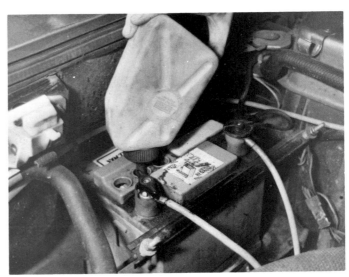

Top-up battery electrolyte level – see Chapter 10

Check the tyre pressures

Top-up the brake master cylinder

Check the correct operation of all lights
Check the operation of the flasher units
Check the operation of the windscreen wipers and washer
Check the operation and efficiency of the horn

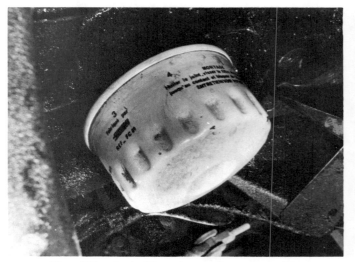

The oil filter in the TL engine – not very accessible

Every 3000 miles (5000 km) or six months – whichever comes first

Undertake all items listed previously, and in addition carry out the following procedures:
Remove, clean and reset the spark plugs
Wipe the ignition leads clean and check their connections for security
Inspect the condition and tension of the alternator drive belt. On TS models, the power steering pump drivebelt must also be checked. Adjust/renew as necessary
Check the fluid level in the brake master cylinder and top-up if necessary (photo). The constant necessity to top-up the fluid level indicates a fault in the brake circuit and this must be looked into without delay – see Chapter 9
Check the transmission oil level. On manual transmissions, there is an oil level plug on the side of the housing, whilst automatic transmissions have a dipstick. Full instructions for checking and topping-up the automatic transmission are given in Chapter 7. The dipstick marker positions are shown in the accompanying illustration
Raise the vehicle and make a brief inspection of the steering and suspension components to ensure they are secure and in serviceable condition. On models with power steering, check the oil level in the power steering reservoir and top-up if necessary, as shown in the accompanying illustration

The engine oil drain plug

Every 6000 to 9000 miles (10 000 to 15 000 km) or twelve months – whichever comes first

Every year, drain the cooling system and renew the anti-freeze solution, see Chapter 2
Renew the engine oil. Drain the oil into a suitable container. This should be done immediately after using the car, as the oil will be hot and flow more easily. When drained, refit the sump plug and refill with the recommended lubricant to the required level (photo)
Renew the oil filter. Wipe the oil filter body with a dry rag to remove any oil, and grip firmly by hand and unscrew to remove (photo). Allow for a certain amount of oil spillage and place a container or rag under the filter. It may be necessary to unscrew the filter using a strap wrench, if it is reluctant to move. Lubricate the new seal and screw the new filter into position, tightening firmly under hand pressure only. When the engine is restarted, check for signs of leakage around the filter joint
Check the carburettor linkages and adjustments as given in Chapter 3
Renew the air filter as given in Chapter 3 (photo)
Check the fuel lines for leaks and security. Clean fuel pump and filter gauze of sediment. Check that the inlet and exhaust manifolds are securely located
Remove distributor cap and check contact points adjustment at 6000 miles (9600 km). Clean and adjust as necessary. At 9000 miles (15 000 km) it is advisable to renew spark plugs and contact points
On automatic transmission models, check around the housing for signs of leakage and, if necessary, make adjustment to the kickdown switch control and the governor computer cable, as given in Chapter 7
At 9000 mile (15 000 km) intervals, drain the differential oil and renew it with the correct grade of lubricant
Check the clutch operating clearance as given in Chapter 5 and, if necessary, adjust
Check (and top-up if necessary) the hydraulic fluid level in the brake master cylinder reservoir
Make an inspection of all rigid and flexible brake hoses and connections, look for signs of leakage and/or deterioration, renew as applicable
Check the disc pad wear detector wiring connections are secure (if fitted)
Inspect the pads for wear and renew if necessary
Check the rear brake shoe linings for wear, and generally clean and inspect each rear brake assembly. Renew any linings worn beyond the specified limit
Check the handbrake adjustment and tape up any excess play, if necessary. Check the cable and linkages for wear or defects
Check the driveshafts for any signs of oil leakage and also for wear in

Renewing the air filter on the TL engine – the TS filter is similar

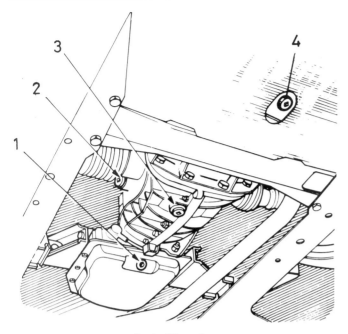

Drain filler plugs

1 Drain plug – automatic transmission
2 Level/filler plug – differential
3 Drain plug – differential
4 Drain plug – engine

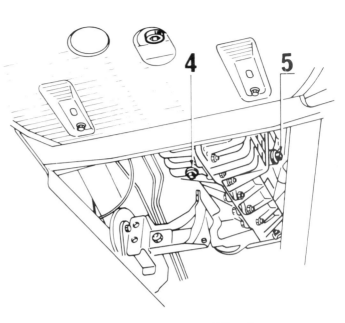

Manual gearbox drain and filler plugs

4 Drain plug   5 Level/filler plug

the joint. Renew if necessary

Check the respective steering and suspension joints for signs of excessive wear. Check the shock absorbers for any signs of leakage and also for security

Check the wheel hubs for play and the wheel retaining nuts for security

Inspect the tyres for signs of excessive or uneven wear. If uneven wear is present, this is due to incorrect pressures or steering alignment.

Make an inspection of the exhaust system. Look for signs of insecurity, leakage, damage or general decay and make repairs or renew as necessary

Check, and repair as necessary, the respective body fittings. In particular, pay attention to the bumpers and mountings, the door and tailgate hinges and catches

Where fitted, check the sunroof drainage channels

Check the seat belt mountings for security

Check around the underbody for signs of corrosion and repair as necessary. Minor repairs to bodywork and paint work are dealt with in Chapter 12

Every 18 000 miles (30 000 km) or two years – whichever comes first

---

Renew the manual gearbox oil. If possible, do this immediately after driving the car, as the oil will be hot and drain more easily. Park the car on flat and level ground. Position a suitable container beneath the gearbox and remove the drain and level/filler plugs. On completion of draining, refit the drain plug and fill the gearbox with oil until the level coincides with the level/filler plug hole. Refit the filler plug

Drain the automatic transmission fluid and renew – see Chapter 7

Remove the brake servo filter and clean or renew it

Every 36 000 miles (60 000 km) or four years – whichever comes first

---

Renew the ohc engine rocker shaft oil filter

Renew the ohc engine timing drivebelt

Chapter 1 Engine

For modifications, and information applicable to later models, see Supplement at end of manual

Contents

Specifications

Overhead valve engine (R1271 20TL models)
Engine (general)
Type:
   With manual transmission 843-20
   With automatic transmission . . . . : . . 843-21
Number of cylinders 4

Bore	79 mm
Stroke	84 mm
Cubic capacity	1647 cm^3
Compression ratio	9.25 to 1
Maximum power	90 bhp (DIN) at 5750 rpm
Maximum torque	97 lbf ft at 3500 rpm
Firing order	1–3–4–2
Static ignition advance	10° ± 1°
Valve gear type	ohv
Valve clearances (cold):	
Inlet	0.20 mm (0.008 in)
Exhaust	0.25 mm (0.010 in)

Cylinder head

Height – standard	93.50 mm (3.681 in)
Minimum after machining	93.00 mm (3.661 in)
Allowable contact face distortion	0.05 mm (0.002 in)

Valve assemblies

Valve seat angles (included):	
Inlet	90°
Exhaust	90°
Valve seat width:	
Inlet	1.5 to 1.8 mm (0.059 to 0.071 in)
Exhaust	1.7 to 2.0 mm (0.067 to 0.079 in)
Outside diameter:	
Inlet	42 mm (1.654 in)
Exhaust	37.1 mm (1.460 in)
Valve stem diameter (inlet and exhaust)	8 mm (0.315 in)
Valve head diameter:	
Inlet	38.7 mm (1.523 in)
Exhaust	34.5 mm (1.358 in)
Valve guides:	
Bore (inlet and exhaust)	8 mm (0.315 in)
Standard outside diameter	13 mm (0.512 in)
Valve spring free length (inlet and exhaust)	40.25 mm (1.58 in)

Camshaft

Number of support bearings	4
Endfloat	0.05 to 0.12 mm (0.002 to 0.004 in)
Valve timing:	
Inlet opens	30° BTDC
Inlet closes	72° ABDC
Exhaust opens	72° BBDC
Exhaust closes	30° ATDC

Tappets

External diameter:	
Standard	12 mm (0.472 in)
Oversize	12.20 mm (0.480 in)

Pushrods

Length – inlet	79 mm (3.125 in)
Length – exhaust	110 mm (4.343 in)
Diameter	6 mm (0.236 in)

Cylinder block liners

Bore diameter	79 mm (3.110 in)
Location diameter at base	84 mm (3.307 in)
Liner projection (less O-ring)	0.10 to 0.17 mm (0.004 to 0.006 in)

Pistons

Type	Alloy – three rings
Gudgeon pin fitting	Press fit in small-end and floating in piston
Piston rings – standard widths:	
Top	1.75 mm (0.069 in)
2nd (taper)	2.0 mm (0.079 in)
Oil scraper	4.0 mm (0.158 in)
Gudgeon pin:	
Outside diameter	21 mm (0.827 in)
Length	69 mm (2.687 in)

Connecting rods

Bearing shell type	Aluminium/tin
Small-end float	0.31 to 0.57 mm (0.012 to 0.022 in)

Crankshaft

Number of main bearings	5
Main bearing shell material	Aluminium/tin
Crankshaft endfloat	0.05 to 0.23 mm (0.002 to 0.009 in)
Thrust washer thicknesses available	2.80 mm (0.110 in)
	2.85 mm (0.112 in)
	2.90 mm (0.114 in)
	2.95 mm (0.116 in)

Main bearing journal diameters:

Standard $\qquad$ $54.80 \text{ mm } {}^{+\,0.013}_{-\,0.011} \, (2.158 \text{ in } {}^{+\,0.0005}_{-\,0.0004})$

Regrind diameter for undersize shells	54.55 mm (2.148 in)

Crankpin diameter:

Standard	48 mm (1.890 in)
Regrind diameter for undersize shells	47.75 mm (1.880 in)

Engine lubrication

Oil capacity	7 pt (4 litres)

Oil pressure:

At idle speed	2 bars (30 lbf/in^2)
4000 rpm	4 bars (60 lbf/in^2)

Torque wrench settings

	Nm	lbf ft
Cylinder head bolts:		
Initial tightening – cold	40.0	30
Final tightening – cold	77.50 to 82.50	55 to 65
Final tightening – hot	85.0 to 90.0	60 to 65
Rocker cover bolts	8.0	6.0
Flywheel bolts – manual transmission	50.0	35
Driveplate bolts – automatic transmission	45.0	35
Connecting rod bolts	45.0	35
Main bearing cap bolts	65.0	45
Crankshaft pulley bolt	60 to 80	45 to 55

Overhead camshaft engine (R1272 20TS models)
Engine (general)

Type:

With manual transmission	829 A7 00
With automatic transmission	829 B7 01
Number of cylinders	4
Bore	88 mm
Stroke	82 mm
Cubic capacity	1995 cm^3
Compression ratio	9.2 to 1
Maximum power	110 bhp (DIN) at 5500 rpm
Maximum torque	127.5 lbf ft at 3000 rpm
Firing order	1–3–4–2
Static ignition advance	$10° \pm 1°$ or $6° \pm 1°$
Valve gear type	ohc

Valve clearances (cold):

Inlet	0.10 mm (0.004 in)
Exhaust	0.25 mm (0.010 in)

Cylinder head

Allowable contact face distortion	0.05 mm (0.002 in)

Valve assemblies

Valve seat angles (included):

Inlet	120°
Exhaust	90°

Valve seat width:

Inlet	1.85 mm (0.072 in)
Exhaust	1.85 mm (0.072 in)

Outside diameter:

Inlet	45 mm (1.772 in)
Exhaust	39.5 mm (1.555 in)
Valve stem diameter (inlet and exhaust)	8 mm (0.315 in)

Valve head diameter:

Inlet	44 mm (1.732 in)
Exhaust	38.5 mm (2.516 in)

Valve guides:

Bore (inlet and exhaust)	8 mm (0.315 in)
Standard outside diameter	13 mm (0.512 in)
Valve spring free length (inlet and exhaust)	47.2 mm (1.858 in)

Camshaft

Number of support bearings 5
Endfloat .... 0.05 to 0.13 mm (0.002 to 0.005 in)
Valve timing:
    Inlet opens .... 20° BTDC
    Inlet closes .... 60° ABDC
    Exhaust opens .... 60° BBDC
    Exhaust closes .... 20° ATDC
Timing belt adjustment deflection .... 5.5 to 7 mm (0.218 to 0.281 in)

Cylinder block liners

Bore diameter .... 88 mm (3.467 in)
Location diameter at base .... 93.6 mm (3.685 in)
Liner projection (less O-ring) .... 0.08 to 0.15 mm (0.003 to 0.006 in)

Pistons

Type .... Alloy – three rings
Gudgeon pin fitting .... Press fit in small-end and floating in piston
Piston rings – standard widths:
    Top .... 1.75 mm (0.069 in)
    2nd (taper) .... 2.0 mm (0.079 in)
    Oil scraper .... 4.0 mm (0.158 in)
Gudgeon pin:
    Diameter (outside diameter) .... 23 mm (0.905 in)
    Length .... 75 mm (2.953 in)

Connecting rods

Bearing shell type .... Aluminium/tin
Small-end endfloat .... 0.31 to 0.57 mm (0.012 to 0.022 in)

Crankshaft

Number of main bearings 5
Main bearing shell material .... Aluminium/tin
Crankshaft endfloat .... 0.045 to 0.23 mm (0.002 to 0.009 in)
Thrust washer thicknesses available .... 2.80 mm (0.110 in)
    2.85 mm (0.112 in)
    2.90 mm (0.114 in)
    2.95 mm (0.116 in)

Main bearing journal diameters .... $62.892 \text{ mm} {}^{+0}_{-0.019}$ ($2.476 \text{ in} {}^{+0}_{-0.0007}$)
Regrind diameter for undersize shells .... 69.762 mm (2.7464 in)
Crankpin diameter:
    Standard .... $52.296 \text{ mm} {}^{+0.010}_{-0.029}$ ($2.058 \text{ in} {}^{+0.0004}_{-0.001}$)
    Regrind diameter for undersize shells .... 51.996 mm (2.0487 in)

Engine lubrication

Oil capacity (at oil change):
    Without filter renewal .... 8.8 pt (5.0 litres)
    With filter renewal .... 9.7 pt (5.5 litres)
Pump pressure:
    At idle speed .... 0.8 bars (11.6 lbf/in²)
    At 3000 rpm .... 3.0 bars (43.5 lbf/in²)
Pump rotor tip-to-housing clearance:
    Minimum .... 0.05 mm (0.002 in)
    Maximum .... 0.12 mm (0.005 in)
Pump rotor endfloat:
    Minimum .... 0.02 mm (0.0008 in)
    Maximum .... 0.10 mm (0.0039 in)
Pump relief valve piston-to-bore clearance:
    Minimum .... 0.03 mm (0.0012 in)
    Maximum .... 0.08 mm (0.0032 in)

Torque wrench settings

	Nm	lbf ft
Cylinder head:		
First initial tightening	50.0	37.0
Second initial tightening	80.0	60
Final tightening	87.5 to 97.5	65 to 71
Camshaft drive pulley bolt	50	37.5
Crankshaft pulley bolt	75 to 85	56 to 64
Connecting rod cap bolts	45 to 50	34 to 37.5
Crankshaft main bearing cap bolts	87.5 to 97.5	65 to 71
Flywheel bolts (manual transmission)	55 to 60	41 to 45
Driveplate bolts (automatic transmission)	65 to 70	49 to 52.5
Oil pump bolts	40 to 45	30 to 34
Intermediate shaft pulley block	50	37.5
Rocker shaft plug	20	15.0

Part A – Overhead valve engine

1 General description (ohv engine)

Both the ohv engine types are four-cylinder in-line units mounted at the front of the vehicle.

Although basically a similar engine to the 807 unit fitted to the Renault 16, the engine and transmission are located in the traditional manner: in-line, with the gearbox at the rear, as shown in Fig. 1.1.

The engine is of the overhead valve type with a crossflow head for maximum efficiency. As the inlet and exhaust valves of each cylinder are transversely opposed to each other, twin rocker shafts are employed.

The camshaft is high mounted in the block and driven via a conventional chain and sprocket from the crankshaft. Chain guides and a tensioner are fitted to give long chain life and quiet operation.

The crankshaft runs in five main bearings – all of renewable shell type – and thrust washers are fitted against the centre web to provide the correct endfloat.

Cooling is by a conventionally front mounted radiator and water circulation system.

Major castings are of light alloy and the cylinder block is fitted with wet liners.

The camshaft also drives the distributor and petrol pump.

A general view of the TL engine is shown in photo 1.9.

2 Major operations possible with engine fitted

1   Where major overhaul or servicing is required it will be wise to remove the complete engine/gearbox-transmission unit and obtain the ease of access provided by mounting the unit on a bench. However, the following operations may be carried out with the engine still in place in the vehicle.

(a) *Removal of the cylinder head, attention to valves, rocker gear and pushrods*
(b) *Removal of the sump, permitting attention to the cylinder liners, pistons, piston rings, connecting rods and big-ends and oil pump*
(c) *Removal of the engine ancillaries including the distributor and starter motor*
(d) *Removal of camshaft (after removal of cylinder head, timing cover, timing chain and crankshaft sprocket)*
(e) *Removal of the transmission unit (see Chapter 6)*
(f) *Removal of the clutch unit (manual transmissions – see Chapter 5)*
(g) *Front crankshaft oil seal in the timing chest replacement*

3 Major operations possible with engine removed

1   With the engine removed from the vehicle, it is possible to achieve all of the items mentioned in the previous Section, plus the following:

(a) *Crankshaft and main bearings – overhaul and refitting*
(b) *Crankcase – renewal or repair*

4 Engine removal – general

1   Where only the engine is to be removed, there are few difficulties as it can be lifted direct from the engine compartment. If, however, the gearbox is to also be removed, it is not advisable to remove the two units combined, due to their size, weight and the gearbox location.
2   Ensure that the lifting tackle, sling and hoist support are up to the job, and that there is sufficient work area.
3   Remember to leave enough room to wheel the vehicle back out of the way once the engine is hoisted high enough. If a trolley hoist is used, it will not be necessary to move the vehicle, but the hoist will have to be moved back. Make sure it is on firm, level ground, with room to manoeuvre.

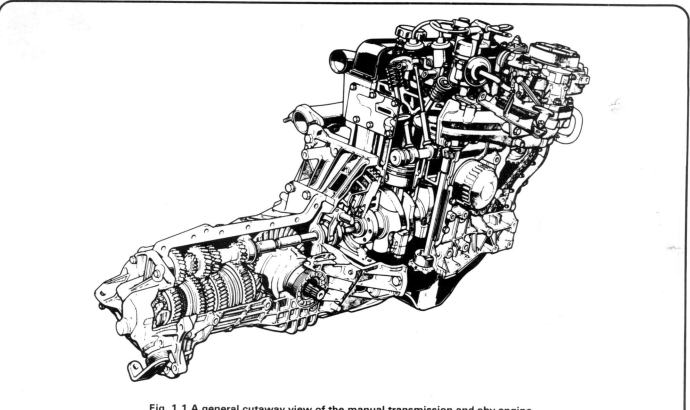

Fig. 1.1 A general cutaway view of the manual transmission and ohv engine layout

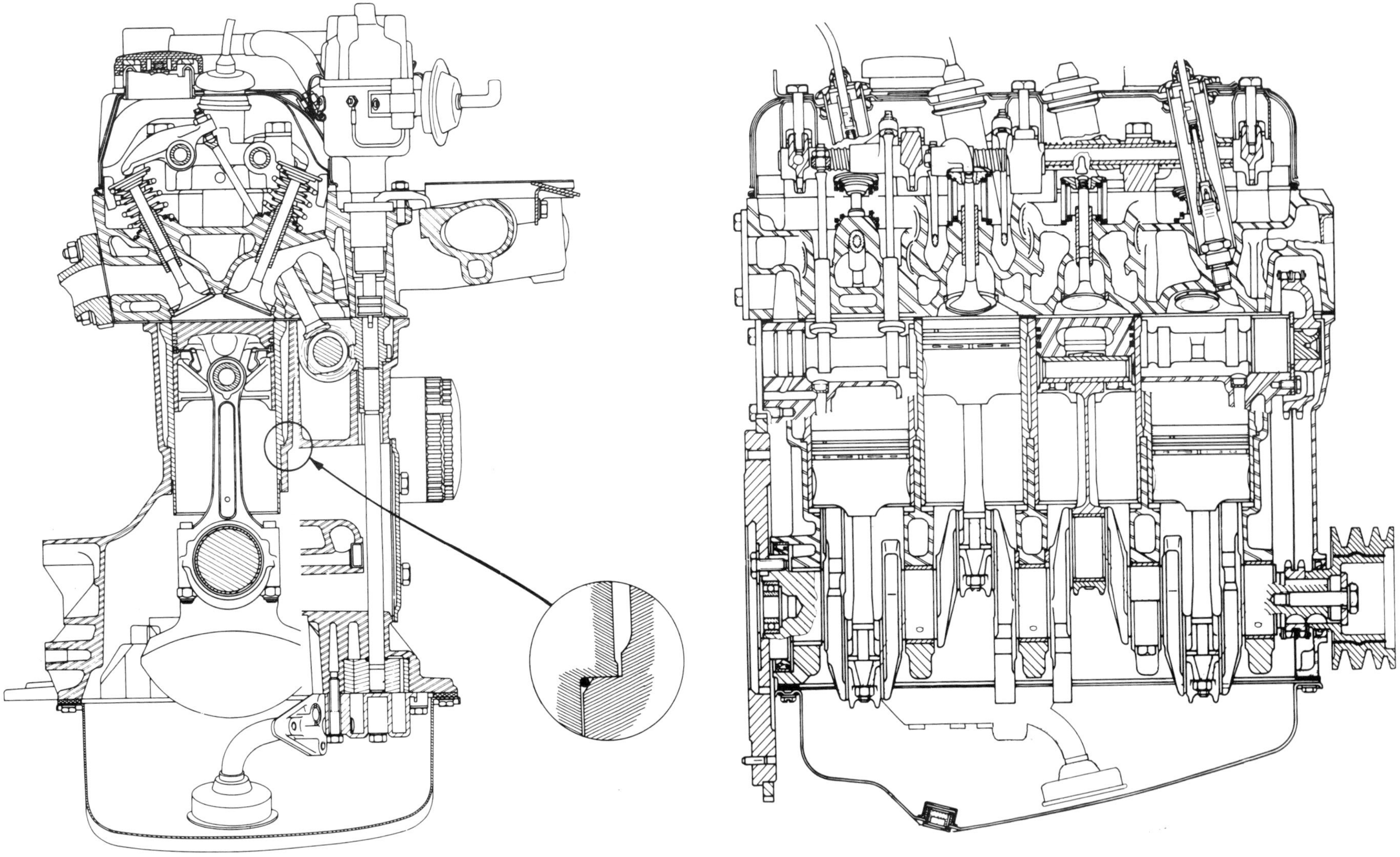

Fig. 1.2 Sectional views of the ohv engine

1.9 The overhead valve engine layout of the TL model

5.2a Disconnect battery earth (negative) lead

5.2b Sump drain plug

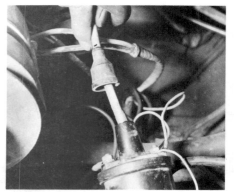

5.4a Detach HT lead from ignition coil

5.4b Detaching the oil pressure transmitter wire

5.4c Detach the starter motor leads

5.4d Unscrew and detach the cylinder block earth lead and bolt

5.5 Detach the fuel pump hoses

5.6 Loosen the alternator adjustment and mounting bolts

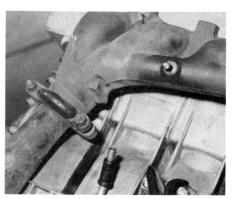

5.11 Exhaust manifold-to-downpipe clamp

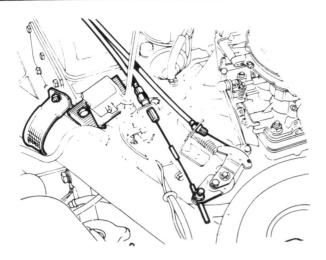

Fig. 1.3 Detach the carburettor controls, the hot air duct and filter trunking

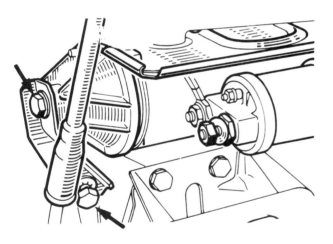

Fig. 1.4 The starter motor end bracket and retaining bolts

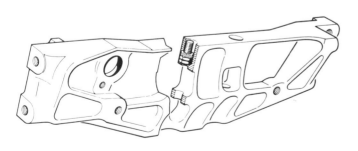

Fig. 1.5 The engine to manual transmission connecting plate with cutaway section to show the captive screw position

5 Engine – removal

1   Raise and support the bonnet. To provide further access, and prevent it being damaged during the removal operations, the bonnet should be detached and placed out of the way where it will not get knocked or scratched.

2   Disconnect the battery earth wire (photo). Unscrew the sump drain plug and empty the oil into a suitable container (photo).

3   Referring to Chapter 2, drain the cooling system, and remove the radiator and its expansion bottle. Save the coolant for reuse if it contains an antifreeze solution.

4   Taking note of their various positions, disconnect the respective ignition wires and associate engine wiring. Take particular note of the leads and wires to the starter motor. Remove or fold the wires back out of the way as applicable (photos).

5   Disconnect the fuel and vacuum supply tubes to the carburettor and fuel pump (photo).

6   Loosen the four fan retaining bolts, whilst applying extra hand pressure to increase the drivebelt tension and prevent the fan rotating. Take care not to damage the plasticfan blades. Next, loosen the alternator mounting bolts (photo) and slacken the drivebelt tension. Remove the drivebelt, fan and pulley.

7   Detach and remove the diagnostic socket and its bracket.

8   Disconnect and remove the hot air ducting inlet pipe and the carburettor/air filter trunking (if not already removed).

9   Disconnect the throttle (and downshift cable, if fitted) from the carburettor.

10 Where fitted, remove the power-assisted steering (PAS) pump return pipe retaining clip, on the right-hand engine mounting bracket.

11 Disconnect the exhaust pipe clamp (photo). Disconnect the starter motor retaining bolts at each end and withdraw it as shown in Fig. 1.4.

12 You will now need to work underneath the front of the car, and therefore will have to raise it and support it accordingly, using suitable stands or blocks. Position the jack and/or stands only under the lifting points on each side, adjacent to the sills. Do not allow the weight of the vehicle to rest on the front suspension arms or transverse member (see the introductory Section concerning jacking-up the vehicle).

13 With the vehicle securely raised, work from underneath and remove the engine undertray bolts. Detach the tray.

14 Where fitted, detach the PAS pump, but do not detach the pipes.

15 Partially remove the engine-to-manual gearbox connecting plate, enabling the two units to be separated. There are two captive sump screws set in this member, as shown in Fig. 1.5. A normal screwdriver is all you need to unscrew them.

16 On automatic transmission models, unbolt and remove the converter cover plate. Then, working through the exposed aperture, unscrew and remove each of the three converter-to-driveplate bolts and check the plate to converter alignment marking is visible – mark accordingly if not, to ensure correct assembly. Rotate the engine, using a spanner located on the crankshaft pulley bolt, to position the converter bolts accordingly, and then jam the starter ring with a suitable screwdriver or similar, to prevent the engine turning whilst undoing each bolt.

17 On manual and automatic transmission models, unscrew and remove the lower engine-to-gearbox retaining bolts.

18 Unscrew and remove the engine mounting nuts.

19 Make a check around the engine, to see if any associate fittings are still attached, then arrange the lifting sling into position and check that it is secure. Lifting plates are fitted, and are shown in Fig. 1.7, being positioned on the right-hand side at the rear, and on the left-hand side at the front.

20 Raise the hoist and take the weight of the engine sufficiently to allow the gearbox to rest on the steering crossmember. Using a suitable wooden wedge, secure the gearbox in this position.

21 Unscrew and remove the upper engine-to-gearbox retaining bolts.

22 The engine can now be pulled carefully from the transmission unit, and when sufficiently clear, raised and removed. On automatic transmission models, take additional care when withdrawing the engine, to avoid pulling on the converter as well. On removal of the engine, take precautions to prevent the converter from becoming dislodged from the transmission whilst the engine is out of the vehicle. Fabricate a suitable retaining plate, or if available, use Renault special tool B. Vi. 465 mark D to secure the converter.

23 On removal of the engine, lower and place it in an area where it can be cleaned externally, prior to dismantling.

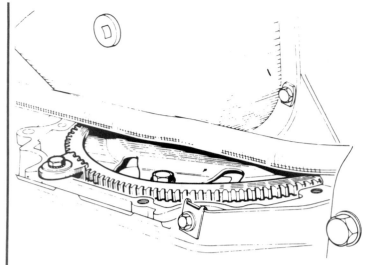

Fig. 1.6 The converter plate is jammed in position with a special Renault tool (Mot 582) to prevent it turning. A similar plate would be easy to fabricate

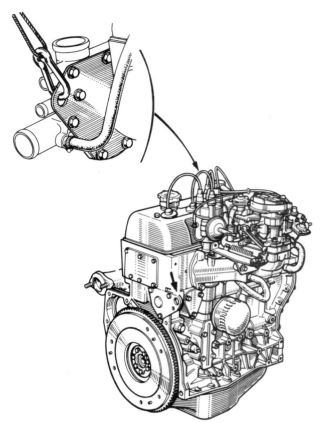

Fig. 1.7 The engine lift plate positions indicated on each side

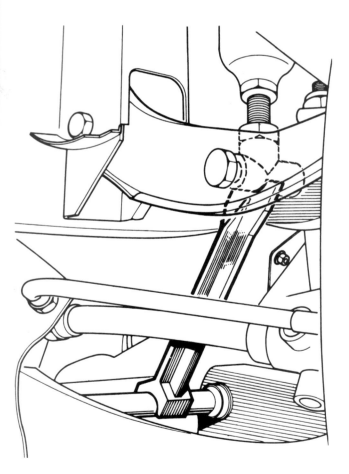

Fig. 1.8 The special spacer leg in position – Renault tool number T Av509
Note: It may be worth buying this tool as it is used for several other operations that require the car front wheels to be raised and suspended

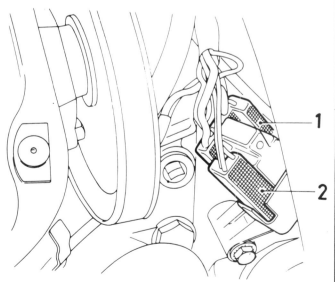

Fig. 1.9 Disconnect the transmission wires at connectors 1 and 2

6   Engine and manual gearbox – removal

It is not generally recommended that the two units be removed together as both are relatively bulky. Therefore, unless suitable lifting gear, a couple of assistants and sufficient working clearance are available below the vehicle to disconnect and manoeuvre the gearbox upwards when lifting the units out, they are best removed individually.

1   Following the procedures given in the preceding Section, disconnect the engine and its associate fittings as described in paragraphs 1 to 18, but excluding paragraphs 15 and 17.

2   Drain the gearbox lubricant into a suitable container.

3   Fabricate a suitable pair of spacers, or if available, use Renault special spacer legs (tool number T. Av. 509). Position them between the front shock absorber lower mountings and the lower suspension arm pivot pins, as shown in Fig. 1.8. See Chapter 11, Section 7, for details on spacer legs.

4   Now raise the front end of the vehicle and support on stands or blocks to allow the front wheels to hang freely. When in this position, make a check to ensure that the spacer legs are securely located, before proceeding further.

5   Unscrew and remove the clutch cable adjusting nuts and detach the cable from the operating lever.

6   Refer to Chapter 8 and disconnect the driveshafts from the sunwheels.

7   Disconnect and remove the top dead centre (TDC) pick-up support plate.

8   Detach the speedometer cable to the transmission and fold it back out of the way.

9   Referring to Chapter 6, disconnect the gearshift control.

10   Position a jack under the gearbox and raise it so that it just supports it without actually lifting it. If available, use a trolley jack, which will provide a mobile support to the transmission during the removal of the engine and gearbox units.

11   Disconnect the gearbox at the mountings on each side.

12   Check around the engine and gearbox to ensure that all associate fittings are disconnected, then attach the engine lifting sling to each of the lift plates as shown in Fig. 1.7.

13   Take the weight of the engine by raising the lift hoist and, with the aid of an assistant, pull it forwards whilst simultaneously adjusting the jack under the gearbox, so that the engine is tilted to the necessary angle for withdrawal. Take care not to damage any of the surrounding components during the engine/transmission removal.

Note: *Do not remove the lower body crossmember.*

7   Engine and automatic transmission – removal

It is not recommended that the engine and automatic transmission be removed together, for the reasons outlined in paragraph 1 of Section 6. However, should you have the necessary assistants and equipment, proceed as follows:

1   Follow the instructions given in Section 5, paragraphs 1 to 18, but excluding paragraphs 15 to 17.

2   Drain the final drive unit lubricant and also the transmission fluid (see Chapter 7).

3   Referring to Fig. 1.9, detach the transmission wiring harness connectors.

4   Referring to the previous Section, follow the instructions given in paragraphs 3, 4 and 7.

5   Unscrew and detach the TDC pick-up unit cover plate, as shown in Fig. 1.10.

6   Disconnect the selector control linkage by loosening the clamp nuts, detaching the rod and unscrewing the control linkage.

7   Disconnect the capsule and governor control cable from the transmission.

8   Position a jack under the transmission for support (see paragraph 10 in previous Section).

9   Disconnect the transmission mountings on each side and follow paragraphs 12 and 13 in the previous Section to remove the engine and transmission units.

10   If the engine and transmission units are to be separated on removal from the vehicle, unscrew the upper and lower retaining bolts and ensure that the three converter-to-driveplate bolts have also been removed. Pull the engine and transmission units apart, taking care not to pull the converter from the transmission housing as well. Once

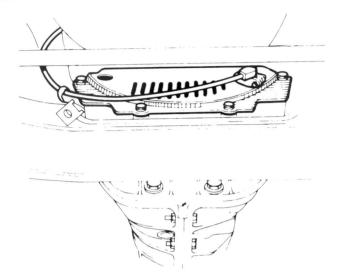

Fig. 1.10 Detach the TDC pick-up

apart, fabricate a retaining plate or means to prevent the converter from becoming detached whilst the transmission is removed.

8   Engine dismantling – general

1   It is best to mount the engine on a dismantling stand, but if one is not available, stand the engine on a strong bench at a comfortable working height. Failing this, the engine can be stripped down on the floor.

2   During dismantling, the greatest care should be taken to keep the exposed parts free from dirt. As an aid to achieving this, it is a sound scheme to first clean down the outside of the engine, removing all traces of oil and congealed dirt.

3   Use paraffin or a good grease solvent. The latter will make the job much easier, as, after the solvent has been applied and allowed to stand for a time, a vigorous jet of water will wash off the solvent and all the grease and filth. If the dirt is thick and deeply embedded, work the solvent into it with a brush.

4   Finally wipe down the exterior of the engine with a rag and only then, when it is quite clean, should dismantling begin. As the engine is stripped, clean each part in a bath of paraffin.

5   Never immerse parts with oilways in paraffin, eg the crankcase, but to clean, wipe down carefully with a solvent dampened rag. Oilways can be cleaned out with wire. If an air line is present all parts can be blown dry and the oilways blown through as an added precaution.

6   Re-use of old engine gaskets is false economy and can give rise to oil and water leaks. To avoid the possibility of trouble after the engine has been reassembled *always* use new gaskets throughout.

7   Do not throw the old gaskets away as it sometimes happens that an immediate replacement cannot be found and the old gasket is useful as a template. Hang up the old gaskets as they are removed on a suitable hook or nail.

8   To strip the engine it is best to work from the top down. The sump provides a firm base on which the engine can be supported in an upright position. When this stage where the sump must be removed is reached, the engine can be turned on its side and all other work carried out with it in this position.

9   Whenever possible, refit nuts, bolts and washers fingertight from wherever they were removed. This helps to avoid later loss and muddle. If they cannot be refitted, lay them out so that it is clear where they came from.

9   Engine dismantling – ancillaries

1   A word of warning at this stage is that you should always be sure that it is more economic to dismantle and overhaul a worn engine rather than simply to exchange it on the Renault Factory scheme. It is

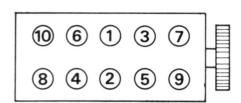

Fig. 1.11 Cylinder head bolts – removal/tightening sequence

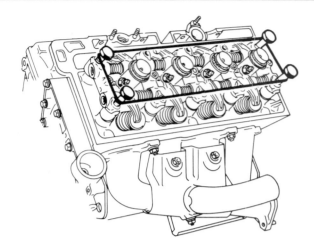

Fig. 1.12 Locate the four projecting corner bolts as shown with an elastic band or string

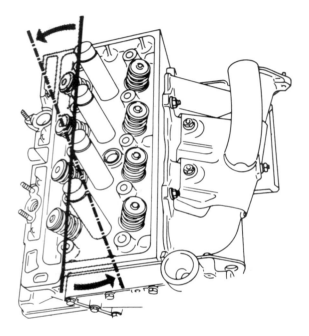

Fig. 1.13 Separate the head from the block by twisting horizontally then lifting clear

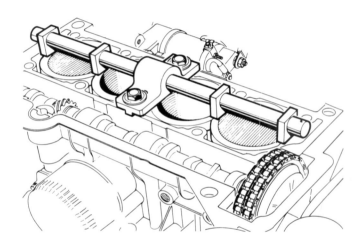

Fig. 1.14 Retain the cylinders in position by fitting a clamp

not always the case.

2   If you are intending to obtain an exchange engine complete, it will be necessary first of all to remove all those parts of the engine which are not included in the exchange. If you are stripping the engine completely yourself in the likelihood of some outside work to be done by specialists, all these items will be taken off anyway.

3   Short engines are not available from Renault. It is as well to check with whoever may be supplying the replacement exchange unit what it is necessary to remove, but as a general guide the following items will have to be taken off. Reference is given to the appropriate Chapter for details of removal of each of these items. Always clean the engine before exchanging:

(a) Alternator – Chapter 10
(b) Distributor – Chapter 4
(c) Thermostat – Chapter 2
(d) Carburettor – Chapter 3
(e) Inlet and exhaust manifolds
(f) Fuel pump – Chapter 3
(g) Distributor/oil pump drive – Chapter 1
(h) Gearbox – Chapter 6 or 7, as applicable
(i) Ignition coil – Chapter 4
(j) Dipstick
(k) Fan and its pulley – Chapter 1
(l) Starter motor – Chapter 10

10 Cylinder head – removal

1   If the engine is still in the vehicle, drain/disconnect/remove (as applicable) the following items:

(a) Drain the cooling system (see Chapter 2)
(b) Disconnect the battery earth cable
(c) Disconnect the ignition and other associate electrical wires from the cylinder head noting their respective positions. Also detach the diagnostic socket
(d) Loosen the alternator and remove the drivebelt
(e) Remove the air cleaner unit and disconnect the carburettor throttle control cable (see Chapter 3)
(f) Remove the radiator together with the expansion bottle (see Chapter 2)
(g) Referring to Chapter 4, remove the distributor
(h) Detach the exhaust downpipe from the manifold connection

2   The procedure for engine fitted or removed is now the same.

3   Unscrew the retaining nut from the dipstick guide tube upper securing clip. The dipstick can be left in position if desired.

4   Remove the rocker cover (photo).

5   Unscrew the respective rocker arm adjustment screws sufficiently to allow each pushrod to be extracted (photo). As the pushrods are removed, lay them out in numerical order or locate them in a piece of

10.4a Remove the rocker cover retaining nuts ...

10.4b ... and remove the cover

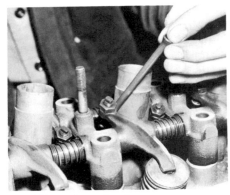
10.5 Lift out the pushrods

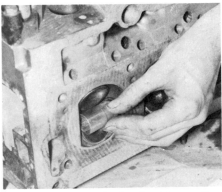
10.7a Remove the spark plug tube washers ...

10.7b ... and cups

11.5a Compressing a valve spring with a piece of slotted tubing

11.5b Support the valve heads with a small wood block

11.6a Detach the valve cup ...

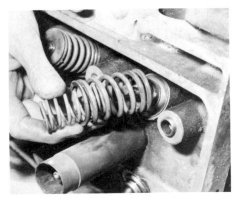
11.6b ... and springs and base washers

12.2 The flywheel retaining bolts and lock tabs

17.3 Big-end cap to rod alignment/number marking

17.6 Withdraw the piston and liner assembly from the block

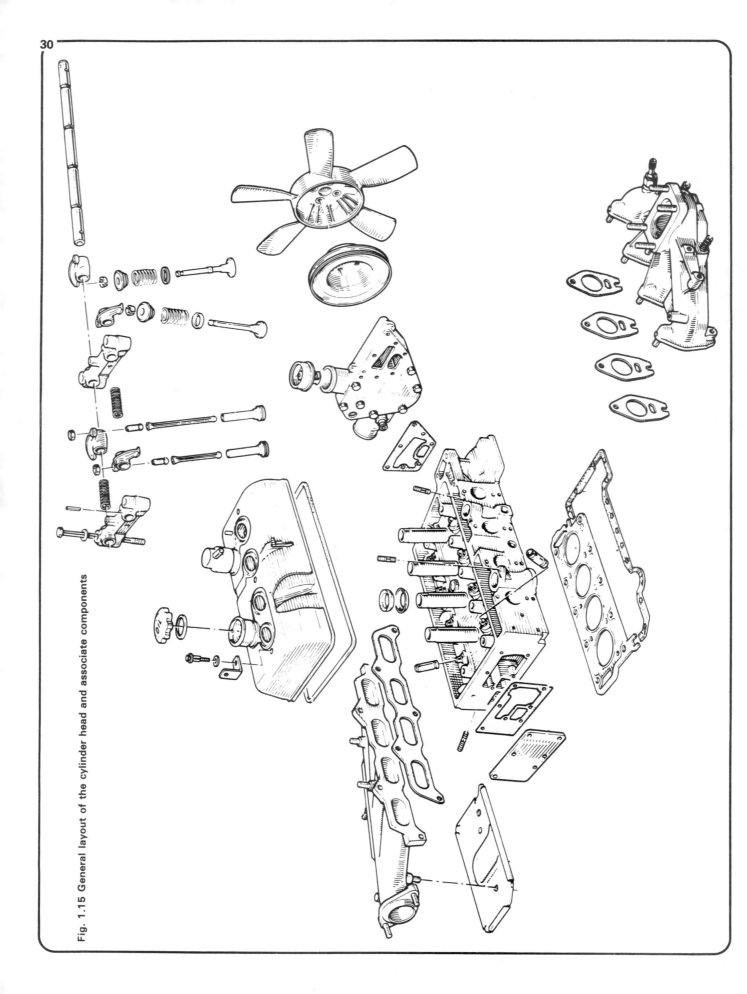

Fig. 1.15 General layout of the cylinder head and associate components

stiff cardboard with eight holes suitably positioned and accordingly marked.

6   Next, loosen the cylinder head bolts in the sequence shown in Fig. 1.11, and extract all bolts except the two at each end.

7   Remove the seals and washers from the spark plug tubes (photo).

8   Locate a large elastic band or piece of string around each of the four remaining bolts, as shown in Fig. 1.12, so that when the rocker assemblies are removed, the bolts do not become dislodged from them and thus retain the assemblies as a unit. Carefully, lift the rocker shaft assemblies clear.

9   Before removing the cylinder head from the block, **note the following**: *Under no circumstances lift the head vertically from the block!* The head and block both stick to the gasket, therefore a lifting action would dislodge the liners in the process and break their lower O-ring seals. If these seals are damaged or distorted in any way it is likely that coolant will leak through to the sump with dire results!

10   The correct pressure to remove the head, without disturbing the cylinders and seals, is to pivot the head in the direction shown in Fig. 1.13. The head will actually pivot round on the location dowel situated in the mating face of the cylinder block on the distributor side.

11   Carefully, tap the head horizontally round, using a soft head mallet or block of wood. When pivoted transversely, the seal between the head and block mating surfaces will be broken and the head can then be withdrawn just sufficiently to extract the tappets (which must be kept in order).

12   The cylinder head can now be withdrawn, together with the tappet chamber seal. If the head is to be removed for any length of time, the cylinder liners must be clamped down in position to prevent them from becoming dislodged. If available, use Renault liner clamp number Mot. 521 as shown in Fig. 1.14. A suitable bar clamp can easily be fabricated and bolted in position if this tool is not available.

11 Cylinder head, rocker assembly and valves – dismantling

1   Provided care is exercised, the water pump, water temperature transmitter and alternator bracket need not be removed from the cylinder head during operations described in this section.

2   Drift out the spring roll pins which retain the rocker shafts to their pillars, as shown in Fig. 1.15.

3   Slide off the rocker arms and springs and clean them, and place them in order for refitting. Do not remove the concave plugs from the shaft ends.

4   Referring to Fig. 1.16, the oil flow route through the rocker assemblies is shown and it should be noted that rocker shaft bearings 1 and 4 incorporate an oil hole (and location dowel), whilst bearings 2, 3 and 5 do not have an oil hole.

5   All valves can be removed with the aid of a conventional type spring compressor, except No 1 inlet. For this, obtain a piece of tubing or an open-ended spanner (photo). With the head laid flat on a bench

and using a small block of wood or metal within the combustion head (photo) to prevent the valve dropping, press down on the spring until the split collets can be removed.

6   Lift off the valve spring top cups, the springs, and the base washers (photo).

7   Withdraw each valve from its guide and keep it in strict order for correct refitting.

12 Flywheel – removal

1   The flywheel can be removed from the engine when in position in the car, providing the transmission and clutch units are first removed (see Chapters 6 and 5 respectively).

2   With the clutch unit removed, bend back the lock tabs from the flywheel retaining bolts. Then unscrew the bolts and remove them (photo). Mark the flywheel and crankshaft in relation to each other.

3   Pull, whilst also supporting the flywheel from the crankshaft flange, taking care not to damage the starter ring gear teeth.

13 Automatic transmission converter driveplate – removal

The procedures described in the preceding section applies to the removal of the torque converter driveplate which is fitted instead of a flywheel with automatic transmission. Note converter/plate mating marks for exact refitting.

14 Sump – removal

1   The sump can be removed from the engine whilst still in position in the vehicle, after first removing the gearbox connecting plate on manual models.

2   Check that the engine oil has been drained, then unscrew and remove the respective sump securing bolts. Loosen them progressively in a diametrically opposed sequence to avoid sump distortion.

3   Withdraw the sump and discard the gasket.

15 Oil pump unit – removal

1   First remove the sump as described above.

2   If working under the car (engine in position) wipe the respective pump crankshaft and internal crankcase items clean of oil, to prevent it dripping down into your face and eyes whilst removing the pump. If the engine is removed from the vehicle, remove the distributor drivegear and then invert the engine.

3   Unscrew and remove the bolts retaining the oil pump unit in posi-

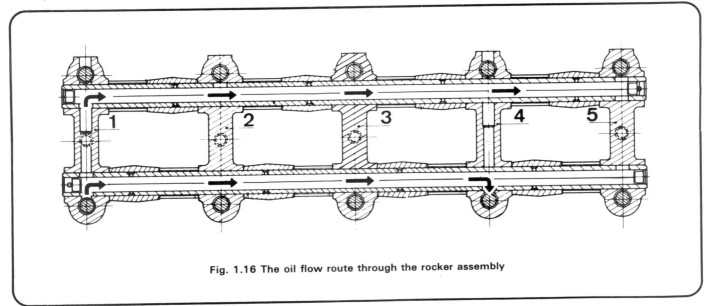

Fig. 1.16 The oil flow route through the rocker assembly

tion and carefully remove the pump.

4   Note their positions and extract the two rotors.

16 Timing cover, timing chain/sprockets and camshaft – removal

1   Unscrew and remove the crankshaft pulley retaining bolt. If the flywheel is still in position, jam it to prevent the crankshaft rotating when unscrewing the pulley bolt. With the flywheel removed, refit two of the retaining bolts into the rear crankshaft, and position a large screwdriver or suitable lever between the bolts to prevent the crankshaft from turning.

2   Unscrew the bolt and withdraw the pulley. Remove the Woodruff key.

3   The timing cover bolts can now be unscrewed and the cover removed. Remove and discard the cover gasket.

4   Unscrew the chain tensioner unit bolts and remove the tensioner, with thrust plate and filter.

5   Unscrew and remove the chain guide (anti-flail) shoes using a suitable Allen key.

6   Using a socket spanner and extension applied through the camshaft sprocket apertures, unscrew and remove the camshaft flange retaining bolts.

7   The timing chain, camshaft and crankshaft pulley are now removed in unison. You will need a suitable puller with which to withdraw the crankshaft pulley. If available, use Renault special tool number Mot. 49 extractor in conjunction with special screw Mot. 525, as shown in Fig. 1.18. If using a standard type puller, take care not to damage the timing chain and/or the crankshaft sprocket. As the crankshaft sprocket is withdrawn, simultaneously extract the camshaft and chain.

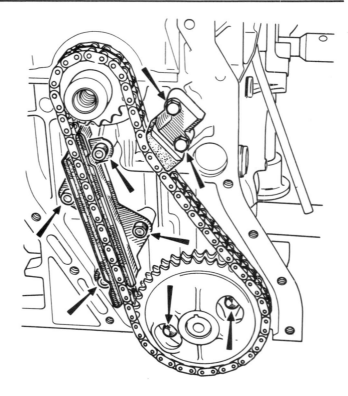

Fig. 1.17 The timing chain tensioner and guide locating bolts

17 Piston/liner assemblies, connecting rods and big-end bearings – removal

1   These components may be removed with the engine in position in the car, if required, after removal of the cylinder head and sump.

2   It is important that where the existing cylinder liners are to be refitted, they are identified for position. Mark the top edges with quick drying paint to indicate each liner's position in the line and also its orientation so that it will be refitted exactly the same way round.

3   Check the numbering of the connecting rods and the big-end caps. These should run from 1 to 4 from the clutch end of the engine and are marked on the camshaft side of the unit, as shown in Fig. 1.20. In the event of these components not being marked, then dot punch them in such a way that the bearing cap will be fitted the correct way round when the mating marks are adjacent (photo).

4   Unscrew and remove the big-end bearing cap nuts.

5   Withdraw the big-end bearing caps complete with shell bearings.

6   Withdraw each cylinder liner/piston/connecting rod assembly upwards from the cylinder block (photo). The lower liner seals will be broken during this operation and must be cleaned from the liner and block mating faces.

7   After removal of each connecting rod, temporarily refit its matching bearing cap and shell bearing.

8   Withdraw each connecting rod/piston assembly from its cylinder liner. Do not allow the piston rings to spring outwards during removal from the liners but restrict them with the fingers to avoid breakage.

18 Piston rings – removal

1   Removal of rings from their grooves is an operation calling for care as they are of cast construction and will snap if opened too wide.

2   Cut three pieces of thin sheet (or use three old feeler gauges) and prise the open ends of the ring apart with the thumb nails just enough to permit the first strip of tin (or feeler) to be slid behind the ring. Slide in the other two pieces of tin and position them equidistantly round the periphery of the piston. The piston ring may now be drawn off as the strips will permit it to ride safely over the lands and other grooves of the piston.

3   The above information is not necessarily applicable if the rings are to be renewed irrespectively, but care should still be exercised to prevent damaging the pistons during removal.

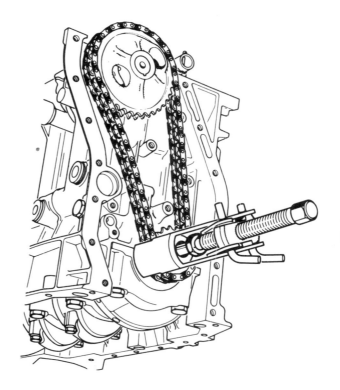

Fig. 1.18 The special Renault tool (Mot 525) used to withdraw the crankshaft sprocket. A standard two-leg puller will suffice

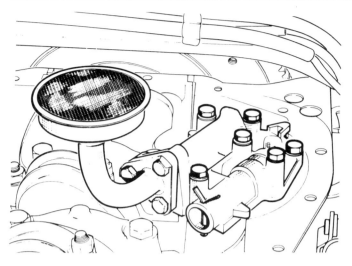

Fig. 1.19 The oil pump location

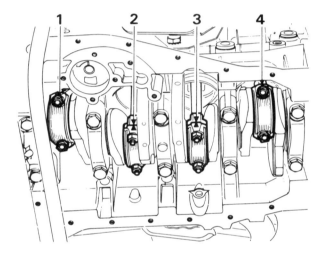

Fig. 1.20 Check the connecting rods and caps for the alignment numbering in the correct order as shown

19 Gudgeon pins – removal

1   The gudgeon pins fitted to these engines are an interference fit in the connecting rod small end but a running fit in the piston. It is preferable that the removal or fitting of gudgeon pins be left to a Renault agent as the connecting rod must first be heated to 250°C (482°F) and a press and special gauge tools employed, as shown in Fig. 1.21.

20 Main bearings and crankshaft – removal

1   Invert the engine block so that the sump flange is uppermost.
2   Mark the five main bearing caps in sequence from the rear either by dot punching or using quick drying paint, as shown in Fig. 1.22 (see also photo). Ensure that the position of the mating marks on both the caps and crankcase will automatically ensure their correct orientation on refitting.
3   Unscrew and remove the main bearing cap bolts and remove all the caps except No 1 which cannot be removed by hand pressure.
4   Tap the No 1 main bearing cap away from the crankshaft and crankcase. Then remove it, using a suitable soft drift.
5   Remove the seal.
6   Remove the two bearing side seals.
7   Carefully, lift out the crankshaft from the halves of the crankcase bearing.
8   Unless the shell bearings are to be renewed, they may be left in position but temporarily screw on the bearing caps which will give some measure of protection to the shell bearings during further servicing operations on the engine block.

21 Oil pump – overhaul

1   The components of the oil pump are shown in Fig. 1.23. It is essential that all parts are in good operative condition for the pump to work effectively, and this applies particularly to the rotors and, of course, the driveshaft.
2   To dismantle the pump, remove the suction pipe bolts. These are retained by lock tabs which must be bent back to release the bolts. Remove the pipe and gasket.
3   Extract the split pin from the pressure relief valve and withdraw the cap and spring, the spring guide and the piston.
4   Clean all components in petrol and wipe or blow dry, ready for inspection.
5   Use a feeler gauge and, referring to Fig. 1.24, check the rotor clearances at the positions shown. Should the clearances exceed the tolerances given, then the pump unit should be renewed, or at least the two rotors.
6   Other items to check are the suction pipe joint flange, the pump

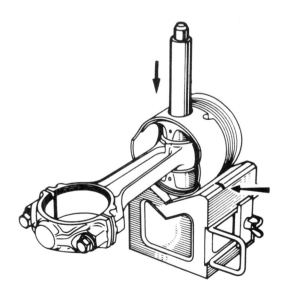

Fig. 1.21 The special tool required to remove the gudgeon pin

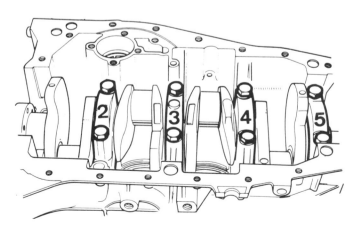

Fig. 1.22 Mark the main bearing caps accordingly

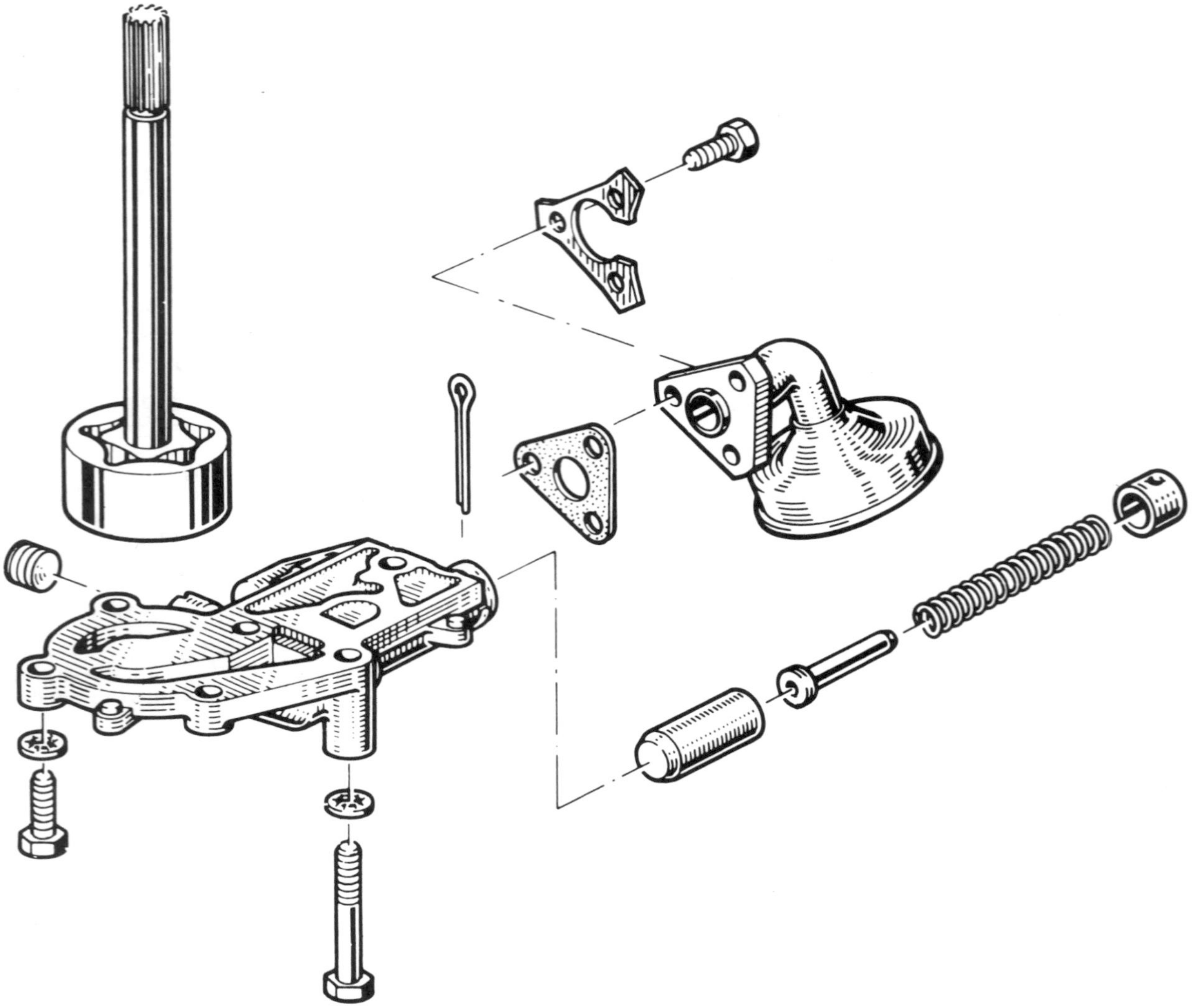

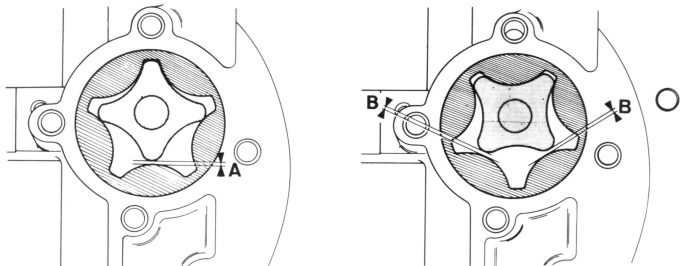

Fig. 1.23 The oil pump components

Fig. 1.24 Check the rotor clearances with a feeler gauge as shown

Clearance in position A: 0.002 in (0.04 mm) minimum
0.012 in (0.29 mm) maximum
Clearance in position B: 0.001 in (0.02 mm) minimum
0.006 in (0.14 mm) maximum

cover joint face and the relief valve piston. Look for signs of wear, scoring or any other defects, and renew as applicable.

7   Reassemble the pump in reverse sequence to dismantling, but lubricate each component in turn with clean engine oil as it is assembled. Use a new gasket at the suction pipe flange.

22 Oil filter – removal and refitting

1   The oil filter is of canister, screw-in, throw-away type located on the right-hand side of the crankcase.

2   The old filter may be very tight to remove and by prising a screwdriver against one of the filter case notches it may be possible to lever it undone.

3   If this fails use a small chain wrench or a worm drive clip to which two bolts have been riveted or welded. After tightening the worm drive screw fully, pressure against the bolts will unscrew the filter from its base.

4   Before fitting a new filter, oil the surface of the rubber sealing gasket and screw it in by hand until it seats, then screw in a further half turn by hand. Do not screw the filter in by using a wrench or rod.

5   Where applicable, start the engine, check for leaks and top up the engine oil level as necessary.

23 Engine components – cleaning and examination

1   After the engine has been stripped, all parts should be cleaned by wiping with a lint-free rag, or in some cases by soaking in a bath of paraffin. However, never immerse parts with oilways in paraffin, eg the crankcase, but to clean, wipe down carefully with a solvent dampened rag. Oilways can be cleaned out with wire. If an air line is present all parts can be blown dry and the oilways blow through as an added precaution.

2   A heavy build-up of carbon on top of the pistons and in the ring grooves will prove difficult to remove in some cases. The carbon must therefore be carefully cleaned off using a suitable scraper, but take care not to scratch the surface of the piston. A blunt hacksaw blade can be used to clean out the ring grooves, but again take great care not to score or damage the ring grooves in any way.

3   When all components are cleaned of oil and dirt, they are ready for inspection.

24 Crankshaft – examination and renovation

1   Examine the crankpin and main journal surfaces for signs of scoring or scratches. Use a micrometer check the crankpins and main journals for excessive wear and ovality.

2   If the crankpins are more than 0.020 mm (0.001 in) out of round then they must be reground.

3   If the main journals are more than 0.013 mm (0.0005 in) out of round then they must also be reground.

4   Specialist automotive engineering firms will carry out this work and supply new shell bearings to the correct undersizes.

5   Renew the spigot bearing if necessary (manual transmission models).

25 Big-end and main bearings – examination and renovation

1   Big-end bearing failure is accompanied by a noisy knocking from the crankcase and a slight drop in oil pressure. Main bearing failure is accompanied by vibration, which can be quite severe as the engine speed rises and falls, and a drop in oil pressure.

2   Bearings which have not broken up, but are badly worn, will give rise to low oil pressure and some vibration. Inspect the big-ends, main bearings and thrust washers for signs of general wear, scoring, pitting and scratches. The bearings should be matt grey in colour. With lead-indium bearings, should a trace of copper colour be noticed, the bearings are badly worn as the lead bearing material has worn away to expose the indium underlay. Renew the bearings if they are in this condition or it there is any sign of scoring or pitting. **Note:** *You are strongly advised to renew the bearings regardless of their condition. Refitting used bearings is a false economy.*

3   The undersizes available are designed to correspond with crank-

shaft regrind sizes, eg -0.25 mm, -0.50 mm and -0.75 mm. The bearings are in fact, slightly more than the stated undersize as running clearances have been allowed for during their manufacture.

26 Cylinder liners – examination and renovation

1   The cylinder bores must be examined for taper, ovality, scoring and scratches. Start by carefully examining the top of the cylinder bore. If they are at all worn a very slight ridge will be found on the thrust side. This marks the top of the piston ring travel. The owner will have a good indication of the bore wear prior to dismantling the engine, or removing the cylinder head. Excessive oil consumption accompanied by blue smoke from the exhaust is a sure sign of worn cylinder bores and piston rings.

2   Measure the bore diameter just under the ridge with a micrometer and compare it with the diameter at the bottom of the bore, which is not subject to wear. If the differences between the two measurements are more than 0.15 mm (0.006 in) then it will be necessary to fit new pistons and liner assemblies. If no micrometer is available remove the ring from a piston and place the piston in each bore in turn about $\frac{3}{4}$ inch below the top of the bore. If a 0.25 mm (0.010 in) feeler gauge can be slid between the piston and the cylinder wall on the thrust side of the bore then remedial action must be taken.

3   Should the liners have been disturbed they must be completely removed from the cylinder block and new seals fitted, otherwise once the seals have been disturbed the chances are that water will leak into the sump.

27 Pistons and rings – examination and renovation

If the old pistons are to be refitted, carefully remove the piston rings and then thoroughly clean them. Take particular care to clean out the piston ring grooves. At the same time do not scratch the aluminium in any way. If new rings are to be fitted to the old pistons then the top ring should be stepped so as to clear the ridge left in the bore above the previous top ring. If a normal but unstepped new ring is fitted it will hit the ridge and break because the new ring will not have worn in the same way as the old, which will have worn in unison with the ridge. The piston rings are supplied pre-gapped for the particular liner diameter and it is not necessary to check them in the liners. It is not necessary to measure the side clearance in the piston ring grooves with the rings fitted as the groove dimensions are accurately machined during manufacture. When fitting new oil control rings to old pistons it may be necessary to have the groove in this instance widened by machining to accept the new wider rings.

28 Connecting rods and gudgeon pins – examination and renovation

1   A visual check only can be carried out to observe whether any movement or play can be seen when the piston is held still and the connecting rod pushed and pulled alternately.

2   If there has been evidence of small-end knock with the engine at normal working temperature then the connecting rod/piston assembly should be taken to a Renault dealer as special tools are required to dismantle and refit these components.

3   Have the connecting rods checked for alignment whenever the gudgeon pins are renewed.

29 Camshaft and camshaft bearings – examination and renovation

1   Examine the chain sprockets. If these are worn or the teeth are hooked, drift out the two securing pins and press off the sprocket.

2   Check the clearance between the camshaft and the flange. Use feelers to measure the gap which should be between 0.05 and 0.12 mm (0.002 and 0.0047 in). If the clearance is incorrect, the flange will have to be pressed off and a new one pressed on.

3   If the sprocket is removed for any reason, it must always be renewed.

4   If the camshaft is renewed as an assembly, then the distributor

drive pinion must also be renewed as both components are supplied as matched pairs.

30 Tappets – examination and renovation

1   Examine the bearing surface of the mushroom tappets which lie on the camshaft. Any indentation in this surface or any cracks indicate serious wear and the tappets should be renewed. Thoroughly clean them out, removing all traces of sludge. It is most unlikely that the sides of the tappets will prove worn, but, if they are a very loose fit in their bores and can readily be rocked, they should be exchanged for new units. It is very unusual to find any wear in the tappets, and any wear is likely to occur at very high mileages.
2   Oversize tappets can be fitted, but the location bores must be reamed out accordingly. This is a task best entrusted to your Renault dealer.

31 Valves and valve seats – examination and renovation

1   Examine the heads of the valves for pitting and burning, especially the heads of the exhaust valves. The valve seatings should be examined at the same time. If the pitting on valve and seat is very slight, the marks can be removed by grinding the seats and valves together with coarse, and then fine, valve grinding paste. Where bad pitting has occurred to the valve seats it will be necessary to recut them and fit new valves. If the valve seats are so worn that they cannot be recut, then it will be necessary to fit new valve seat inserts. These latter two jobs should be entrusted to the local Renault agent or engineering works. In practice it is very seldom that the seats are so badly worn that they require renewal. Normally, it is the exhaust valve that is too badly worn for refitting, and the owner can easily purchase a new set of valves and match them to the seats by valve grinding.
2   Valve grinding is carried out as follows. Smear a trace of coarse carborundum paste on the seat face and apply a suction grinder tool to the valve head. With a semi-rotary motion, grind the valve head to its seat, lifting the valve occasionally to redistribute the grinding paste (photo). When a dull matt even surface finish is produced on both the valve seat and the valve, wipe off the paste and repeat the process with fine carborundum paste, lifting and turning the valve to redistribute the paste as before. A light spring placed under the valve head will greatly ease this operation. When a smooth unbroken ring of light grey matt finish is produced on both valve and valve seat faces, the grinding operation is completed.
3   Scrape away all carbon from the valve head and the valve stem. Carefully clean away every trace of grinding compound, taking great care to leave none in the ports or in the valve guides. Clean the valves and valve seats with a paraffin soaked rag then with a clean rag, and finally, if an air line is available, blow the valves, valve guides and valve ports clean.

32 Valve guides – examination and renovation

1   Examine the valve guides internally for wear. If the valves are a very loose fit in the guides and there is the slightest suspicion of lateral rocking using a new valve, then new guides will have to be fitted. If the valve guides have been removed compare them internally by visual inspection with a new guide as well as testing them for rocking with a new valve.
2   Valve guide renewal should be left to a Renault agent who will have the required press and mandrel. Work of this kind in a light alloy head without the correct tools can be disastrous.

33 Timing sprockets and chain – examination and renovation

1   Examine the teeth on both the crankshaft gearwheel and the camshaft gearwheel for wear. Each tooth forms an inverted 'V' with the gearwheel periphery, and if worn, the side of each tooth under tension will be slightly concave in shape when compared with the other side of the tooth, ie one side of the inserted 'V' will be concave

20.2 Mark the main bearing caps

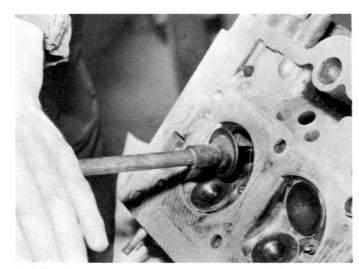

31.2 Grinding a valve

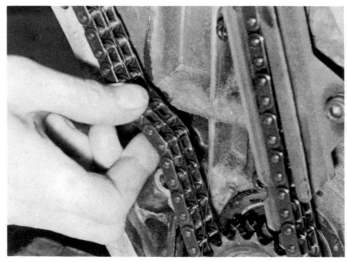

33.2 Inspecting the timing chain for wear

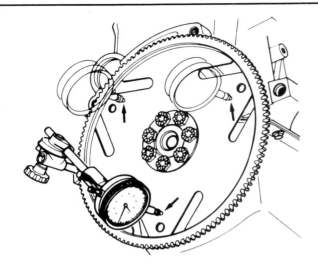

Fig. 1.25 Check the converter driveplate run-out using a clock gauge, positioned as shown

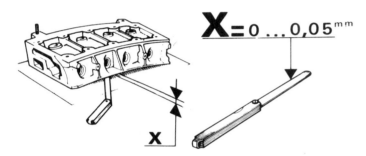

$$X = 0 \ldots 0{,}05^{mm}$$

Fig. 1.26 Check the cylinder head face for distortion – the maximum permissible (X) should not exceed 0.002 in (0.05 mm)

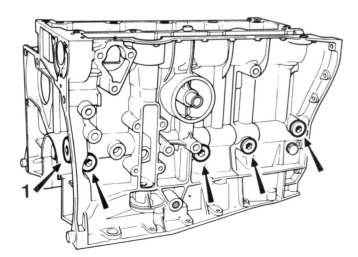

Fig. 1.27 The cylinder block oilway plugs – note position of No 1 plug

when compared with the other. If any sign of wear is present the gearwheels must be renewed.

2   Examine the links of the chain for side slackness and renew the chain if any slackness is noticeable when compared with a new chain (photo). It is a sensible precaution to renew the chain at about 30 000 miles (48 000 km) and at a lesser mileage if the engine is stripped down for a major overhaul. The actual rollers on a very badly worn chain may be slightly grooved.

34 Timing chain tensioner – examination and renovation

1   If the timing chain is badly worn it is more than likely that the tensioner will be too.
2   Examine the face of the tensioner which bears against the chain and renew it if it is grooved or ridged.

35 Cylinder block – examination and renovation

Check for cracks. The cost of welding the alloy material must be weighed against a new casing. Threaded holes which have stripped, may have proprietary thread inserts installed to rectify.

36 Rockers and rocker shafts – examination and renovation

1   Check the shafts for straightness by rolling on a smooth surface. It is most unlikely that they will deviate from normal, but, if they do, a judicious attempt must be made to straighten them. If this is not successful purchase a new shaft. The surface of the shafts should be free from any worn ridges caused by the rocker arms.
2   If any wear is present, renew the offending shaft/s. Wear is only likely to have occurred if the rocker shaft oil holes have become blocked.
3   Check the rocker arms for wear of the rocker bushes, for wear of the adjusting ball-ended screws. Wear in the rocker arm bush can be checked by gripping the rocker arm tip and holding the rocker arm in place on the shaft, noting if there is any lateral rocker arm shake. If shake is present, and the arm is very loose on the shaft, a new bush or rocker arm must be fitted.
4   Check the tip of the rocker arm where it bears on the valve head for cracking or serious wear on the case hardening. If none is present reuse the rocker arm. Check the lower half of the ball on the end of the rocker arm adjusting screw.
5   Renew any defective spacer springs.

37 Flywheel/converter plate and starter ring – examination and renovation

1   If the teeth on the flywheel starter ring gear (manual transmission) or torque converter driveplate (automatic transmission) are excessively worn, it will be necessary to obtain complete new assemblies. It is not possible to obtain separate ring gears.
2   On manual transmission models, examine the clutch mating surface of the flywheel and renew the flywheel if scoring or cracks are evident.
3   On automatic transmission models, the converter plate face should be checked for run-out, using a dial gauge. The maximum permissable run-out is 0.3 mm (0.012 in). Renew the plate if this figure is exceeded.

38 Cylinder head and piston crowns – decarbonisation

1   This can be carried out with the engine either in or out of the car. With the cylinder head off carefully remove with a wire brush and blunt scraper all traces of carbon deposits from the combustion spaces and the ports. The valve head stems and valve guides should also be freed from any carbon deposits. Wash the combustion spaces and ports down with petrol and clean the cylinder head surface free of any gasket cement or foreign matter with a suitable solvent.
2   Clean the pistons and top of the cylinder bores. If the pistons are still in the block then it is essential that great care is taken to ensure

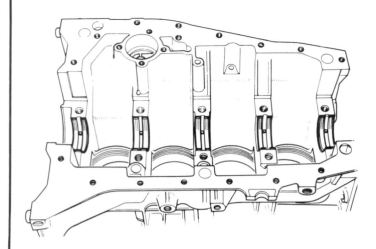

Fig. 1.28 Locate the shells

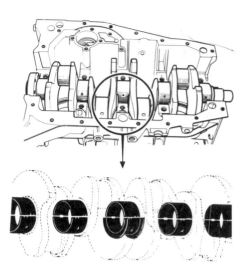

Fig. 1.29 The crankshaft main bearing shell location positions; the central thrust washers adjust the endfloat

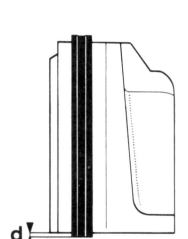

Fig. 1.30 Locate the side seal with 'd' equal to 0.008 in (0.20 mm)

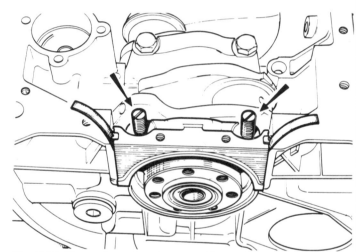

Fig. 1.31 The end cap fitted over guide studs – note protruding shim or protecting tape each side

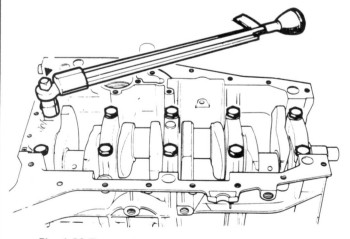

Fig. 1.32 Torque tighten the main bearing cap bolts

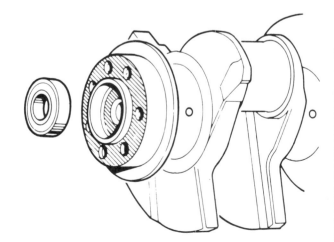

Fig. 1.33 The clutch shaft spigot bearing location in the crankshaft

that no carbon gets into the cylinder bores as this could scratch the cylinder walls or cause damage to the piston and rings. To ensure this does not happen, first turn the crankshaft so that two of the pistons are at the top of their bores (having clamped the liners in position). Stuff rag into the other two bores or seal them off with paper and masking tape. The waterways should also be covered with small pieces of masking tape to prevent particles of carbon entering the cooling system and damaging the water pump.

3   There are two schools of thought as to how much carbon should be removed from the piston crown. One school recommends that a ring of carbon should be left round the edge of the piston and on the cylinder bore wall as an aid to low oil consumption. Although this is probably true for older engines with worn bores, on newer engines the thought of the second school can be applied, which is that for effective decarbonisation all traces of carbon should be removed.

4   If all traces of carbon are to be removed, press a little grease into the gap between the cylinder walls and the two pistons which are to be worked on. With a blunt scraper carefully scrape away the carbon from the piston crown, taking great care not to scratch the aluminium. Also scrape away the carbon from the surrounding lip of the cylinder wall. When all carbon has been removed, scrape away the grease which will now be contaminated with carbon particles, taking care not to press any into the bores. To assist prevention of carbon build-up the piston crown can be polished with a metal polish. Remove the rags or masking tape from the other two cylinders and turn the crankshaft so that the two pistons which were at the bottom are now at the top. Place a rag or masking tape in the cylinders which have been decarbonised and proceed as just described. If a ring of carbon is going to be left round the piston then this can be helped by inserting an old piston ring into the top of the bore to rest on the piston and ensure that carbon is not accidentally removed. Check that there are no particles of carbon in the cylinder bores. Decarbonising is now complete.

5   Check the cylinder head gasket for any sign of distortion. Lay a straight edge across it and along it. If a 0.05 mm (0.002 in) feeler gauge can be inserted between the head and straight edge, then the head must be distorted and in need of resurfacing. The very maximum amount of resurfacing depth permissable is 0.5 mm (0.020 in) and work must be entrusted to an automotive machinist.

39 Engine reassembly – general

1   To ensure maximum life with minimum trouble from a rebuilt engine, not only must everything be correctly assembled, but all the parts must be spotlessly clean, all the oilways must be clear, locking washers and spring washers must always be fitted where indicated and all bearing and other working surfaces must be thoroughly lubricated during assembly. Before assembly begins renew any bolts or studs, the threads of which are in any way damaged, and whenever possible use new spring washers. **Note**: *Before fitting the cylinder head bolts check that the holes and threads in the block are clean and free of oil – this is most important.*

2   Apart from your normal tools, a supply of clean rags, an oil can filled with engine oil (an empty plastic detergent bottle thoroughly cleaned and washed out will invariably do just as well), a new supply of assorted spring washers, a set of new gaskets and a torque wrench should be collected together.

40 Cylinder block – preparation for reassembly

1   Where regular oil changing has been neglected or a bearing has broken up then it will be wise to clean out the oilways of the block using a wire probe and a paraffin syringe, and finally blowing through with air from a tyre pump or a compressed air line.

2   Access to the oilways is obtained by unscrewing and removing the socket screws arrowed in Fig. 1.27. When refitting these plugs, tighten to a torque of 30 lbf ft (45 Nm) except No 1, which should be tightened to 60 lbf ft (83 Nm).

41 Engine reassembly – crankshaft

1   Fit the main bearing upper shells into their crankcase locations, engaging the lock tabs fully into the cut-outs in the bearing recesses as shown in Fig. 1.28.

2   Locate a thrust washer each side of the centre main bearing, with

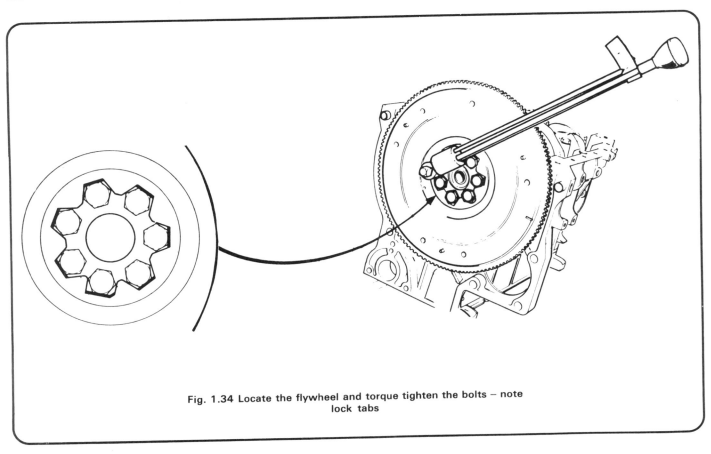

Fig. 1.34 Locate the flywheel and torque tighten the bolts – note lock tabs

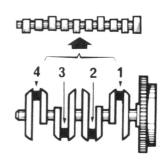

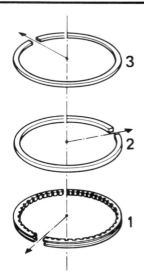

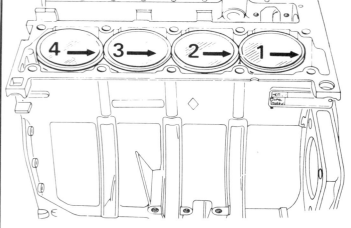

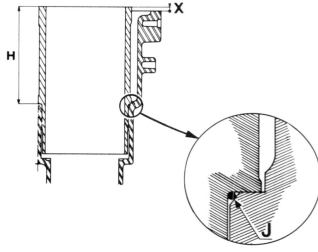

Fig. 1.36 Stagger the ring gaps as shown when fitted

Fig. 1.35 The correct piston positions

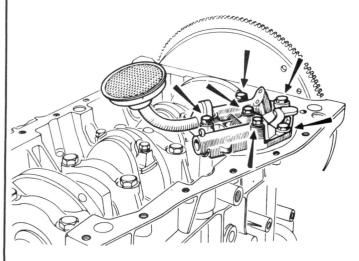

Fig. 1.37 The oil pump location bolts

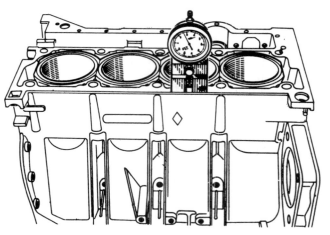

Fig. 1.38 Check the cylinder heights 'H' in position and calculate the protrusion 'X'. Seal 'J' must be correctly located

the white metal face towards the crankshaft webs. Smear them with grease to hold in position.

3 Oil the bearings and crankshaft journals and lay the crankshaft carefully in position in the crankcase.

4 Locate the lower half bearing shells into the bearing caps. Note that no oil holes are provided in the lower halves of bearing Nos 2, 3, 4 and 5. Fit the respective bearing caps into their original positions and semi-tighten the bolts to retain them. Do not fit the No 1 bearing cap at this stage.

5 Check the crankshaft endfloat. This may be done by using either a dial gauge or feeler gauges and prising the crankshaft first in one direction and then the other. The total permissible endfloat must be between 0.05 and 0.23 mm (0.002 and 0.009 inch) and if outside these tolerances, then the thrust washers must be changed for ones of different thicknesses as listed in Specifications.

6 Referring to Fig. 1.30, locate the No 1 main bearing side seals into the cap with the seal groove facing out as shown. When fitted, the seal should protrude from the joint face by about 0.203 mm (0.008 in).

7 Lubricate and insert the bearing shell into position. The bearing seal should also be lubricated at this stage.

8 The bearing cap assembly can now be carefully fitted into position. To protect the seal during assembly, insert a piece of thin shim between the seal and block on each side of the bearing. Renault suggest the use of guide studs to assist the critical fitting of the bearing cap and these are easily fabricated from old, cut down bolts. Once the bearing cap is in position, the studs can be removed, the bolts inserted and the protection shims removed. When in position check that the seal strips still project slightly on each side.

9 Tighten the main bearing cap bolts to the specified torque and then ensure that the crankshaft rotates freely. Recheck the endfloat.

10 The oil seal can now be located to the No 1 main bearing. To ease assembly, lubricate the seal lips and its periphery before fitting. Use a suitable tube drift to drive the seal into position. If the old seal is still available, this can be located between the drift and the new seal to protect the new seal during assembly.

11 Where a new crankshaft has been supplied, insert a new clutch shaft spigot bearing, as shown in Fig. 1.33, using a suitable diameter tube drift. **Note:** *It applies only to manual transmission models.*

42 Flywheel/converter driveplate – refitting

1 Locate the flywheel/converter driveplate (as applicable) onto the crankshaft. Then fit the retaining bolts which must be lightly smeared with a thread-locking compound.

2 On manual transmission models, use a new lockplate. When the bolts are tightened to the specified torque bend over the respective tabs to lock each bolt in position.

3 Referring to Chapter 5, refit the clutch unit.

43 Pistons, connecting rods and cylinder liners – reassembly

1 As previously explained, the fitting of the pistons to the connecting rods will have been carried out by the Renault agent due to the difficulty of removing and inserting the gudgeon pin. Check that the pistons have been fitted correctly, however, by noting that the arrows on the piston crowns will face towards the rear (flywheel end) of the engine when the connecting rod identification markings are facing the camshaft, as shown in Fig. 1.35.

2 If new piston and liner assemblies have been supplied, they must be cleaned of the anti-rust coating. Soak them in a suitable solvent to remove the protective coating – do not scrape it off.

3 Keep the respective pistons and rings with their mating cylinder: They are carefully matched sets.

4 Fit the piston rings to each piston in turn, reversing the process for removal as described earlier in this Chapter. Where new ring sets are being fitted to old pistons and liners, follow the manufacturer's instructions supplied with the rings. *It is most important that the rings are assembled in the correct manner (photo).* Once fitted into their ring grooves, check that the rings are free to rotate around the piston and that they do not bind in the groove when fully compressed. If they do, then it is likely that a piece of carbon still remains on the ring land and it needs further cleaning.

5 Liberally oil the rings and ring grooves and turn the rings so that the gaps are at three different points of circle, as shown in Fig. 1.36.

6 Locate the shell bearings in the connecting rod and cap big-end bearings (photo).

7 Attention must now be given to fitting the liners. Fit each liner in its correct position in the block, having first thoroughly cleaned the mating surfaces.

8 Using a straight edge and feeler gauge, check that each liner protrudes between 0.10 and 0.17 mm (0.004 and 0.0067 in) above the top face of the cylinder block. If incorrect, the liner is faulty.

9 Remove the liners, keeping them identified for positioning.

10 Oil the interior of the liner bore, and then using a clamp (photo) slide the piston/connecting rod assembly into the liner, fitting from the bottom of the liner upwards. The use of plenty of oil and striking blows with the hand will facilitate this operation (photo). Ensure that fitting takes into account the liner, piston crown and connecting rod alignment marks.

11 Fit one O-ring seal to the base of each liner. Place the liner/piston/connecting rod assembly into position in the cylinder block with all locating marks correctly aligned (piston crown facing rear, connecting rod numbers facing camshaft, liner positioning marks correct).

12 Oil the crankpins and pull each connecting rod down so that the respective (numbered) big-end bearing cap complete with shell bearing can be fitted to the crankpin and the big-end bolts tightened to a torque of 35 lbf ft (45 Nm). Washers are not fitted under the big-end nuts (photos).

13 Fit the remaining three piston/liner assemblies in the same way and then apply clamps to keep the liners and seals in position during the remaining engine reassembly operations as shown in Fig. 1.14.

14 Once the piston and liner assemblies are in position, the connecting rods and caps located on the crankshaft and the liners clamped in position, rotate the crankshaft to ensure that it revolves without excessive tight spots. Leave the cylinder clamps in position for subsequent operations until the cylinder head is ready to be fitted.

44 Oil pump – refitting

1 Locate the inner (complete with driveshaft) and outer rotors in the crankcase recess.

2 Fit the oil pump body and screw in and tighten the securing bolts as shown in Fig. 1.37.

3 For further operations with the engine in an upright position, stand the lower faces of the crankcase on blocks of wood in order to protect the oil pump and strainer from damage.

45 Camshaft and timing sprockets – reassembly

1 With the engine in an upright position, oil the camshaft bearing surfaces in the crankcase. Slide the camshaft into position but projecting from the face of the engine by approximately 75 mm (3 in).

2 Place the chain on the camshaft sprocket.

3 Fit the crankshaft sprocket within the loop of the timing chain. Locate the Woodruff key with the groove in the crankshaft.

4 By turning the crankshaft and the camshaft and repositioning the crankshaft sprocket teeth in the links of the chain, a position will be reached where the crankshaft sprocket can be slid onto its key and the timing marks on both sprockets will be in exact alignment with the shaft centres as shown in Fig. 1.40.

5 Drive on the crankshaft sprocket using a tubular drift and at the same time push in the camshaft to its final position, keeping the chain as straight as possible (photo).

6 Screw in the two camshaft flange bolts and bend down the tabs of the locking plates (photo).

7 Locate the plunger filter, and spring into the slipper of the chain tensioner.

8 Fit the tensioner assembly (two bolts) together with its thrust plate. Use an Allen key to release the plunger. Fit the chain anti-flail guards so that there is a parallel gap between the guards and the chain of 0.8 mm (0.032 in).

9 Assuming a new oil seal is to be fitted to the timing cover (in the crankshaft aperture), carefully prise out the old one without distorting the cover. Note which way round the seal is fitted. Support the timing cover underneath the aperture, lubricate the new seal periphery and carefully tap it into position using a suitable diameter tube drift. If the new seal is distorted or damaged in any way during assembly, it must

42

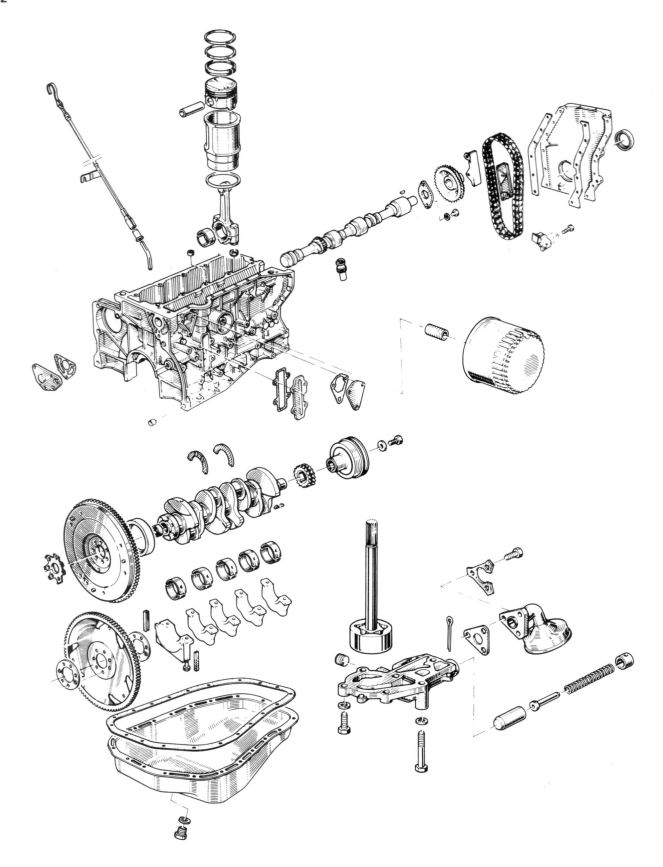

Fig. 1.39 General view of the cylinder block and associate components

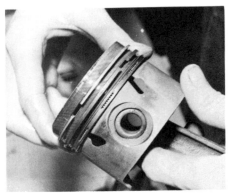

43.4 Correctly fitted piston rings

43.6 Locate the big-end bearing shells

43.10A Fit piston ring clamp

43.10B Slide piston rod assembly into its respective liner

43.10C Direction arrow on piston crown faces rear (flywheel)

43.12A Oiling the crankpins

43.12B Locate the big-end caps

45.5 Drive the crankshaft sprocket into position

45.6 Tightening the camshaft flange bolts

50.2A Insert the tappets ...

50.2B ... and tap lightly to retain in position

50.6 Locate the new cylinder head gasket

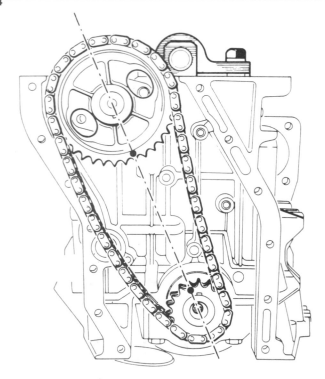

Fig. 1.40 Align the camshaft and crankshaft sprocket timing marks

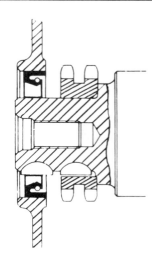

Fig. 1.41 The seal position in the timing chest is important

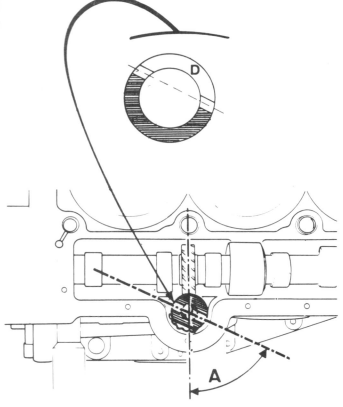

Fig. 1.42 Align the oil pump/distributor drive gear with slot as shown (A = 53°). The slot is offset and the small Section 'D' is towards the camshaft

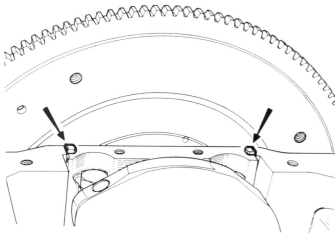

Fig. 1.43 Trim the protruding sections of seal flush to the block face

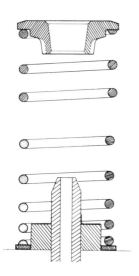

Fig. 1.44 Position the valve springs with close set coils downwards

be renewed. When in position, the seal should be flush with the inner timing case surface, as shown in Fig. 1.41. Lubricate the seal lips with grease before fitting the cover.

10 Stick new timing cover gaskets into position with grease and fit the cover and securing bolts finger tight after inserting the crankshaft pulley Woodruff key. Check that the edge of the timing cover is in alignment with the cylinder head mating surface of the crankcase before finally tightening the timing cover bolts.

11 Locate the crankshaft pulley onto the end of the shaft and make secure with the retaining bolt, which must be tightened to the specified torque. Apply a thread-locking compound to the threads of the bolt.

46 Sump – refitting

1 Where new main bearings and side seals have been fitted, cut off the protruding seal ends. Also trim the timing cover gaskets back, should they protrude beyond the sump/crankcase mating face.

2 Smear the mating surfaces of the crankcase with grease or sealant and stick the sump gaskets in position, aligning the respective bolt holes.

3 Carefully, locate the sump and screw in the bolts fingertight. At the same time, refit the gearbox connecting plate (on manual models). Then tighten the bolts progressively in a diametrically opposed sequence to secure.

4 Fit and tighten the sump drain plug.

47 Distributor drivegear – refitting

1 Turn the engine so that No 1 piston (flywheel end) is at TDC (firing), which will position the cams of No 4 cylinder in the 'rocking' position.

2 Insert the oil pump/distributor drivegear, aligning the offset slot/dog, as shown in Fig. 1.42, with the smaller section towards the camshaft. The slot will be angled at 53° to a right-angled line from the camshaft.

3 Complete this operation by pouring some clean engine oil into the cavity below the camshaft and locating the camshaft rear bearing closure plate with new gasket.

48 Valves – refitting

1 Apply engine oil to the valve stems and slide them back into their original position in the cylinder head.

2 Fit the base washers, the valve springs and the spring cap. The springs must be fitted so that the closer coil gap ends are towards the cylinder head.

3 Using a compressor, compress the valve springs so that the split collets may be located in the recess in the valve stem. The use of a little grease will help to keep the collets in position while the compressor is released.

4 Once all the valves have been reassembled, tap the ends of the stems with a soft-faced hammer to ensure that the collets are correctly seated.

49 Rocker shafts – reassembly

1 Lubricate the rocker shafts located in the clutch end pillar and drive the rollpin into the pillar and inlet rocker shaft concerned, as shown in Fig. 1.45.

2 Next, fit the spring and rockers to their respective shafts, following the illustration as a guide. Note: The inlet and exhaust rocker arms are different, the inlet arm being slightly more curved at the valve stem end.

3 Fit the second distance support pillar and repeat the above procedure, fitting the next rocker arm and spring to each shaft followed by the next pillar, and so on. Lubricate each item in turn as it is assembled.

4 When all the rocker arms, springs and the final pillars are in position, align the hole and drive a new rollpin into the pillar and exhaust rocker shaft at the diagonally opposing end to the other rollpin, fitted earlier.

50 Cylinder head – refitting

1 Before fitting the cylinder head into position, make sure that all the mating surfaces are perfectly clean.

2 Insert the tappets into their original cylinder head locations and tap each one lightly to retain it in its bores when the head is being lowered (photos). Application of some stiff grease to the tappets will assist their retention.

3 Tap the cylinder head locating dowel into position in the top face of the cylinder block. Remove the liner clamps.

4 Clean out the cylinder block blind bolt holes as any trapped oil will prevent correct head fitting.

5 The following operations require extreme accuracy and care, if the fitting of the cylinder head is to give a leak-free installation and the maintenance of good performance. *Do not use gasket cement.*

6 Carefully position a new gasket on the top face of the cylinder block. Check that all the bolt and water holes are clear (photo).

7 Fit the rubber seal round the edge of the tappet chamber ensuring that its ends dovetail into (not overlap) the cylinder head gasket.

8 The rocker shaft assemblies should be positioned on the cylinder head before it is fitted, using the four other rocker bolts and an elastic band (as in the removal procedure).

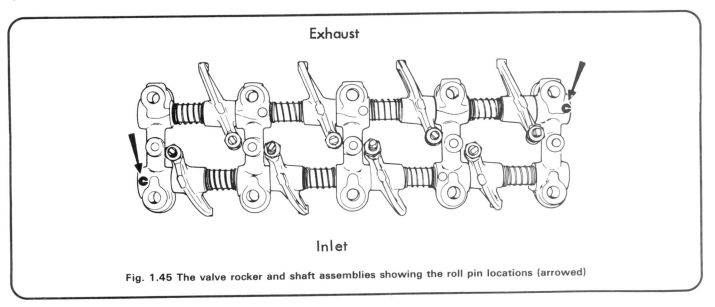

Fig. 1.45 The valve rocker and shaft assemblies showing the roll pin locations (arrowed)

50.10 Fit the rocker assembly and cylinder head bolts

51.2 Checking a valve clearance

51.3 Adjusting a valve clearance

55.3 Reconnect the accelerator cable and linkage to carburettor

9   Lower the cylinder head with extreme care into position on the block, then recheck the alignment of the distributor hole by testing the distributor in position and adjusting the head fractionally until the distributor has a perfect sliding fit into its location. Fit the sparking plug tubes.

10   Smear the cylinder head bolt threads and washers with heavy grease and locate them with the rocker assembly (photos). Screw them into position. Note that the two shooter ones are located at the timing cover end.

11   Slacken off the rocker adjuster nuts and screws, then relocate the pushrods between their respective tappets and rockers. Note that the inlet side pushrods are shorter than those at the exhaust side.

12   Use a torque wrench to tighten the cylinder head bolts in three separate stages, in the sequence shown in Fig. 1.48, to the torque wrench settings given in the Specifications. Final tightening takes place after the engine has been restarted and has reached normal running temperature. Switch off and allow it to cool for 50 minutes. Unscrew the bolts (in sequence) about a quarter of a turn and then retighten them in the prescribed sequence to the final torque wrench setting (hot) given in the Specifications. Repeat the final stage of tightening after the vehicle has covered 300 to 500 miles (500 to 1000 km), and recheck the valve clearances.

13   Check, and adjust as necessary, the valve clearances as given in the following Section.

51 Valve/rocker clearances – adjustment

1   Final and precise adjustment of the valve stem to the rocker arm clearances will be carried out with the engine temperature as described for the final stage of cylinder head bolt tightening in the preceding section. Approximate settings made when the engine is on the bench will require rotation of the engine and this may be done by turning the exposed flywheel or connector plate. When the engine is in the car and a manual gearbox is fitted, top gear should be engaged and front road wheel jacked up and turned. With automatic transmission cars, 'inching' the engine while using the starter motor will have to be resorted to.

2   If fitted, remove the rocker cover and then turn the engine by one of the methods described above until No 1 piston is at TDC on the compression stroke. This may be ascertained by placing a finger over No 1 plug hole and feeling the build-up of pressure. A rod placed in the plug hole will indicate the highest point of travel of the piston which will be for all practical purposes TDC. Both valves for that particular cylinder will now be fully closed and the clearances should be checked using feeler gauges (photo). The clearances should be as specified.

3   If the clearance requires adjustment, loosen the locknut, and with the feeler in position turn the adjuster screw until the feeler blade is nipped and will not move. Now unscrew the adjuster until the feeler

blade is a stiff sliding fit. Tighten the locknut and recheck the clearance (photo).

4   Repeat the adjustment procedure on the other valves bearing in mind the engine firing order (1 – 3 – 4– 2), as if the cylinders are tackled in this sequence, much less engine turning will be required. The inlet valves are on the left when viewed from the front of the car.

52 Inlet and exhaust manifolds – refitting

1   Clean the contact surfaces of both the inlet and exhaust manifolds, also the cylinder head.
2   Check that the coolant passages in the manifold are clear – remove any scale or sludge.
3   Locate the gaskets onto the studs. It is not necessary to apply any sealant solution.
4   Fit the manifolds and secure with washers and nuts.

53 Engine-to-gearbox/transmission – refitting

1   If not already fitted, refer to Chapter 5 and refit the clutch unit to the flywheel. Check that the release bearing and lever are correctly located and lubricate the clutch shaft splines with grease.
2   Adequately support the engine and gearbox/transmission units at

the same relative height so that the gearbox primary shaft will slide in horizontally into the splined hub of the friction disc.
3   The help of an assistant to keep the engine still will be useful. Keep the gearbox/transmission quite level and push it into engagement with the engine. In order to engage the primary shaft of the gearbox with the driven plate splines and finally with the flywheel bush, it may be necessary to turn the gearbox unit slightly or to raise or lower it fractionally, but on no account allow the weight of the gearbox/transmission unit to hang upon the clutch assembly while the primary shaft is passing through it, and support it at all times.
4   Refit the bellhousing securing bolts and fit the starter motor (lower securing bolts only).
5   Locate the rocker cover using a new gasket if required.
6   The combined engine/gearbox/transmission unit is now ready for refitting to the engine compartments.
7   Before coupling an automatic transmission, remember to remove the connector retaining plate fixed on dismantling.
8   When the converter and driveplate are reattached (with the three bolts), ensure that the paint alignment marks correspond to get the correct distributor timing mark position on the converter.

54 Engine – refitting

1   Clean the engine compartment and tie back any cables and wires

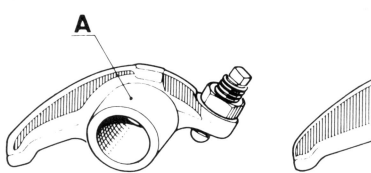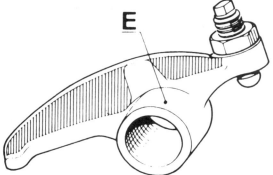

Fig. 1.46 The inlet rocker arm (A) and the exhaust rocker arm (E) differ in profile

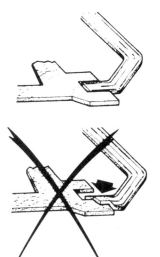

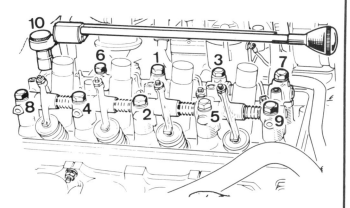

Fig. 1.48 Cylinder head bolt tightening sequence (see special instructions concerning this operation)

Fig. 1.47 Locate the seal and gasket in dovetail fashion

which might interfere with the refitting.

2 Prior to commencing refitting, check the condition of the engine mountings (and gearbox/transmission as applicable). If the rubber mountings show any signs of deterioration or are oil soaked, renew them.

3 Locate and arrange the lifting sling so that when the engine (and transmission as applicable) are lowered into position, they can be suitably angled for easy refitting.

4 Using the hoist, lift the unit/s into the engine compartment, and carefully lower and guide into position. It will be particularly useful to have an assistant during this operation. Raise or lower the height of the transmission accordingly as the unit/s are refitted. Where the gearbox is already in the car, pay particular attention to paragraphs 1 to 3 in the previous Section.

5 Once in position, refit the bellhousing bolts, refit the starter motor, the gearbox mountings (if applicable) and referring to Chapter 8, reconnect the driveshafts, using new rollpins.

6 On automatic transmission models, the engine must be turned over with the starter motor prior to torque tightening the three converter/plate retaining bolts. Therefore do not relocate the converter housing bottom cover until this is achieved. Referring to Chapter 7, reconnect the governor cable which will have to be adjusted.

55 Ancillaries and connections – refitting

1 The engine ancillary items and fittings are reassembled in reverse order to removal. See Section 5, paying particular attention to the following:

   (a) When reconnecting the TDC pick-up unit, adjust its position as described in Chapter 4

   (b) Reconnect and adjust the accelerator cable, as in Chapter 3 (photo)

   (c) When all hoses and pipes are reconnected, refill the cooling system and check for any signs of leakage

   (d) Double-check the respective electrical connections as they are reattached – a mistake could be expensive

   (e) Re-tension the alternator drivebelt (see Chapter 10) and, where fitted, the PAS pump belt (see Chapter 11)

   (f) Reconnect the manual gearbox gear lever assembly

   (g) Reconnect and adjust the clutch cable to release arm (see Chapter 5)

56 Engine – initial start-up after major overhaul

1 Refill the engine and gearbox/transmission units with the correct grade and quantity of oil.

2 Check that there is fuel in the tank and turn the engine over on the starter to prime the fuel pump.

3 Start the engine with the carburettor set to a fast tick-over and then inspect for leaks.

4 Give the car a test run and with the engine at the normal working temperature adjust the carburettor as described in Chapter 3.

5 Check the torque of the cylinder head bolts as described for Section 50, adjust the valve clearances as given in Section 51.

6 Repeat the operations described in the preceding paragraph after 500 miles (800 km) and change the engine oil.

Part B – Overhead camshaft engine

57 General description (ohc engine)

The ohc engine type is a four-cylinder in-line unit mounted at the front of the vehicle. It incorporates a crossflow design head, having the inlet valves and manifold on the left-hand side of the engine and the exhaust on the right.

The inclined valves are operated by a single rocker shaft assembly which is mounted directly above the camshaft. The rocker arms have a stud and locknut type of adjuster for the valve clearances, providing easy adjustment. No special tools are required to set the clearances.

The camshaft is driven via its sprocket pulley from the timing belt, which in turn is driven by the crankshaft sprocket pulley. This belt also drives an intermediate shaft which actuates the petrol pump and oil pump shafts, the actuation being cam and gear respectively. The camshaft drives the distributor direct from its opposing end to the pulley sprocket.

A spring-loaded jockey wheel assembly provides the timing belt tension adjustment.

A single, twin or triple pulley is mounted on the front of the crankshaft and this drives the alternator/water pump drivebelt, the power steering pump drivebelt and the air conditioning compressor drivebelt, as applicable.

The crankshaft runs in the main bearings which are shell type aluminium/tin material. The crankshaft endfloat is taken up by side thrust washers.

The connecting rods also have aluminium/tin shell bearing type big-ends.

Aluminium pistons are employed, the gudgeon pins being a press fit in the connecting rod small-ends and a sliding fit in the pistons. The No 1 piston is located at the flywheel end of the engine (at the rear).

As is typical with Renault engines, removable wet cylinder liners are employed, each being sealed in the crankcase by a flange and O-ring. The liner protrusion above the top surface of the crankcase is crucial; when the cylinder head and gasket are tightened down they compress the liners to provide the upper and lower seal of the engine coolant circuit within the engine.

The cylinder head and crankcase are manufactured in aluminium and the engine is inclined at an angle of 15° when installed in the car.

58 Engine and transmission – removal methods

If only the engine is to be removed, there are no special problems. It can be withdrawn in the normal manner: forwards to disconnect it from the transmission and then upwards through the engine compartment.

Where the transmission is also to be removed, the following points should be noted.

The official Renault Workshop manual suggests that the engine and transmission can be removed together as a unit. It also mentions, however, that the front side members must not be removed.

In our workshop, we found that this crossmember – together with the upper crossmember (in front of the steering rack) – severely restricts the movement of the gearbox when disconnected, since they limit the necessary angular movements required for their joint removal. These crossmembers also make things difficult when removing the gearbox separately to the rear from underneath. In view of the above, we therefore removed the engine first and then the gearbox separately. Both were removed through the engine compartment. This method proved easier and is therefore recommended. The engine removal details are given in Section 61. To remove the gearbox, refer to Chapter 6 or 7 as applicable.

59 Major operations possible with engine fitted

The following major operations can be carried out on the engine, whilst still in place in the vehicle:

   (a) Cylinder head removal

   (b) Camshaft removal

   (c) Timing sprockets and belt removal

   (d) Timing belt tensioner removal

   (e) Intermediate shaft removal

   (f) Inlet and exhaust manifolds removal

   (g) Sump removal

   (h) Big end bearings removal

   (j) Oil pump removal

   (k) Pistons and connecting rod assemblies, and cylinder liners removal

60 Major operations possible with engine removed

The following major operations can be carried out with the engine out of the bodyframe on the bench or floor:

   (a) All items listed in the previous Section

   (b) Crankshaft and main bearings – removal, overhaul and refitting

Fig. 1.49 Cutaway view of the overhead camshaft engine fitted to the TS models

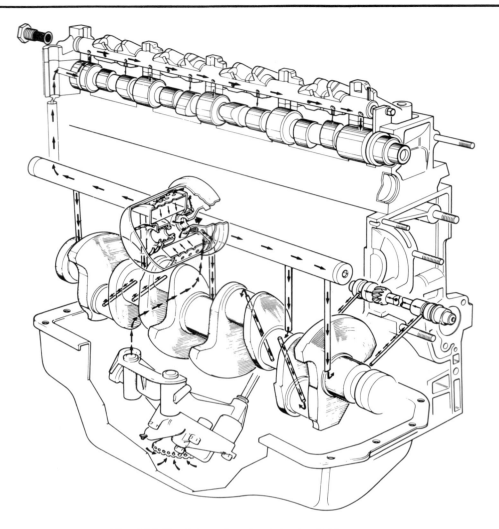

Fig. 1.50 The lubrication circuit in the OHC engine

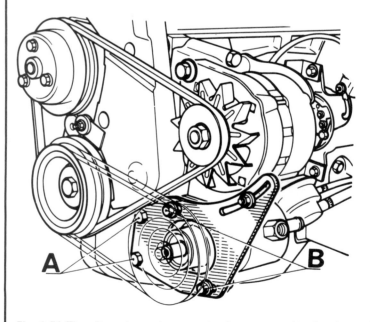

Fig. 1.51 The alternator and power steering pump units showing the respective drivebelts and mounting bolts A and B for the mounting plate

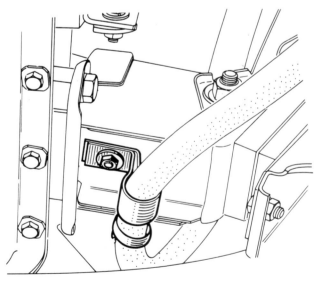

Fig. 1.52 The power steering pipe location bracket under the left-hand engine mounting

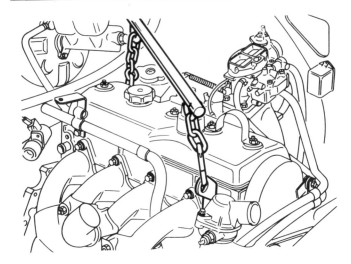

Fig. 1.53 Locate the engine lifting sling as shown

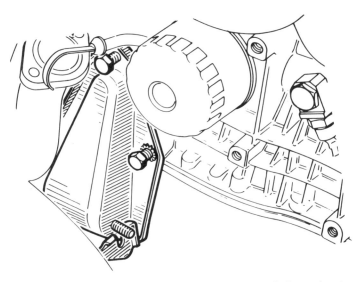

Fig. 1.54 Detach the right-hand engine mounting bolts and nuts

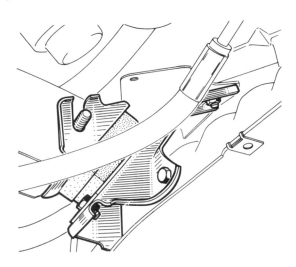

Fig. 1.55 Detach the left-hand mounting

61 Engine – removal

1   Refer to Section 5 in Part A of this Chapter and follow the instructions given in paragraphs 1 to 4 inclusive (photo).

2   Remove the carburettor air filter unit, disconnecting the inlet and outlet pipes and noting their relevant positions. Unclip the filter container retaining strap and lift the filter unit clear.

3   Detach the heater and carburettor hot spot pipes, noting their respective locations.

4   Detach the vacuum pipe to the servo unit at the inlet manifold.

5   Disconnect the breather pipes to the rocker cover.

6   Open the throttle and retain in the open position to slacken the inner cable, thus enabling it to be detached from the quadrant on the carburettor throttle mechanism. Unbolt the cable retainer clamp to the bracket on the rocker cover and fold the cable back, out of the way.

7   Unbolt the clutch slave cylinder and remove it from the clutch housing, by pulling it free from the operating rod attached to the lever. The hydraulic pipe can be left attached to the cylinder and folded back, out of the way.

8   Unscrew the three retaining nuts and detach the exhaust downpipe from the manifold flange joints (photo).

9   Disconnect the inlet and outlet pipes from the fuel pump, located on the bottom front left-hand side of the cylinder block. Plug the pipes to prevent fuel leakage.

10 You will now need to work underneath the car. It should therefore be positioned over a work pit; if possible, or raised and supported with axle-stands and/or blocks. Before working underneath, make sure the vehicle is supported securely and the handbrake is fully applied. Place a wheel chock at each side of a rear wheel to prevent any possibility of the vehicle rolling off the stands.

11 Unscrew and remove the six bolts securing the engine undertray. Do not remove the crossmember.

12 The alternator can be removed from its mounting brackets and placed out of the way at the base of the nearside inner wing panel with the wiring left connected. Remove the mounting/adjuster bolts, hinge the alternator inwards to detach the belt and withdraw the alternator. Alternatively, leave the alternator attached for removal with the engine and simply disconnect the wires.

13 Where power steering is fitted, the alternator belt can only be removed completely after removing the power steering pump drivebelt. The power steering pump must be detached when removing the engine. The pump bracket mounting bolts underneath are most accessible via the vent slots in the engine underpanel at the front. Do not disconnect the pump hoses but position the pump to one side.

14 Remove the starter motor, which is retained by a bracket and two bolts at the front end and three bolts to the clutch housing at the rear. Accessibility is not very good and care must be taken.

15 Detach the TDC pick-up unit (photo), and cover plate (photo). Then unscrew the engine-to-clutch housing retaining bolts. Note that one bolt is hidden from view under the rubber dust cover of the clutch operating lever aperture. Detach the power steering pipe securing bracket from its location under the left-hand engine mounting.

16 Lower the car and then position a jack under the front end of the gearbox. Raise it to support (not lift) the gearbox.

17 Check around the engine to ensure that all associate fittings and connections are detached.

18 Arrange the engine lifting sling, hooking it onto the two lift brackets, one of which is at the front near the thermostat housing and the other diagonally opposite on the side at the rear of the engine, as shown in Fig. 1.53 (photo).

19 Disconnect the right and left-hand engine mounting brackets as indicated in Figs. 1.54 and 1.55.

20 Raise the engine to take its weight and ease it forward away from the clutch housing to disconnect the input shaft from the clutch. When completely disengaged, raise the engine by manoeuvring it forwards and upwards out of the engine compartment to clear the front body crosspanel (photo).

21 Remove the engine to the work area and clean it down prior to any dismantling tasks.

62 Engine dismantling – general

Refer to Section 8 of Part A in this Chapter for full information.

61.1 Remove the radiator

61.8 Detach the exhaust downpipe

61.15a Detach the TDC pick-up

61.15b Remove the coverplate

61.18 Locate the lifting sling

61.20 Lift the engine clear

63.2a Remove the exhaust manifold

63.2b Remove the inlet manifold

63.2c Remove the oil pressure switch

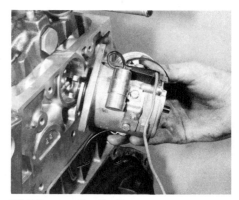
63.5 Remove the distributor

64.9 Clamp the cylinder liners in position

65.2 The No 5 rocker bearing pedestal removed. Note rollpin hole for identification

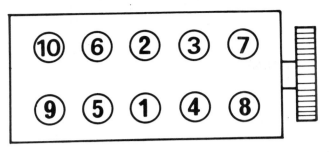

Fig. 1.56 The cylinder head bolts removal/tightening sequence

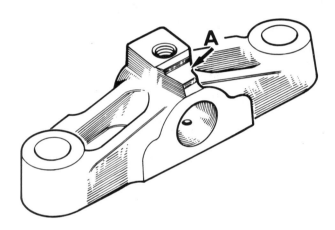

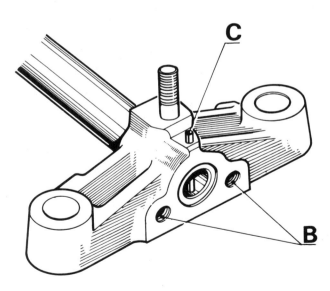

Fig. 1.57 Rocker bearing pedestals

A = Pedestals 1 to 4
B = Pedestal No 5 showing the shim retaining bolt holes and the rollpin location (C)

63 Engine dismantling – ancillaries

1   Before starting to dismantle the ancillary items on the engine, refer to Section 9, paragraphs 1 to 3 concerning replacement engines. If the engine is to be fully dismantled, proceed as follows:
2   Remove the following items, taking note of how they are secured and located (photos):

(a) *The coolant feed pipe to heater from water pump*
(b) *Exhaust manifold*
(c) *Water pump and thermostat housing*
(d) *Inlet manifold and carburettor, noting in particular the interconnecting hot spot pipe layout from the water pump, to the automatic choke manifold and cylinder head*
(e) *If not already disconnected, remove the petrol pump unit with gaskets and spacer plate*
(f) *Unscrew and remove the oil pressure and coolant temperature sender switches*
(g) *Unscrew and remove the oil filter, using a strap wrench if necessary*
(h) *Remove the clutch unit (see Chapter 5)*

3   Before removing the distributor, turn the engine to the top dead centre (TDC) position. This is indicated by the marks on the camshaft and intermediate shaft sprockets being aligned with the timing indicators in the respective apertures in the timing cover. When both marks are in alignment with their pointers, and the No 1 cylinder piston on TDC (firing stroke), scribe a mark on the end of the cylinder block opposite that of the timing mark on the flywheel.
4   Note the position of the distributor rotor arm and make an alignment mark between the distributor flange and the cylinder head. This will act as a timing guide when refitting.
5   Unscrew and remove the three distributor retaining bolts and withdraw the distributor (photo).

64 Cylinder head – removal

1   If the engine is still in the vehicle, drain, disconnect or remove (as applicable) the following items:

(a) *Disconnect the battery earth lead*
(b) *Drain the cooling system (see Chapter 2)*
(c) *Disconnect the wires, pipes and leads to the cylinder head, noting the respective connections*
(d) *Remove the air filter, carburettor and inlet manifold (see Chapter 3)*
(e) *Remove the exhaust manifold, disconnecting it from the cylinder head and exhaust downpipe flange*
(f) *Remove the undertray beneath the engine*
(g) *Where fitted detach the power steering pump drivebelt (see Chapter 11)*
(h) *Detach the alternator drivebelt*
(i) *Remove the diagnostic socket*
(j) *If the cylinder head is to be dismantled and the distributor removed, refer to Chapter 4 and check TDC before unbolting the distributor*

2   The procedure for cylinder head removal with engine fitted or removed is now the same.
3   Unbolt and remove the timing cover.
4   Remove the rocker cover.
5   With the engine set at TDC, the timing belt tensioner bolts can be loosened and the tensioner pivoted to slacken the belt tension. Remove the timing belt.
6   The cylinder head retaining bolts can now be progressively loosened, and with the exception of the front right-hand bolt, removed. Loosen off the bolts in the sequence shown in Fig. 1.56.
7   The cylinder head is now ready for removal from the block, and it is essential that it is detached in the correct manner. Do not lift the head directly upwards from the block. The head must be swivelled from the rear in a horizontal manner, pivoting on the remaining head bolt at the front. You will probably have to tap the head round on its rear corner, using a soft-headed mallet or wood block to break the seal between the head, gasket and block. Once the head is pivoted round and the seal broken, it can be lifted clear. This action is necessary

because if the head were to be lifted directly from the block, the seal between the head, gasket and block would be unbroken and the liners would thus be disturbed. Each liner has a seal around its lower flange; where the liners are not being removed, it is essential that this seal is not broken or disturbed. If the liners are accidentally disturbed they must be removed and new lower seals fitted.

8 The rocker shaft assembly and final bolt can be removed from the cylinder head once it is withdrawn from the engine.

9 To prevent the possibility of movement by the respective cylinder liners whilst the head is removed, it is advisable to place a clamp-plate over the top edges of the liners. A suitable plate (or bar) can be fastened temporarily in position using the existing head bolt holes, using shorter bolts of the desired thread and diameter with large, flat washers under the heads. Alternatively, use a block of wood with two bolts and spacers, clamping it in position in diagonal fashion as shown (photo).

65 Rocker assembly – dismantling

1 Unscrew the end plug from the shaft and extract the plug and filter. This filter must be renewed at 36 000 mile (60 000 km) intervals.

2 Number the rocker arms and pedestals/bearings. Note that bearing No 5 has two threaded holes to retain the shim which adjusts the rocker shaft endfloat, and a hole for the rollpin which locates the shaft and pedestal (photo).

3 Keep the respective parts in order as they are removed from the shaft and note their respective locations. Note also that the machined flat section on top of pedestals 1 to 4 all face towards the camshaft sprocket.

66 Camshaft – removal

1 The camshaft can be removed with the engine fitted in the car. Where this is the case, proceed as follows in paragraphs 2 to 8. Where the engine/cylinder head are removed, proceed from paragraph 9.

2 Disconnect the battery earth lead.

3 Drain the engine coolant (see Chapter 2)

4 Detach the throttle cable from the carburettor and bracket on the rocker cover.

5 Remove the radiator and, where fitted, the electric cooling fan (see Chapter 2).

6 Unscrew and withdraw the front grille panel.

7 Remove the engine undertray.

8 Detach the warm air trunking.

9 Remove the drivebelts to the alternator and, where fitted, the power steering pump and air conditioning pump.

10 Unbolt and remove the timing cover.

11 Disconnect the respective HT leads and remove the sparking plugs. Next, rotate the crankshaft to locate the No 1 piston (flywheel end) at TDC on firing stroke. This can be checked by ensuring the timing mark on the flywheel is in line with the 'O' graduation marked on the aperture in the clutch housing. Rotate the crankshaft by means of a spanner applied to the crankshaft pulley retaining bolt.

12 Next, turn the crankshaft from the TDC a further quarter of a turn clockwise (viewed from the front).

13 Loosen the timing belt tensioner, release the tension and withdraw the belt.

14 To remove the camshaft sprocket, pass a suitable hardwood dowel rod or screwdriver through a hole in the sprocket and jam against the top surface of the cylinder head to prevent the camshaft from turning. Unscrew the retaining bolt and remove the sprocket. Take great care as the sprocket is manufactured in sintered metal and is therefore relatively fragile (photo). Also, take care not to damage or distort the cylinder head. Remove the Woodruff key.

15 Remove the rocker cover and unscrew the cylinder head retaining bolts in a progressive manner in the sequence shown in Fig. 1.56. With the bolts extracted, remove the rocker assembly and relocate some of the bolts with spacers to the same depth as the rocker pedestals fitted under the bolt heads, to ensure that the cylinder head is not disturbed during subsequent operations. If for any reason the head is disturbed, then the head gasket and respective liner seals will have to be renewed – see Section 64, paragraph 7. Remove the distributor (see Chapter 4).

16 Unscrew and remove the two bolts retaining the camshaft location fork plate. Remove the plate from the groove in the camshaft.

17 The camshaft front oil seal can now be extracted from its housing. Carefully prise out from the front or preferably drift out from the rear. Take great care not to damage the seal location bore in the head.

18 The camshaft can now be withdrawn carefully through the seal

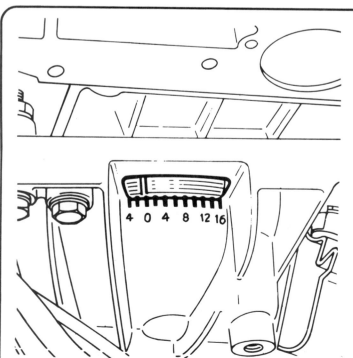

Fig. 1.58 The timing graduation marks in the clutch housing and aperture showing flywheel TDC position mark

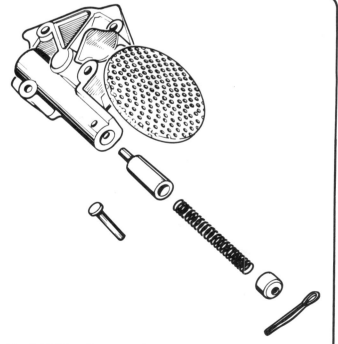

Fig. 1.59 The oil pump unit showing relief valve components removed

66.14 Remove the camshaft sprocket

67.8 The crankshaft pulley, bolt and washer

68.12 The tensioner spring and piston

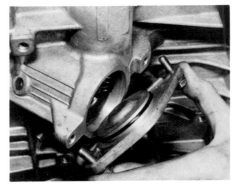

69.8a Unscrew and remove the side cover ...

69.8b ... and extract the oil pump drive

aperture in the front of the cylinder head. Take care during its removal not to snag any of the lobe corners on the bearings as they are passed through the cylinder head.

67 Camshaft pulley, sprocket and front seal – removal

1   The camshaft pulley and front oil seal can be removed with the engine fitted as given below. When removing these items with the engine removed, proceed from paragraph 5.
2   Remove the engine undertray panel.
3   Remove the power steering pump driveshaft (where fitted) and the alternator drivebelt.
4   Remove the clutch shield plate.
5   Turn the engine over to the TDC position (see Chapter 4), with the mark on the flywheel and ' 'O' mark on the clutch housing in alignment.
6   Remove the timing cover.
7   Loosen the timing belt tensioner and remove the belt.
8   Now remove the crankshaft pulley which is secured by a large bolt and washer (photo). To prevent the shaft turning when measuring the bolt, join the flywheel starter ring teeth with a large screwdriver blade jammed against a convenient spot on the cylinder block or clutch housing (engine in position).
9   With the pulley bolt removed, the pulley can be withdrawn from the shaft using a puller, or levering free, but take special care. The timing sprocket is located directly onto the pulley rear face and this sprocket, like its counterparts, is relatively fragile, being manufactured of sintered metal. Remove the sprocket from the crankshaft.
10 Prise the key from the keyway in the shaft. Remove the spacer or air conditioning pulley wheel if fitted.
11 Carefully prise out the old seal using a screwdriver blade but do not damage the seal housing or shaft in the process.
12 The timing sprocket is located onto the rear of the pulley by a couple of rollpins, and the two components can be prised apart with care if desired.
13 Seal refitting (engine fitted) is a reversal of the removal process.

Lubricate the new seal before fitting with clean engine oil and drive it into position using a suitable pipe drift. The seal must be fitted 'squarely' and accurately or it will leak. If distorted in any way during fitting, renew it.
14 When refitting the pulley retaining bolt, smear the threads with a thread locking compound. Readjust the tension of the timing belt and the respective drivebelts, as applicable. **Note**: *Do not get any oil onto the timing belt during the above operations. If it is oil impregnated it must be renewed before refitting.*

68 Timing belt/tensioner – removal

1   If the engine is fitted and only the timing belt and tensioner are to be removed, proceed as given in paragraphs 2 to 13. Where the engine is being dismantled, as given previously, proceed from paragraph 11.
2   Raise the front of the car so that the wheels clear the ground and support it with suitable stands.
3   Unbolt and remove the engine undertray.
4   Remove the power steering pump drivebelt, loosening the pump retaining/adjuster bolts to loosen the tension.
5   Loosen the alternator retaining bolts and remove its drivebelt.
6   Remove the rocker cover.
7   Detach the battery earth terminal.
8   Remove the spark plugs and keep them in order for refitting.
9   Turn the engine over (see Section 63) to the TDC position.
10 Drain the cooling system or clamp the inlet manifold heater hose close to the manifold and detach the outlet hose from the manifold at the timing case end. Remove the timing cover.
11 Loosen the tensioner retaining bolts and remove the belt.
12 Take care when removing the tensioner as it is operated by a spring and piston in the crankcase side and the tensioner is under considerable pressure. As the tensioner is unbolted, take care that the spring and piston (photo) don't fly out of their aperture at high speed!
13 If the engine is installed, ensure that the timing is not disturbed whilst the belt and tensioner are removed.

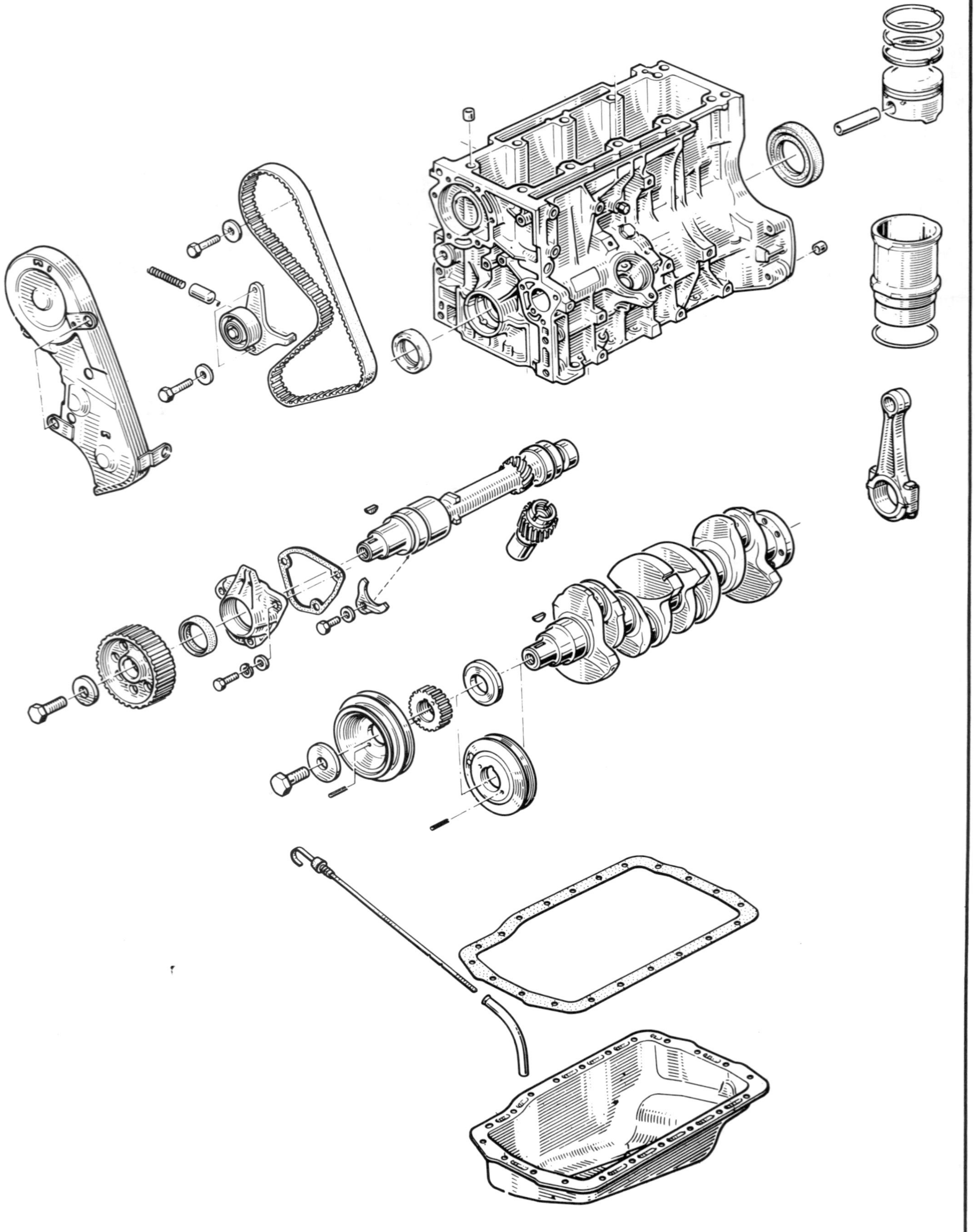

Fig. 1.60 The crankcase and relative components

69 Intermediate shaft and oil seal – removal

1   Where the engine is fitted, refer to the previous Section and follow paragraphs 3 to 6, then continue as follows in paragraphs 2 and 3. Where the engine is removed, continue from paragraph 4.
2   Clamp the inlet manifold heat hose to prevent circulation. Clamp it as close as possible to the inlet manifold and then detach the outlet hose on the manifold.
3   Loosen the timing belt tensioner and remove the timing belt, taking care not to get oil or grease on it.
4   Unscrew the intermediate shaft sprocket bolt, passing a screwdriver shaft or rod through one of the holes in the sprocket to lock against the front of the block and retain the sprocket in position whilst it is being unscrewed.
5   Withdraw the sprocket and remove the Woodruff key from the shaft.
6   Unbolt and remove the intermediate shaft housing.
7   The oil seal can now be extracted. Prise it free with a screwdriver but take care not to damage the housing.
8   Before the intermediate shaft can be withdrawn, the oil pump drive pinion must first be extracted. To do this, unscrew the two side cover retaining bolts and remove the cover. The oil pump drive pinion is now accessible and can be extracted (photos).
9   The intermediate shaft can now be removed from the front of the block.

70 Flywheel – removal

1   The flywheel/converter driveplate is retained in position by seven bolts on the end of the crankshaft.
2   To loosen these bolts, lock the starter ring with a screwdriver blade or similar implement inserted between the teeth of the starter ring and against a portion of the block.
3   With the flywheel 'jammed' to prevent it turning, unscrew the retaining bolts. A thread-locking compound has been applied during assembly and they will therefore be tight to unscrew.
4   The bolt holes are not equidistant and so there is no need to mark the flywheel and crankshaft flange alignment positions prior to removal.
5   If the flywheel/converter driveplate is to be removed or inspected and the engine is in the car, the engine and clutch will have to be removed for access. It is not possible to withdraw the gearbox.

71 Sump and oil pump – removal

1   If the engine is still fitted, drain the engine oil, remove the engine undertray and the flywheel coverplate with TDC pick-up unit.
2   Unscrew the respective sump bolts and prise the sump free.
3   The oil pump is now accessible for removal. First, lift the driveshaft upwards and remove it.
4   Unscrew the two pump unit retaining bolts and withdraw the pump. Note that the pump is also located by dowels.
5   Unscrew the four pump cover bolts to inspect the rotors.
6   Extract the relief valve split pin and withdraw the cup, spring, guide and piston.

72 Piston/liner assemblies, connecting rods and big-end bearings – removal

The general procedures for the above mentioned items are the same as for the ohv engine version given in Part A of this Chapter, Section 17. Note the following additional points:

(a)   If necessary, mark the connecting rods numerically from No 1 (flywheel end) to No 4 on the intermediate shaft side
(b)   If removing the big-end bearings with the engine in situ, it is essential to remove the oil pump for better accessibility

73 Piston rings – removal

Refer to Section 18 of Part A in this Chapter for full information.

74 Gudgeon pins – removal

Refer to Section 19 of Part A in this Chapter for full information.

75 Main bearings and crankshaft – removal

Refer to Section 20 of Part A in this Chapter for full information.

76 Oil pump and lubrication system

1   The engine lubrication system and circuit is shown in Fig. 1.50.
2   Oil from the sump is sucked into the circuit via the pump to the oil filter. From there the oil is passed into the main oil gallery, where it is distributed under pressure to the respective crankshaft main bearings, big-end bearings and at the front end is circulated via the intermediate shaft. Oil to the camshaft and rocker shaft assemblies is fed up from the rear end of the main gallery. The rocker shaft has a small gauze filter at its oilway entrance. The oil passes along the oilway in the rocker shaft and is dispersed from various interspaced holes to the lobes and bearings of the camshaft.
3   The oil pressure is regulated by a valve unit within the oil pump unit. The main oil filter is of the disposable cartridge type and is easily accessible for renewal at the specified intervals.
4   The oil pump can be removed with the engine fitted but due to its location in the underside of the crankcase, the sump must first be removed for access. Once removed, overhaul the pump as described in Section 80, renewing any defective components.

77 Oil filter – removal and refitting

1   The oil filter is a disposable cannister type, horizontally located in the cylinder block on the right-hand side (photo).
2   If the old filter proves too tight to be removed by hand pressure, use a strap wrench to unscrew it. Alternatively, a Jubilee clip (or two joined together to make up the required diameter) strapped around the cannister will provide a better grip point. If necessary, the cannister can be tapped round using a small hammer.
3   Once the old filter is removed, wipe clean the joint area in the

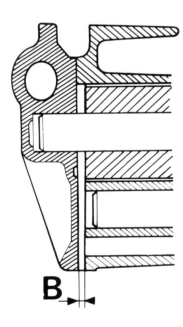

Fig. 1.61 Check the oil pump endfloat at 'B'

77.1 The oil filter location

79.4 View showing the crankshaft pulley to timing sprocket location arrangement

80.2 Remove the pump cover bolts

80.4 Check the rotor clearance

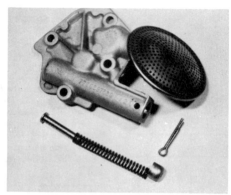

80.7 The relief valve components

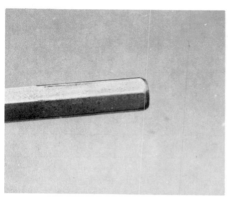

80.8 Check the end of the oil pump driveshaft for signs of wear

83.1 Locate the main bearing shells in the crankcase ...

83.2a ... and lubricate them

83.2b Locate the crankshaft into position

83.3 Fit the shells to the main bearing caps engaging the location tabs

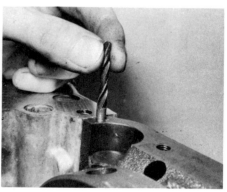

83.6 Use a drill to gauge the seal requirement

83.8 Slide the end caps into position – note the shims each side between the seals and crankcase (arrowed)

cylinder block and lubricate the new seal ring.

4   Screw the filter carefully into position by hand, ensuring that the seal does not twist or distort as it is tightened.

5   Do not overtighten the filter; it need only be tightened by firm hand pressure.

6   Check and top up the engine oil as required, then run the engine to check for any signs of leakage around the filter seal.

78 Engine components – cleaning, examination and renovation

The following engine components should be cleaned, examined for wear and/or damage, and renovated or renewed as applicable. To avoid duplication of text, the components listed below refer to the relevant Section in Part A of this Chapter, but refer to the Specifications for dimensions and clearance checks.

Crankshaft – examination and renovation – see Section 24
Big-ends and main bearings – examination and renovation – see Section 25
Cylinder liners – examination and renovation – see Section 26
Pistons and rings – examination and renovation – see Section 27
Connecting rods and gudgeon pins – examination and renovation – see Section 28
Camshaft and camshaft bearings – examination and renovation – see Section 29
Valves and valve seats – examination and renovation – see Section 31
Valve guides – examination and renovation – see Section 32
Cylinder block – examination and renovation – see Section 35
Rockers and rocker shafts – examination and renovation – see Section 36
Flywheel/converter plate and starter ring – examination and renovation – see Section 37
Cylinder head and piston crowns – decarbonisation – see Section 38

79 Timing case components – examination and renovation

1   The principal items of concern in the timing case components are the timing belt, sprockets and belt tensioner unit.

2   If the timing belt, is obviously worn, shows any signs of cracking or is coated in oil or grease, it must be renewed. The manufacturers recommend that the belt be renewed every 36 000 miles (60 000 km).

3   Clean and inspect the respective belt sprockets. They are manufactured in sintered metal and as such are relatively fragile – so handle with care. If they show any signs of wear or damage they must be renewed. Any slight burrs made by the puller during removal must be removed, using a fine file.

4   The crankshaft sprocket is attached to the pulley wheel by two roll pins and the two components can therefore be separated if necessary. Take care not to damage either component (photo).

5   Examine the timing belt tensioner unit, in particular the jockey wheel tensioner spring and piston. Renew any components showing signs of defects.

6   Where the engine has been dismantled, the front oil seals of the crankshaft, camshaft and intermediate shaft must automatically be renewed on assembly. Failure to do this could cause leakage through one or possibly more of them within a relatively short time and this will in turn ruin the timing belt.

80 Oil pump – overhaul

1   It is essential that all parts of the pump are in good condition for the pump to work effectively.

2   To dismantle the pump, remove the cover retaining bolts and detach the cover (photo).

3   Extract the gears and clean the respective components.

4   Inspect for any signs of damage or excessive wear. Use a feeler gauge and check the clearance between the rotor (gear) tips and the inner housing as shown (photo).

5   Also, check the gear endfloat using a straight-edged rule laid across the body of the pump and feeler gauge inserted between the rule and gears.

6   Compare the clearances with the allowable tolerances given in the Specifications at the start of this Chapter and, if necessary, renew any defective parts, or possibly the pump unit.

7   Do not overlock the relief valve assembly. To extract it, remove the split-pin and withdraw the cup, spring, guide and piston. Again, look for signs of excessive wear or damage and renew as applicable (photo).

8   Check the pump driveshaft for signs of wear or distortion and renew if necessary (photo).

81 Intermediate shaft assembly – examination and renovation

1   Clean and inspect the intermediate shaft, the oil pump drive pinion and associate components.

2   Check the front housing for any signs of cracks or distortion.

3   Check the drive pinion teeth for any signs of damage.

4   Renew any defective components.

82 Engine reassembly – general

Refer to Sections 39 and 40 (Part A) before starting on the engine reassembly. The oilway plugs in the TS engine are shown in Fig. 1.62. If they have been removed, refit them and tighten to the specified torque.

83 Engine reassembly – crankshaft and main bearings

1   Invert the block and locate the main bearing upper shells into position, engaging the lock taps into the cut-outs in the bearing recesses (photo). Note that the bearing shells for bearing Nos 1, 3 and 5 are identical and have two oil holes in them whilst the Nos 2 and 4 bearing shells have three holes and an oil groove in them.

2   Lubricate the shells with clean engine oil and carefully lower the crankshaft into position (photos).

3   Locate the shells to the main bearing caps in a similar manner to that of the block and lubricate (photo). Fit the thrust washers to No 2 main bearing with the dots facing the crankshaft.

4   Fit the respective bearing caps into position (without the side seals at this stage) and torque tighten the retaining bolts.

5   Now check the crankshaft endfloat using a clock gauge or feeler gauges. Note the total endfloat, and then, referring to the Specifications subtract the specified endfloat. Select a thrust washer of suitable thickness to provide the correct endfloat. Washers are available in the thicknesses given in the Specifications.

6   Before removing the crankshaft bearing caps to insert the selected thrust washers check the clearance between the block and the bottom of the seal groove on the No 1 and No 5 bearing caps. This clearance can be checked using twist drills to gauge the clearance (photo). Where the clearance (C) is 5 mm (0.197 in) or less use a seal of 5.15 mm (0.202 in) thickness. Where the clearance (C) is in excess of 5 mm (0.197 in) select a white code seal of 5.40 mm (0.212 in) thickness.

7   Remove the main bearing caps and insert the selected thrust washers, with their slotted faces towards the crankshaft. When relocating the bearing caps, fit the side seals to the grooves of the Nos 1 and 5 main bearings. The grooved seal must face out and protrude from the joint face of the cap by approximately 0.20 mm (0.008 in).

8   When fitting the No 1 and No 5 main bearing caps, locate a feeler gauge blade or shim between the crankcase and the seal on each side to ensure that the cap and seals are fitted and do not become dislodged (photo). Take due care when tackling this awkward operation. When fitting the seal into the groove each side, leave a small amount of seal protruding at the bottom so that it does not slide up the groove as the bearing cap is being fitted.

9   When the end caps are fitted, insert the retaining bolts and check that the crankshaft rotates freely. Tap the bearing housings with a mallet, should the shaft bind. If it continues to bind, a further inspection must be made. Also check that, once in position, there are no gaps between the seals and the crankcase when the shim is removed.

10 Tighten the retaining bolts down to the specified pressure, and recheck the endfloat (photo).

11 Once the shim is removed, the side seals can be trimmed to within 0.5 to 0.7 mm (0.020 to 0.028 in) of the sump joint face. Use a feeler

83.10a Tighten the main bearings and ...

83.10b ... recheck the endfloat

83.11 Trim the seals

83.12 Fit the new seals

84.3 Tighten the flywheel bolts to the specified torque setting

85.3 Check the liner protrusions

85.8a Arrows to flywheel end

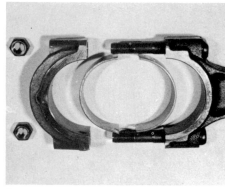
85.8b The connecting rod bearings and cap laid out ready for assembly

85.8c Ensure that rod and cap number markings correspond ...

85.8d ... and fit the caps and bearings

85.8e Torque tighten the big-end bearing cap nuts

86.2 Insert the rotors into the pump

86.5 Refit the pump unit – note driveshaft and C-clip (arrowed)

87.1 Insert the intermediate shaft

87.2 Refit the lockplate

87.3 Insert the new oil seal into the cover

87.4 Relocate the timing belt tensioner assembly

87.5 Fit the cover (note new seal gasket)

87.6 Locate the sprocket and retain with bolt and flat washer

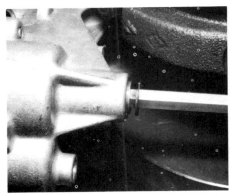

87.8 Check that the circlip is in position on the driveshaft (oil pump end)

87.9 The side cover – note the seal location

88.3 Refit the sump

89.3a Insert the valve ...

89.3b ... and locate the base washers, springs and spring cap

gauge blade of the required thickness to act as a guide when trimming off the seal (photo).

12 Lubricate the new front and rear main bearing oil seals and carefully locate them into their apertures, tapping them fully into position using a tube drift of a suitable diameter (photo). Ensure that the seals face the correct way round, with the cavity/spring side towards the engine. Should the seal lip accidentally become damaged during fitting, remove and discard it and fit another new seal.

13 If a new clutch spigot bearing is being fitted now is the time to do it. Drive it home using a suitable diameter tube drift.

Note: *When fitting this bearing to the crankshaft, on an engine in which the flywheel bolts are not retained by locktabs, smear the outer bearing surface with a suitable thread locking compound.*

84 Flywheel/converter driveplate – refitting

1 Locate the flywheel or converter driveplate (as applicable) onto the crankshaft and align the bolt holes (which are not equidistant).

2 If the retaining bolts are fitted with a lockplate, use a new plate, and when the bolts have been tightened to the specified torque, bend over the tabs to lock each bolt in position.

3 Where no lockplate is fitted, smear the bolt threads with a thread-locking compound and tighten to the specified torque (photo).

4 On manual transmission models, refit the clutch unit as described in Chapter 5.

85 Cylinder liners, pistons and connecting rods – refitting

1 Before fitting the piston and connecting rod assemblies into the liners, the liners must be checked in the crankcase for depth of fitting. This is carried out as follows.

2 Although the cylinder liners fit directly onto the crankcase inner flange, O-ring seals are fitted between the chamfered flange and the lower cylinder section as shown in Fig. 1.64. New O-rings must always be used once the cylinders have been disturbed from the crankcase.

3 First, insert a liner into the crankcase without its O-ring and measure how far it protrudes from the top face of the crankcase. Lay a straight edge rule across its top face and measure the gap to the top face of the cylinder block with feeler gauges. It should be as given in the Specifications (photo).

4 Now check the height on the other cylinders in the same way and note each reading. Check that the variation in protrusion on adjoining liners does not exceed 0.04 mm (0.0016 in).

5 New liners can be interchanged for position to achieve this if necessary, and when in position should be marked accordingly 1 to 4 from the flywheel end.

6 Remove each liner in turn and position an O-ring seal onto its lower section so that it butts into the corner, taking care not to twist or distort it.

7 Wipe the liners and pistons clean and smear with clean engine oil, prior to their respective fitting.

8 The instructions covering the fitting of the piston rings, pistons and connecting rods are covered in Section 43 of Part A, paragraphs 1 to 6 and 10 to 14 inclusive. Make sure that the following points are adhered to:

(a) *The arrows on top of the pistons must point towards the flywheel (photo)*

(b) *The connecting rods and caps must be tightened to the specified torque with the numbered markings in alignment (photos)*

(c) *When assembled, reclamp the liners and rotate the crankshaft to ensure it rotates smoothly*

86 Oil pump – refitting

1 Lubricate the respective parts of the oil pump and reassemble.

2 Insert the rotors (photo) and refit the cover. No gasket is fitted on this face.

3 Tighten the retaining bolts to secure the cover.

4 Insert the oil pressure relief valve assembly, fitting the piston into the spring and the cup over the spring at the opposing end. Compress into the cylinder and insert a new split-pin to retain the valve assembly

in place.

5 Fit the assembled pump unit into position, together with the driveshaft. Ensure the driveshaft has the C-clip fitted into its groove, and that this is fitted at the pump end of the shaft (photo). Tighten the retaining bolts.

87 Intermediate shaft – refitting

1 Lubricate the shaft and insert it through the front of the crankcase (photo).

2 Slide the lockplate fork into the protruding shaft location groove and secure the plate with bolt and washer. Check that the shaft is free to rotate on completion (photo).

3 Fit the new oil seal into the intermediate shaft front cover and lubricate its lips (photo).

4 The timing belt tensioner can also be fitted at this stage (photo). Insert the spring into its housing in the side of the crankcase and locate the plunger over it. Compress the spring and locate the tensioner jockey wheel arm, retaining it with bolts. The spring tension is quite strong and an assistant will probably be required here.

5 Fit the front cover carefully into position with a new gasket, and retain it with the bolts (photo).

6 Fit the Woodruff key into its groove in the shaft and carefully locate the intermediate shaft drive sprocket into position with its large offset inner face towards the crankcase (photo). Use a suitable diameter drift to tap the sprocket into position over the key.

7 Prevent the sprocket from rotating by inserting a screwdriver blade or similar through a sprocket hole, and tighten the retaining nut (complete with flat washer) to the specified torque.

8 If not already located, the oil pump drive pinion and shaft can now be inserted through the side cover hole in the crankcase. Make sure that the limiting circlip is in position on the oil pump end of the shaft (photo). Once in position, lubricate with engine oil to prevent pinion 'pick-up' on restarting the engine.

9 Ensure that the intermediate shaft and oil pump drive rotate freely, then refit the side cover with seal and secure with bolts (photo).

10 Refit the petrol pump.

88 Sump – refitting

1 Check that the mating surfaces of the sump and crankcase are perfectly clean, with no sections of old gasket remaining.

2 Smear an even layer of sealant round the two mating flange surfaces and locate the gasket.

3 Fit the sump carefully into position and locate the retaining bolts (photo). Tighten the bolts progressively by hand in a diagonally opposed sequence, and finally, tighten to the recommended torque setting.

4 Fit and tighten the sump drain plug.

89 Valves – refitting

1 Lubricate the valve stems and guide bores with clean engine oil prior to inserting them into their respective positions. All traces of grinding paste around the valve seat and cylinder head seating faces must be removed – check this before each valve is fitted.

2 As each inlet valve is relocated in its guide, fit a new O-ring seal over the stem. These O-rings are not fitted to the exhaust valves.

3 Fit the base washers, springs and spring cap (photo). The springs must be located with the close coil gaps downwards (to the head) as in Fig. 1.65.

4 Using a valve spring compressor, compress the valve springs sufficiently to allow the split collets to be located in the groove of the valve stem, then release the compressor (photo). The use of a little grease will retain the collets in position as the compressor is removed.

5 When all the valves are reassembled, tap the end of each stem in turn with a soft-faced hammer to ensure that the collets are correctly seated.

90 Rocker shaft – reassembly

1 Lubricate each component as it is assembled with engine oil. Lay

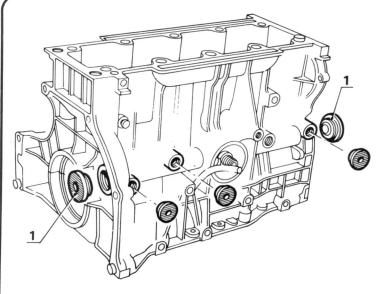

Fig. 1.62 The crankcase oilway plug locations – note positions of No 1 plugs

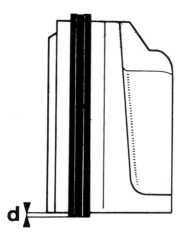

Fig. 1.63 Check seal protrusion from cap joint face at 'D' – this must be 0.008 in (0.20 mm)

Fig. 1.64 The liner seal location (J) when fitted – measure protrusion X

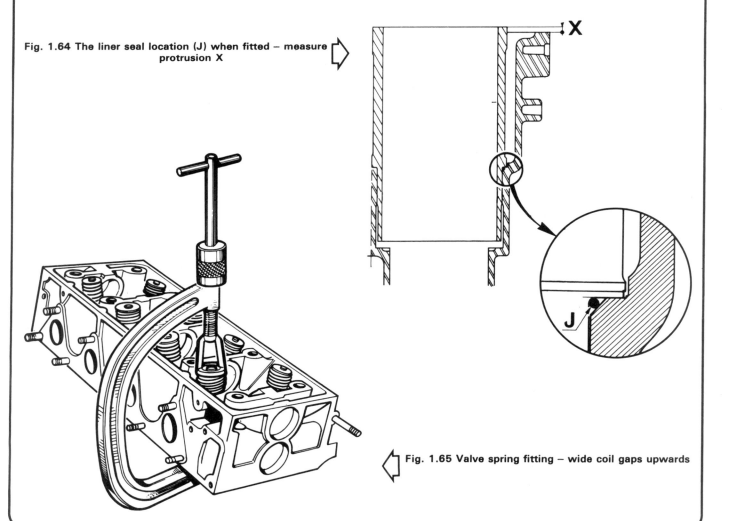

Fig. 1.65 Valve spring fitting – wide coil gaps upwards

89.4 Compress the springs and locate the collets

90.2 Insert the filter and retaining bolt

90.3 The pedestal retaining pin

91.2 Insert the camshaft

92.4 Locate the gasket

92.5a Lower the cylinder head into position, and ...

92.5b ... locate the rocker shaft assembly

92.7a Fit the camshaft retaining plate ...

92.7b ... and check the endfloat of the camshaft

92.8 Refit the camshaft sprocket

93.4 The crankshaft spacer washer and Woodruff key

93.10 Check belt tension at point arrowed

the pedestals, spacers, springs and rockers out in order of appearance.

2 Support the rocker shafts in a soft-jawed vice and insert the new filter into the end of it (photo), fit the retaining bolt and tighten it to the specified torque.

3 Assemble the respective pedestals, rocker arms springs and spacers onto the shaft. When the shaft assembly is complete, compress the last pedestal to align the retaining pin hole in the shaft and pedestal. Drive a new pin into position to secure (photo). Early models fitted with a hollow type roll-pin should have the later solid type pin fitted on reassembly.

91 Camshaft – refitting

1 Check that the respective camshaft location bearings in the cylinder head are perfectly clean and lubricate with some engine oil. Similarly lubricate the camshaft journals and lobes.

2 Insert the camshaft carefully into the cylinder head, guiding the cam sections through the bearing apertures so as not to score the bearing surfaces (photo).

3 With the camshaft in position, the front oil seal can be carefully drifted into position. Lubricate the seal lips with oil and drive into its location using a suitable tube drift.

92 Cylinder head – refitting

1 Before refitting the cylinder head, check that all the mating surfaces are perfectly clean. Loosen the rocker arm adjuster screws fully back. Also ensure that the cylinder head bolt holes in the crankcase are

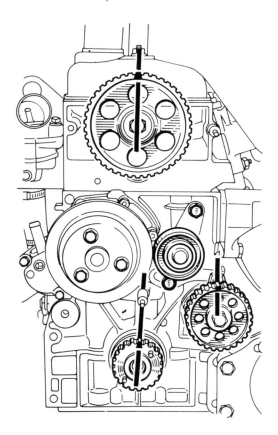

Fig. 1.66 The timing sprocket marks aligned at their respective timing positions

Mark on camshaft sprocket in line with rocker cover stud
Mark on crankshaft sprocket in line with central timing case stud
Mark on intermediate shaft sprocket in line with edge of crankcase

clean and free of oil. Syringe or soak up any oil left in the bolt holes, and in the oil feed hole on the rear left-hand corner of the block. This is most important in order that the correct bolt tightening torque can be applied.

2 Prior to removing the liner clamps, rotate the crankshaft to locate the pistons halfway down the bores. Check that the location dowel is in position at the front right-hand corner.

3 Remove the liner clamps.

4 Fit the cylinder head gasket onto the cylinder block (photo) upper face and ensure that it is exactly located. If possible, screw a couple of guide studs into position: They must be long enough to pass through the cylinder head so that they can be removed when it is in position.

5 Lower the cylinder head into position, engaging with the dowel, and then locate the rocker assembly (photo). Remove the guide studs if they were used.

6 Lubricate the cylinder head bolt threads and washers with engine oil, then screw them into position. Tighten them progressively in the sequence given in Fig. 1.56. Tighten all the bolts to the initial torque specified then further tighten the second torque specified. Now slacken off each bolt a quarter of a turn and retighten to the final torque specified.

7 Locate the camshaft retaining plate in the groove of the camshaft and retain it with bolts and washers. Check the camshaft endfloat and, if necessary, adjust by fitting a retainer plate of an alternative thickness.

8 Refit the camshaft sprocket and tighten the retaining bolt and flat washer to the specified torque (photo). When fitting the sprocket, ensure that the keyway is in exact alignment with the key. The sprocket inner hub is offset to the camshaft.

9 The valve rocker clearance adjustment can now be made (see Section 95).

93 Timing sprockets, tensioner and belt – refitting and adjustment

1 Referring to Chapter 2, refit the water pump with its pulley and outlet pipe.

2 Refit the thermostat (see Chapter 2), and relocate the hose between the water pump housing and the thermostat housing, securing with jubilee clips.

3 Refit the timing belt tensioner unit (if not already assembled). Insert the spring and piston into the crankcase aperture. Locate the jockey wheel. Fitting the top bolt first and pushing it inwards, compress the piston and spring, then screw in the lower adjustment bolt. Do not tighten it at this stage.

4 Refit the crankshaft pulley unit comprising a spacer washer (or air compressor drive pulley where fitted), the Woodruff key and the timing sprocket and pulley (photo).

5 Rotate the crankshaft to the TDC position with No 1 piston on firing stroke. The bottom sprocket timing mark should be in alignment with the timing case retaining stud, as shown in Fig. 1.66. Check this at the rear end by the mark on the flywheel, which should be opposite the mark on the rear face of the crankshaft when dismantled.

6 Set the camshaft sprocket with its timing mark aligned with the rocker cover stud.

7 Align the intermediate shaft sprocket vertically in line with the crankcase web.

8 The timing belt can now be relocated over the sprockets and with its outer face bearing on the adjuster jockey wheel. If using the old belt (which is *not* recommended), it should be fitted facing the same way as when removed.

9 To adjust the tensioner, loosen the tensioner bolts about a quarter of a turn to allow the tensioner to automatically take up any belt slack under the spring tension. Tighten the tensioner retaining bolts.

10 Next check the timing belt tension at the mid-point of its longest run (between the camshaft and intermediate shaft pulleys). The correct amount of deflection is about 6 mm ($\frac{1}{4}$ in) (photo).

11 As a double check on the tension, turn the engine through two complete revolutions in a clockwise direction (when facing the sprockets), loosen the tensioner bolts and allow the tensioner to readjust itself, if at all. Then recheck the belt tension after retightening the bolts. **Note:** *Do not turn the engine in an anti-clockwise direction!*

12 Refit the timing cover to complete. Do not forget the spacer tube, which fits onto the stud immediately above the crankshaft pulley and the hose clips on the upper left-hand bolt (photo).

93.12 Timing cover location stud and spacer

95.4 Adjust the valve clearances

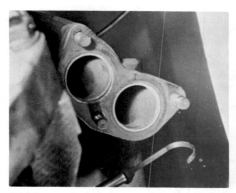

97.5 Locate the exhaust manifold gasket over the studs

94 Inlet and exhaust manifolds – refitting

1   Check that the mating faces of the respective manifolds and cylinder head are perfectly clean.
2   Fit the combination gasket onto the exhaust manifold studs and the individual gaskets onto the inlet manifold studs.
3   Refit the manifolds and secure with washers and nuts.

95 Valve rocker clearances – adjustment

1   The precise adjustment of the valve/rocker clearances is of utmost importance for two main reasons. The first, to enable the valves to be opened and fully closed at the precise moment required by the cycle of the engine. The second, to ensure quiet operation and minimum wear of the valve gear components.
2   Settings made when the engine is on the bench will require rotation of the engine and this may be done by turning the exposed crankshaft pulley bolt with a 22 mm spanner. If the engine is in the car and a manual gearbox fitted, select top gear, then jack-up the front so that a front wheel is clear of the ground and can be turned. With automatic transmission, this method is not possible and 'inching' the engine using the starter motor will have to be resorted to.
3   Turn the engine by means of one of the methods described until No 1 piston is at TDC on the compression stroke. This may be ascertained by placing a finger over No 1 plug hole and feeling the build-up of pressure. A rod placed in the plug hole will indicate the highest point of travel of the piston which will be for all practical purposes TDC. Both valves for that particular cylinder will now be fully closed and the clearances should be checked using feeler gauges (photo). The clearances should be as given in the Specifications.
4   If the clearance requires adjustment, loosen the locknut, and with the feeler in position turn the adjuster screw until the feeler blade is nipped and will not move. Now unscrew the adjuster until the feeler blade is a stiff sliding fit. Tighten the locknut and recheck the clearance (photo).
5   Repeat the adjustment procedure on the other valves bearing in mind the engine firing order (1-3-4-2), as if the cylinders are tackled in this sequence, much less engine turning will be required.

96 Engine – refitting

1   The engine refitting procedures are similar to those of the ohv version engine, therefore refer to the relevant Section in Part A of this Chapter. Note the following additional points, however:

2   If removed, re-engage the clutch release arm, attaching to the ball-head bolt in the clutch housing. Prise open the spring in the rear of the arm using a suitable screwdriver, and push the arm down into position, engaging with the ball-head.
3   Arrange the engine lifting sling so that the engine tilts downwards at the rear and is inclined to the left side.
4   When lowering the engine into position, do not forget to guide the lower power steering pipe underneath the engine mounting.
5   Raise the front of the gearbox as much as possible initially, to assist in aligning the two units until the input shaft is engaged. The engine and clutch housing can then be drawn together using retaining bolts and the respective units jointly lowered. Guide the engine over the mountings and engage the retaining bolts. A mirror will be of assistance to align the mounting holes on the right-hand side.
6   Where power steering is fitted, locate the pipe retainer under the left-hand mounting. When secure, ensure that the pipe does not chafe against any of the surrounding components.
7   The refitting procedures are otherwise a direct reversal of the removal process.

97 Ancillaries and fittings – refitting

1   The engine ancillary items and fittings are reassembled in the reverse order to removal as given in Section 63. When refitting the following items, attend to the respective adjustments and special fitting instructions with due care.
2   When the engine is refitted to an automatic transmission, re-attach the driveplate bolts before assembling the lower coverplate and TDC pick-up unit. Ensure that the converter and driveplate are realigned as when removed.
3   Reattach the starter motor with the three bolts at the rear and two at the front. Make sure that the wiring connections are correctly made.
4   Fit the power steering pump and bracket, followed by the alternator and respective drivebelts, which must be retensioned.
5   Reconnect the exhaust downpipe, applying some suitable sealant to the pipe joint connections (photo). Use new clamps where the old ones are suspect at the bottom end.
6   Reconnect the radiator and the respective coolant hoses, a layout of which is given in Chapter 2.
7   Reconnect the throttle cable. Any adjustments that may be necessary can be made when the engine is restarted.
8   Top up the engine and gearbox with the relevant oils on completion. Refill the cooling system and bleed it as described in Chapter 2.
9   Before restarting the engine, check that all fittings and ancillaries have been securely located. Do not leave tools lying around the engine area, and wipe up any spillages clean.
10 See the briefnotes in Section 56 prior to starting up.

Part C – Fault diagnosis

98 Fault diagnosis – engine

Symptom	Reason/s
Engine will not turn over when starter switch is operated	Flat battery Bad battery connections Bad connections at solenoid switch and/or starter motor Starter motor jammed Defective solenoid Starter motor defective
Engine turns over normally but fails to start	No spark at plugs No fuel reaching engine Too much fuel reaching the engine (flooding)
Engine starts but runs unevenly and misfires	Ignition and/or fuel system faults Incorrect valve clearances Burnt out valves Worn out piston rings
Lack of power	Ignition and/or fuel system faults Incorrect valve clearances Burnt out valves Worn out piston rings
Excessive oil consumption	Oil leaks from gaskets or seals Worn piston rings or cylinder bores resulting in oil being burnt by engine Worn valve guides and/or defective valve stem seals
Excessive mechanical noise from engine	Wrong valve to rocker clearances Worn crankshaft bearings Worn cylinders (piston slap) Slack or worn timing chain and sprockets (ohv models)
Poor idling	Leak in inlet manifold gasket

Note: *When investigating starting and uneven running faults, do not be tempted into snap diagnosis. Start from the beginning of the check procedure and follow it through. It will take less time in the long run. Poor performance from an engine in terms of power and economy is not normally diagnosed quickly. In any event, the ignition and fuel systems must be checked first before assuming any further investigation needs to be made.*

Chapter 2 Cooling system

Contents

Specifications

System type .... Sealed and pressurised, with centrifugal circulation pump, fan and thermostat

Coolant capacity (including heater)
ohv engines – types 843–20 and 843–21 (20TL) .... 7.2 litres (12.7 pints)
ohv engines – versions with air conditioning .... 7.7 litres (13.5 pints)
ohc engines – types 829–A700 and 829–B701 (20TS) .... 7.8 litres (13.7 pints)
ohc engine – versions with air conditioning .... 8.2 litres (14.5 pints)

Drivebelts – maximum deflection adjustments
TL models:
    Water pump/alternator belt .... 4.5 to 5.5 mm ($\frac{11}{64}$ to $\frac{7}{32}$ in)
    Power-assisted steering pump belt and air conditioning
    compressor belt .... 5.5 to 6.4 mm ($\frac{7}{32}$ to $\frac{1}{4}$ in)
TS models:
    Water pump/alternator belt .... 5.5 to 6.5 mm ($\frac{7}{32}$ to $\frac{1}{4}$ in)
    Power-assisted steering pump belt and air conditioning
    compressor belt .... 4.0 to 5.5 mm ($\frac{5}{32}$ to $\frac{7}{32}$ in)

Thermostat (TL and TS models)

	Temperate climate	Hot climate
Opening temperature	83°C (182°F)	75°C (167°F)
Fully open	95°C (203°F)	87°C (189°F)

1 General description

1 The system is of pressurised type and sealed, but with the inclusion of an expansion bottle to accept coolant displaced from the system when hot and to return it when the system cools.

2 Coolant is circulated by thermosyphon action and is assisted by means of the impeller in the belt-driven water pump.

3 A thermostat is fitted in the outlet of the water pump. When the engine is cold, the thermostat valve remains closed so that the coolant flow which occurs at normal operating temperatures through the radiator matrix is interrupted.

4 As the coolant warms up, the thermostat valve starts to open and allows the coolant flow through the radiator to resume.

5 The engine temperature will always be maintained at a constant level (according to the thermostat rating) whatever the ambient air temperature.

6 The coolant circulates around the engine block and cylinder head and absorbs heat as it flows, then travels in an upward direction and out into the radiator to pass across the matrix. As the coolant flows across the radiator matrix, air flow created by the forward motion of the car cools it and it returns via the bottom tank of the radiator to the cylinder block. This is a continuous process, assisted by the water pump impeller.

7 Later models are fitted with an electric cooling fan which is actuated by the thermostatic switch according to coolant temperature.

8 The car interior heater operates by means of water from the cooling system.

9 Carburettors fitted to the Renault are fitted with water connections from the cooling system for the purpose of choke operation or hot spot heating and the models are dealt with in Chapter 3.

2 Cooling system – draining

1 If the coolant is known to be in clean condition and of the correct constituency of antifreeze mixture, arrange suitable containers to hand

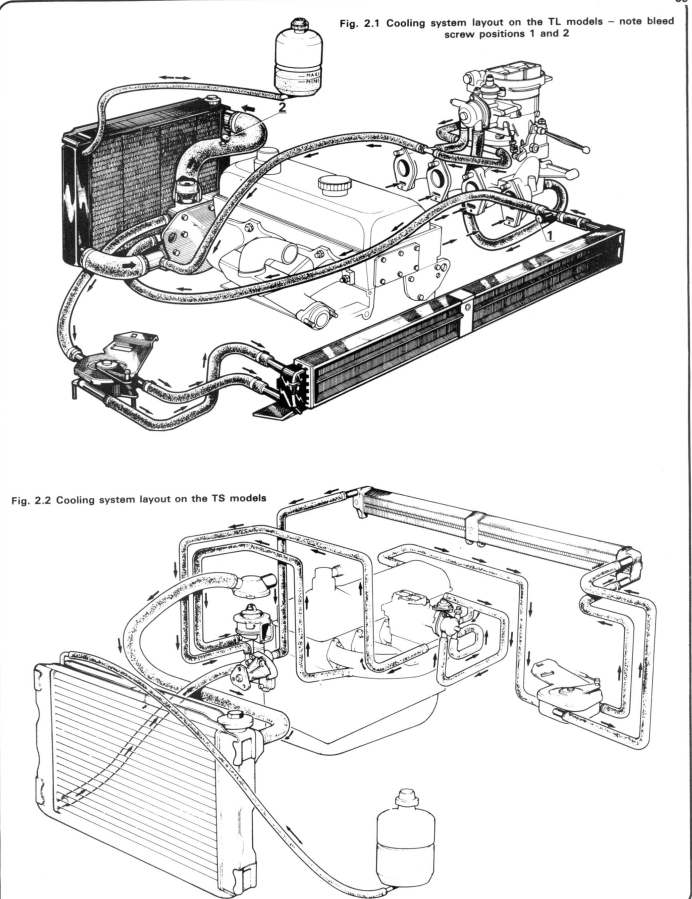

Fig. 2.1 Cooling system layout on the TL models – note bleed screw positions 1 and 2

Fig. 2.2 Cooling system layout on the TS models

before commencing draining.

2   Where one object of draining is to flush the system then it is to be recommended that the engine is at normal operating temperature as sludge and dirt will then be in suspension and more readily removed. If the engine is drained hot, flush with hot water *not* cold or distortion or cracking of internal engine components may occur.

3   Set the facia heater control to 'hot'.

4   Remove the air vent valve from the expansion bottle (photo).

5   Open the drain tap at the bottom rear face of the radiator and drain. The coolant will flow slowly at first and as the expansion bottle empties it will flow faster. As this stage, unscrew and remove the radiator filler cap (photo).

Note: *Where there is no drain plug or tap fitted to the radiator base, unscrew and detach the radiator bottom hose connection to drain the system. Due to the uncontrolled flow of coolant when the hose is disconnected, extra care must be taken when the coolant is hot.*

6   To drain the cylinder block on TL engine versions, unscrew the plug shown in Fig. 2.3.

7   To drain the cylinder block on the TS engine versions, unscrew and remove the drain plug on the exhaust side of the engine for partial draining, as shown in Fig. 2.4, and the drain plug on the inlet side of the engine (Fig. 2.5) for full draining.

8   Open the bleed screws located in the heater return hose, and the radiator top hose (20 TL engines) or the automatic choke housing and thermostat housing on the TS versions.

3   Cooling system – flushing

1   Remove the thermostat from its water pump location as described in Section 10.

2   Temporarily reconnect the hose to the water pump outlet.

3   Check that the drain plugs are open and that the heater control is on 'hot'.

4   Insert a hose in the radiator filler cap and flush through until the water emerges clean. Use hot water if the engine was drained hot.

5   The accumulation of sludge or scale may necessitate removal of the radiator (Section 6) and reverse flushing. This is carried out by inverting the radiator matrix and placing a hose in the outlet pipe so that water flows in a reverse direction to normal.

6   The use of chemical descaler should only be used in a cooling system if scale and sludge formation are severe and then adhere strictly to the manufacturers instructions.

7   Leakage of the radiator or cooling system may be temporarily stopped by the use of a proprietary sealant but in the long term, a new cylinder head or other gasket, water pump, hoses or radiator matrix must be installed. Do not attempt to solder a radiator yourself. The amount of local heat required will almost certainly melt adjacent joints. Take the radiator to a specialist or exchange it for a reconditioned unit.

4   Cooling system – filling and bleeding

1   Have ready a sufficient quantity of coolant mixture as described in Section 5. Close the radiator and block taps and/or reconnect the bottom hose.

2   Turn the heater control lever to 'hot'.

3   Check that the bleeder screws are fully open (photos).

4   Loosen the expansion bottle clip and lift the bottle temporarily as high as possible (whilst still connected to the hose).

5   Next refill the radiator to the 'full' mark and refit the radiator cap. Complete the filling of the system by pouring into the expansion bottle, from where it will circulate round the system.

6   When the coolant exits from the bleed screws they can be retightened.

7   The level of the coolant in the expansion bottle should be roughly 70 mm (2¾ inches) above the 'MAXI' mark.

8   Relocate the expansion bottle cap (with valve and seal).

9   Run the engine at a fast tickover for a couple of minutes to warm up the coolant and enable the thermostat to commence opening. Next, open up the bleed screws again, and when the coolant flows out of them, retighten the bleeder screws and stop the engine.

10   Refit the expansion bottle into position and make secure with the clip. After a short period (once the engine has again cooled down)

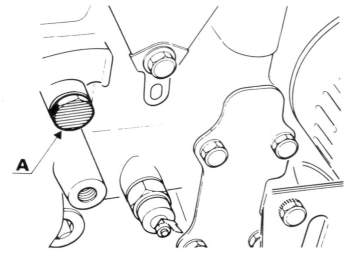

Fig. 2.3 The cylinder head drain plug (A) for the TL engine

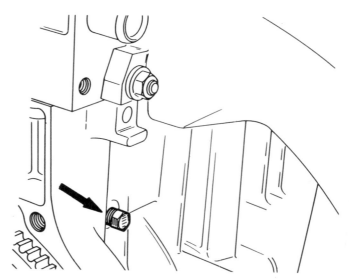

Fig. 2.4 The partial drain plug – TS engine

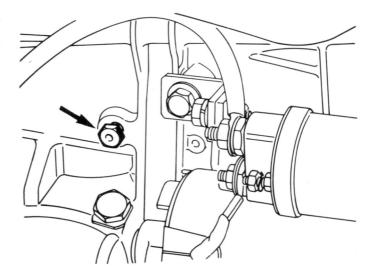

Fig. 2.5 The full drain plug – TS engine

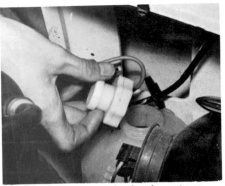

2.4 Remove the expansion bottle vent cap and ...

2.5a ... open the radiator drain plug

2.5b Remove the radiator filler plug

4.3a Bleed screw at carburettor – TS models

4.3b Hose bleeder valve – TS models

4.3c Thermostat housing bleeder valve (TS), also showing the respective hose connections to water pump, and the coolant temperature sender switch location in thermostat housing

6.4 The electric cooling fan unit – note cable location clips round hose

6.6a Remove the retaining bolt at top of radiator ...

6.6b ... and lift it clear

recheck the coolant level in the expansion bottle and, if necessary, top up to the level given in paragraph 7. If coolant passes through the expansion bottle valve at any time then the valve must be renewed.

5   Coolant and antifreeze mixture

1   The original coolant in the sealed system is of 'long-life' type and with antifreeze characteristics. It is preferable to mix a new coolant solution every year however, as apart from the antifreeze properties, rust and corrosion inhibitors (essential to a light alloy engine) will, after this period of usage, tend to lose their effectiveness.

2   Mix the antifreeze with either distilled water or rain-water in a clean container. Drain and flush the system as previously described and pour in the new coolant. Do not allow antifreeze mixture to come in contact with vehicle paintwork, and check the security of all cooling system hoses and joints as antifreeze mixture has a 'searching' action.

3   The following amounts of antifreeze (as a percentage of the total coolant – see Specifications) will give positive protection down to the specified temperatures.

Percentage of antifreeze	Protection to (°C)
50%	–37
40%	–25
30%	–16
25%	–13
20%	–9
15%	–7
10%	–4

A mixture of less than 20% strength is not recommended as anti-rust and anti-corrosion action is not effective.

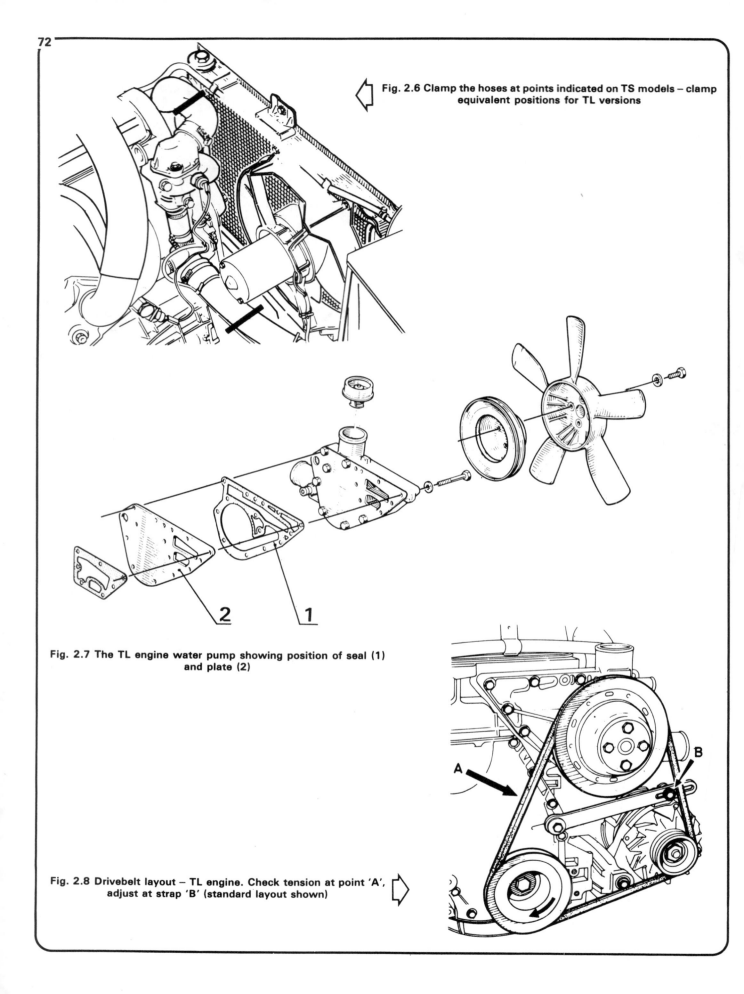

Fig. 2.6 Clamp the hoses at points indicated on TS models – clamp equivalent positions for TL versions

Fig. 2.7 The TL engine water pump showing position of seal (1) and plate (2)

Fig. 2.8 Drivebelt layout – TL engine. Check tension at point 'A', adjust at strap 'B' (standard layout shown)

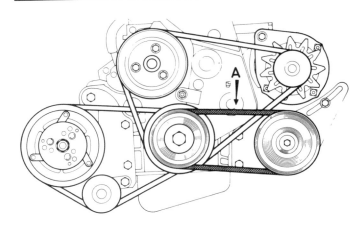

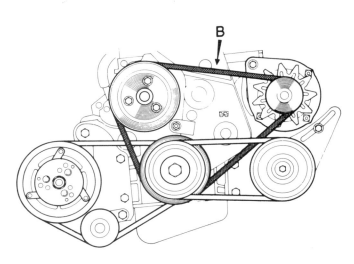

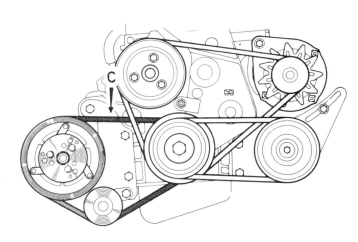

Fig. 2.9 Drivebelt layouts – TS engine. Check tension where indicated by arrow

A *Power steering pump drivebelt*
B *Water pump and alternator drivebelt*
C *Air conditioning compressor drivebelt (where fitted)*

6 Radiator (and electric cooling fan, where fitted) – removal and refitting

1   On models fitted with an electric cooling fan, disconnect the battery earth lead.
2   Assuming only the radiator (and electric cooling fan, where fitted) is being removed, it is not necessary to drain the complete cooling system. Instead, locate clamps at the position indicated in Fig. 2.6 and tighten to compress the top and bottom hoses, thereby retaining the coolant in the engine and heater systems. A pair of G-clamps and some flat pieces of wood will do the job. The hoses must of course be in good condition or they will crack when compressed. If no clamps are available, drain the system.
3   Drain the radiator coolant through the drain plug or detach the bottom hose from the radiator connection as applicable.
4   Where an electric cooling fan is fitted, detach the wires from the connectors, and unclip from the hose (photo). Also disconnect the leads from the thermal switch in the base of the radiator.
5   Disconnect the expansion bottle-to-radiator hose, and the top and bottom hoses.
6   Remove the radiator retaining bolt/s and carefully, lift the radiator clear (photos).
7   Refitting is a reversal of the removal procedure, but check before fitting that the location mountings are in good condition and renew if necessary.
8   When the radiator is in position and the hoses reconnected, top up the radiator with coolant before releasing the hose clamps. Run the engine and bleed the system (see Section 4) to complete and check for leaks.

7 Electric cooling fan unit – removal and refitting

1   The fan unit may be removed from the radiator without removing the radiator from the engine. This of course obviates the need to drain the coolant.
2   Disconnect the battery earth terminal.
3   Detach the motor wire to the connectors near the right-hand headlight.
4   Unscrew and remove the three motor bracket retaining bolts and withdraw the bracket and motor.
5   The fan normally has a very long trouble-free life and apart from the renewal of brushes, any wear occuring in other components will indicate the need for an exchange replacement unit.
6   Refitting is a reversal of the removal procedure.

8 Water pump (TL models) – removal and refitting

1   Disconnect the battery earth lead.
2   Referring to Section 2, drain the coolant.
3   Unscrew the hose clips and detach the heater hoses and the radiator hoses, and remove the radiator as described in Section 6.
4   Loosen the four fan retaining bolts.
5   Slacken the alternator mounting bolts and pivot inwards to loosen the belt tension.
6   Remove the fan and drivebelt.
7   The water pump retaining bolts can now be unscrewed and the pump unit detached from the front of the engine. Lightly tap it with a piece of wood or soft head mallet to break the seal.
8   It is not possible to repair the pump if it is faulty in any way, and it must therefore be renewed as a complete unit.
9   Before refitting the pump, carefully remove any old gasket from the mating surfaces and locate a new seal between the pump and the plate, as shown in Fig. 2.7.
10 Always use a new joint gasket, and do not use any form of sealant with it as it must be fitted dry.
11 Refit the pump and tighten the retaining bolts.
12 Refit the fan and pulley, retension the drivebelt and then relocate the radiator. Connect up the hoses and the battery. Refill the cooling system as given in Section 4 and check for any signs of leakage from the hoses and pump unit.

9 Water pump (TS models) – removal and refitting

1   Disconnect the battery earth lead.

2   Drain the cooling system (see Section 20).

3   Referring to Section 6, remove the radiator.

4   Disconnect the power steering pump drivebelt, where fitted.

5   Loosen the alternator mounting bolts, pivot it inwards and remove the drivebelt. Unscrew and remove the three retaining bolts and remove the water pump pulley (photo). To prevent the pulley from turning, locate the drivebelt round it and grip it tightly by hand – but do not get oil or grease onto the belt.

6   Detach the hose from the carburettor at the water pump, and the coolant return pipe (photo).

7   Unscrew the retaining bolts and detach the pump unit. Lightly tap it free using a piece of wood or a soft-headed mallet to break the seal.

8   Since the water pump is a sealed unit, it cannot be repaired if defective and must therefore be renewed.

9   Prior to refitting the pump unit, clean the joint faces of any old gasket. Always use new gaskets on assembly, but do not use any sealant (photo).

10   Fit the pump unit, and reassemble the associate items disconnected during removal in the reverse sequence.

11   Top up the cooling system and bleed it to complete (see Section 4). Check around the hoses and pump connections for signs of leakage.

10 Thermostat – removal, testing and refitting

1   The thermostat is located within the outlet pipe of the water pump housing. On TL models the thermostat unit is located within the top hose and retained by the hose clip. The hose is in turn secured to the pump outlet by another clip. On TS models the thermostat unit is retained within its own housing, located on top of the water pump, the top hose being secured to the thermostat housing cover.

2   Before removing the thermostat, drain sufficient coolant to enable the coolant level to fall below the top radiator hose.

3   On TL models, unscrew the top hose clips to the water pump outlet and extract the thermostat.

4   On TS models, unscrew the thermostat housing cover retaining screws and lift the cover clear (whilst still attached to the hoses). Extract the thermostat (photo).

5   Suspend the thermostat in a pan of water in which a thermometer has been placed. The thermostat should commence opening within 3 or 4 degrees of its opening temperature and continue to its fully open position. Transfer the fully open thermostat to cold water and observe that it closes within 20 seconds. If the unit does not operate correctly within the specified temperatures, renew it. Top up the coolant level and bleed the system as given in Section 4. Check for signs of leaks.

11 Drivebelts – adjustment and renewal

1   The drivebelts are driven from the engine crankshaft pulley, which is of a single, double or treble track type, depending on the number of belts fitted. The ancillaries depending on the drivebelt/s are:

     (a) *Cooling system water pump*
     (b) *Alternator*
     (c) *Air conditioning pump*
     (d) *Power assisted steering pump*

The last two items are not fitted to all models.

2   It is most important that the drivebelt tension be correctly adjusted. A tight fitting will reduce the belt life and also that of the drive bearings of the component concerned. A loose fitting will also reduce the belt life, will slip and consequently also reduce the efficiency of the unit it drives

3   The belts can be adjusted independently but the rear one can only be removed after withdrawal of the front belt.

4   Inspect the condition of the belts occasionally and renew them if they show any signs of fraying, or have stretched so that available adjustment has been fully used.

5   Belts are correctly adjusted when there is a total deflection of the

9.5 Remove the water pump pulley and drivebelt

9.6 The coolant return pipe housing

9.9 Fit pump with new gasket – timing cover removed for clarity only

10.4 Removing the thermostat – TS model

13.1 The radiator electric cooling fan temperature switch

specified amount (see Specifications), under a moderate thumb pressure at the centre of the longest run of the belt concerned as shown in Figs. 2.8 and 2.9.

6 To make adjustment to the drivebelt of a particular system, loosen the alternator/pump/compressor (if applicable) and pivot the unit inwards or outwards to slacken or tighten the tension respectively. Retighten the mounting bolts of the unit concerned and recheck the tension of the belt.

7 Whenever a new belt has been fitted, its tension should be rechecked after the engine has been run for a short initial period. New belts normally stretch a fraction during the early stage of usage and will probably be in need of further adjustment after a short time.

8 To remove and refit a belt, loosen the mounting bolts of the alternator/power assisted steering pump/compressor, as applicable, and slacken off the adjustment of the belt for removal. Refitting of the belt is a reversal of the above procedure and it must, of course, be adjusted for tension.

12 Engine coolant temperature transmitter – testing

1 Where an engine coolant transmitter unit is suspected of being faulty, the only simple way to test it is by substitution.

2 Removal necessitates partial draining of the cooling system, whilst the gauge removal necessitates removal of the instrument panel (see Chapter 10).

3 A simple test of the gauge may be made by touching the sender unit wire to earth (ignition on) whilst an assistant observes the gauge.

The gauge should read 'hot'; if not, either there is a break in the wiring or the gauge itself is at fault.

4 It is not possible to repair the gauge or sender unit and they must therefore be renewed if faulty.

13 Radiator electric cooling fan temperature switch – testing

1 The thermal switch which regulates the operation of the electric radiator cooling fan is fitted into the base of the radiator as shown (photo). Ideally, tests to the switch should be carried out after it has been removed from its location. If this is done, the cooling system will have to be drained and refilled, but the following alternative method may be substituted.

2 Connect a test light to the fan switch. Where the engine is cold, it should not light up.

3 Start the engine and blank off the radiator to ensure quick warming up.

4 Hold a thermometer in contact with the radiator and when the temperature reaches 92°C (197.6°F) the bulb should light up (allow a margin of 5°C either side).

5 Switch off the engine and allow the temperature of the radiator to drop to 82°C (179°F) when the light should go out (with the ignition 'ON'). Differential between lamp ON or OFF should be 6–20°C (11–36°F).

6 If the switch does not operate within the test limits, renew it.

7 If the switch does operate correctly, then the fault must lie in the fan assembly or the connecting wiring or relay.

14 Cooling system – fault diagnosis

Symptom	Reason/s
Loss of coolant but no overheating	Small leaks in system
Overheating and loss of coolant only when overheated	Faulty thermostat
	Fan belt slipping/electric fan faulty
	Engine out of tune due to ignition and/or fuel system settings being incorrect
	Blockage or restriction in circulation of cooling water
	Radiator cooling fins clogged up
	Blown cylinder head gasket or cracked cylinder head
	Sheared water pump impeller shaft
	Cracked cylinder
	New engine still tight
Engine runs too cool and heater inefficient	Thermostat missing or stuck open

Chapter 3 Fuel and exhaust systems

For modifications, and information applicable to later models, see Supplement at end of manual

Contents

Specifications

Fuel pump .... AC or SEV mechanical diaphragm type

Carburettors

Engine:	Carburettor type	Carburettor mark
843–20	Weber 32 DARA 4	6500
843–21	Weber 32 DARA 5	6600
829–A–7–00	Weber 32 DARA 8	—
829–B–7–01	Weber 32 DARA 9	—

Weber 32 DARA 4 and 5	**1st barrel**	**2nd barrel**
Choke tube	24	26
Main jet	132	150
Idle jet	50	45
Air compensation jet	180	145
Emulsifier	F53	F6
Accelerator pump	60	
Needle valve	175	
Float level	7 mm ($\frac{9}{32}$ in)	
Float weight	11g	
Initial throttle butterfly opening (cold):		
Mark 6500	1.40 mm (0.055 in)	
Mark 6600	1.60 mm (0.063 in)	
Adjustment gauge thickness:		
DARA 4	7 mm (0.275 in)	
DARA 5	8 mm (0.315 in)	

Weber 32 DARA 8 and 9	**1st barrel**	**2nd barrel**
Choke tube	26	26
Main jet	132	140
Idle jet	60	50
Air compensation jet	155	145
Emulsifier	F58	F6
Diffuser	3.5	4
Accelerator pump jet	60	
Needle valve	175	
Float level	7 mm (0.276 in)	
Float weight	11g	
Initial throttle opening (cold):		
Weber 32 DARA 8	1.55 mm (0.218 in)	
Weber 32 DARA 9	1.65 mm (0.276 in)	

Idle speed (TS engines):	
Weber 32 DARA 8	800 ± 25 rpm
Weber 32 DARA 9	675 ± 25 rpm
Idle speed (TL engines):	
Automatic transmission models	625 ± 25 rpm
Manual transmission models	700 ± 25 rpm

Fuel tank capacity

TL models	52 litres (11.0 gallons)
TS models	64 litres (14.0 gallons)

Torque wrench settings

	lbf ft	Nm
Inlet manifold	15.0 to 22.5	20 to 30
Exhaust manifold	15.0 to 22.5	20 to 30

1 General description

The Renault 20 fuel system is basically conventional in principle. The fuel tank unit is mounted on the underside of the car, just forward of the rear suspension assembly. From the tank the fuel is drawn to the carburettor via a mechanically operated diaphragm pump, mounted on the engine. The pump unit also incorporates a filter to prevent any sediment drawn from the tank reaching the carburettor.

The carburettors fitted to all models, incorporate an automatic choke system. This utilises redirected engine coolant which is used to warm up the carburettor inlet manifold and autochoke device.

A crankcase emission control system is employed whereby unwanted crankcase fumes are redirected via tubes from the camshaft/rocker cover to the carburettor and inlet manifold so they can be drawn into the engine combustion chambers and burnt off.

and the element removal and service details are therefore the same.

2   To remove the air filter element, unscrew the end cover retaining nut or unclip the cover (as applicable) and lift the cover clear to extract the element (photo). It cannot be washed or cleaned and must be renewed at the specified intervals.

3   Before fitting the replacement element, clean out the filter housing using a clean non-fluffy cloth, but take care not to damage the carburettor preheat device in the lower part of the cylinder (photo).

4   When the new element is in position, refit the cap and retaining screw and ensure that they are securely located.

5   To remove the element assembly completely, disconnect the respective air intake and outlet ducting tubes, unclip the cannister retaining clips and remove the unit complete.

6   Refitting is a direct reversal of the removal process, but ensure that the ducting tubes and unit retaining clips are secure, and renew defective clips or ducting sections, if defective.

2 Air cleaner – removal, servicing and refitting

1   The air cleaner fitted to both TL and TS models is of similar design,

3 Fuel pump – routine servicing

1   The fuel pump is bolted to the side of the crankcase on TS models,

2.2 Removing the filter (TL engine)

2.3 The interior of the cleaner canister showing the preheat device

3.1 The fuel pump and connections (TS model)

3.3a Remove the cap and seal ...

3.3b ... followed by the filter for cleaning

5.3 Removing the pump (TS engine)

and to the upper left-hand face of the cylinder head on TL models. On TL models, the fuel pump is driven by a cam on the forward end of the camshaft, while on TS models it is driven by the auxiliary shaft (photo).

2   Check the fuel hoses are secure to the pump inlet and outlet pipes and the circle of screws which secure the pump flanges together are tight (where applicable).

3   Every 9000 miles (15 000 km) remove the pump top cover, taking care not to break the seal gasket. Extract the filter and clean through. Wash the chamber of the pump out to remove any sediment. Always use clean petrol for washing out the pump components (photo).

4   When refitting the cover, check the condition of the gasket and renew if necessary. Do not overtighten the cover screw.

4 Fuel pump – testing

1   Uncouple the fuel pipe at its connection with the carburettor.

2   Spin the engine on the starter and observe if a well defined spurt of petrol is ejected from the hose. If this occurs then the fuel pump is serviceable.

3   An alternative method is to remove the pump from its location and place a thumb over the inlet port and actuate the operating lever when fitted. A substantial suction should be felt and heard if the pump is in good order.

4   Where these tests prove positive then lack of fuel at the carburettor must be due to blocked fuel lines, blocked tank vent or a sticky carburettor needle valve.

5 Fuel pump – removal, dismantling, reassembly and refitting

1   Disconnect the pump inlet fuel line and plug the fuel line so that fuel does not escape from the tank.

2   Disconnect the pump fuel line to the carburettor. On TS models, remove the engine undertray and return hose.

3   Unscrew and remove the two pump securing nuts, bolts and washers. Withdraw the pump and retain any gaskets or insulating washers which are fitted between the pump flange and the engine block or head (photo).

4   If the pump has seen considerable service it will almost certainly be realistic to exchange it for a factory reconditioned unit, if no obvious and easily repairable faults are apparent.

5   If it is decided to repair the pump, then before dismantling, file an alignment mark across the edges of the two mating flanges to facilitate reassembly.

6   Remove the cover and filter and the flange screws and separate the two halves of the pump body.

7   Withdraw the diaphragm by disengaging the operating rod from the pump operating lever.

8   The diaphragm and valve assemblies may be renewed if necessary as these components are available in kit form.

9   If wear has occurred in the operating lever or its spindle, then a new pump unit should be obtained.

10 Reassembly is a reversal of dismantling but ensure that the valves are correctly orientated and staked in position.

6 Carburettors – general description

1   The TL models are equipped with a Weber 32 DARA type carburettor, which is of a twin choke downdraught design, incorporating a semi-automatic choke device.

2   The semi-automatic choke is operated by a bi-metallic spring, which opens or closes the choke progressively according to the temperature of the coolant. The base of the carburettor is heated by engine coolant which flows through separate passages in the inlet manifold, and this is designed to assist the carburettor efficiency during the warm-up period.

3   ·The TS models are also fitted with a Weber 32 DARA carburettor (photo). On both models, the initial cold start choke setting is made by pressing down the throttle pedal fully and then allowing it slowly to return.

4   TS models with automatic transmission and air conditioning have a Weber 32 DARA 9C carburettor which incorporates a throttle butterfly opener, operated by vacuum from the inlet manifold. An electrically operated solenoid valve in the vacuum circuit is activated

6.3 The Weber 32 DARA is fitted to TS models with manual transmission

8.3 Disconnect the throttle cable from the quadrant (a), the return spring (b) and solenoid wire, where fitted (c)

8.7 Remove the flange nuts on each corner and then remove the carburettor

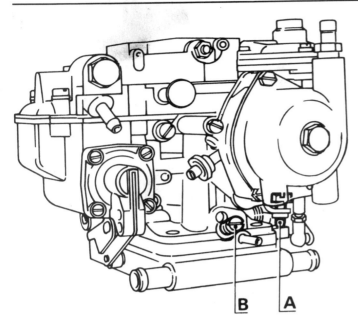

Fig. 3.1 Weber 32 DARA 4 and 5 carburettor idle speed screws

A   Throttle adjuster screw   B   Fuel volume screw

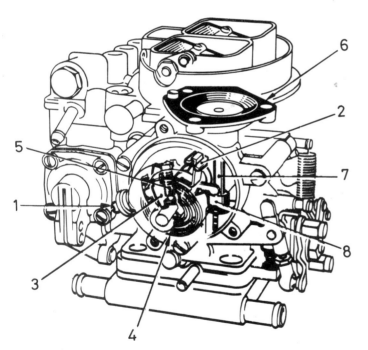

Fig. 3.2 The thermostatic choke assembly

1   Fast idle setscrew   5   Coil spring (cam lever)
2   Spindle lever   6   Diaphragm (cover removed)
3   Cam lever   7   Connecting rod
4   Thermostat spring   8   Compensator

when the air conditioning compressor is working. Adjustments for the 32 DARA 9C are the same as for the 32 DARA 9 (as are the other specifications).

5   On the 32 DARA 9C models a solenoid valve closes the idle circuit whenever the ignition is switched off.

7   Weber 32 DARA 4 and 32 DARA 5 carburettors – idle speed adjustment

1   There are two adjustment screws fitted; the throttle adjuster screw and the fuel volume screw. Both of these are indicated in Fig. 3.1.

2   Before making any adjustments, run the engine up to its normal operating temperature.

3   On manual transmission models, turn the throttle screw to set the engine speed at about 675 rpm. On automatic transmission models, turn the throttle screw to set the engine speed at about 600 rpm ('A' selected, handbrake on). You will need the aid of a tachometer to adjust the engine speed accurately.

4   Next, locate the fuel volume screw and adjust it to give the highest possible engine idle speed, without the engine stalling or 'hunting'.

5   Next, tighten the fuel volume screw, weakening the mixture down until the engine speed is reduced by about 20 to 25 rpm for manual transmission models, or 20 to 50 rpm for automatic transmission models to set the idle speed at the recommended figure given in the specifications.

6   At the prescribed idle speed, the engine should run smoothly. Any further adjustments to the speed should be made with the throttle screw.

7   If difficulties are encountered in adjusting the idle speed, check the fuel level in the carburettor float chamber – see Section 9.

8   Weber 32 DARA carburettor – removal and refitting

1   Disconnect the battery earth terminal.

2   Disconnect the air filter trunking from the carburettor.

3   Detach the throttle cable linkage to the carburettor (photo).

4   Detach the fuel pipe at the carburettor from the fuel pump.

5   Fit clamps to the coolant pipes connecting the carburettor to the water pump, and the appropriate coolant intake pipes to the carburettor. Disconnect the hoses at the carburettor.

6   Detach the vacuum tube from the carburettor (to the distributor).

7   Unscrew and remove the four carburettor flange retaining nuts and carefully, lift the carburettor clear of the inlet manifold (photo). Try not to break the flange gasket as the carburettor is removed, in case a replacement is not available, in which case the existing one can be reused, or at least used as a pattern to make a new one.

8   Refitting is a reversal of the removal process, but use a new flange gasket if possible. With the coolant hoses reconnected, remove the clamps and check the coolant level. Top up and bleed if necessary (see Chapter 2, Section 4).

9   Readjust the carburettor when the engine has been restarted and warmed up.

9   Weber 32 DARA 4 and 5 carburettors – general adjustments

Initial throttle opening – check and adjustment

1   Remove the air filter ducting from the carburettor.

2   Check that the choke flaps are in the fully shut position.

3   To check the adjustment you will need a gauge rod of the specified clearance for your model carburettor (see Specifications). A drill of the correct diameter will suffice, but take care not to score the surface of the carburettor with it.

4   Measure the clearance between the primary butterfly flap and the carburettor and, if necessary, adjust the clearance to the specified amount by screwing the adjuster screw in the choke housing accordingly.

Automatic choke adjustment

5   To make any adjustment to the automatic choke, it will be necessary to remove the cover which is retained by three retaining screws. Clamp the coolant hoses to the cover prior to removal. **Note:**

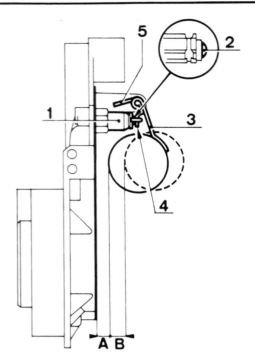

Fig. 3.3 Check the float clearance holding cover in vertical position shown

1 Needle valve
2 Ball
3 Arm
4 Tongue to needle valve
5 Adjustment tongue
A Gasket to float dimension
B Float travel

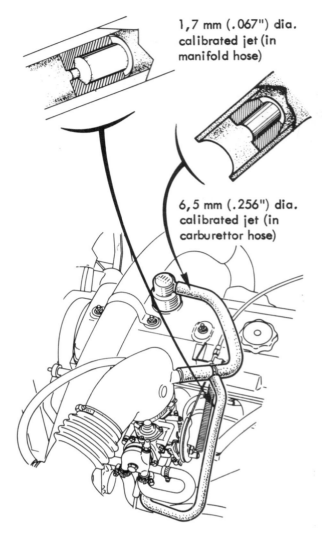

1,7 mm (.067") dia. calibrated jet (in manifold hose)

6,5 mm (.256") dia. calibrated jet (in carburettor hose)

Fig. 3.4 The calibrated jet locations in the TS model

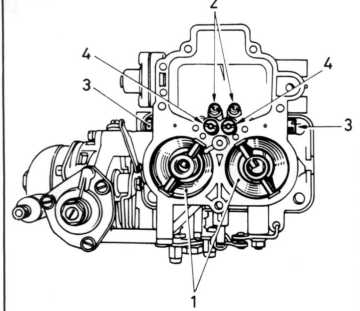

Fig. 3.5 Choke and jet positions on the Weber 32 DARA carburettor

1 Choke tubes
2 Main jets
3 Idle jets
4 Air compensator jets

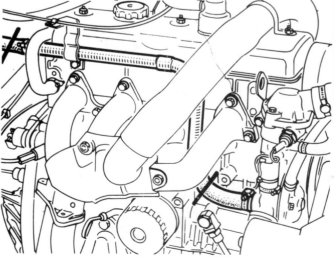

Fig. 3.6 Clamp the hoses at points indicated (TS models)

9.5 Note the alignment marks on the choke housing

10.1 The cover inverted to show float, needle valve and gasket locations

11.3 The idle damper solenoid valve incorporated into the Weber 32 DARA carburettor fitted to the TS series

15.1a The crankcase emission control tubes on the TS engine

15.1b The crankcase emission control tubes on the TL engine

When removing the cover check that the thermostatic spring cover and housing have alignment marks (photo).

6 With the cover removed, close the choke flap valves by pushing on the spindle lever.

7 Next, move the diaphragm rod so that it is in contact with the pneumatic capsule, and hold the choke flap closure lever against the diaphragm rod.

8 Using gauge rods or drills, measure the part open setting of the choke flaps at the point between the long part of the flap tops and the housing wall. Check the adjustment against that given in the Specifications and, if necessary, adjust the clearance by means of the screw recessed into the top of the diaphragm unit.

9 When the adjustment is completed, refit the thermostatic spring cover housing and ensure that the identification marks are aligned as shown in photo 9.5.

Float level – check and adjustment

10 To check the float level, it will be necessary to remove the carburettor upper Section. To do this, detach the air cleaner ducting and unscrew the upper section retaining screws. Detach the choke valve control rod, then carefully lift the cover clear, trying not to break the gasket seal; it can be reused if undamaged and in good condition.

11 Support the top cover vertically, enabling the float to close the needle valve without allowing the ball to enter into the valve.

12 In this position, calculate the clearance between the float and the float chamber gasket, which should be 7 mm ($\frac{9}{32}$ in).

13 If adjustment is necessary, bend the float arm accordingly but ensure that the tongue stays at a right angle to the needle valve centre-line. Next, check the extent of the float travel, which should be 8 mm ($\frac{5}{16}$ in). This is adjusted by bending the tongue accordingly.

10 Weber 32 DARA 4 and 5 carburettors – dismantling and reassembly

1 Unscrew and remove the upper body screws and disconnect the choke control rod. Withdraw the upper assembly which contains the needle valve choke control mechanism, and float (photo).

2 Empty the float chamber. To remove the float, extract the hingepin, then unhook the needle valve.

3 Do not dismantle the choke butterflies or spindles unless essential. Check the security of the inlet valve, but do not add to or remove any of the washers located beneath it.

4 Remove the four screws and withdraw the accelerator pump.

5 If the automatic choke has failed, remove the complete unit and fit a new one.

6 Refer to Fig. 3.5 and remove the jets. Clean them by blowing air from a tyre pump through them, never use wire to probe them.

7 Reassembly is a reversal of dismantling, but use new gaskets and check that any interconnecting linkage is correctly located.

11 Weber 32 DARA 8 and 9 carburettors – adjustment

1 The adjustment procedures for the Weber 32 DARA 8 and 9 are similar to those given for the DARA type 4 and 5 as described in Section 7. Note, however, that the adjustment specifications differ and therefore, although the descriptions are identical, reference must be made to the specification figure for the particular setting or adjustment for your carburettor type.

2 Automatic transmission models equipped with air conditioning are fitted with a Weber 32 DARA 9C carburettor. This differs from the others, in that it has a throttle butterfly opener operated by vacuum pressure supplied from the inlet manifold. The vacuum circuit has a solenoid valve which is operated electrically whenever the air conditioner compressor is working.

3 The fuel cut (idle damper) solenoid valve (photo) cuts the idle supply whenever and as soon as the ignition is switched off. This solenoid can easily be checked for operation by running the engine and simply disconnecting the solenoid wire terminal, at which point the engine will stop – or should! If the solenoid is defective, renew it.

4 The idle speed on this type of carburettor is adjusted with the gear

selection lever set in the 'A' position. The engine must be at its normal operating temperature. Adjust the fuel and throttle stop screws to give the specified idle speed of 675 ± 25 rpm.

5   Leaving the selector lever in the 'A' engagement, and with the air conditioner compressor in operation, rotate the throttle butterfly screw to set the idle speed at 675 ± 25 rpm.

6   Oil fume rebreathing circuits are also fitted to the above type carburettors systems and care must be taken when dismantling to ensure that the calibrated jets in the manifold and carburettor hoses (shown in Fig. 3.4) are refitted correctly. Do not leave the jets out or the idle speed will be upset, and normal running will be affected too.

12 Weber DARA 8 and 9 carburettors – dismantling and reassembly

The instruction for dismantling and reassembly of the DARA 8 and 9 series carburettors closely follows that of the DARA 4 and 5 series given in Section 10, but note the following:

(a) *When removing the top section, unscrew the retaining screws and then detach the butterfly swivel rod to lever C-clip, by prising it free*

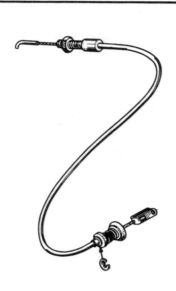

Fig. 3.7 Throttle cable (TS models)

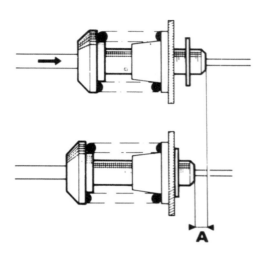

Fig. 3.8 Compress the compensator so that A = 0.078 in (2 mm)

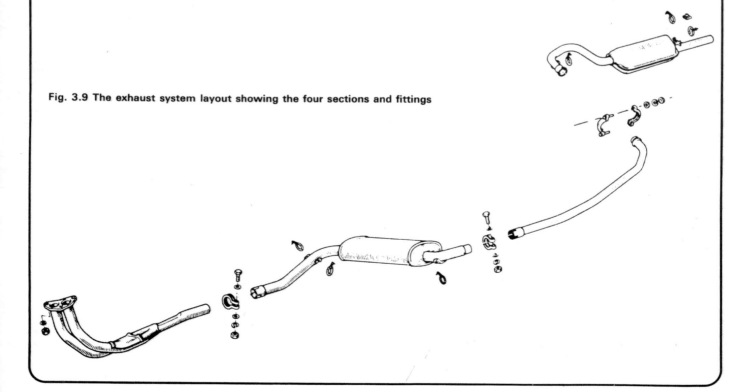

Fig. 3.9 The exhaust system layout showing the four sections and fittings

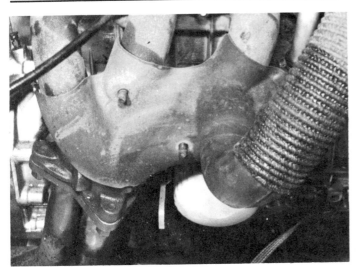

19.1 The 'preheat' cowl in position on the manifold

19.4 Exhaust system location rings and section clamp (typical)

(b) Loosen, but do not remove, the three screws retaining the automatic choke housing unit to the main carburettor body, enabling the choke housing to be withdrawn sufficiently to allow the top section to be detached

(c) With the top section removed the carburettor can be cleaned inspected and reassembled as described in Section 10

13 Manifolds/gaskets – renewal

Inlet manifold

1 This manifold can be removed complete with carburettor, leaving the heater hoses attached (on TS models) to avoid draining if only the gaskets are in need of renewal. On TL models, the cooling system must be drained.
2 If the manifold itself is to be detached, remove the air filter and carburettor as described previously and then unbolt the manifold at the cylinder head and downpipe connections. Both TS and TL cooling systems must be drained and hoses disconnected.
3 Remove all traces of the old manifold gaskets and fit new ones over the studs. Fit the manifold and retain with nuts and washers. Refit the carburettor and air cleaner.

Exhaust manifold

4 On TS models, first unbolt the metal return pipe from the heater unit. Clamp the heater hose at the points indicated in Fig. 3.6 to avoid draining the cooling system. Detach the heater return pipe.
5 Unscrew the manifold retaining nuts and washers and detach the downpipe. Then withdraw the manifold. Remove the old gasket.
6 Clean the joint faces of the manifold and cylinder head, fit a new gasket and reassemble in the reverse order. Finally bleed the cooling system and check for leaks.

14 Throttle cable – removal and refitting

1 Disconnect the battery earth lead.
2 Detach the cable from the throttle quadrant and remove the cable adjuster and fitting from the cam cover.
3 At the pedal end of the cable, withdraw the clevis pin and prise free the circlip that retains the compensator to the bulkhead panel.
4 If the vehicle is fitted with automatic transmission detach the wire from the governor (downshift) control, if necessary.
5 Withdraw the cable.
6 Refitting is a reversal of the removal procedure. When relocated, check that when the throttle pedal is fully pressed downwards that the carburettor butterfly is fully open and against its stop. Hold the throttle in this position and adjust the cable to compress the compensator about 2 mm (0.078 in) as shown in Fig. 3.8.
7 On automatic transmission models, ensure that the kickdown switch is fully operational.

15 Crankcase emission control device

1 All types of engine are fitted with this device to reduce the emission of fumes from the crankcase to atmosphere.
2 The system comprises a circuit of hoses with a valve incorporated. When the engine is running, crankcase fumes are drawn up through a tie piece mounted on the rocker box cover and sucked through one of the two hoses which connect with the carburettor and the inlet manifold (photos).
3 The direction of fume flow is controlled by jets within the hoses to the carburettor and manifold.
4 Servicing is restricted to checking the security of the hose unions and occasionally disconnecting and blowing through with an air line. If the hoses are defective and need renewing at any time, be sure to insert the correct jets, which are recognisable by their inside diameter measurements. If the jets are left out, it will upset the carburettor adjustments and will provide uneven idling.

16 Fuel gauge and transmitter unit – fault finding

1 If the fuel gauge fails to give a reading with the ignition on or reads 'full' all the time, then a check must be made to see if the fault is in the gauge, sender unit, or wire in between.
2 Turn the ignition on and disconnect the wire from the fuel tank sender unit. Check that the fuel gauge needle is on the empty mark. To check if the fuel gauge is in order now earth the fuel sender unit wire. This should send the needle to the full mark.
3 If the fuel gauge is in order, check the wiring for damage or loose connections. If none can be found, then the sender unit will be at fault and must be renewed.

17 Fuel tank cleaning

1 With time it is likely that sediment will collect in the bottom of the fuel tank. Condensation, resulting in rust and other impurities, will usually be found in the fuel tank of any car more than three or four years old.
2 When the tank is removed it should be vigorously flushed out and turned upside down and, if facilities are available, steam cleaned.
3 To remove the tank see Section 18.

18 Fuel tank – removal and refitting

1 The fuel tank is located underneath the car, attached to the floor directly in front of the rear suspension area. Access for removal leaves a lot to be desired, so therefore run the car onto ramps or over a pit if available. Failing this, raise it as high as possible at the rear and ensure that the vehicle is secure on chassis stands or similar.

2   The tank should preferably be removed when the fuel level is very low; if not, syphon the contents into a suitable container and store in a safe place.

3   Disconnect the battery earth lead. Raise the rear seat and detach the sender unit and withdraw it from the tank.

4   Working underneath, first detach and remove the handbrake cable assembly situated directly underneath the tank (see Chapter 9).

5   Unbolt and remove the diagonal crossmembers to the rear suspension central mounting.

6   Disconnect the fuel pipes at the lower right-hand side corner.

7   Disconnect the filler and vent pipes through the rear wheel arch.

8   The tank can now be unbolted around its retaining flange. **Note**: *One of the bolts secures the earth wire.* Support the tank as it is unbolted, then carefully lower and remove it.

9   Should the fuel tank be in need of repair, consult your Renault dealer or a fuel tank repair specialist. Do not attempt to repair the tank yourself by welding or similar methods requiring heat; even if the tank is empty the fumes are highly explosive!

10 Refitting of the tank is a reversal of the removal procedure. Check that all pipe connections are secure and when the tank is refilled check for any signs of leakage.

11 Reconnect the suspension arms and handbrake cable. Readjust the handbrake as given in Chapter 9.

19 Exhaust system – description, removal and refitting

1   The exhaust system comprises four sections, being the front section to the manifold, the expansion box section, the intermediate pipe, and at the rear the silencer and pipe. A preheat cowl and pipe leads from the exhaust manifold to the air filter as shown in the photo.

2   Each pipe section is joined by clamps which vary in type according to location.

3   Each section is removable for individual renewal when necessary, but due to corrosion around the clamps and jointed sections you will probably have to use a wire brush to remove the surface rust, and penetrating oil to ease detachment at the joints. If necessary, cut through the joint bolts with a hacksaw.

4   The exhaust system is suspended and located by 'doughnut' rings (photo) and a bracket from the rear gearbox mounting. These retaining rings will become perished in time, and should therefore be inspected periodically, and where defective or damaged, renewed.

5   When assembling each section, smear the joint with an exhaust pipe sealant to safeguard against small leakages from the joint.

6   When the sections and system is reassembled, make a final check to ensure that no part of the system can chafe against adjacent fittings and body sections. Check for any signs of leaks.

20 Fault diagnosis – fuel system

Unsatisfactory engine performance and excessive fuel consumption are not necessarily the fault of the fuel system or carburettor. In fact they more commonly occur as a result of ignition faults. Before acting on the fuel system it is necessary to check the ignition system first. Even though a fault may lie in the fuel system it will be difficult to trace unless the ignition is correct. The table below, therefore, assumes that the ignition system is in order.

Symptom	Reason/s
Smell of petrol when engine is stopped	Leaking fuel lines or unions Leaking fuel tank
Smell of petrol when engine is idling	Leaking fuel line unions between pump and carburettor Overflow of fuel from float chamber due to wrong level setting or ineffective needle valve or punctured float
Excessive fuel consumption for reasons not covered by leaks or float chamber	Worn jets Choke stuck
Difficult starting, uneven running, lack of power, cutting out	One or more jets blocked or restricted Float chamber fuel level too low or needle valve sticking Fuel pump not delivering sufficient fuel Intake manifold gasket leaking, or manifold fractured

Chapter 4 Ignition system

For modifications, and information applicable to later models, see Supplement at end of manual

Contents

Specifications

Firing order .... 1 – 3 – 4 – 2

Ignition system type .... 12v battery, coil and distributor

Spark plugs
843-20 and 843-21 engine (TL) .... AC 41-2XLS
829 A700 and 829 B701 engines (TS) .... AC 42-LTS or Champion BN6Y
Spark plug gap .... 0.55 to 0.65 mm (0.022 to 0.026 in)

Distributor
843-20 and 843-21 engines (TL) .... R258 D60 or R307 D60
829 A700 and 829 B701 engines (TS) R303 D59
Distributor contact breaker settings (vacuum capsule disconnected, engine idling):
    Dwell percentage .... 63% ± 3%
    Dwell (cam) angle .... 57° ± 3°
Flywheel timing:
    TL (ohv engine) .... 10° ± 1° BTDC
    TS (ohc engine) .... 6° ± 1° BTDC
Contact breaker points gap .... 0·4 mm (0·016 in)
Distributor rotation:
    TL (ohv engine) .... Clockwise
    TS (ohc engine) .... Anti-clockwise

Torque wrench setting

	lbf ft	Nm
Spark plugs:		
Taper seat type	11 to 15	15 to 20
Conventional type	19 to 26	26 to 35

1 General description

1   In order that the engine may run correctly it is necessary for an electrical spark to ignite the fuel/air mixture in the combustion chambers at exactly the right moment in relation to engine speed and loading. The ignition system is based on feeding low tension voltage from the battery to the coil where it is converted to high tension voltage. The high tension voltage is powerful enough to jump the gap between the electrodes of the sparking plugs in the cylinders many times a second under high compression, providing that the system is in good condition and all the adjustments are correct.

2   The system is divided into two circuits; the low tension and high tension.

3   The low tension (sometimes called primary) circuit consists of the battery, lead wire to the starter solenoid, lead from the starter solenoid to the ignition switch, lead from ignition switch to the coil low tension windings (SW or + terminal) and from the coil low tension windings (CB or – terminal) to the contact breaker points and condenser in the distributor.

4   The high tension circuit comprises the high tension or secondary windings in the coil, the heavily insulated lead from the coil to the distributor cap centre contact, the rotor arm, and the leads from the four distributor cap outer contacts (in turn) to the sparking plugs.

5   low tension voltage is stepped up by the coil windings to high tension voltage intermittently by the operation of the contact points and the condenser in the low tension circuit. High tension voltage is then fed via the centre contact in the distributor cap to the rotor arm.

6   The rotor arm rotates clockwise (TL engine) or anticlockwise (TS engine) at half engine revolutions inside the distributor. Each time it

comes in line with one of the outer contacts in the cap, the contact points open and the high voltage is discharged, jumping the gap from rotor arm to contact and thence along the plug lead to the centre electrode of the plug. Here it jumps the other gap – sparking in the process – to the outer plug electrode and hence to earth.

7   The static timing of the spark is adjusted by moving the outer body of the distributor in relation to the distributor shaft. This alters the position at which the points open in relation to the position of the crankshaft (and thus the pistons).

8   The timing is also altered automatically by a centrifugal device, which further alters the position of the complete points mounting assembly in relation to the shaft when engine speed increases, and by a vacuum control working from the inlet manifold which varies the timing according to the position of the throttle and consequently load on the engine. Both of these automatic alterations advance the timing of the spark at light loads and high speeds. The mechanical advance mechanism consists of two weights, which move out from the distributor shaft as engine speed rises due to centrifugal force. As they move out, so the cam rotates relative to the shaft and the contact breaker opening position is altered.

9   The degree to which the weights move out is controlled by springs, the tension of which significantly controls the extent of the advance to the timing.

10   The vacuum advance device is a diaphragm and connecting rod attached to the cam plate.When the diaphragm moves in either direction the cam plate is moved, thus altering the timing.

11   The diaphragm is actuated by depression (vacuum) in the inlet manifold and is connected by a small bore pipe to the carburettor body.

12   On both engine variants the firing order is 1–3–4–2 and the No 1 cylinder is at the flywheel end of the engine as shown in Figs 4.1 and 4.2.

13   A diagnostic socket is fitted (photo) to enable Renault mechanics to quickly pinpoint any problem within the ignition system and also to time it accurately. Unfortunately, without the necessary associate equipment, the diagnostic socket is of little use to the home mechanic.

2   Routine maintenance

1   *Spark plugs:* Remove the plugs and thoroughly clean away all trace of carbon. Examine the porcelain insulation round the central electrodes inside the plug, and if damaged discard the plug. Reset the gap between the electrodes. Do not use a set of plugs for more than 9000 miles. It is false economy. At the same time check the plug caps. Always use the straight tubular ones normally fitted. Good replacements are normally available at your local Renault agency.

2   *Distributor:* Every 9000 miles remove the cap and rotor arm and put one or two drops of engine oil into the centre of the cam recess. Smear the surfaces of the cam itself with petroleum jelly. Do not over lubricate as any excess could get onto the contact breaker points surfaces and cause ignition difficulties. Every 9000 miles examine the contact breaker point surfaces. If there is a build-up of deposits on one face and a pit in the other it will be impossible to set the gap correctly and they should be refaced or renewed. Set the gap when the contact surfaces are in order.

3   *General:* Examine all leads and terminals for signs of broken or cracked insulation. Also check all terminal connections for slackness or signs of fracturing of some strands of wire. Partly broken wire should be renewed. The HT leads are particularly important as any insulation faults will cause the high voltage to 'jump' to the nearest earth and this will prevent a spark at the plug. Check that no HT leads are loose or in a position where the insulation could wear due to rubbing against part of the engine.

3   Distributor breaker points (ohv engines) – adjustment

1   Prise back and release the distributor cap retaining clips and detach the cap.

2   Withdraw the rotor arm from the cam spindle and remove the dust shield.

3   The contact points are now accessible for inspection and if necessary adjustment (photo). Prise the points apart by levering the moving contact away from the fixed contact, using a small screwdriver. If the circular contact faces are pitted or badly worn they

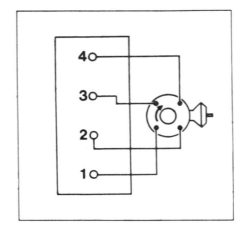

Fig. 4.1 Distributor and spark plug HT lead positions – TL engine

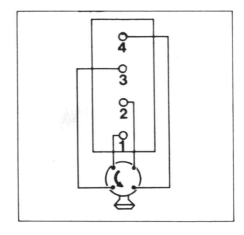

Fig. 4.2 Distributor and spark plug HT lead positions – TS engine

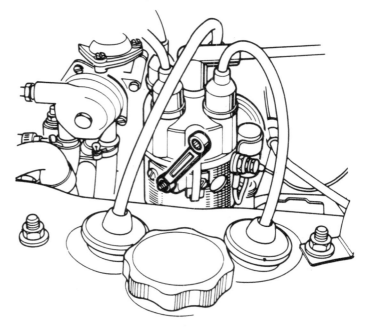

Fig. 4.3 Adjusting the points externally on the TL engine (remove cap to check with feeler gauges)

1.13 The distributor (cap removed) and diagnostic socket on the TL engine

3.3 Internal view of distributor on the TL engine showing (1) external points adjuster nut, (2) retaining screw, (3) LT connector, (4) condenser, (5) advance/retard diaphragm and (6) moving contact point

3.5 Checking the contact gap (TL engine)

5.2 An upper body retaining screw (arrowed) and LT lead and connection from the condenser (TS engine)

5.5 Internal view of TS distributor with upper section removed showing (1) moving contact pivot, (2) contact points, (3) fixed contact screw and (4) external adjuster

5.13 Checking the contact gap on the TS distributor

7.2 Detach the vacuum pipe (arrowed) from the diaphragm body (TL engine shown)

7.4 The TS distributor drive dog with offset segments for correct fitting

cannot be accurately adjusted and must therefore be removed for cleaning or renewal, as applicable.

4   Assuming the contact faces to be in order, turn the engine to position the moving contact arm cam lug against the peak of one of the four cam spindle lobes. The engine can be turned by engaging a gear and moving the car accordingly.

5   Select a feeler gauge blade of the specified clearance, and insert it between the contact faces. The selected blade should be a fine interference sliding fit (photo). If the gap is incorrect, rotate the adjuster nut on the outside of the distributor, shown in Fig. 4.3, in the desired direction to open or close the points as required.

6   Check the inside of the distributor cap before replacing it, and verify that the four contact segments are clean, and also that the central spring-loaded carbon brush is clean and moves freely in its housing.

7   Further fine adjustment of the points can be made with the engine running (at its normal operating temperature) if necessary with

reference to the Specifications.

4   Distributor contact breaker points (ohc engine) – adjustment

1   It will be seen that the distributor on the TS engine is mounted horizontally on the bulkhead end of the engine and is driven directly by the camshaft.

2   This limits accessibility to the contact breaker points and associate fittings within the distributor, and it is therefore suggested that if the points are to be inspected, serviced and adjusted using feeler gauges, the distributor be removed.

3   A fine adjustment of the points can be made without removing the distributor and with the engine running, by turning the external adjustment nut (photo 5.5) in the desired direction.

4   If the distributor has been removed (see Section 7), the contact breaker points can be inspected and adjusted in the same manner as given in the previous Section, paragraphs 3 to 7 respectively.

5 Distributor contact breaker points – removal and refitting

1 The removal and refitting of the contact breaker points on the distributor in both types of engine is basically the same. However, as previously mentioned, on the ohc (TS) engine it will be necessary to remove the distributor.

2 Remove the distributor cap and withdraw the rotor arm and dust shield. On TS models remove the two upper bearing body retaining screws and withdraw the upper bearing body (photo). Detach the low tension lead.

3 Unscrew and remove the adjuster nut as shown in Fig. 4.3 and photo 5.5 (as applicable).

4 On TL models, unscrew and remove the retaining screws each side of the adjuster on the outer body.

5 Prise free the small dust cover from the outer face of the distributor body (adjacent to the condenser) and, using a small screwdriver or similar suitable implement, extract the retaining lug through the hole in the body.

6 Next, remove the adjustment rod and spring.

7 Unscrew and remove the fixed contact retaining screw and withdraw the contact.

8 Loosen the LT terminal (TL models). Detach the low tension lead and, with a pair of needle nose pliers, withdraw the moving point retaining clip and insulating washer from the pivot post. Extract the moving contact, pressing the spring arm inwards to release it from its mounting.

9 Examine the point faces for a 'pip' on one and a corresponding 'pit' on the other and/or possibly uneven wear. The faces of both contacts, where this is apparent, should be cleaned and resurfaced using an oilstone. Keep the faces to their original contour and remove all surface deformity on each contact.

10 Where severe burning has occurred (usually caused by a defective condenser or poor earth connections) or possibly severely worn contact faces, they must be renewed.

11 Clean the faces of both contacts, whether old or new, prior to refitting, using methylated spirit. This removes any oil or protective coating that may be present.

12 Refitting is a direct reversal of the removal procedure, but ensure that the fibre washer located above the moving contact breaker is relocated.

13 Adjust the contact breaker gap as described in the preceding Sections to complete (photo).

6 Condenser – removal, testing and refitting

1 Faulty ignition resulting in misfiring and uneven running can be caused by a faulty condenser which is mounted externally on the body of the distributor.

2 If the contact breaker points show signs of excessive burning and pitting on the faces of the contacts, it is an indication that the condenser has probably broken down and should be renewed.

3 To check the efficiency of the condenser remove the distributor cap and rotor arm. Then rotate the engine so that the points are closed – that is with the breaker arm resting between two high points on the cam.

4 Switch on the ignition and with a non-conductive article such as a splinter of wood, move the contacts open by levering on the spring of the moving breaker. If there is a severe flashing spark it indicates that the condenser has probably failed.

5 An additional test to confirm condenser failure on TL models is to open the points (this can be done by placing a piece of paper of postcard between the contacts) and disconnecting the condenser lead from the breaker terminal post. Then put a voltmeter or 12v bulb with two wander leads between the terminal post and the condenser lead. Switch on the ignition, and if there is a reading or the bulb lights the condenser is faulty and must be renewed.

6 To renew the condenser, detach the wire from the terminal post, remove the mounting screw and replace the old unit with a new one. Check that arcing has been virtually eliminated by testing as already described.

7 Distributor – removal and refitting

1 Disconnect the HT leads from the spark plugs and between the distributor cap and the coil.

2 Disconnect the LT lead from the terminal on the side of the distributor body. Pull off the hose from the vacuum unit (photo).

3 The method of retaining the distributor in position varies according to distributor type. On the ohv (TL) engine it is retained by a clamp plate and bolt, whilst on the ohc (TS) engine it is secured by three setscrews, equally spaced around the distributor flange. Before removing the retaining bolt/setscrews, mark the relative positions of the distributor to the block or cylinder head as applicable, which will act as a guide when retiming the distributor on refitting, (if necessary). Remove the setscrews/bolt and withdraw the distributor.

4 Refitting is a reversal of the removal procedure, and provided the distributor driveshaft has not been removed, the ignition timing will automatically be correct when the unit is refitted, as the offset shaft segments will engage to give the correct timing position (photo).

5 If the distributor driveshaft has been withdrawn or partially withdrawn and rotated, then it will be necessary to refit the driving gear as described in Section 4 of Chapter 1 before the distributor unit is located in the engine block or cylinder head.

8 Distributor (ohv engine) – dismantling and reassembly

1 Remove the distributor cap, rotor, contact breaker arms and externally mounted condenser, all as previously described. Note the location of the serrated cam in relation to the vacuum capsule rod, then remove the spring clip and lift the points pivot post unit from the baseplate. Remove the screws and withdraw the vacuum capsule.

2 Remove the spring clip from the end of the driveshaft.

3 Mark the drive dog in relation to the upper cam slot, then withdraw the pin and slide off the washers and bush from the driveshaft. Remove the baseplate securing screws and withdraw the baseplate assembly.

4 The shaft and counterweight assembly can now be extracted from the distributor body.

5 If wear is evident in the bushes or counterweight holes, or the springs are stretched then it will be economical to exchange the complete distributor unit for a factory exchange one. Ensure that the replacement unit carries the same index number as the original. The appropriate index numbers, and vehicle and engine applications, are listed in the specifications section of this Chapter.

6 Reassembly is a reversal of dismantling but clean and lubricate all components first.

9 Distributor (ohc engine) – dismantling and reassembly

1 Remove the distributor cap, rotor, contact breaker arms and externally mounted condenser, as previously described.

2 Remove the spring clip and lift the points pivot post unit from the baseplate, after noting the location of the serrated cam in relation to the vacuum capsule rod.

3 Detach and remove the baseplate from the centrifugal unit on the driveshaft and remove the vacuum capsule.

4 Remove the drive dog spring, then extract the retaining pin from the drive dog on the bottom of the driveshaft, having marked it in relation to the upper cam slot. Remove the washer assemblies, noting their order of fitting.

5 Withdraw the driveshaft upwards through the distributor body and note the washers under the centrifugal unit.

6 Clean and inspect the respective components as given in paragraph 5 in the previous Section.

7 Reassembly is a reversal of the removal procedure, but ensure that all parts are clean and, where applicable, lubricated.

10 Ignition timing

1 It is necessary to time the ignition when it has been upset due to overhauling or dismantling which may have altered the relationship between the position of the pistons and the moment at which the distributor delivers the spark. Also, if maladjustments have affected the engine performance it is very desirable, although not always essential, to reset the timing starting from scratch. In the following procedures it is assumed that the intention is to obtain standard performance from the standard engine which is in reasonable condition. It is also

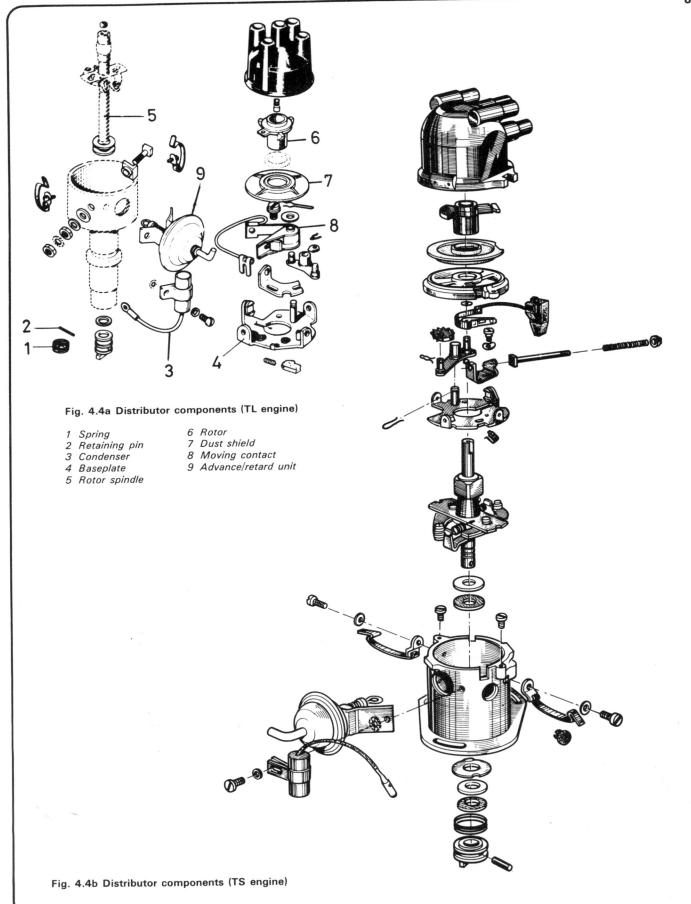

Fig. 4.4a Distributor components (TL engine)

1 Spring
2 Retaining pin
3 Condenser
4 Baseplate
5 Rotor spindle
6 Rotor
7 Dust shield
8 Moving contact
9 Advance/retard unit

Fig. 4.4b Distributor components (TS engine)

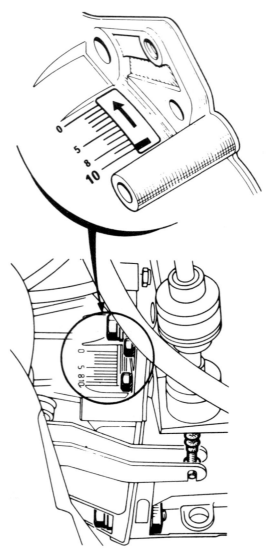

Fig. 4.5 The flywheel timing mark aperture on transmission
housing aperture – manual transmission models

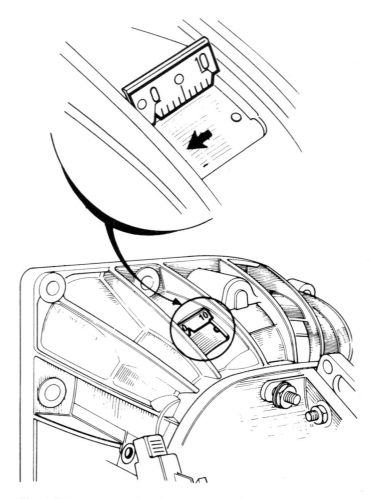

Fig. 4.6 The converter housing timing check aperture – automatic
transmission models

assumed that the recommended fuel octane rating is used.

2   Renault now fit a diagnostic socket and this device is designed to enable the Renault dealers to quickly analyse the condition of the ignition circuit, and to diagnose any defects in it. Unfortunately, for the private owner/DIY mechanic, specialised equipment is needed to utilize this device and it is therefore of little use to him.

3   The static or datum timing is getting the spark to arrive at a particular position on the crankshaft. Most manufacturers stick to the convention of using No 1 cylinder for this adjustment and the Renault is no exception. Note, however, that No 1 is at the flywheel end. The respective spark plug lead positions are shown in Figs 4.1 and 4.2 for both engine types in relation to the distributor.

4   On manual transmission models, the timing mark on the flywheel must be aligned with the 'O' graduation marking on the flywheel housing to set the static timing at TDC (top dead centre of the firing stroke for the No 1 cylinder), as shown in Fig. 4.5. On automatic transmission models there is a timing check aperture in the converter housing as indicated in Fig. 4.6, and the timing hole in the converter plate is at TDC when aligned with the 'O' marking in the fixed graduations. To check the TDC on No 1 piston, turn the engine over by hand using a suitable spanner on the crankshaft pulley. Remove the spark plugs to relieve the compression. With the flywheel/converter plate set in the TDC position, remove the distributor cap and check that the rotor arm tip is in alignment with the contact segment in the cap of No 1 cylinder plug lead. If it is, good! If not then the engine must be turned another complete revolution to the TDC mark again. The rotor

arm should then be in the correct position. Should the rotor arm still be way out, check whether the distributor body can be rotated enough to compensate by slackening the clamp and trying it. It may be possible, with alterations to plug lead lengths, but this should not be necesary.

5   Now the engine should be set at the correct static advance position with reference to Specifications.

6   As discussed in the opening section, the spark is produced when the contact points in the LT circuit open. It is now necessary to slacken the distributor clamping screw(s) so that the body of the distributor may be turned (whilst the rotor spindle stays still). The distributor should now be turned slightly, one way or the other, so that the contact points are fully open on the cam. The contact gap *must* be set correctly. It is difficult to see exactly when the points are fully open on the cam, and it is similarly difficult to see exactly when the points are just closed so a means of doing this electrically is necessary. Use a continuity tester or a 12 volt bulb and a jumper lead. If the latter is used, put one lead to the terminal where the coil LT lead joins the distributor and the other to a good earth on the engine block. With the ignition switched on the bulb will now light. Turn the body of the distributor anticlockwise (TS) or clockwise (TL) until the light just goes out. Then, turn the body back again until the light just comes on. Then tighten the clamping screw(s). If desired the correctness of the setting can be checked with a strobosccpic timing light but such a device is not essential for accurate setting of the static timing.

7   The performance of the engine should now be checked by road testing.

Measuring plug gap. A feeler gauge of the correct size (see ignition system specifications) should have a slight 'drag' when slid between the electrodes. Adjust gap if necessary

Adjusting plug gap. The plug gap is adjusted by bending the earth electrode inwards, or outwards as necessary until the correct clearance is obtained. Note the use of the correct tool

Normal. Grey-brown deposits, lightly coated core nose. Gap increasing by around 0.001 in (0.025 mm) per 1000 miles (1600 km). Plugs ideally suited to engine, and engine in good condition

Carbon fouling. Dry, black, sooty deposits. Will cause weak spark and eventually misfire. Fault: over-rich fuel mixture. Check: carburettor mixture settings, float level and jet sizes; choke operation and cleanliness of air filter. Plugs can be re-used after cleaning

Oil fouling. Wet, oily deposits. Will cause weak spark and eventually misfire. Fault: worn bores/piston rings or valve guides; sometimes occurs (temporarily) during running-in period. Plugs can be re-used after thorough cleaning

Overheating. Electrodes have glazed appearance, core nose very white — few deposits. Fault: plug overheating. Check: plug value, ignition timing, fuel octane rating (too low) and fuel mixture (too weak). Discard plugs and cure fault immediately

Electrode damage. Electrodes burned away; core nose has burned, glazed appearance. Fault: pre-ignition. Check: as for 'Overheating' but may be more severe. Discard plugs and remedy fault before piston or valve damage occurs

Split core nose (may appear initially as a crack). Damage is self-evident, but cracks will only show after cleaning. Fault: pre-ignition or wrong gap-setting technique. Check: ignition timing, cooling system, fuel octane rating (too low) and fuel mixture (too weak). Discard plugs, rectify fault immediately

Fig. 4.7 The diagnostic socket leads

A Contact breaker
B Ignition coil +
C Pick-up
D Earth
1 TDC signal pick-up
2 Earth (distributor)
3 Contact breaker
4 TDC pick-up signal
5 TDC pick-up (screening)
6 Ignition coil +

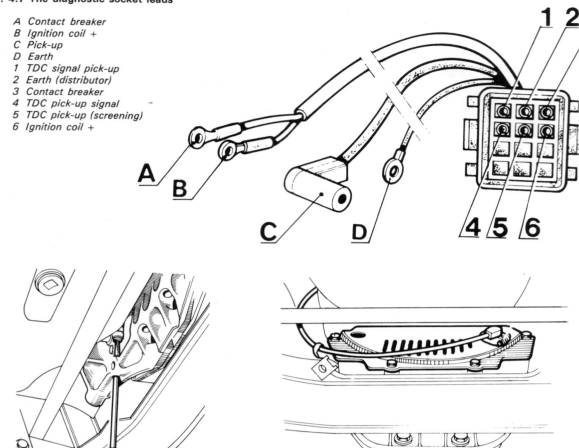

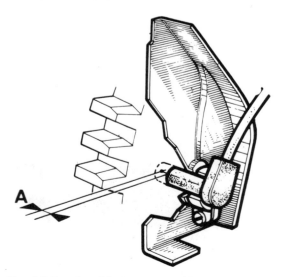

Fig. 4.8 The diagnostic pick-up cable clamp types

A Manual transmission
B Automatic transmission

Fig. 4.9 Set the pick-up clearance (A) from flywheel

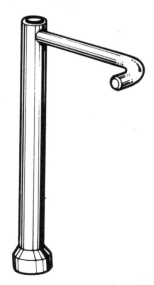

Fig. 4.10 Special spark plug spanner

8   Should the owner wish, he may check the centrifugal advance of the distributor. For this he will need to employ an accurate tachometer and a stroboscopic timing light. The timing can then be set observing the flywheel timing marks. The engine must be at its normal operating temperature, the vacuum detached and the engine idling. The relevant cam, dwell and flywheel timing angles are given in the Specifications for each engine type. The initial advance figure is on a clip attached to an HT lead at the distributor end.

9   Should the timing prove difficult due to a possible defective distributor, have it checked out by your Renault dealer or auto-electrician. The testing and possible repairs may amount to the price of a new distributor however, so make careful enquiries first and explain the symptoms before going ahead with this.

10   An easy check can be made to see if the vacuum advance is operational, by detaching the vacuum pipe from the carburettor manifold, and sucking on the tube. With the distributor cap removed, observe whether the vacuum spring has any movement. If there is no movement, it is defective and the vacuum unit must be renewed.

11   Diagnostic socket – removal and refitting

1   Disconnect the battery earth lead from its terminal.

2   Remove the diagnostic socket leaving the support plate in position. Detach the socket cover and disconnect the earth wire, the contact breaker wire and the ignition coil wire noting their respective connections as shown in Fig. 4.7.

3   Unscrew the pick-up unit retaining screw and remove the pick-up, working under the car.

4   Unscrew the clamp and detach the pick-up cable from its clutch/transmission housing location. This varies according to transmission type as shown in Fig. 4.8.

5   Refitting is a reversal of the removal procedure, but when inserting the pick-up unit, it must be adjusted to give the necessary clearance from the flywheel. When refitting the existing pick-up unit, push it home so that it is in contact with the flywheel, then mark its location. Extract the unit by about 1 mm (0·040 in) and tighten the clamp screw, as shown in Fig. 4.9.

6   Where a new pick-up unit is being fitted, it is pushed into position so that the three lugs make contact with the flywheel and then the clamp screw is tightened.

12   Spark plugs and HT leads – general

1   With the development of modern technology and materials, spark plugs are generally very reliable and require minimal attention. When they are due for checking and cleaning it is good practice to have them thoroughly sand blasted, gapped and checked under pressure on the machine that most garages have installed.

2   They can also be used as good indications of engine condition, particularly as regards the fuel mixture being used and the state of the pistons and cylinder bores. Check each plug as it is possible that one cylinder condition is different from the rest. Plugs come in different types to suit the particular type of engine. A 'hot' plug is for engines which run at lower temperatures than normal and a 'cold' plug is for the hotter running engines. If plugs of the wrong rating are fitted they can either damage the engine or fail to operate properly. Under normal running conditions a correctly rated plug in a properly tuned engine will have a light deposit of brownish colour on the electrodes. A dry, black, sooty deposit indicates an over-rich fuel mixture. An oily, blackish deposit indicates worn bores or valve guides. A dry, hard, whitish deposit indicates too weak a fuel mixture. If plugs of the wrong heat ranges are fitted they will have similar symptoms to a weak mixture together with burnt electrodes (plug too hot) or to an over-rich mixture caked somewhat thicker (plug too cold). Do not try and economise by using plugs beyond 9000 miles. Unless the engine remains in exceptionally good tune, reductions in performance and fuel economy will outweight the cost of a new set.

3   The standard plug recommended for the Renault 20TS models is a washerless type which has a taper seating. It is important when fitting these plugs that the seating faces are clean and the plugs are tightened to the specified torque or with the special spanner.

4   The HT leads and their connections at both ends should always be clean and dry and, as far as possible, neatly arranged away from each other and nearby metallic parts which could cause premature shorting

in weak insulation. The metal connections at the ends should be a firm and secure fit and free from any signs of corrosive deposits. If any lead shows signs of cracking or chafing of the insulation it should be renewed. Remember that radio interference suppression is required when renewing any leads. **Note:** *It is advisable when removing spark plugs from this engine to use a fully cranked 'short' spark plug remover. Be especially careful when refitting plugs to do so without force and screw them up as far as possible by hand first. Do not over-tighten. The aluminium head does not take kindly to thread crossing and extra force. The proprietary non-cranked plug caps should always be used to ease fitting and to ensure against HT lead shorting.*

13   Fault diagnosis – ignition system

Engine troubles normally associated with, and usually caused by faults in, the ignition system are:

(a) *Failure to start when the engine is turned*
(b) *Uneven running caused by misfiring or mistiming*
(c) *Even running at low engine speeds, but misfiring when engine speed rises or when the engine is under load*
(d) *Even running at higher engine speeds and misfiring or stoppage at slow speed*

For (a), first check that all wires are properly connected and dry. If the engine fails to catch when turned on the starter do not continue turning or the battery will be flattened and the problem made worse. Remove one spark plug lead from a plug and turn the engine again and see if a spark will jump from the end of the lead to the top of the plug or the engine block. It should jump a gap of $\frac{1}{4}$ inch with ease. If the spark is there ensure that the static ignition timing is correct and then the fuel system. If there is no spark at the plug lead proceed further and remove the HT lead from the centre of the distributor which comes from the coil. Try again by turning the engine to see if a spark can be obtained from the end. If there is a spark the fault lies between the contact in the distributor cap and the plug. Check that the rotor arm is in good condition and making proper contact in the centre of the distributor cap and that the plug leads are properly attached to the cap. The four terminals inside the cap should be intact, clean and free from corrosion. If no spark comes from the coil HT lead, check next that the contact breaker points are clean and the gap is correct. If there is still no spark obtainable it may be assumed that the low tension circuit is at fault. To check the low tension circuit properly it is best to have a voltmeter handy or a 12v bulb in a holder with two wander leads attached. The procedure now given is arranged so that the interruption in the circuit – if any – can be found. Starting at the distributor, put one of the two leads from the tester (be it lamp or voltmeter) to the moving contact terminal and the other to earth. A reading (or light) indicates that there is no break in the circuit between the ignition switch and the contact point (which should be open). Check next that the condenser is OK as described in Section 6. If this is satisfactory it means that the coil is not delivering HT to the distributor and must therefore be renewed. If there is no LT reading on the first check point repeat the test between the CB (–) terminal of the coil and earth. If a reading is now obtained there must be a break in the wire between the CB (–) terminal and the contact points. If there is no reading at this second check point repeat the test between the SW (+) terminal of the coil and earth. If this produces a reading then the low tension post of the coil windings must be open-circuited and the coil must be renewed. If there is no reading at this third check point there must be a break between the ignition switch and the coil. If this is the case, a temporary lead between the + terminals of both coil and battery will provide the means to start the engine until the fault is traced.

For (b) uneven running and misfiring should be checked first by ensuring that all HT wires are dry and properly connected. Ensure also that the leads are not short circuiting to earth against metal pipework or the engine itself. If this is happening an audible click can usually be heard from the place where the unwanted spark is being made.

For (c), misfiring occurs at high speeds the points gap is too small or the spark plugs need renewal due to failure under more severe operating pressures.

For (d), if misfiring is occuring at low engine speeds and the engine runs satisfactorily at high speeds, the points gap is probably the cause – being too great. If not, check the slow running adjustment of the car-burettor (see Chapter 3).

Chapter 5 Clutch

Contents

Specifications

Type	Single dry plate with diaphragm spring pressure plate. Hydraulically actuated on TS models; cable operated on TL models

Identification

On 843-20 (TL) engine	200 DBR 350
On 829-A700 (TS) engine	215 DBR 410

Clutch operating clearances

TL model (measured at end of operating lever)	2 to 3 mm ($\frac{3}{32}$ to $\frac{1}{8}$ in)
TS model (measured at clutch pedal)	5 mm ($\frac{3}{16}$ in)
TS models only: clutch fork pushrod travel	11·5 mm ($\frac{29}{64}$ in)

1 General description

On TL models, the clutch is cable operated, the cable running from the clutch pedal to the operating lever protruding from the clutch housing. The cable is adjustable to take up the wear of the driven plate in the clutch unit. TS models differ in that the clutch is actuated hydraulically, the slave cylinder being mounted adjacent to the operating lever where it protrudes from the clutch housing.

The clutch pedal pivots on the same shaft as the brake pedal. The release arm activates a thrust bearing (clutch release bearing) which bears on the diaphragm spring of the pressure plate. The diaphragm then releases or engages the clutch driven plate which is splined onto the gearbox primary shaft. The clutch driven plate (disc) spins in between the clutch pressure plate and the flywheel face when it is released, and is held there when engaged, to connect the drive from the engine to the transmission unit.

As wear takes place on the driven plate the clearance between the clutch release bearing and the diaphragm decreases. This wear is compensated for, up to the point where the driven plate is worn out, by altering the length of the clutch cable (TL models only). This adjustment takes place next to the release arm with an adjuster nut on the cable.

On TS models clutch pedal pushrod clearance must be periodically checked and, if necessary, adjusted.

Note: *At the time of completion of this manual, no information was available concerning the clutch mounted cylinder other than that service parts were not available.*

2 Clutch operating clearance – checking and adjustment

TL models

1 The operating clearance of the clutch is checked at the end of the operating lever and the clearance should be as specified.

2 Should adjustment be necessary, unscrew the locknut and then screw the adjuster nut in or out as required, to achieve the correct clearance (photo). Retighten the locknut whilst retaining the adjuster nut in the set position.

TS models

3 The clutch is hydraulically actuated and therefore the clearance of the pushrod must be periodically checked. The clearance between the end of the pushrod and the piston in the master cylinder must be between 0.2 to 0.5 mm (0.008 to 0.020 in) and this is shown more clearly in Fig. 5.2.

4 This clearance is obtained by checking the distance from the end of the pushrod to the pushrod-to-pedal clevis pin which should be about 115 mm (4.5 in). If adjustment is necessary, loosen the pushrod locknut away from the clevis, rotate the pushrod accordingly to set the clearance, then retighten the locknut.

3 Clutch unit (TL models) – removal, inspection and refitting

1 The clutch unit can be removed for inspection and/or renewal without removing the engine or gearbox. The instructions given below

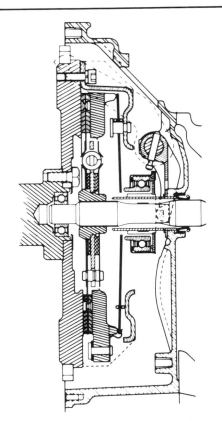

Fig. 5.1 Cross-section of TL model clutch assembly

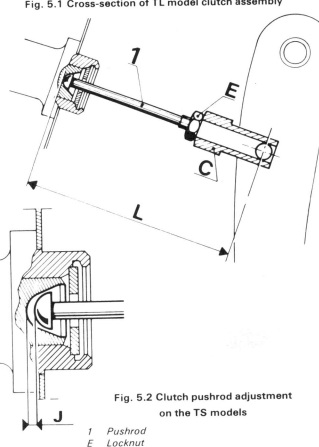

**Fig. 5.2 Clutch pushrod adjustment
on the TS models**

1   Pushrod
E   Locknut
C   Clevis
L   must equal 115 mm (4.5 in)
J   must equal 0.2 to 0.5 mm (0.008 to 0.020 in)

assume that neither of these major units are to be removed. If they are, follow the instructions for their removal in Chapter 1 or 6 as applicable.

2   During the following procedure it will be necessary to disconnect the driveshafts from the gearbox. Refer to Chapter 8, Section 2 and prepare the vehicle. Make sure the vehicle is secure before working underneath.

3   Commence by disconnecting the battery earth cable.

4   Disconnect the exhaust downpipe at the manifold and support out of the way.

5   Unscrew and remove the starter motor retaining bolts.

6   Unscrew and remove the upper gearbox-to-engine retaining bolts.

7   Detach the cable retaining clips, noting their positions.

8   Unscrew and remove the clutch operating cable filter module and detach the cable from the lever.

9   Disconnect each driveshaft from the gearbox. Remove the TDC pick-up support plate.

10   Unscrew and remove the lower engine-to-gearbox retaining bolts.

11   Detach the speedometer cable from the gearbox.

12   Referring to Chapter 6, disconnect the gear lever.

13   Position a jack (preferably a trolley type) under the rear casing of the gearbox and then raise it to support – not lift – the gearbox.

14   Unbolt and remove the gearbox mountings on each side.

15   Next, carefully manoeuvre the gearbox rearwards to the point where there is sufficient clearance to carry out the clutch removal.

16   Mark the position of the clutch pressure plate cover in relation to its location on the face of the flywheel.

17   Unscrew the clutch cover securing bolts as shown in Fig. 5.4. These should be unscrewed in diametrically opposite sequence, a few turns at a time, until the diaphragm spring pressure is released and the pressure plate assembly can be withdrawn. During withdrawal of the pressure plate assembly, do not let the driven plate fall.

18   Examine the driven plate friction linings for wear and loose rivets. Check the disc for distortion, cracks, broken hub springs or worn splines in its hub. The surface of the linings may be highly glazed but provided the woven pattern of the friction material can be clearly seen, then the plate is serviceable. Any signs of oil staining will necessitate renewal of the driven plate and investigation and rectification of the oil leak (probably crankshaft rear main bearing and seals) being required.

19   Check the amount of wear which has taken place on the friction linings and, if they are worn level with or to within 1.6 mm ($\frac{1}{16}$) of the heads of the securing rivets, the driven plate should be renewed as an assembly. Do not attempt to re-line it yourself as it is rarely successful.

20   Examine the machined faces of the flywheel and the pressure plate and if scored or grooved, renew both components on a factory exchange basis.

21   Check the segments of the pressure plate diaphragm spring for cracks and renew the assembly if apparent.

22   Where clutch engagement has been fierce or clutch slip has occurred in spite of the driven plate being in good condition, renew the pressure plate assembly complete.

23   Check the clutch release bearing which is located in the fork of the release lever. See that it spins freely without shake or slackness and that its pressure face is not scored or chipped. Renew if defective, or as a matter of course during major overhaul.

24   Before refitting the clutch unit, check that all friction contact faces are clean and free from oil and grease. Clean the machined face of the flywheel with a petrol soaked rag.

25   Locate the driven plate on the face of the flywheel so that the longer projection of the splined hub is on the gearbox side.

26   Locate the pressure plate assembly on the flywheel (sandwiching the driven plate) so that the cover/flywheel mating marks are in alignment.

27   Screw in the securing bolts in diametrically opposite sequence until they are slightly more than finger tight.

28   The driven plate must now be centralised by inserting either an old gearbox first motion shaft or a suitably stepped mandrel or dowel which will pass through the hub of the driven plate and engage with the spigot bush in the centre of the flywheel. As the pressure plate securing bolts have not yet been tightened, the insertion of the centralising tool will cause the driven plate to move sideways or up and down as necessary until it is centralised. Try the tool in two or three different positions to ensure perfect centralising and to enable the gearbox first motion shaft to pass through the clutch driven plate during refitting of the gearbox to the engine.

29   Fully tighten the pressure plate assembly to flywheel bolts in

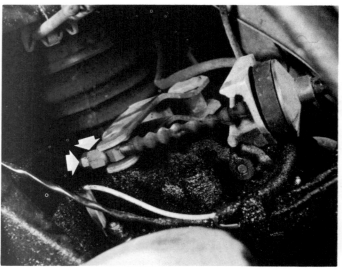

2.2 The clutch cable and operating lever assembly on the TL showing the locknut and adjuster nut (arrowed)

4.2a Locate the driven plate and cover (TS models)

4.2b Centralising the driven plate (TS models)

6.2 The clutch thrust bearing and operating lever shown in position (TS models)

8.1 Clutch operating cylinder (TS models) – unscrew bolts (1) and withdraw cylinder from actuating rod (2) – note bleed nipple (3)

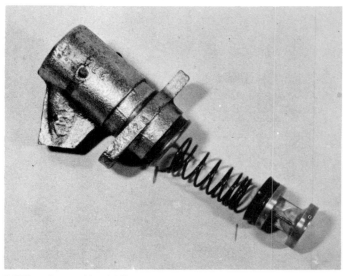

8.6 The piston with seal fitted and spring showing orientation to cylinder

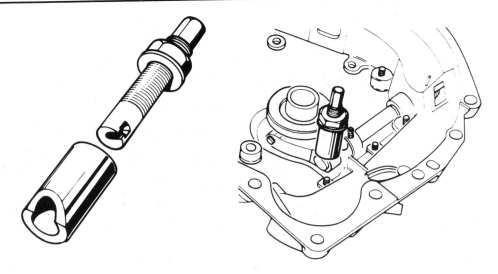

Fig. 5.3 Renault special tool Emb 384 used for removing the withdrawal fork retaining pins on TL models

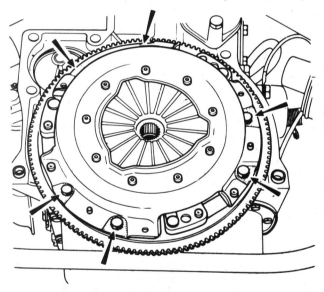

Fig. 5.4 The clutch cover securing bolts (arrowed)

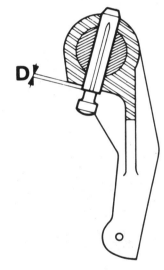

Fig. 5.5 The withdrawal fork retaining pin protrusion (D) must equal 1 mm (1/32 in) – TL models

diametrically opposite sequence.

30 Refit the gearbox to the engine in the reverse sequence to removal and tighten the respective retaining bolts to the specified torque ratings (where given).

31 Readjust the clutch operating clearance to complete.

---

4 Clutch unit (TS models) – removal, inspection and refitting

1 It is not possible to inspect or remove the clutch unit without first removing the engine, therefore refer to Chapter 1, Part B for the engine removal instructions.

2 With the engine and clutch removed, refer to the previous Section, paragraphs 16 to 29, for details of clutch unit removal, inspection and assembly (photos).

3 Refit the engine as described in Chapter 1, Part B.

---

5 Clutch withdrawal mechanism (TL models) – removal and refitting

1 Separate the gearbox from the engine as described in Section 3, paragraphs 1 to 15.

2 Detach the spring from the withdrawal pad and fork, and remove

the withdrawal pad from the shaft.

3 To remove the withdrawal fork the gearbox must first be removed. It will then be necessary to extract the retaining pins. They are an interference fit and could prove difficult to remove using ordinary methods. You may therefore have to either borrow Renault special tool number Emb 384 or take the gearbox into your Renault dealer for removal of the pins.

4 With the pins removed, the shaft can be withdrawn and the fork and spring removed; but note how the spring is located.

5 Renew any worn or defective parts.

6 Prior to refitting the fork, lubricate the shaft with Molykote BR 2 grease (or equivalent).

7 Insert the shaft with rubber seal and locate the fork and spring. Align the shaft and fork retaining pin holes and drive the pins into position so that they are located with the shoulders protruding by 1 mm ($\frac{1}{32}$ in) as shown in Fig. 5.5.

8 Relocate the withdrawal pad and lubricate the fork fingers and pad guide groove with Molykote BR2 grease (or equivalent).

9 Fit the spring with its ends locating into the holes in the withdrawal pad support and fork.

10 Smear the contact area of the diaphragm spring (to withdrawal pad) with a small amount of Molykote BR2 grease (or equivalent).

11 Refit the gearbox to the engine, and finally adjust the operating clearance.

6 Clutch withdrawal mechanism (TS models) – removal and refitting

1　Remove the engine from the car as described in Chapter 1, Part B.
2　Disconnect the clutch operating lever from the ball head in the clutch housing by withdrawing it outwards initially, and when detached, extract the lever and rod from within the housing (photo).
3　Withdraw the clutch thrust bearing.
4　Check the thrust bearing for wear and/or binding and renew if necessary.
5　Grease the ball and fork fingers prior to reassembly.
6　Refitting is a reversal of the removal procedure.

7 Clutch operating cable (TL models) – removal and refitting

1　To remove the cable, first unscrew the locknut and adjuster nut at the operating lever end. Withdraw the cable from the lever and refit the nuts and retain the rubber block as shown in Fig. 5.6.
2　At the pedal end of the cable, detach the inner cable end nipple from the clevis fork, sliding it clear of the slot, and remove the cable.
3　Refitting is a reversal of the removal procedure, but on completion, adjust the operating clearance as given in Section 2.

8 Clutch operating cylinder (TS models) – removal, overhaul and refitting

1　Clean the area around the housing and unscrew the two retaining bolts from the clutch housing (photo).
2　Swivel the pump upwards and pull it free from the operating lever and rod for removal. Unless the cylinder is to be dismantled for overhaul it is not necessary to detach the hydraulic line.
3　Where the cylinder is to be dismantled, remove it to a clean work area, having first detached the hydraulic line. Plug or clamp the line to prevent fluid spillage.
4　Prise the dust cover free from the end of the cylinder, then apply a limited amount of air pressure into the hydraulic hose connection aperture. Hold a cloth over the exposed end of the cylinder in which to catch the piston assembly and spring when they exit.
5　With the piston and spring removed, wash the respective components in methylated spirit and wipe dry with a non-fluffy cloth. The seal and dust cover should always be renewed when removed. If the piston and/or cylinder bore are damaged, scored or excessively worn, they must be renewed.
6　Before reassembly, smear the piston seal and cylinder bore with hydraulic fluid. Locate the new seal on the piston with tapered flange as shown (photo).
7　The wider spring coils are located at the opposing end to the piston. Insert them into the cylinder, taking care not to damage the seal lips. Locate the dust cover.
8　Locate the operating rod into the piston and reattach the cylinder

to the clutch housing. Tighten the two retaining bolts, which are fitted with shakeproof washers.
9　Refit the hydraulic line and bleed the circuit in the same manner as that prescribed for the brakes; see Chapter 9, Section 8.

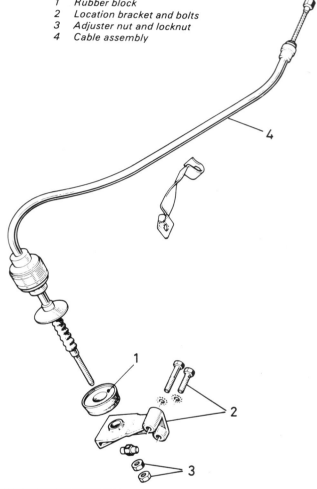

Fig. 5.6 The clutch cable components (TL models)

1　Rubber block
2　Location bracket and bolts
3　Adjuster nut and locknut
4　Cable assembly

9 Fault diagnosis – clutch

Symptom	Reason/s
Judder when taking up drive	Loose engine/gearbox mountings or over-flexible mountings Badly worn friction surfaces or friction plate contamination with oil carbon deposit Worn splines in the friction plate hub or on the gearbox input shaft
Clutch spin (or failure to disengage) so that gears cannot be meshed	Clutch actuating cable clearance too great (TL models) Clutch friction disc sticking because of rust on splines (usually apparent after standing idle for some length of time) Damaged or misaligned pressure plate assembly Incorrect release bearing fitted Air in hydraulic circuit (TS models)
Clutch slip – (increase in engine speed does not result in increase in car speed – especially on hills)	Clutch actuating cable clearance from fork too small resulting in partially disengaged clutch at all times (TL models). Clutch friction surfaces worn out (beyond further adjustment of operating cable) or clutch surfaces oil soaked
Squealing noise when clutch pedal depressed	Release bearing worn

Chapter 6 Manual gearbox

For modifications, and information applicable to later models, see Supplement at end of manual

Contents

Specifications

Four-speed gearbox
Type . . . . Four forward gears, one reverse. Synchromesh on all forward gears. Central floor-mounted gear lever

Renault type number
TL models . . . . 352-41 (LH drive) or 352-42 (RH drive)
TS models . . . . 367-01 or 367-08

Gear ratios

	352-42	367-01
1st	3·82	3·36
2nd	2·26	2·05
3rd	1·48	1·31
4th	1·03	0·93
Reverse	3·07	3·18
Final drive ratio	9 x 34	8 x 33

Crownwheel and pinion backlash . . . . 0·12 to 0·25 mm (0·005 to 0·010 in)

Differential bearings pre-load . . . . 2 to 7 lbf (1 to 3 da N).

Torque wrench settings

	lbf ft	Nm
367 and 369 types		
Gearcase half housing bolts:		
8 mm	20 to 30	30 to 40
10 mm	30 to 40	45 to 55
Rear cover bolts:		
8 mm	15 to 20	20 to 30
10 mm	30 to 40	45 to 55
Clutch housing bolts	30 to 40	45 to 55
Secondary shaft nut	85 to 110	120 to 150
Reverse gear selector bolt	20 to 30	30 to 40
Primary shaft nut (later models)	85 to 110	120 to 150
352 type		
Gearcase half housing bolts:		
7 mm	15	20
8 mm	20	30
Rear cover bolts	10	12
Clutch housing bolts:		
8 mm	17	24
10 mm	25	35
Reverse gear selector retaining bolt	20	28
Speedometer worm nut	75 to 85	100 to 120

Five-speed gearbox
Type . . . . Five forward gears, one reverse. Synchromesh on all forward gears

Renault type number 369

Gear ratios
1st . . . . 3·36
2nd . . . . 2·06
3rd . . . . 1·38
4th . . . . 1·06
5th . . . . 0·82
Reverse . . . . 2·09
Final drive ratio . . . . 8 x 33 or 9 x 35

Torque wrench settings

	lbf ft	Nm
Half housing bolts:		
8 mm	20	30
10 mm	30 to 40	45 to 55
Rear cover screws:		
8 mm	15 to 20	20 to 30
10 mm	30 to 40	45 to 55
Reverse gear screw	20 to 30	30 to 40
Clutch housing screws	30 to 40	45 to 55
Crownwheel bolt	85 to 100	120 to 140
Secondary shaft end nut	85 to 110	120 to 150
Bearing plate screw	30 to 40	45 to 55
Mainshaft end nut	85 to 110	120 to 150

1 General description and modifications

Two types of manual four-speed gearbox are fitted to the Renault 20, the type 352 as fitted to the TL model and the type 367 as fitted to the TS variant. A five-speed gearbox is also available, designated the type 369.

On all three types, the layout and design is similar. The aluminium gearcasing comprises four sections, being the clutch housing, the right- and left-hand housings, (housing the main gear assemblies and also the differential unit), and the rear cover unit (containing the selector control shaft and selector finger). On the 369 gearbox, the rear cover also houses the fifth gear and its synchromesh assembly. All forward gears on all three gearbox types are fitted with synchromesh. Drive to the gears from the flywheel and clutch unit is via the clutch shaft, which is engaged with the primary shaft splines. The clutch shaft passes through the differential compartment. The primary shaft

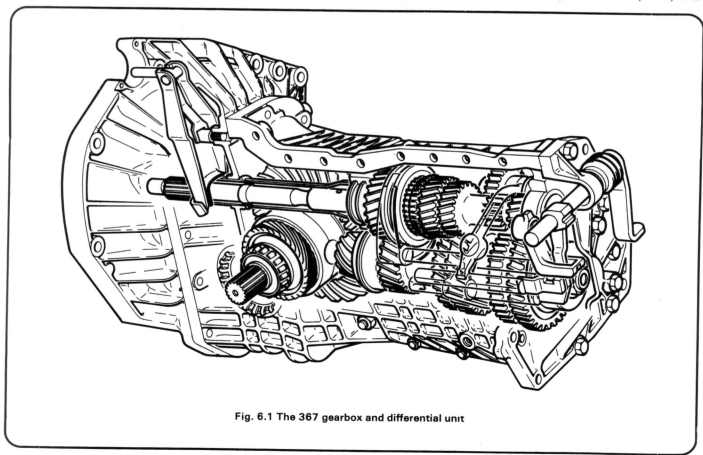

Fig. 6.1 The 367 gearbox and differential unit

transmits motion via the respective gears to the pinion (secondary) shaft. The reverse idler gear is located on a separate shaft in the rear of the main casing.

Motion is transmitted when a particular gear is engaged transferring the drive from the primary to the secondary shaft, which in turn drives the differential unit and consequently the driveshafts.

The gear selector forks and shafts are located in the side of the gear casing and are actuated by the selector rod shift mechanism located in the rear casing. The selector forks are in constant engagement with the synchro sliding hubs which move to and fro accordingly to engage the gear selected.

The speedometer drivegear is attached to the differential unit on 367 and 369 models and to the end of the secondary shaft on 352 models and this is turn drives the drive gear unit to which the drive cable is attached. Both the speedometer cable and driven gear unit can be removed with the gearbox in place. Removal of the drivegear, however, necessitates removal of the gearbox.

Inspection of the gear assemblies and the differential unit can only be made with the gearbox removed from the vehicle and the respective casing sections separated. Only the rear cover can be removed with the gearbox in the vehicle. On the 369 type gearbox this means that the fifth gear can be inspected/refitted with the gearbox in place.

Although the transmission unit is basically simple in operation, certain dismantling, adjustment and reassembly operations require the use of specialised tools. Therefore, if you are contemplating overhauling the gearbox it is essential that you read through the relevant sections concerning your gearbox before starting any work.

Another point to consider is the availability of necessary parts. You will not really know what you require until the casing sections are separated. It is at this stage that an assessment should be made on the extent of work required and any parts that will be needed, do check with your Renault dealer before proceeding further. In some instances, certain items are only supplied as complete assemblies, and in many cases the simplest course of action is to reassemble the casings and get an exchange unit — usually the most satisfactory and economical solution.

TS models from vehicle fabrication No 93000 are fitted with a modified primary shaft. This has a nut and double-track ball bearing at the rear end and a plain roller bearing at the differential end. The torque wrench setting of the nut is given in the Specifications and there is no adjustment required. Photos of the later type primary shaft are shown in Section 5.

2   Gearbox – removal and refitting

1   Although the gearbox is located behind the engine in the conventional manner, it is a relatively bulky unit and removing it rearwards and downwards, whilst possible, can prove difficult. The main problem with removal in this manner is that the upper and lower body crossmembers, situated immediately to the rear of the clutch housing, cannot (and must not) be removed. They therefore tend to restrict movement of the gearbox. Removal in this manner necessitates the aid of a couple of fit assistants to work underneath the vehicle and help in manoeuvring the gearbox free. The engine must also be disconnected and tilted at an acute angle (upwards at the front). As the gearbox also contains the differential assembly it is quite a heavy unit. This method of removal is therefore not generally recommended. We found that the best method was to remove the engine first. The gearbox can then easily be disconnected and withdrawn through the engine compartment. Referring to Chapter 1, remove the engine and then detach and remove the gearbox as follows.
2   Drain the transmission oil.
3   Raise and support the front of the vehicle, and remove the front roadwheels.
4   A spacer leg must now be located between the suspension lower arm pivot pin and the lower shock absorber mounting on each side. Renault dealers use special tool No T AV 509/T AV 603 for 369 gearbox) as shown in Fig. 6.2. However, should you decide to fabricate your own spacers, make sure they are securely located.
5   Detach the exhaust downpipe from the location strap attached to the gearbox.
6   If removing the gearbox with the engine in position, detach the exhaust downpipe from the manifold, and the starter motor from its housing. Also remove the TDC pick-up unit. On TL models, disconnect

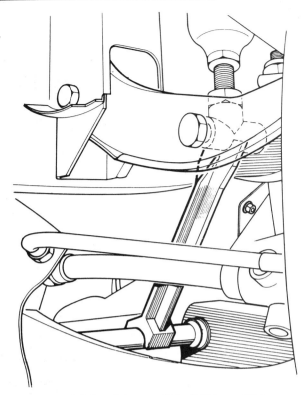

Fig. 6.2 Special spacer T Av 509 in position

the clutch cable at the operating lever and unscrew the two bolts retaining the cable filter module to the clutch housing. On TS models, unbolt and detach the clutch slave cylinder and withdraw it from the operating rod, but do not disconnect the hydraulic hose. The cylinder can be positioned out of the way, but support it to prevent the hose being stretched.
7   Referring to Chapter 8, disconnect the driveshafts from the differential sunwheel shafts. When disconnected each side, pivot the stub axle carrier units downwards to disconnect each driveshaft.
8   Referring to Section 9, disconnect the gear lever control linkage.
9   Detach the speedometer cable by withdrawing the retaining clip and extracting the cable from its location housing.
10 Detach the reversing light wire spade connector from the switch (photo).
11 Position a jack (preferably a trolley type) under the gearbox and raise it to support – not lift – the gearbox.
12 Unbolt and remove the mounting bolts on each side of the gearbox. Loosen off the side-mounting-to-chassis bolts each side. Ensure that the jack is supporting the gearbox securely and remove the side mounting on one side. This makes gearbox removal and refitting much easier.
13 Next, check that all gearbox attachments are free, then, with the aid of an assistant, manoeuvre it forwards into the engine compartment and lift it clear.
14 Remove the gearbox to the area of dismantling and clean it externally for inspection and overhaul.
15 Refitting is a reversal of the removal procedure. When the gearbox is lowered into position, reconnect it to the mountings and the removed mounting to the chassis. The gearbox and mountings can then be slid back in the slotted adjuster holes in the chassis to the original position (photo).
16 When the selector lever linkage is reconnected, check its adjustment as given in Section 8.
17 Note that when reconnecting the driveshafts to the sunwheel shafts, the rollpin holes are slightly offset. If the rollpin is difficult to drive through, disconnect the shaft and rotate it 180°, then relocate it to align the holes. Always use new rollpins.
18 When the engine and gearbox are being reunited, smear the clutch shaft splines with a light coating of Molykote BR2 grease or equivalent.
19 Refer to Routine Maintenance and replenish the gearbox with oil.

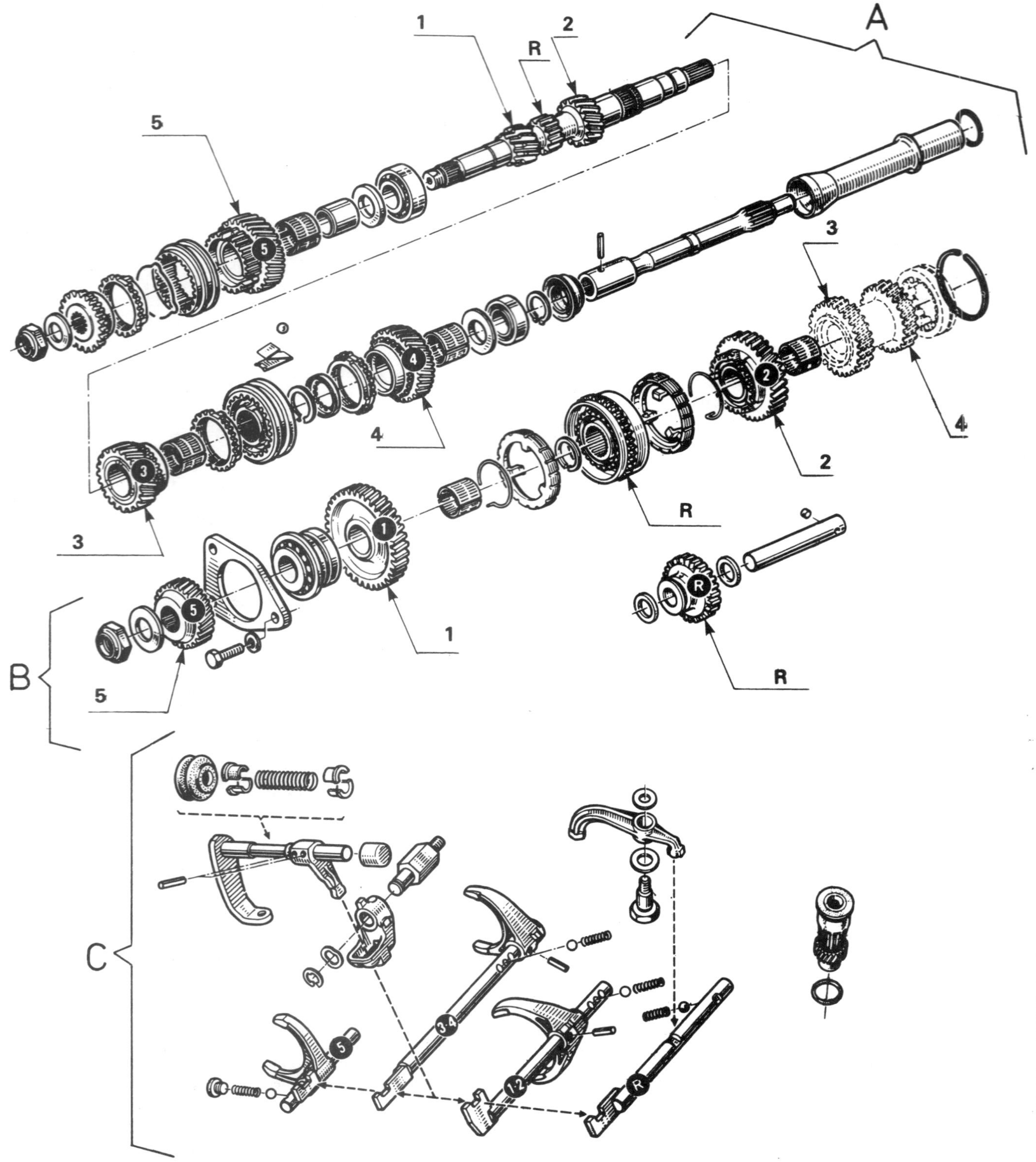

Fig. 6.3 The 369 (5-speed) gearbox components

A Primary/clutch shaft
   assembly

B Secondary (pinion) shaft
   assembly

C Selectors

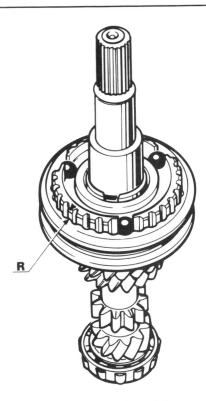

Fig. 6.4 Mark the relative positions of the sliding gear and synchro hub at 'R'

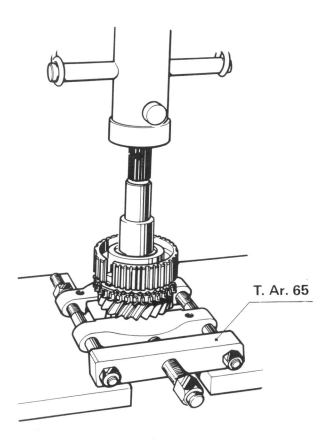

Fig. 6.5 Special tool T Ar 65 used for removing the driveshaft

3   Gearbox (Types 367 and 369) – dismantling

1   The types 367 and 369 gearbox are similar in construction, the principle difference being the 5th gear assembly in the type 369 gearbox. The gear and differential assemblies are housed in the gearcase, which comprises of four sections: the clutch housing at the front, the rear cover and the right- and left-hand casing halves. All casings must be separated for access to the gears and differential unit. Proceed as follows.

2   First remove the clutch housing, but before removing the retaining bolts, punch-mark or scribe an identification mark on the two 'dowel bolt' positions (these have recessed bolt heads). This will ensure correct reassembly. Next, unscrew and remove the twelve bolts retaining the housing.

3   Carefully, tap the housing free from the rear using a soft-headed mallet (photo), or piece of wood and remove the gasket.

4   Detach the gearbox mountings on each side at the rear.

5   On type 369 gearbox, unscrew and remove the 5th gear screw, spring and interlock ball of the shaft.

6   Unscrew the rear housing retaining bolts, taking note of their respective lengths/positions. Do not forget the bolt in front of the control lever.

7   Lightly tap the rear housing free, using a soft headed hammer, and manoeuvre the gear control lever free from the selector rods and remove the cover.

8   Before separating the gearcase halves, consideration should be given as to whether or not the primary and secondary shaft assemblies are likely to require attention. If it is decided they will require attention, then on type 367 models (from vehicle fabrication No 93000) and all type 369 gearboxes, the respective primary and secondary shaft rear locknuts must be loosened. This is best done at this stage as the shafts can be prevented from turning by tapping the selector rods to 'in gear' positions to lock the shafts.

9   Once the shafts are locked, relieve the nut lock flange from the secondary and primary shafts (photo). Get an assistant to steady the gearbox whilst you loosen off the primary and secondary shaft locknuts. You will need 36 mm and 30 mm box spanners respectively.

10   On the type 369 gearbox, remove the nuts from each shaft and then withdraw the washer; also remove the 5th gear dog clutch and synchro ring from the primary shaft. Before removing the hub from the sliding pinion, their relative positions must be marked (if not so already) for correct reassembly positions. Remove the slider pinion with fork arm and shaft. Withdraw the 5th gear and retain the half-needle roller bearings. Remove the spacer links and double ball bearing support washer. From the secondary shaft, withdraw the washer and 5th driven gear. Remove the 'tilting lock' and the biconical bearing plate.

11   Detach and remove the speedometer drive pinion unit.

12   Unscrew and remove the half casing central retaining bolts (two off) (photo). Position the gearbox on its side, with the crownwheel teeth facing upwards. Unscrew the sixteen outer flange bolts and nuts from the casing halves and, as each is removed, note its length and location. When the bolts are removed invert the gearbox, (crownwheel teeth downwards) and carefully tap the housings apart using a soft-headed mallet or piece of wood against the protruding flange sections. Once the seal is broken, the housings can be separated from the location dowel and the right-hand side case lifted clear.

13   The differential unit and gear assemblies can now be lifted out of the half casing (photos). To remove the reverse idler, press down the retaining peg and withdraw the shaft, gear (noting the direction of fitting) and the thrust washer. Retain the lock peg and spring.

14   The respective assemblies are now ready for cleaning, inspection and further dismantling/overhaul as necessary.

Primary shaft dismantling

15   To separate the primary shaft from the input (clutch) shaft, withdraw the sleeve and drive out the rollpin that locates the two shafts, then slide them apart.

16   Withdraw the bearing at the differential end of the shaft. A suitable puller is essential here – Renault suggest the use of special puller number Mot 49 and adaptor Rou 407.

17   Extract the circlip and remove the roller bearing cages. Withdraw the 4th gear and synchromesh ring. Keep the needle roller bearings in a safe place.

18 Before removing the 3rd/4th sliding gear, mark its relative position to the synchro hub at mark 'R' shown in Fig. 6.4. Remove the sliding gear and retain the three balls with it.

19 Remove the 3rd gear synchromesh hub retaining circlip.

20 Next, support the assembly in a soft-jawed vice so that the rear end face of the large gear section rests on top of the vice. If available, use the special Renault tool T Ar 65 as shown in Fig. 6.5. Press or drive the shaft assembly through and remove the synchromesh hub, the synchro ring and 3rd gear. Retain the needle roller half bearings in a safe place.

21 Remove the taper bearing or ball bearing (as applicable) in a similar manner using tool T Ar 65 if available.

22 On type 367 gearboxes produced from vehicle fabrication No 93000, the rear bearing of the primary shaft was modified and a locknut and tab washer fitted to the end of the shaft. When the nut and tab washer are removed, extract the inner rear ball race of the biconical bearing unit (photo), then withdraw the bearing using a puller, (noting which way round it is fitted).

Secondary shaft dismantling

23 First, remove the nut from the rear end of the shaft. If not already loosened off as suggested earlier, fit the gear train in a soft jaw vice and grip the 3rd/4th gear cluster. Unscrew the nut and remove it with the washer.

24 Withdraw the bearing assembly. On type 367 gearboxes, this is a double taper roller bearing and the rear cone and outer race are removed first. Then withdraw the inner bearing race and spacer using a suitable puller. As the bearing is a flush fit, there is little room in which to engage the puller legs. Therefore hold the assembly in the hand and tap the end of the shaft downwards onto a wooden block (bearing end down). This shock treatment should ease the bearing down the shaft sufficiently to allow the puller legs to engage fully behind the bearing to draw it off. Take care not to damage the bearing and check that the balls of the synchro unit are not allowed to fall out.

25 The 1st speed gear and needle roller bearings can now be withdrawn – keep them together. Remove the synchro ring.

26 Mark the relative positions of the 1st/2nd sliding gear to the hub and remove it.

27 Extract and remove the synchro hub retaining circlip from its groove. Use a puller and remove the synchro hub and ring followed by the synchro ring and 2nd gear. Keep the needle roller half bearings with the 2nd gear.

28 This is as far as the shaft can be dismantled and no attempt should be made to remove the 3rd and 4th gear cluster (photo).

Gear control selectors dismantling

29 Centralise the respective shafts, then drive out the fork arm retaining pins from the 1st/2nd and 3rd/4th forks.

30 Withdraw each shaft in turn (1st/2nd then 3rd/4th) and keep each with its selector fork and interlock balls and springs.

31 To remove the reverse selector, unscrew the retaining screw and withdraw the selector and shaft.

32 To remove the reverse pinion gear on the early type 367 gearbox, press out the lockpin and withdraw the shaft, pinion and the friction washers. Retain the spring pin and locking spring.

33 On the later type 367 gearbox and also the type 369, pull the shaft to the rear to remove, and keep the pinion with its friction washers.

Rear casing dismantling

34 On the early type 367 gearbox, extract the circlip and drive out the control finger retaining pins. If the outer breather is removed, the pins can be punched out through the breather hole. Withdraw the shaft and keep with the selector finger, spring and bellows. The seals and rings can now be removed from the casing.

35 On later type 367 gearboxes and also the type 369, a forked spring compressing tool will be needed to relieve the spring tension and enable the four half shells to be extracted (see Fig. 6.6). Drive out the retaining pins and remove the rear casing cap. Remove the control finger, the spring and lipped seal.

---

4   Inspection for wear of transmission components

Once the gearbox has been dismantled into its major sub-assemblies, it can be cleaned and inspected. Clean the respective components in petrol or other suitable cleaning solvent, then wipe dry, ready for inspection.

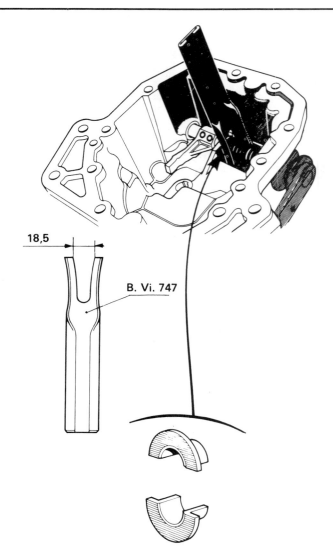

18,5

B. Vi. 747

Fig. 6.6 Use special forked spring compressor to relieve spring tension in the 369 gearbox rear cover

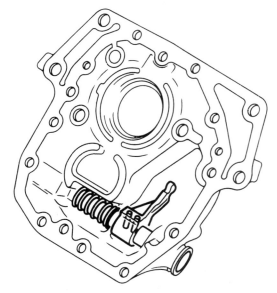

Fig. 6.7 The 367 rear cover and selector shaft/finger, showing rollpin positions

2.10 Detach the reversing light switch wires

2.15 Slide the mounting rearwards in direction of arrow to its original position

3.3 Tap protruding flanges to separate housing joints

3.9 Prise the nut flange from the shaft flat face (arrowed) to release

3.12 Remove the central retaining bolts

3.13a General view of the primary and secondary shaft assemblies in position in gearcase half housing (the clutch shaft having been separated)

3.13b Note location of seals and washer as they are removed for access to bearing and 4th gear

3.22 The double track ball bearing fitted to later TS models from vehicle fabrication No 93000

3.28 The secondary shaft dismantled as far as is possible

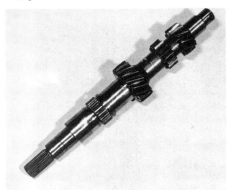

4.2 Check the gears and splines for damage

4.4 Inspect the synchromesh units and sliding gears for wear

4.7a The speedometer drivegear (A) is retained by the large C-clip arrowed (B) (on 367 and 369 models only)

4.7b Check the differential bearing cones for wear or damage ...

4.7c ... also the bearing cups in the half housings

4.11 Clean and inspect the mountings and renew if necessary

1   Check the casting for cracks or damage, particularly near the bearing housings and on the mating surfaces. Casings are only available in matched pairs so both will have to be renewed.
2   Check all the gears for chips and possible cracks and renew where necessary (photo). You should be able to tell whether this should be so from the initial diagnosis before dismantling.
3   Check all the shafts and splines for wear and flat spots and renew if necessary. The gears through which the shafts pass should be a good slide fit and not rock about.
4   Carefully, inspect the synchromesh units for signs of damage or excessive wear (photo). Once the gearbox is fully dismantled, it is always advisable to renew the synchro rings as a matter of course, since their relative cost is quite low.
5   On the type 352 gearbox (TL models), the hub/sliding gear renewal necessitates obtaining the correct replacements as they are available in two tolerance sizes, according to your pinion shaft. The hub and crownwheel and pinion are colour-coded to suit as follows:

Final drive pinion tolerance	less than 16.63 mm (0.6547 in)	over 16.63 mm (0.6547 in)
1st/2nd synchromesh hub . .	Red/Yellow	White
3rd/4th synchromesh hub . .	Blue/Blue	Red
Final drive pinion colour . . .	Red/Blue	Yellow

To measure the tolerances, use a micrometer and measure the dimension between the outer edges of the two splines as shown in Fig. 6.8. Note the reading, then make several similar checks across other splines to obtain an average reading in order to decide the most suitable hub requirement.
6   Carefully inspect the differential unit and its bearings for signs of wear and/or damage. Although the outer bearings may be renewed by the home mechanic, he may well have difficulty in setting up the final drive in the casing afterwards.
7   Any failure within the final drive unit will necessitate renewal of the complete assembly, with the possible exception of the outer bearings and of course the speedo drive gear (photos). We did not dismantle the crownwheel and pinion because it is not a task which can be undertaken, at least at the reassembly stage, by the home mechanic. The cost of purchasing a new crownwheel without a new pinion, madness anyway, is again approximately half that of a new exchange transmission unit. Purchasing the two together, crownwheel assembly and pinion assembly, to enable them to mesh and set-up correctly is approximately the cost of the exchange transmission and you will not get the guarantee.
8   Check that the nylon speedometer drive gearwheel is in good condition and running easily in its bush.
9   Check the selector forks for wear. Measure them with a pair of calipers and compare their ends with the thickest point; if in doubt renew them. They should only be fractionally worn.
10   Check the gearshift mechanism. The tongue which slots into the selectors may have worn considerably, in which case this too must be renewed. Failure to do so will promote difficulty in gear changing caused by a sloppy action.
11   Inspect the casings for signs of damage and cracks. Always renew the seals and gaskets as a matter of course when reassembling and do

not forget to check the transmission unit mountings (photo). Renew them if the rubber is perished or oil impregnated.

5   Gearbox (Types 367 and 369) – reassembly

1   Before starting to reassemble the gearbox it pays to spend some time in preparing plenty of clean space. If your work bench is rough, cover it with hardboard or paper for a good non-gritty surface. Do not start until you have all the necessary parts and gaskets assembled and make sure that all the ones you have obtained are going to fit. Gasket sets often contain items covering other models so you will not need them all – this is why it helps to keep the old gaskets you take off until the job is eventually finished. All parts must be kept meticulously clean during assembly, and as each component/sub-assembly is refitted, lubricate it with clean gearbox oil. The gear clusters must be assembled before they are refitted. The assembly of each cluster is time consuming and requires patience and accuracy; do not try to rush things! Start by reassembling the secondary shaft.

Secondary shaft assembly
2   Grease and assemble the two halves of the roller bearing cage to the shaft (photo).
3   Slide the 2nd gear into position and locate the synchro spring as shown (photo) with the hooked spring located into the hole in the shouldered segment of the gear.
4   Locate the synchro ring (photo) to the 2nd gear, but take care not to confuse the 1st speed gear ring with that of the 2nd, as the two differ dimensionally as shown in Fig. 6.13.
5   The synchro hub is now fitted with its offset shoulder facing towards the 3rd gear (photo). When fitting the hub, Renault recommend it be preheated to a temperature of 250°C (482°F). A domestic oven can be used to heat up the hub accordingly, then press it into position on the shaft. Not having a cooker at hand we pressed our hub on cold using a suitable tube drift, but extra care must be taken when 'cold fitting' to avoid damage. Once in position, check that the hub abuts the stop shoulder, with the lugs below the shoulder level.
6   Locate the new retaining circlip (photo).
7   The 1st/2nd sliding gear is now fitted with the gear section offset to the rear (photo) and the alignment markings corresponding.
8   Fit the synchro ring (photo).
9   Smear the half cage needle roller bearings with grease and locate together with the 1st gear (photo) and synchro ring.
10   Fit the double taper roller bearing inner cone and spacer (photo).
11   Next, fit the double taper roller bearing cup and outer bearing cone (photo).
12   The dished washer is now fitted onto the shaft with its concave face towards the bearing.
13   Screw a new locknut into position on the end of the shaft. The nut can either be tightened at this stage, by holding the gear assembly firm in a soft-jawed vice and tightening the nut to 85 to 110 lbf ft (120 to 150 Nm), or it can be left until the gearbox is reassembled so that the gears can be locked in position and the nut tightened (prior to refitting the rear cover) (photos).

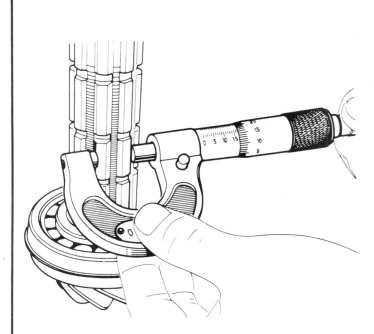

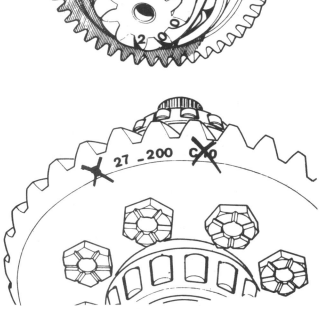

Fig. 6.8 Method of calculating the pinion spline measurement for hub refitting (type 352 gearbox)

Fig. 6.9 The crownwheel and pinion match markings

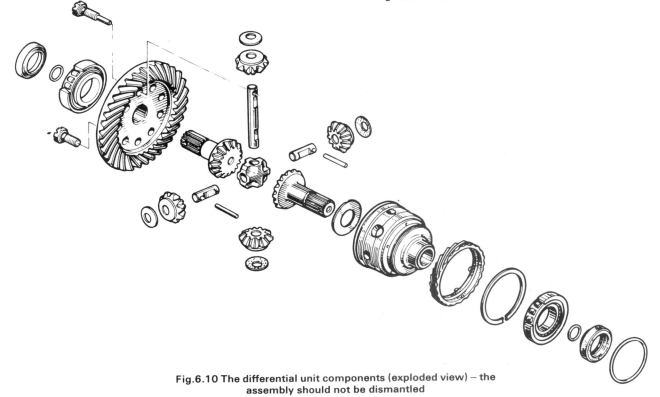

Fig.6.10 The differential unit components (exploded view) – the assembly should not be dismantled

5.2 Locate the needle roller bearing

5.3 Fit 2nd gear and locate the synchro spring

5.4 Locate the synchro ring followed by ...

5.5 ... the synchro hub with offset shoulder to 3rd gear

5.6 Fit the retaining clip (arrowed)

5.7 Locate 1st/2nd sliding gear ...

5.8 ... and synchro ring

5.9 Assemble the needle roller halves to the shaft and slide 1st gear into position

5.10 Fit the taper bearing cone ...

5.11 ... followed by its outer cone and cup assembly

5.13 The fully assembled secondary shaft unit

5.15 Fit the twin roller bearing, washer and locknut onto the primary shaft (later models)

5.17 Assemble the 3rd gear needle roller bearings and fit the 3rd gear

5.18 Locate the synchro ring followed by ...

5.19 ... the synchromesh hub

5.21a Insert the spring and ball ...

5.21b ... and locate the sliding gear

5.22 Locate the circlip (arrowed)

5.23 Fit the synchromesh ring

5.24 Locate the needle bearings

5.25 Slide the 4th gear into position

5.26 Locate the thrust washer

5.27 Fit the bearing and secure with circlip

5.29 Reverse idler gear in position

Primary shaft assembly

14 On type 367 gearboxes up to vehicle fabrication No 93000, support the shaft and press or drive the taper roller bearing cone into position on the rear of the shaft.

15 On type 367 gearboxes from vehicle fabrication No 93000, relocate the special ball bearing onto the shaft, pressing the main section of the bearing into position with a suitable tube drift. Locate the bearing half-track, the washer and locknut, (photo). To tighten at this stage, grip the 3rd/4th gear cluster in a soft-jawed vice and tighten the nut to a torque of 85 to 110 lbf ft (120 to 150 Nm).

16 On the type 369 gearbox, relocate the bearing so that it butts against the 1st gear. Slide the washer down and fit flush to the bearing.

17 To the front end of the shaft, assemble the 3rd gear needle roller bearing half casings (smear with grease) (photo).

18 Slide the 3rd speed gear into position and locate its synchro ring (photo).

19 On the early type 367 gearbox, heat up the synchro hub to about 250°C before fitting if possible. Where a new hub is being used, it can be fitted any way round. If employing the old hub however, fit it so that it is located as when removed, this being shown by the alignment mark which should be towards the 3rd speed gear. The notches of the hub must of course align correspondingly the synchro ring bosses when fitted (photo). When the hub is pressed into position, allow it to cool naturally before continuing. Relocate the hub locating circlips.

20 On later, type 367 gearboxes and also the type 369 the hub must be fitted so that the alignment marks correspond. Where a new hub is to be used, locate it so that the large recess is to the 4th gear and be sure to align the hub notches with the synchroniser ring bosses. Locate the circlip to retain the hub.

21 Refit the 3rd/4th sliding gear carefully into position and, smearing grease into the hub spring and ball locations, insert the balls and springs. As the hub is fitted ensure that the relative markings are in alignment where the original gear and hub are being used. Compress

5.30 Reverse gear selector arm and shaft in position

5.31a Insert the 3rd/4th selector shaft interlock ball and spring and press down as shown to allow the shaft to pass through

5.31b Then locate the selector fork

5.32 The assembled selector rods and forks

5.33a Insert reverse gear selector shaft interlock ball and spring and ...

5.33b ... make secure by fitting the reverse light switch

5.34 Relocate the selector control shaft assembly

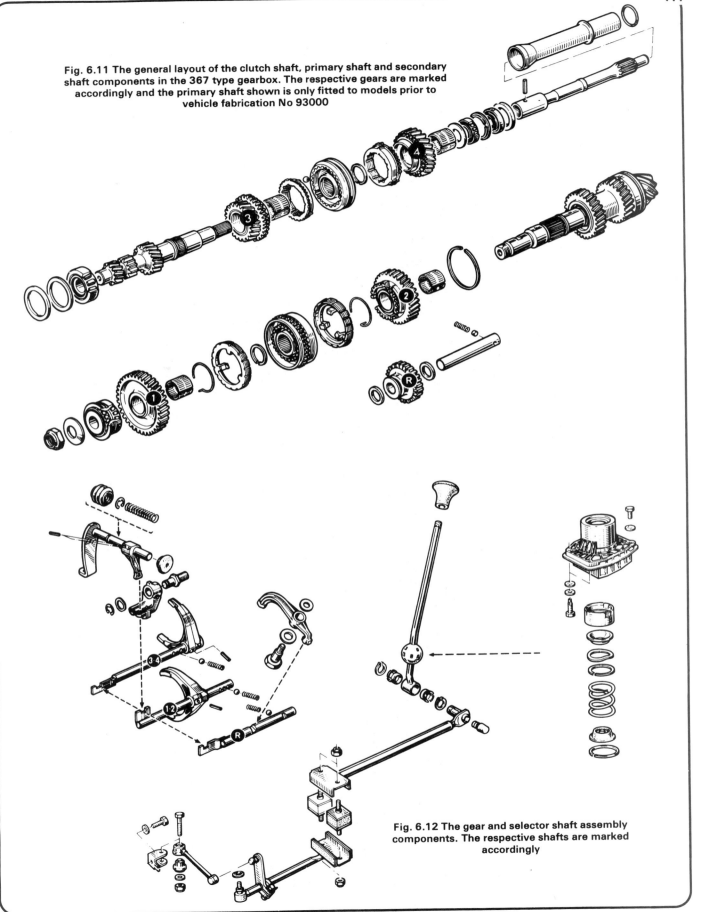

Fig. 6.11 The general layout of the clutch shaft, primary shaft and secondary shaft components in the 367 type gearbox. The respective gears are marked accordingly and the primary shaft shown is only fitted to models prior to vehicle fabrication No 93000

Fig. 6.12 The gear and selector shaft assembly components. The respective shafts are marked accordingly

the balls and springs with a screwdriver to ease assembly (photos). During the subsequent operations be careful not to allow the springs and balls to eject from their locations, should the sliding gear be dislodged.

22 Locate the circlip into position between the hub and the sliding gear, (photo).

23 Fit the 4th speed synchro ring (photo).

24 Smear the half-needle roller bearing with grease and locate them onto the shaft (photo).

25 Slide the 4th gear into position over the beerings (photo).

26 Next, locate the thrust washer with its flat face flush to the gear (photo). Drive it into position using a suitable drift.

27 Drive the roller bearing into position in a similar manner and make secure by fitting the retaining circlip (photo). The primary and secondary shafts are now ready for fitting into the gearbox.

Reverse idler gear

28 On the early type 367 gearbox the shaft is inserted into position and engages the 3mm friction washer, the idler gear, the pinion and the 5mm friction washer. Locate the spring and pin through the shaft recess and casing to secure as shown in Fig. 6.14.

29 On the later type 367 and all type 369 gearboxes, recess the pin into the shaft to a depth of 8 mm (0.314 in), then insert the shaft locating the 3 mm thick friction washer, the idler gear and the 5 mm friction washer (photo).

Gear selectors

30 Slide the reverse gear selector shaft into position and locate the reverse gear selector arm, engaging with the slot in the shaft. Screw in the retaining bolt with special washers and tighten to the specified torque (photo).

31 Fit the 3rd/4th selector shaft interlock ball and spring, then slide the shaft into position and locate the selector fork. Align the fork and shaft rollpin hole and drive in a new rollpin with its slot facing rearwards (photos).

32 Fit the 1st/2nd speed selector interlock ball and spring. Slide the shaft into position, locating the fork as it is fitted. Align the fork and shaft rollpin hole and drive a new pin into position with its slotted face to the rear (photos).

33 Prior to refitting the reversing light switch on the outside of the cover, insert the reverse gear selector shaft interlock ball and spring (photo). Then fit the switch to retain the ball and spring, (photo).

Rear cover

34 Insert the rings and seals into the endcase, then locate the bellows onto the control shaft. Fit the shaft and engage with the spring and selector finger. Using new rollpins, drive them through the finger and shaft to secure the two (photo). To fit the half-shells compress the spring sufficiently enough to insert them.

6   Gearbox (Types 367 and 369) – final assembly

1 Whenever the gearbox is being reassembled, irrespective of what work has been undertaken, it is important that the differential unit bearing preload is checked and adjusted as necessary.

2 First check that the two half-casings are perfectly clean and the bearing cups of the differential taper bearings are seated fully in their housings. The right-hand housing cup should be fitted so that it is slightly below the casing inner face.

3 Locate the differential unit into the left-hand half housings, carefully lower the right-hand casing into position and then insert and tighten the retaining bolts to the correct torque specified and in the sequence shown in Fig. 6.16.

4 Smear the adjustment nut thread with CAF33 or equivalent solution then locate the nut into the half-housing so that it butts against the bearing cup. Adjustment is made by the right-hand nut.

5 Screw the nut in, to the point where the differential unit can be rotated with a slightly stiff motion where new bearings have been fitted. If the old bearings are being reused, simply screw in the nut to the point where the differential can be rotated without any slack.

6 The differential pre-stress or loading must now be checked. To do this you will need a spring balance and some cord. Tie the cord to the balance and wind the cord round the differential case as shown in Fig. 6.35. Pull the spring balance until the differential starts to rotate and note the loading of the balance. The loading is correct when the

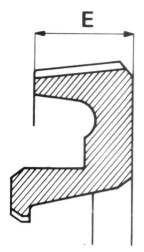

Fig. 6.13 The 1st and 2nd synchromesh rings differ dimensionally – measure across Section E to identify

1st gear ring = 14 mm (0.551 in)
2nd gear ring = 12 mm (0.472 in)

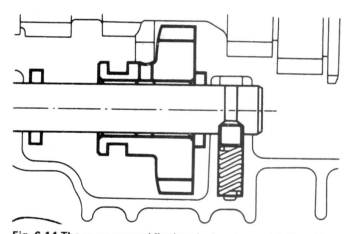

Fig. 6.14 The reverse gear idler interlock spring and ball position

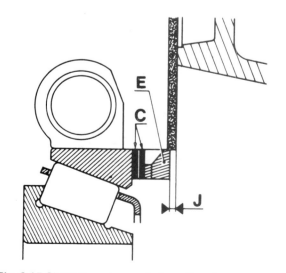

Fig. 6.15 Check the primary shaft endfloat (early models). Clearance at J must be 0.10 mm (0.004 in)

E   Distance piece   C   Shims

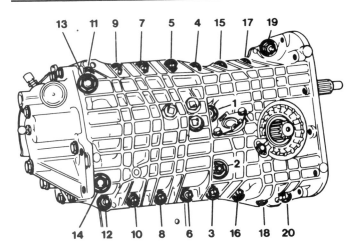

Fig. 6.16 Tighten casing bolts numerically in sequence shown

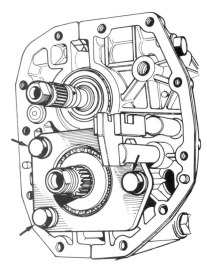

Fig. 6.17 Relocate the bearing stop plate onto the rear face of the 369 gearbox

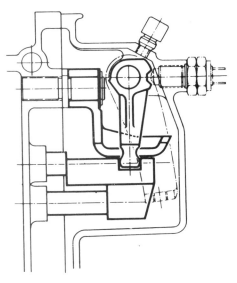

Fig. 6.18 Locate the selector finger as the cover is fitted

balance reads 2 to 7 lbf (1 to 3 da N). If required, screw the nut in or out accordingly to achieve the correct bearing preload.

7   Once the preload is set, unscrew and remove the bolts retaining the right-hand casing in position and separate the two half housings.

8   Locate the seals and location washer (with lug) onto the front of the primary gear shaft, then slide the clutch shaft into position aligning the rollpin holes. Drive a new rollpin into position to secure the two shafts, then fit the guide tube.

9   Into the right-hand housing fit the differential unit, the pinion shaft and the primary shaft assembly (photos). When in position, ensure that the guide tube drain hole points downwards.

10   Smear the mating surfaces of each half housing with a suitable sealant, then carefully assemble the two. As they are assembled, check that the locating lug of the washer on the front end of the primary shaft is engaged in its location hole in the half housing. Also ensure that the location pin protruding from the rear of the left-hand housing is aligned with the corresponding location slot in the periphery of the secondary shaft rear bearing (photo).

11   Insert the respective housing bolts to secure, but on models prior to vehicle fabrication No 93000, do not fully tighten the bolts yet, as the primary gear endfloat must be checked. To do this refer to Fig. 6.15. Relocate any adjustment shims removed during dismantling, together with the distance washer. Lightly tap the washer to seat the bearings, then locate the rear cover gasket. You will need a dial indicator gauge to check the endfloat clearance, which should be 0.10 mm (0.004 in). The clearance is measured to ensure correct free play between the space link and seal external face as shown at 'J'. If the clearance is incorrect, add or subtract shims as applicable.

12   Tighten the half housing retaining bolts to the specified torque and in the sequence shown in Fig. 6.16 (photos).

13   On the later type 367 gearboxes, the primary and secondary shaft tail nuts can now be retightened. Engage two gears to lock them in position for tightening to the specified torques. When the nuts are tightened, peen over the end flange of each nut to lock it in position (photos). Unlock the gears and check that the gears rotate freely.

14   On the type 369 gearbox, relocate the bearing stop plate and its three retaining bolts as shown in Fig. 6.17. Tighten the bolts and then fit the 5th gear, flat washer and retaining nut onto the secondary shaft. Assemble the following in order of appearance onto the primary shaft: flat washer, spacer collar, half needle roller bearings (smeared with grease) and the 5th drivegear together with the synchromesh unit. Refit the flat washer and the special retaining nut, tighten the nut to the specified torque and peen over the end flange to lock it in position. The secondary shaft assembly tail nut can also be tightened and peened over to lock in position, but refer to the Specifications for its torque setting. Lock the two shafts by engaging two gears at once. This prevents the shafts turning when tightening the nuts. Once tightened, neutralise the gears and check the shafts for freedom of rotation.

15   The rear cover for both types of gearbox can now be refitted. Smear the faces of the gearbox rear end and the rear cover with sealant and locate the gasket. Ensure that the selectors are in neutral end engage the selector control finger as the cover is fitted (photo).

16   Insert the rear cover retaining bolts and at the same time refit the right- and left-hand rear gearbox mountings. The right-hand mounting is fitted together with the exhaust pipe hanger bracket, (photo).

17   Torque tighten the cover bolts to the specified torque.

18   On the type 369 gearbox, relocate the interlock ball and spring for 5th gear, apply some sealant to the retaining bolt thread and insert it to secure.

19   Fit the speedometer driven gear unit into the gearbox housing and retain in position with the plate and bolts (photos).

Clutch housing

20   Locate the new O-ring seal onto the clutch pad guide sleeve flush to the flange (photo).

21   Smear the front face of the gearcase with sealant; also the mating face of the clutch housing. Locate the gasket onto the face of the gearcase and carefully refit the clutch housing (photo). Check that the clutch shaft guide sleeve drain hole is still facing downwards, then insert the retaining bolts, not forgetting that the special dowel bolts must be inserted into their original locations. You may recall that these two bolts are recognisable by their recessed heads (photo). One bolt is located at the top right side (in a row of three bolts) and the other on the bottom left-hand corner (in a row of four bolts).

22   The gearbox should now be ready for refitting, apart from fitting

6.9a Locate the primary shaft into the gearcase

6.9b Engage the clutch shaft and sleeve and drive in new rollpin to secure

6.9c Fit the clutch pad guide sleeve with oil hole downwards (arrowed)

6.9d Relocate the differential unit

6.10 Align the bearing slot and location pin for engagement

6.12a Tighten the primary (where applicable) and secondary shaft nuts ...

6.12b ... and peen over the flanges to secure (arrowed)

6.15 Fit the rear cover

6.16 The right-hand mounting and exhaust hanger bracket

6.19a Insert the speedometer drive pinion ...

6.19b ... and secure with lockplate and bolts

6.20 Fit the O-ring seal onto the clutch pad sleeve

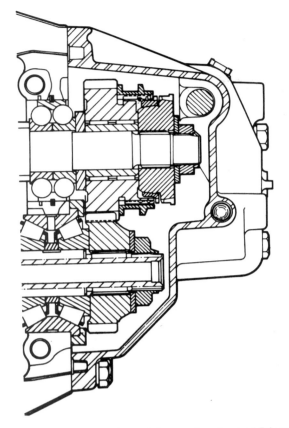

Fig. 6.19 Cross-section view of the rear housing and 5th gear assemblies of the 369 gearbox

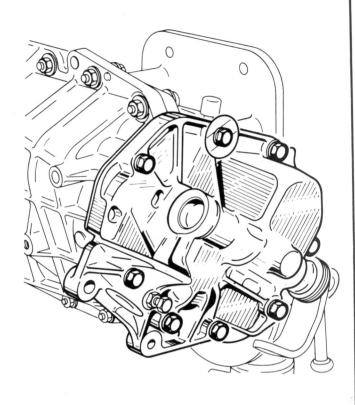

Fig. 6.20 The rear cover and retaining bolts

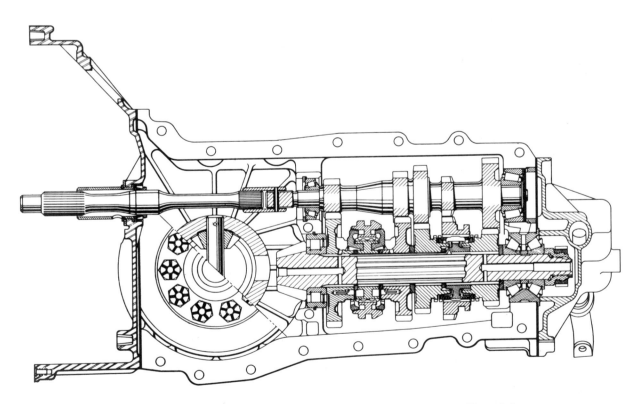

Fig. 6.21 Cross-section view of the 352-41 gearbox as fitted to the TL models

6.21a Refit the clutch housing

6.21b Special 'dowel' bolt (arrowed)

the clutch withdrawal lever, as given in Chapter 5. If the reversing light switch is still to be fitted do not forget to also fit the reverse gear selector interlock ball and spring at the same time. Refit the drain plug and tighten to secure.

7 Gearbox (Type 352) – dismantling

1   The gearbox casing comprises four main sections: The clutch housing, the right- and left-hand half housings and the rear cover. Access to any of the gear assemblies or differential unit necessitates separating the respective housings. Proceed as follows:
2   Unscrew and remove the clutch housing retaining bolts. Carefully, tap the housing away from the gearbox using a soft-headed hammer.
3   Remove the rear cover bolts and carefully, remove the cover in a similar manner.
4   With the cover removed, extract any bearing adjustment shims together with the distance washer from the primary shaft.
5   Unscrew and remove the respective half housing securing bolts and separate the housings by carefully, tapping the protruding flange sections with a soft-headed mallet.
6   The differential unit, secondary gear unit and primary gear unit can now be removed from the half casing, as applicable. The secondary gear is removed with the stop peg from the double taper roller bearing cup.
Note: *When the differential is lifted out, inspect briefly the crownwheel and pinion for signs of excessive wear or damage. They cannot be renewed individually as they are a matched pair. Therefore, should their renewal be necessary, it is advisable to reassemble the gearbox and exchange it for a replacement unit from your Renault dealer. Further information concerning the differential unit is given in Section 4. Refer to this before proceeding further.*

Primary shaft dismantling
7   Disengage the bearing track rings and adjuster washers.
8   Support the shaft at the front and drive the rollpin through to separate the clutch shaft, as shown in Fig. 6.23.
9   Supporting the gear assembly in a soft-jawed vice, use a suitable puller and remove the respective taper roller bearings from each end of the shaft. If the bearings are judged to be in serviceable condition, they can be left on the shaft.

Secondary shaft dismantling
10   Support the shaft in a soft-jawed vice, retaining it by the 1st speed gear. Select 1st gear and unlock the speedometer drive pinion, using a suitable open end spanner.
11   Next, withdraw the double taper roller bearing followed by the final drive pinion adjusting washer.
12   Remove the 4th gear and synchromesh ring.
13   Remove the 3rd/4th gear sliding synchromesh unit. Mark the relative position of the gear to the shaft and retain the hub keys.

14   To remove the 3rd/4th synchro hub you will need to support the hub carefully so that it does not get damaged and drive the shaft on the end with a soft-headed mallet. Alternatively and preferably, use Renault special tool number T Ar 65 (extractor).
15   Extract the gearwheel stop washer retaining key as shown in Fig. 6.24.
16   Remove the 3rd speed gear stop washer and the gear with synchro ring.
17   Withdraw the stop washer, 2nd gear and its synchro ring.
18   Mark the 1st/2nd sliding synchro gear in relation to its hub and remove it together with the hub stop washer.
19   Remove the synchro hub in a similar manner to that of the 3rd and 4th hub, but as it is removed take care not to dislodge the front roller bearing outer track.
20   Withdraw the 1st gear synchro ring, stop washer and gear.
21   The front roller bearing cannot be renewed as the inner track is bonded to the final drive pinion. To prevent the rollers and outer track becoming dislodged, fit a suitable retaining clip or clamp over the bearing as shown in Fig. 6.25.

Rear cover dismantling
22   Extract the rollpins retaining the selector control finger and withdraw the shaft removing the bushes, spring, finger and bellows.
23   Extract the oil seal by prising carefully with a screwdriver.
24   To remove the speedometer drive, unscrew and withdraw the retaining bolt and extract the pinion unit and seal.
25   Inspect the respective components as described in Section 4.

8 Gearbox (Type 352) – reassembly

1   Refer to the introductory paragraph in Section 5 before proceeding.
2   Where new synchromesh hubs and sliding gears are being fitted, they must be marked in relation to each other before dismantling, as they are carefully matched. On the 1st/2nd synchro unit, mark the assembly on the chamfered side of the sliding gear so that it can be seen when assembled. When marked, separate the sliding gear/s from the hub/s and clean thoroughly.

Secondary shaft assembly
3   Engage the 1st gear synchro spring as shown in Fig. 6.27 so that it contacts the three segments.
4   Slide the 1st speed gear into position on the shaft (against the pinion bearing) and locate the synchro ring. Fit the stop washer and rotate it to align the keyway. A suitable temporary key should now be slid into position down the keyway in the shaft to hold the washer in position during subsequent operations. This 'dummy' key can be fabricated from an old washer retaining key by removing the hooked lug. Ensure that the keyway spline chosen is one with an oil hole as shown in Fig. 6.28.

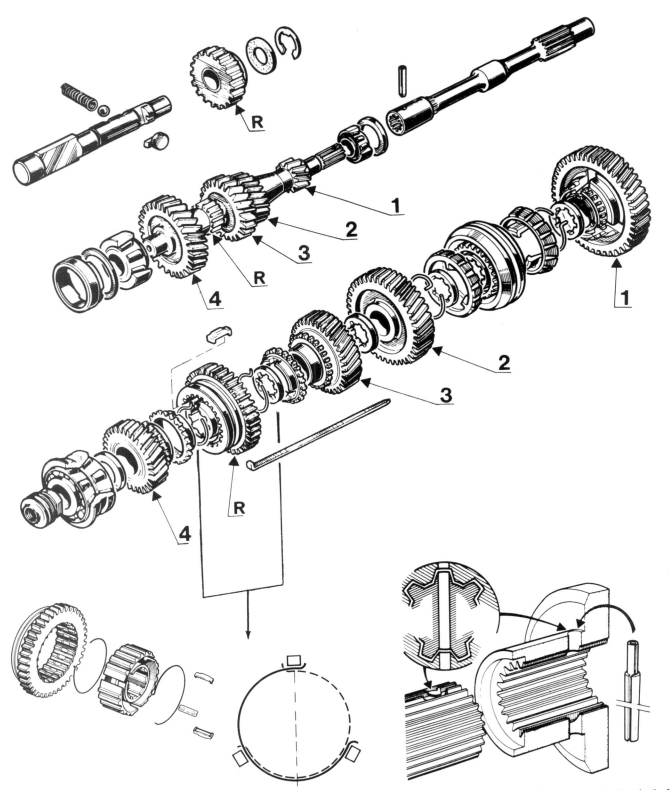

Fig. 6.23 Drive out the rollpins to separate the clutch shaft

Fig. 6.22 The clutch shaft, primary shaft and secondary shaft assembly (352 models). Each gear is marked accordingly. The insert indicates 3rd/4th synchro hub spring location positions

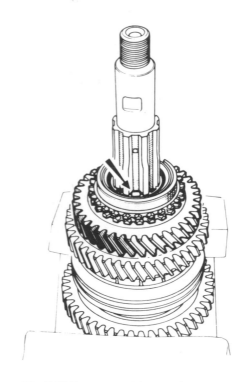

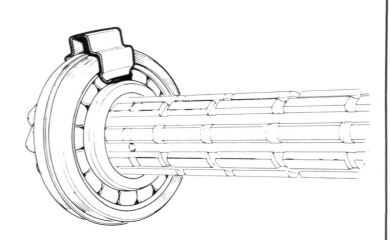

Fig. 6.25 Retaining clip in position to prevent bearing collapsing

Fig. 6.24 Extract retaining key (arrowed)

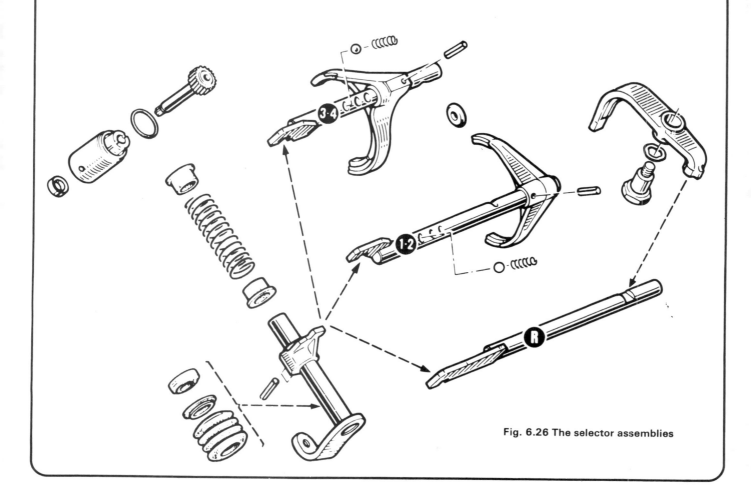

Fig. 6.26 The selector assemblies

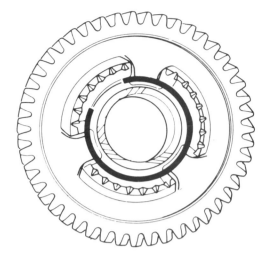

Fig. 6.27 Locate the spring as shown

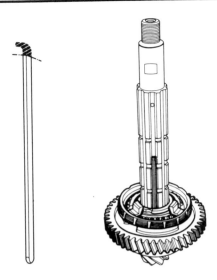

Fig. 6.28 Fit the dummy key into spline with oil hole. Remove hooked end of old key (shaded)

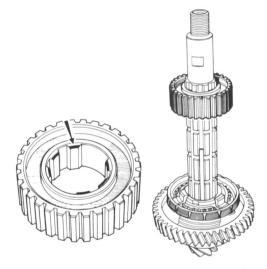

Fig. 6.29 Chamfered splines sections to face the 1st gear

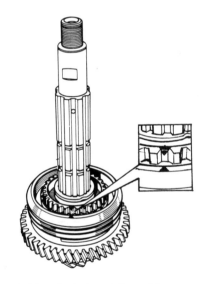

Fig. 6.30 Align the hub match markings

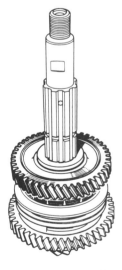

Fig. 6.31 Fit the 2nd gear and stop washer

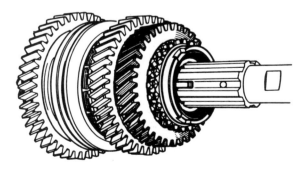

Fig. 6.32 Fit the 3rd gear, retaining ring and stop washer

5   Detach the bearing outer race retaining clip.
6   When fitting the 1st/2nd speed synchro hub, first heat it up to an electric oven temperature of 250°C. Leave the hub in the oven at this temperature for about 15 minutes, then extract and assemble it onto the pinion shaft so that an unsplined section is aligned with the dummy key. The chamfered section of the splines in the hub must face towards the 1st gear, as shown in Fig. 6.29. Press the hub fully into position so that it just comes into contact with the stop washer. As the hub is pressed into position, centralise the synchro ring with the lugs below the stop washer level in order not to damage the spring. Withdraw the dummy key and allow the hub to cool.
7   Next, assemble the synchro hub sliding gear with the chamfered side facing the 2nd gear and the relative hub match markings in alignment.
8   Locate the stop washer with its splines aligned with those on the shaft.
9   Fit the synchro spring to the 2nd gear (in a similar fashion to that for the 1st) and assemble the 2nd gear with synchro ring, as shown in Fig. 6.31. Fit the stop washer and align the splines with those of the shaft.
10   Next, assemble the 3rd gear and synchro ring.
11   Slide the stop washer into position and rotate it to align the splines.
12   Slide the stop washer location key into position down a keyway in the shaft, (choose a keyway with an oil hole in it).
13   Press or drive the 3rd/4th synchro hub into position, so that it is flush against the 3rd gear stop washer. Check when fitting that the notch on the hub is facing the 3rd gear and is aligned with the stop key. The three synchro ring notches must be aligned with the keys.
14   Locate the 4th gear and its synchro ring.
15   Fit the pinion protrusion adjustment washer and double taper roller bearing.
16   Fit the speedometer worm drivegear.
17   Support the shaft assembly vertically in a vice with soft jaws, fastened to the 1st gear, as shown in Fig. 6.33. Select the 1st gear to lock the shaft, and torque tighten the speedometer worm pinion to the specified setting. When tightened, do not lock the nut until the pinion shaft is adjusted on assembly.

Primary shaft assembly

18   Check that the bearings and their surface areas on the shaft are perfectly clean before fitting.

19   Press each bearing onto its respective end of the shaft and ensure that they are fully located.
20   If the crownwheel and pinion assembly components have been dismantled and/or refitted, it is essential that their mesh positions be checked and, if necessary, adjusted before the complete final reassembly of the gearbox takes place. Whilst Renault dealers have special tools to effect this procedure, it can be achieved by checking the backlash of the gears with a dial indicator gauge, if available and if you feel proficient enough to carry out this check and adjustment.
21   To check with a dial gauge, first locate the pinion shaft assembly into the right-hand gearcase half. Locate the differential assembly and fit the left-hand casing, retaining with a few securing bolts, but do not fully tighten them yet. Locate the rear cover to retain the double taper roller bearing track. Now fully tighten the half casing bolts.
22   Clamp the dial indicator to the front of the casing and check the backlash between the crownwheel and pinion. This should be between 0.12 mm to 0.25 mm (0.005 to 0.010 in).
23   Any adjustment to the pinion is made by fitting an alternative pinion protruding adjustment washer, as necessary. These are available in varying thicknesses.
24   If the differential bearings have been removed and refitted or renewed, check the fitting adjustment using a spring pressure gauge and a suitable length of cord. Coil the cord around the differential housing as shown in Fig. 6.35 and check the pressure requirement needed to rotate the differential. If using the old bearings, the differential should be free to turn without play. If new bearings have been fitted, the differential should rotate under a preloading of 2 to 7 lbf (1 to 3 da N).
25   Adjustment to the differential bearings is made by rotating the ring nuts on each side in the desired direction. When fitting the ring nuts, smear their threads with a suitable thread sealant. The nut on the differential housing side is turned slightly more than its opposite number to give more backlash. Mark each ring nut adjustment position on completion, as shown in Fig. 6.36.
26   Remove the rear cover, separate the left- and right-hand gearbox half casings and remove the differential unit.

Gearbox final assembly

27   Grease the tapered bearings of the primary shaft and assemble the outer tracks (cups). Fit the adjustment washer to the front against the bearing – smear it with grease to locate.
28   Locate the primary and secondary (pinion) shafts into position in

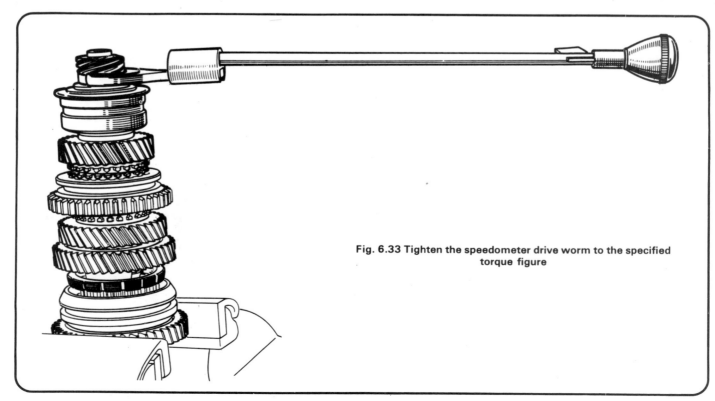

Fig. 6.33 Tighten the speedometer drive worm to the specified torque figure

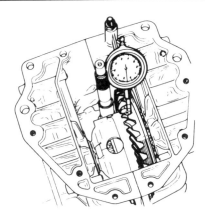

Fig. 6.34 Check the crownwheel to pinion backlash

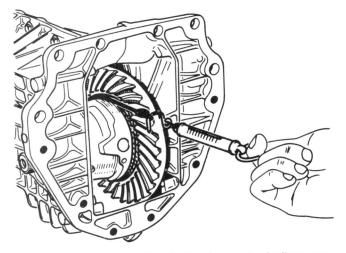

Fig. 6.35 Method of checking the bearing pre-load adjustment

the right-hand casing. When in position, check that they are fitted in correct alignment as shown in Fig. 6.37. Do not forget the lock peg in the secondary shaft. Any adjustment necessary to align the gears is made by fitting a primary shaft washer of an alternative thickness of which there are several variations.

29 If the selectors have been dismantled, reassemble as follows. First, slide the reverse gear shaft into the casing, engaging the reverse gear selector, with its end locating in the reverse gear shaft slot. Tighten the pivot bolt to the specified torque.

30 Insert the 1st/2nd gear interlock spring and ball, then slide the 1st/2nd selector shaft into position, locating the fork with the offset hub rearwards as shown in Fig. 6.38. Drive a new rollpin in to secure the fork to the shaft. The rollpin split section must face rearwards.

31 Insert the lock disc between the shafts.

32 Repeat the above procedure with the 3rd/4th selector shaft fork and interlock spring and ball, but note that the fork hub faces forwards (towards the differential).

33 Insert the reverse gear lock ball and spring into the left-hand casing, slide the shaft through and engage the idler gear and friction washer. Fit the gear with the offset hub facing forwards, and the friction washer bronze face likewise. Locate the key guide from inside the bore and push the shaft fully home. Fit the snap ring to secure.

34 Reassemble the rear cover. Drift the new oil seal into the housing and locate the rubber bellows onto the control shaft. Slide the shaft into the housing and engage the bushes, spring and control finger as shown in Fig. 6.40. Align the holes in the shaft and finger, then carefully drift new rollpins into position to secure.

35 Insert the differential unit into the right-hand casing.

36 Smear the respective casing half facing joints with sealant and locate the left-hand casing into position on the right-hand casing. Ensure when fitting that the reverse gear selector locates in the slot in reverse gear.

37 Locate the retaining bolts around the housings but do not fully tighten yet as the primary shaft endplay must be checked and possibly adjusted.

38 To do this, locate the adjuster washers (the same amount that were removed). Lightly tap the distance washer with a section of suitable tubing to seat the bearings, locate the rear cover gasket and then calculate the clearance between the gasket outer face and the distance washer face. This should read 0.02 to 0.12 mm (0.001 to 0.005 in). Should adjustment be necessary, add or subtract adjuster washer thicknesses as applicable.

39 Smear the rear cover and endface of the gear housings with sealant and locate the rear cover, engaging the selector finger into the slots of the selector shafts.

40 The half casing bolts can now be tightened in the sequence shown

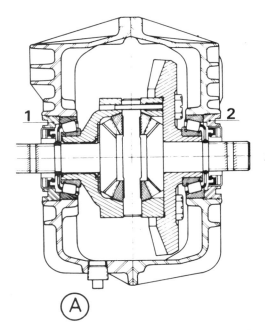

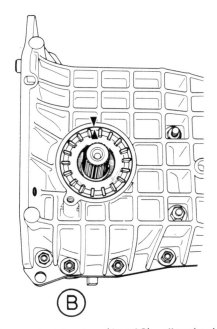

Fig. 6.36 Differential unit cross-section view (A) showing the ring nut locations against bearings (1 and 2) – align the ring nut with the relevant adjustment marking on the casing as shown in view B

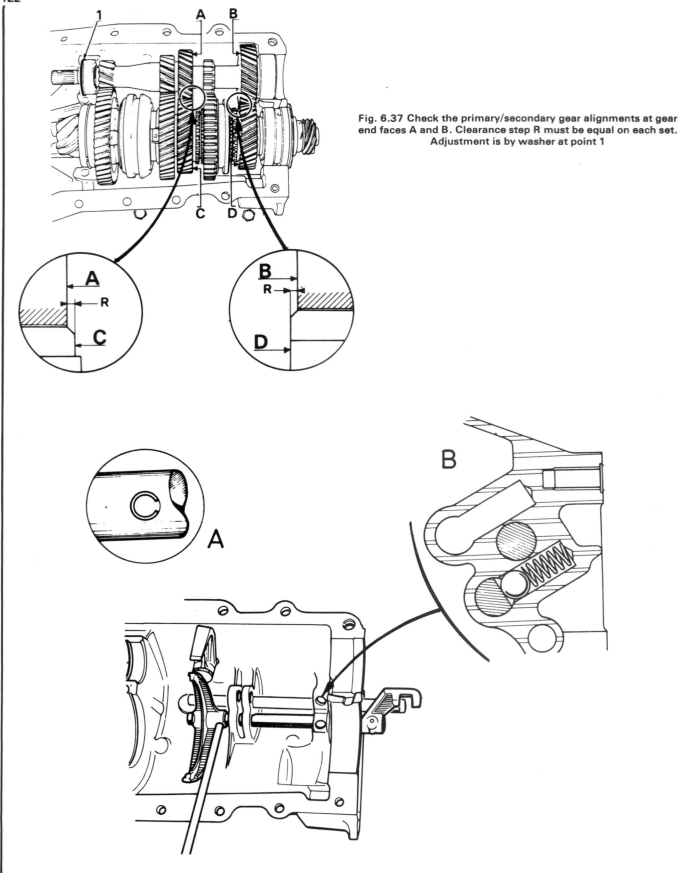

Fig. 6.37 Check the primary/secondary gear alignments at gear end faces A and B. Clearance step R must be equal on each set. Adjustment is by washer at point 1

Fig. 6.38 Location of fork onto shaft – note rollpin split to face rear (A) and interlock spring and ball location (B)

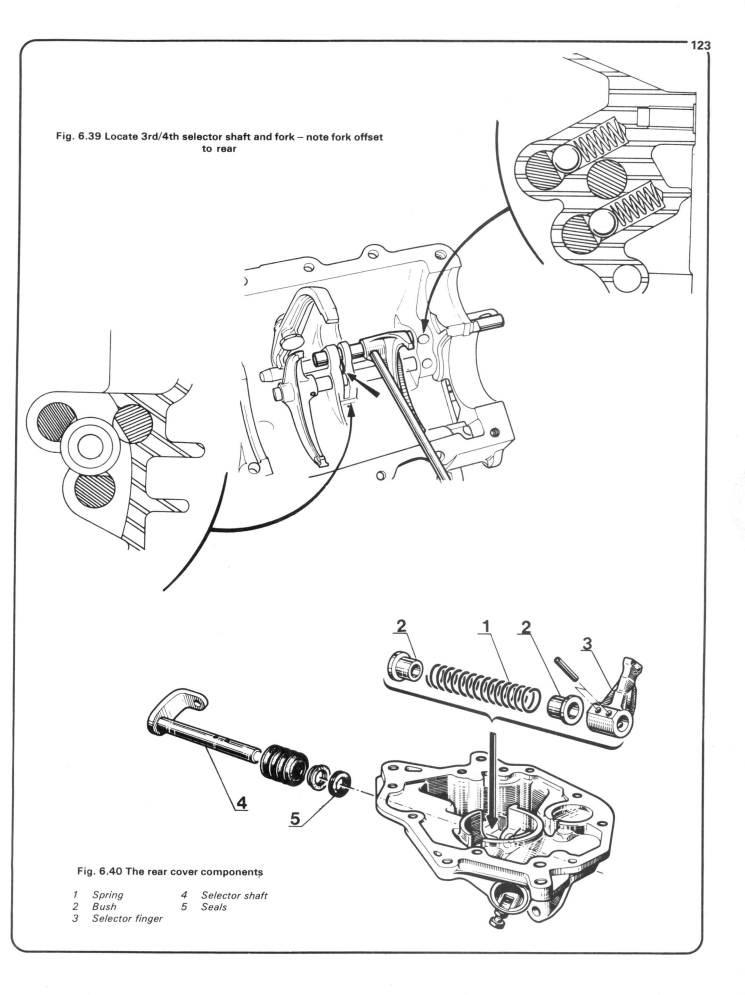

Fig. 6.39 Locate 3rd/4th selector shaft and fork – note fork offset to rear

Fig. 6.40 The rear cover components

1 Spring   4 Selector shaft
2 Bush   5 Seals
3 Selector finger

in Fig. 6.41 to the specified torque wrench settings.

41 Tighten the rear cover bolts to the specified torque.

42 With the gearbox assembled, recheck the crownwheel and pinion backlash as described earlier, then make any further minor adjustments that may be necessary. When complete, lock the differential ring nuts in position by fitting the lockplate and retaining bolts.

43 Drive the new oil seals into the clutch housing, using a tube drift of suitable diameter.

44 Smear the clutch housing gasket with sealant and locate on the front gearcase face. The clutch housing can now be fitted, but special care is needed when sliding it into position over the splines of the primary shaft, to avoid damaging the seal lips. Lubricate the lips of the seal and, if possible, wrap a shim round the splines to protect the seal while fitting the housing.

45 With the housing in position, insert the retaining bolts and tighten them. Remove the protector shim (if used).

46 Check that all gearcase bolts are secure and all external fittings in position. Operate the selector rod, using a pair of grips and ensure the gear selection action is smooth and positive.

47 Reassemble the clutch withdrawal mechanism (see Chapter 5). The gearbox is now ready to be refitted into the car.

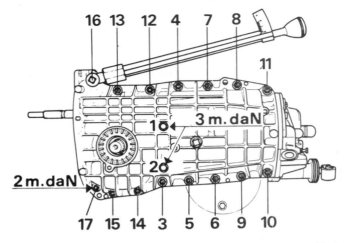

Fig. 6.41 Tighten the casing bolts in sequence shown to specified torque

---

9 Gearlever and control rod – removal, refitting and adjustment

1 Working inside the car, unscrew and remove the lever bellows retaining screws.

2 Unscrew the four floor frame plate bolts and the two bolts retaining the lever housing.

3 As removal now continues underneath the vehicle, it must be raised and supported securely on chassis stands.

4 Unscrew and remove the four undertray retaining screws. Detach the undertray.

5 Unscrew the lever housing bolts, then disconnect the control rod from its linkage at the gearbox end and withdraw it (photo).

6 Reassembly is a reversal of the removal procedure.

7 On earlier models, adjust the linkage control by selecting neutral and loosening the clamp arm nut to allow the control rod to move freely. On later models, select neutral and loosen the nut (2) shown in Fig. 6.42b to free the rod.

8 On the type 352 and 367 gearboxes, the dimension X must equal 2 mm. For the type 369 gearbox it must equal 13 mm. A feeler gauge of the appropriate thickness is inserted between faces F and Q as indicated, and the locknut tightened to set the clearance: See Fig. 6.43.

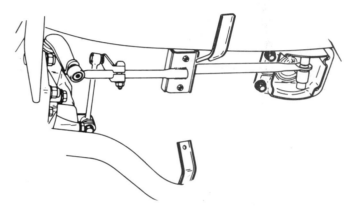

Fig. 6.42A Control linkage layout (earlier type)

---

10 Differential unit – removal and refitting

1 Access to the differential unit is only available after removal and separation of the gearbox casings, as described previously in this Chapter.

2 Once the gearbox has been removed and the right- and left-hand half casings separated the differential unit can be lifted clear for inspection.

3 The differential unit can now be cleaned and inspected for signs of excessive wear and/or damage. Where this is readily apparent, it is recommended that the unit be repaired or exchanged by your Renault dealer as it is not a task for the DIY mechanic. Further inspection notes on this are given in Section 4.

4 Items that can be removed and renewed include the taper roller bearings (using a suitable puller) and, on TS models, the speedometer drivegear which is secured by a large circlip. Extract the circlip and prise the nylon gear free for refitting.

5 If renewing the taper roller bearings, the respective cups (outer races) must also be removed from the gearcase half housings. This necessitates removal of the adjuster rings and seals from the outside in order to drive the cups out of their housings. Mark the positions of the adjuster ring in relation to the gearcase halves as an approximate guide to adjustment on reassembly as in Fig. 6.36.

6 New taper roller bearings must be pressed carefully into position, and once removed, always use new seals on reassembly. On later models also fit new O-rings to the adjuster ring as shown in Fig. 6.44.

7 If the speedometer drivegear is badly worn or damaged also check the driven gear; it too will probably be in need of renewal.

8 When refitting the differential unit, the crownwheel and pinion

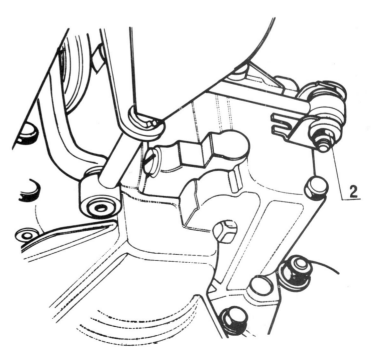

Fig. 6.42B Control linkage attachment (2) (later type)

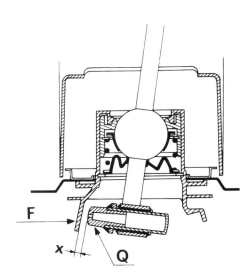

Fig. 6.43 The control lever position for adjustment

F   Housing face   X   2 mm (Type 352 and 367)
Q   End fitting   or 13 mm (Type 369)

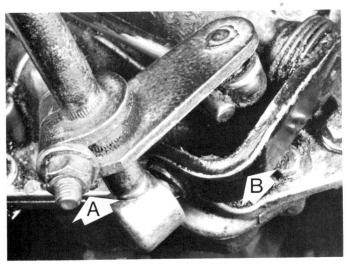

9.5 The adjuster clamp (A) and control rod (B)

mesh clearance must be checked and adjusted together with the bearing preload adjustment – see Sections 6 and 8.
9   Reassembly and refitting of the gearbox is described in Sections 5 or 8 (as applicable) and Section 2 respectively.

11 Differential-to-driveshaft oil seals – refitting

1   Partially drain the oil in the final drive housing to lower the level and thus prevent spillage through the seal housing.
2   The driveshaft on the side concerned must now be disconnected as described in Chapter 8. Note the position of the ring nut (make an alignment mark to the casing) and unscrew it.
3   The offending oil seal can now be hooked and prised out of its location within the ring adjuster nut (photo).
4   Clean the inside diameter of the ring adjuste nut before inserting the new seal. Lubricate the new seal with oil to assist refitting.
5   Use a tube drift of suitable diameter and drive the new seal into position, cavity side inwards so that when fully fitted, the outer face of the seal is flush to the ring nut seal housing edge. Refit the ring nut to its original position, and make secure with lockplate and bolt (photo).
6   Relocate and attach the driveshaft, then top up the final drive housing oil level.
7   TL models from 1978 onwards have an O-ring seal fitted to the adjuster ring outside diameter as shown in Fig. 6.44.
8   To renew the O-rings, proceed as in paragraphs 1 to 3 above, then mark the relative positions of the adjuster ring to half casing. Remove the adjuster locking plate and unscrew the ring, noting the exact number of turns required. Refitting is a reversal of the removal process. Lubricate the O-rings before fitting and screw in the adjuster the same number of turns to the position marked and refit the lockplate.

11.3 Differential housing seal with ring nut removed

12 Speedometer cable

1   The speedometer cable is a conventional inner/outer driven cable. It is fixed at the gearbox by a clamp (TL models) or retaining spring clip (TS models) (photo) and at the speedometer head by a knurled nut, on the outer cable. It is easily renewed. The whole cable must be renewed; 'inners' and 'outers' are not available separately. Make sure it

11.5 Ring nut and lock plate

12.1 The speedometer drive cable connection at the gearbox (manual – TS) showing the retaining clip

passes through its original passage. Speedometer failure is inevitably the result of a broken speedo cable. Fluttering and whining is quite common, and a sign of impending cable failure.

2   When refitting a cable, make sure that it is located in the same manner as the original with no sharp bends and ensure that the clip is securely located.

13 Fault diagnosis – manual gearbox

1   Faults can be sharply divided into two main groups: Some definite failure with the transmission not working: Noises implying some component worn, damaged, or out of place.

2   The failures can usually be tracked down by commonsense and remembering the circumstances in which they appeared. Thus if the car will not go at all, a mechanical failure will occur in different circumstances to a broken linkage from the gear lever!

3   If there is a definite fault within the transmission then it has to be removed and dismantled to repair it, so further diagnosis can wait till the parts can be examined.

4   If the problem is a strange noise, the decision must be taken whether in the first place it is abnormal, and if so whether it warrants action.

5   Noises can be traced to a certain extent by doing the test sequence as follows:

6   Find the speed and type of driving that makes the noise. If the noise occurs with engine running, car stationary, clutch disengaged, gear engaged, the noise is not in the transmission. If it goes after the clutch is engaged in neutral, halted, it is the clutch.

7   If the noise can be heard faintly in neutral, clutch engaged, it is in the gearbox. It will presumably get worse on the move, especially in some particular gear.

8   Final drive noises are only heard on the move. They will only vary with speed and load, whatever gear is engaged.

9   Noise when pulling is likely to be either the adjustment of preload of the differential bearings, or the crownwheel and pinion backlash.

10 Gear noise when free-wheeling is likely to be the relative positions

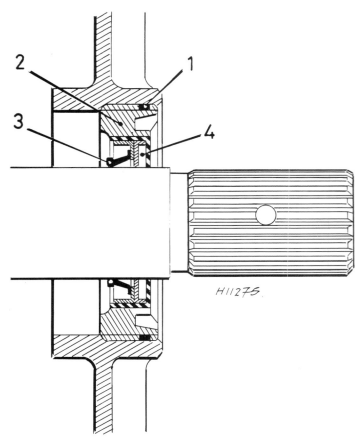

Fig. 6.44 The modified differential ring nut assembly fitted to TL models from 1978 on

| 1 | O-ring | 3 | Lip seal |
| 2 | Ring nut | 4 | Felt section |

of crownwheel and pinion.

11 Noise on corners implies excessive tightness or excessive play of the bevel side gears or idler pinions in the differential.

12 In general, whining is gear teeth at the incorrect distance apart. Roaring or rushing or moaning is bearings. Thumping or grating noise suggests a broken gear tooth.

13 If subdued whining comes on gradually, there is a good chance the transmission will last a long time to come, but check the transmission oil level!

14 Whining or moaning appearing suddenly, or becoming loud, should be examined quickly.

15 If thumping, or grating noises appear stop at once. If bits of metal are loose inside, the whole transmission, including the casing, could quickly be wrecked.

16 Synchromesh wear is obvious. You just 'beat' the gears and crashing occurs.

17 Difficulty in engaging gears can be caused by an incorrectly adjusted selector control mechanism, so check this before assuming the problem is within the gearbox.

Chapter 7 Automatic transmission

For modifications, and information applicable to later models, see Supplement at end of manual

Contents

Specifications

Gearbox type
TL . . . . 4141-10, or 4141-12 (1978 on)
TS . . . . 4141-20 or 4141-13 (1978 on)

Gears . . . . 3 forward, 1 reverse

Gear ratios
1st . . . . 2·4 : 1
2nd . . . . 1·48 : 1
3rd . . . . 1·00 : 1
Reverse . . . . 1·92
Final drive ratio . . . . 8 x 33

Lubricant capacities
Gearbox . . . . 10·5 pt (6 l) – approx total capacity
Final drive . . . . 3 pt (1·6 l)

Torque wrench settings

	lbf ft	Nm
Converter casing bolts	30 to 33	40 to 45
Final drive case to gearcase bolts	13·5 to 16·5	18 to 22
Sump bolts (gearcase)	2·25 to 3·0	3 to 4
Converter driveplate to crankshaft bolts:		
TL models	30 to 37	40 to 50
TS models	49 to 52·5	65 to 70
Converter to driveplate bolts	22 to 26	30 to 35

1 General description

1 The automatic transmission systems fitted to both the TL and TS versions are basically the same in design and actuation. On both types, fully automatic gearchanging is provided without the use of a clutch, but over-ride selection is still available to the driver.

2 The automatic transmission comprises of three main assemblies; the converter, the final drive and the gearbox. A cutaway view of the transmission unit with the three main assemblies sub-divided is shown in Fig. 7.1.

3 The converter takes the place of the conventional clutch and transmits the drive automatically from the engine to the gearbox, providing increased torque when starting off.

4 The converter receives its lubricant from the pump mounted on the rear of the gearcase, and is driven direct by the engine. This pump also distributes fluid to the respective gears, clutch and brake assemblies within the gearbox.

5 The gearbox comprises an epicyclic gear train giving three forward and one reverse gear, selection of which is dependent on the hydraulic pressure supplied to the respective clutches and brakes. The hydraulic pressure is regulated via the engine speed by the hydraulic distributor, and gear selection is determined by two solenoid valves. These are actuated by the electrically operated governor/computer. The exact hydraulic pressure is regulated by a vacuum capsule and pilot valve operating according to engine loading.

6 The clutches (E1 and E2) and brakes (F1 and F2) are multi-disc oil bath type and, according to the hydraulic loading, engage or release the epicyclic gear train components.

7 The governor is in effect a low output alternator which provides variable current to the computer. It is driven by a worm gear on the final drive pinion and its output depends on the vehicle speed and engine loading.

8 The computer acts upon the variation of current from the governor combined with the selected lever position to open or close the

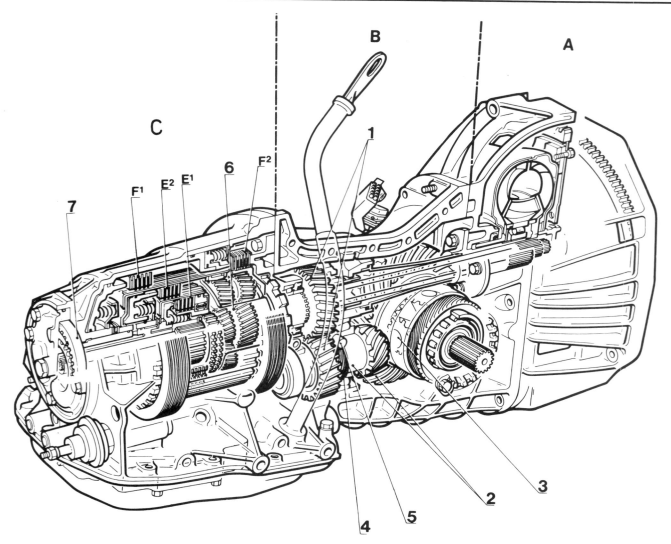

Fig. 7.1 Cutaway view of the Renault 4141 automatic transmission showing the main sections, 'A' converter housing, 'B' final drive and 'C' gearbox

1	Step down gears	7	Oil pump
2	Crownwheel and pinion	E1	Multi-disc clutches
3	Differential	E2	Multi-disc clutches
4	Worm gear	F1	Brake discs
5	Governor	F2	Brake discs
6	Epicyclic gear train		

solenoid valves accordingly. In addition it acts as a safety device to prevent the 1st gear 'hold' position being selected at a speed in excess of 22 mph (35 kph) at light throttle.

9 The system also incorporates a kickdown switch, operated by pressing the throttle pedal to its fully open position, at which point under certain engine loading and speeds, the computer will be activated and a lower gear automatically selected.

10 The drive selected in the gearbox is transferred to the differential unit via stepdown gears, which counteract the difference in levels between the main gear assemblies in the gearbox and the level of the crownwheel and pinion in the differential housing.

11 The selector lever is centrally situated within the car and has six positional alternatives, being as follows:

P (Park): With the lever in this position, the transmission is neutralised and the drive wheels are locked
R (Reverse): Reverse gear position, which when selected also actuates the reversing light switch
N (Neutral): The transmission is in neutral
1 (1st gear): 1st gear hold position
2 (2nd gear): 2nd gear hold position
A (Automatic): Gears engage automatically according to engine loading and car speed

12 In addition to the above, the kickdown switch causes a lower speed to be selected at a higher speed than normal when the throttle pedal is suddenly pressed fully down. This device is designed to give sudden acceleration when required such as for overtaking.

13 Because of the obvious hazards of starting the car when in gear, a starter inhibitor switch is fitted and only allows the starter to be operated when the selector is in Park or Neutral position. The inhibitor switch is fitted below the transmission governor/computer unit. Its removal necessitates withdrawal of the oil sump plate – not a DIY mechanic job. Another safety feature built into this transmission on models from 1977, is the design of the selector lever handle which must be compressed by hand before Park, Reverse or 1st gear can be selected. This locking device prevents accidental selection of those gears when the engine is running. It should be noted that in certain countries, the automatic position is marked as 'D' (drive).

14 The automatic transmission is a relatively complex unit and therefore should problems occur, it is recommended that the fault be discussed with your Renault dealer, who should be able to advise you on the best course of action to be taken. Items that can be attempted by the home mechanic are given in the following Sections in this Chapter. To obtain trouble-free operation and maximum life expectancy from your automatic transmission, it must be serviced as described and its operation not be subjected to abuse.

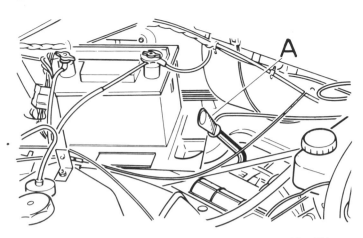

Fig. 7.2 The automatic transmission dipstick position 'A'

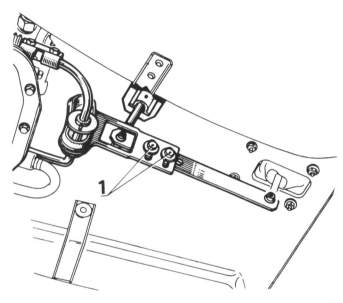

Fig. 7.3 The selector control shaft showing the adjuster bolts (1)

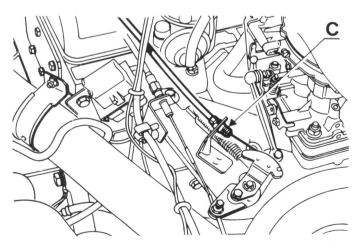

Fig. 7.4 The governor control cable to quadrant – the outer cable
location and nuts are indicated at C

2 Automatic transmission vehicles – towing

1   Should your car need to be towed (due to a breakdown in the automatic transmission or otherwise) it is important that the front wheels be raised clear of the ground. This is necessary because the oil pump within the transmission unit is actuated by drive from the engine and it would therefore be non-operational in the event of a breakdown.
2   If circumstances do not allow the car to be towed in this fashion, or only a limited mileage is to be covered, the car can be towed in the normal manner but only providing that the following precautions are taken:

(a)   *The mileage to be covered does not exceed a distance of 30 miles (50 km)*

(b)   *An additional quantity of 2 Imp qts (2 litres) of the recommended transmission oil (see Specifications) is added to the transmission*

(c)   *The maximum permissible towing speed under these conditions is 18mph (30 km/h)*

3   On arrival at the towing destination, do not forget to drain off the surplus lubricant.

3 Maintenance – transmission and differential

Transmission

1   The automatic transmission fluid level must be checked regularly between 1200 and 3000 miles (2000 to 5000 km) intervals.
2   When checking oil level, position the vehicle on flat ground and place the hand control in 'P'. Start the engine and run it for two minutes to allow the converter to fill up.
3   Allow the engine to tick over and, with the lever still in 'P', check the oil level on the dipstick, as shown in Fig. 7.2.
4   Dependent on whether the car has just finished a run and the engine/gearbox is thoroughly hot or whether it has been started from cold, check as follows.

COLD – *Minimum 1 or Maximum 2*
HOT – *Minimum 2 or Maximum 3*

Do not allow the oil level to drop below the minimum mark and never overfill as this may cause overheating.
5   The transmission fluid must be drained and renewed at regular intervals of 18 000 miles (30 000 km). If the vehicle is used for towing, the change should be at more frequent intervals.
6   The transmission fluid must be drained whilst hot but with the engine stopped. When draining, do not confuse the transmission and differential drain plugs, both of which are shown in an illustration in the maintenance section at the start of the manual. Remove the plug and drain the fluid into a suitable container for disposal. Drain the fluid up to as maximum period of five minutes, then refit the drain plug, making certain that it is secure.
7   Insert a suitable funnel into the dipstick tube and top-up the fluid level. Although the capacity is about $9\frac{1}{2}$ pints (5.5 litres), the normal topping-up requirement after draining is only about $5\frac{1}{2}$ to $6\frac{1}{2}$ pints (3 to 4 litres). Top-up using only the lubricant type specified for the transmission (not the differential) and take care not to overfill.

Differential (final drive unit)

8   The differential unit has a combined level check and filler plug on the side of the casing.
9   The plug should be removed and the level checked /topped-up – if necessary every 3000 miles (5000 km). The oil level should be maintained to the bottom of the filler plug hole.
10   Every 9000 miles (15 000 km), remove the differential drain plug and empty the old lubricant into a suitable container. Refit the drain plug, remove the level plug and refill with new oil of the specified grade to the level required. Then refit the level plug. The differential case should take 3 pints (1.6 litres) when being refilled.

4 Selector control – removal, refitting and adjustment

1   Unscrew the control lever handle retaining screw and remove the handle.
2   Detach and remove the control cover.

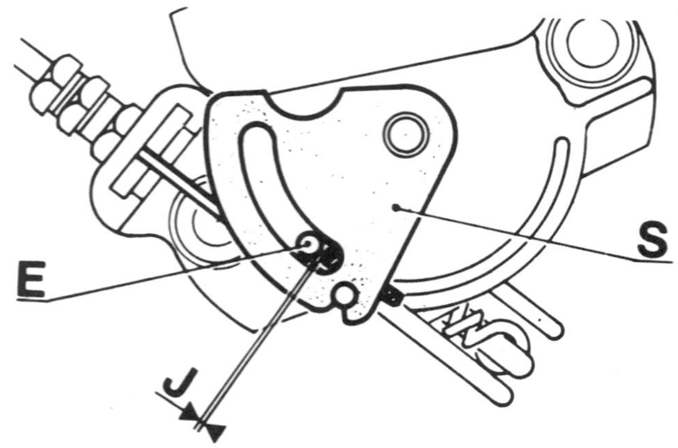

Fig. 7.5 Clearance point 'J' between stop peg 'E' and quadrant 'S'

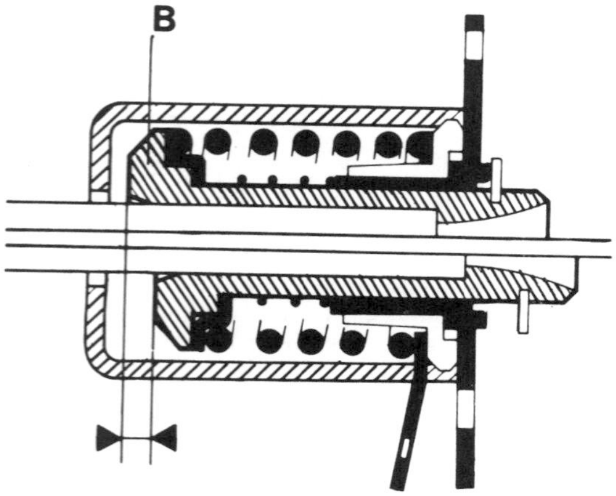

Fig. 7.6 Check the throttle cable free play adjustment at
stop sleeve (B) with accelerator pedal fully down – clearance
to equal 3 to 4 mm (0.125 to 0.156 in)

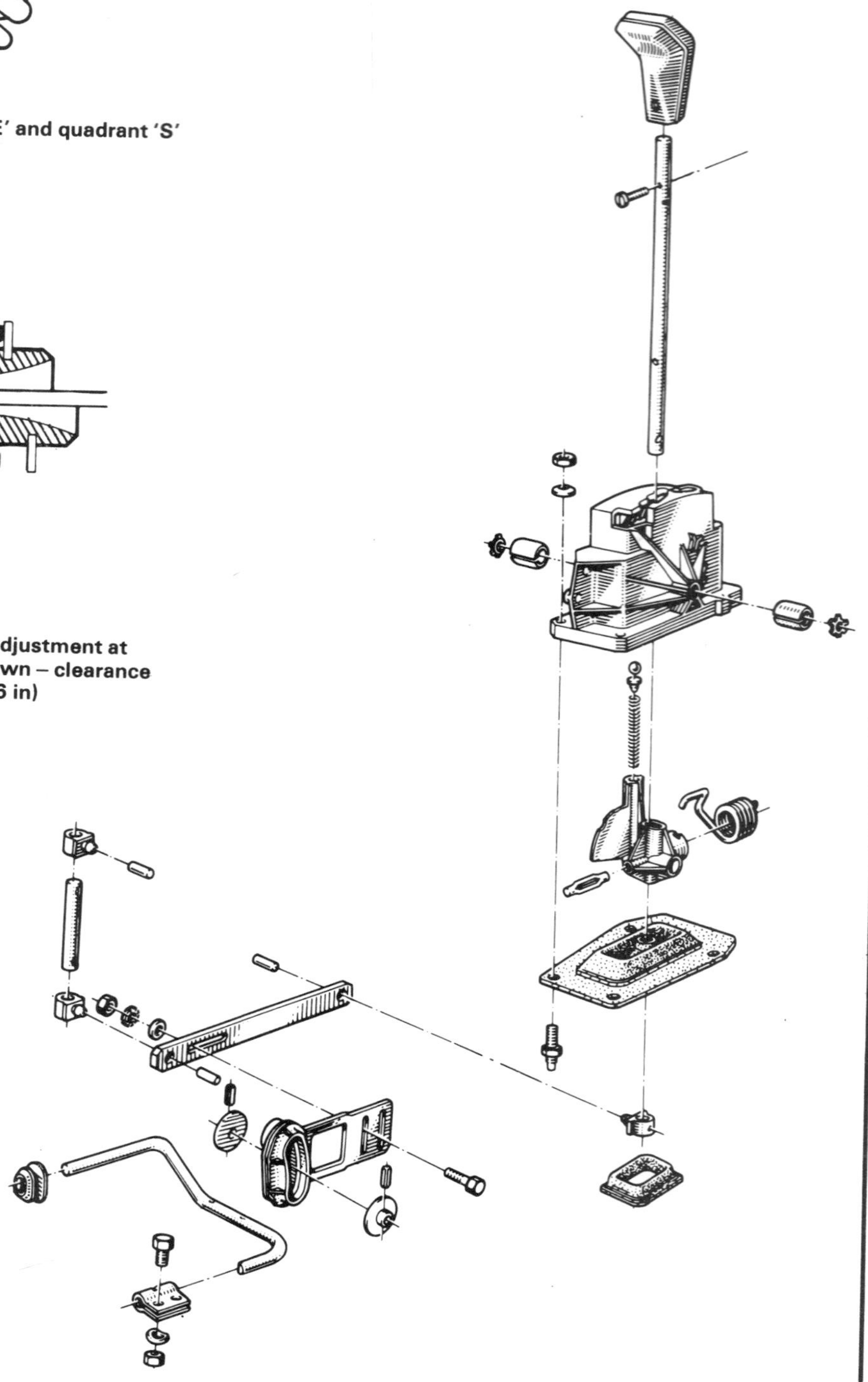

Fig. 7.7 The selector lever and control assembly components

3   Working underneath the car, disconnect the selector control rod to connector arm.

4   Detach the centre bridge section and housing, unscrew the retaining nuts and withdraw the lever.

5   To remove the linkage assembly, detach the cover and unscrew the rod clamp nuts. Detach the rod connections to the lever and frame.

6   Reassembly is a reversal of the removal procedure, but ensure that the control shaft and linkage abut to each other and adjust the selector mechanism as follows.

7   Position the selector lever in the 2nd gear 'hold' location. Push the control shaft fully inwards (to the 2nd gear 'hold' position), then extract it by one notch. Slacken off the adjuster bolts as shown in Fig. 7.3, and have an assistant check that the selector lever is still engaged in the 2nd gear 'hold' position. Retighten the two retaining bolts, then roadtest the car to ensure correct selection adjustment has been achieved.

5   Governor control cable – renewal and adjustment

1   To remove the governor control cable, unhook it from the quadrant location at the governor and unscrew the outer cable retaining nuts.

2   From the engine end of the cable, unhook the inner cable from the throttle connecting quadrant cam near the carburettor as shown in Fig. 7.4. Detach the outer cable from the bracket.

3   Refitting is a direct reversal of the removal procedure but the cable must be adjusted.

4   Turn the outer cable adjuster at the governor end to allow the maximum cable extension and locate the control cable into the quadrant. At the other end, locate the cable to the carburettor connecting quadrant.

5   To adjust the cable get an assistant to press the throttle pedal down fully whilst you retension the cable at the carburettor end. Rotate the outer cable sleeve at its location bracket so that the quadrant is fully opened.

6   At the governor end of the cable, loosen the outer cable location nuts, then adjust the cable to give a clearance of 0.3 to 0.5 mm (0.012 to 0.020 in) between the quadrant and the stop peg as indicated in Fig. 7.5. Tighten the locknut to secure to cable.

7   Check the adjustment of the throttle cable – see next Section.

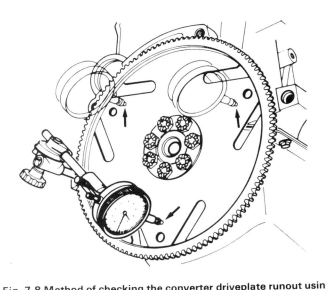

Fig. 7.8 Method of checking the converter driveplate runout using a clock gauge. Note respective check positions (arrowed)

6   Kickdown switch/throttle cable – checking, renewal and adjustment

1   To check the kickdown switch for operation, connect a test light and lead between the switch and battery. When the throttle pedal is pressed hard down the test light should glow; if it does not the switch is faulty.

2   Renewal of the switch necessitates renewal of the throttle cable also, as the two are combined.

3   Disconnect the cable at the carburettor end and also at the throttle pedal end (see Chapter 3) and remove with the switch.

4   Refit in the reverse order but ensure the throttle cable has sufficient free play to allow 3 to 4 mm ($\frac{1}{8}$ to $\frac{5}{32}$ in) movement of the stop sleeve (as shown in Fig. 7.6) as the throttle is fully pressed.

5   Check the adjustment of the governor cable as described in the previous Section.

7   Automatic transmission – removal and refitting

1   Experience has shown that the best method of removing the automatic transmission unit is forward and up through the engine compartment, but not attached to the engine. Renault specify that the lower body crossmember must not be removed, and it is this that limits the manoeuvrability of the transmission unit when removing.

2   Although Renault suggest that the transmission can be withdrawn rearwards and from underneath, this should not be attempted unless a vehicle lifting hoist or work pit are available to provide sufficient working area beneath the vehicle for the awkward manoeuvering procedures involved. In addition, the engine would have to be tilted at an extreme angle upwards at the front end to allow disengagement of the two units.

3   Removal of the engine and transmission combined is described in Chapter 6, Section 2. If removing by this method, take into consideration the considerable weight to be raised and ensure that your lifting tackle is up to the job. Do not leave it until the assemblies are half out before finding out! To remove the units separately proceed as follows.

4   Referring to Chapter 1, remove the engine.

5   With the engine removed, place a bridge piece or clamp across the transmission torque converter housing to prevent the torque converter becoming dislodged during removal of the transmission.

6   Referring to Chapter 1, Section 7, follow the instructions given in paragraphs 2 to 8 inclusive to disconnect the respective associate transmission attachments. Where an oil cooler unit has been fitted, disconnect and plug the pipe connections to the transmission.

7   The transmission should now be ready for removal. You will require an assistant to help guide it forward whilst supporting it and then to help lift it from the engine compartment.

8   Refitting is a reversal of the removal procedure. When the engine and transmission are refitted, reconnect and adjust the governor cable, the throttle cable and selector control linkage. Do not forget to top up the transmission fluid level and also the final drive oil.

8   Differential unit driveshaft oil seal – renewal

Refer to Chapter 6, Section 11.

9   Converter driveplate – removal and refitting

1   This is bolted to the rear end of the engine crankshaft and therefore the engine must be removed from the car first. This is described in Chapter 1.

2   Normally, there are only two reasons for removing the converter driveplate; to inspect and renew due to worn starter ring teeth and to inspect and check the run-out of the plate.

3   To check the run-out, clamp a clock gauge to a fixed location on the cylinder block. Turn the driveplate, take readings at each converter bolt hole in turn and note any variation. The maximum run-out permissible is 0.3 mm (0.012 in) as shown in Fig. 7.8 (if exceeded renew the driveplate).

4   To remove the converter driveplate, support or jam it to prevent rotation and unscrew the seven retaining bolts. Withdraw the plate from the crankshaft.

5   Refit in the reverse sequence and tighten the bolts to the specified torque.

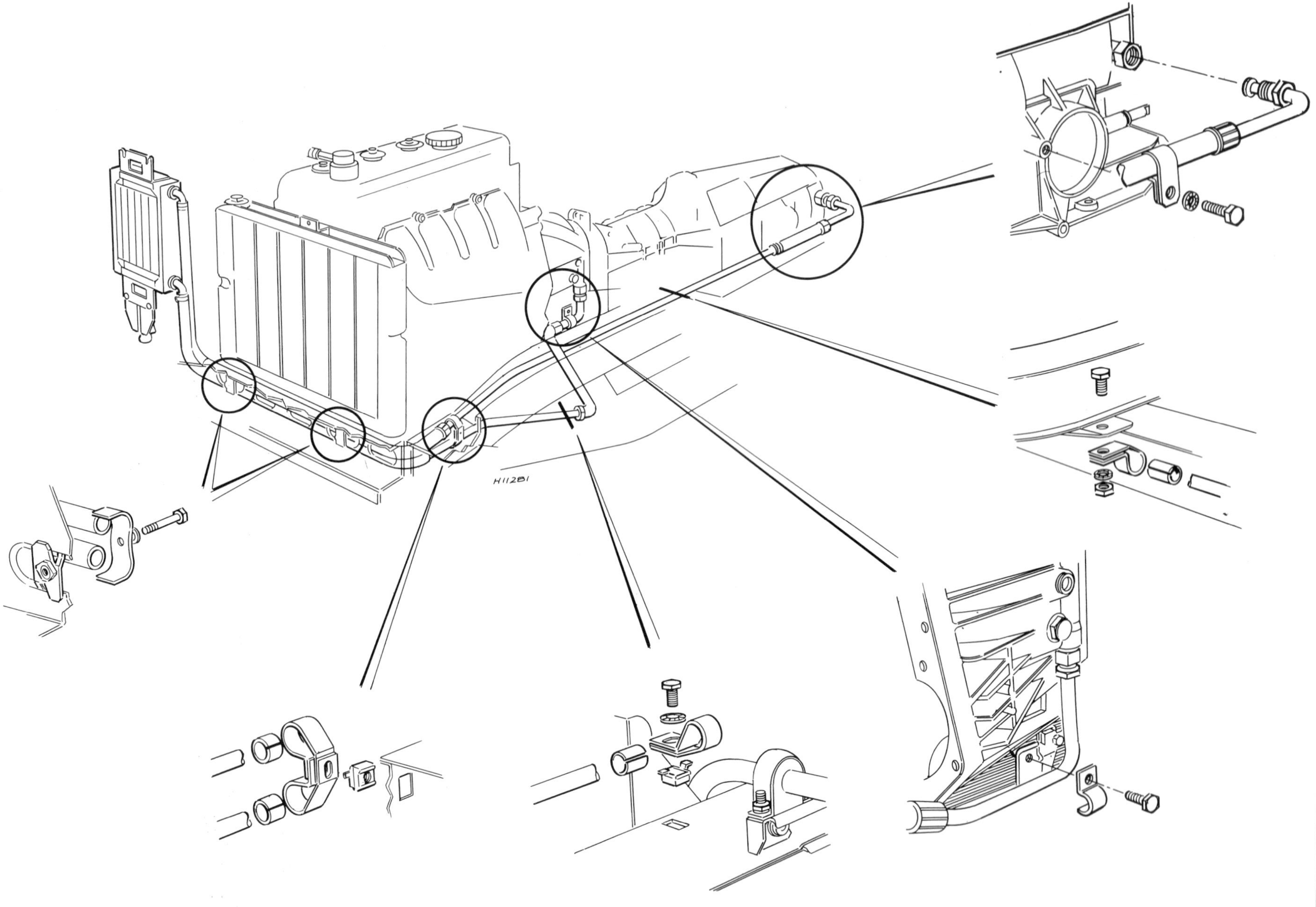

Fig. 7.9 The oil cooler, interconnecting pipes and associate fittings

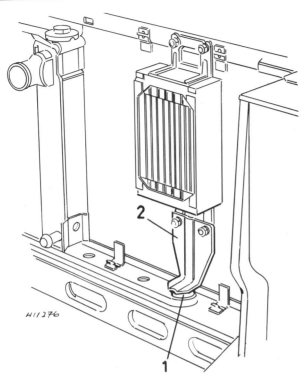

Fig. 7.10 The oil cooler matrix – note the lower bracket (2) and its bottom location (1)

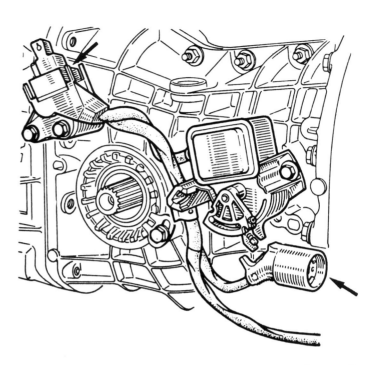

Fig. 7.11 The transmission wiring harness connections (arrowed) to be checked if a fault occurs in the starter circuit

10 Oil cooler – general information

1   Some automatic transmission models are equipped with an oil cooler unit. This is a particularly useful and, in certain instances, essential fitting where the vehicle is used for towing.

2   The maximum towing weight for a vehicle fitted with an oil cooler should not be exceeded however, and Renault specify the following towing maximums:

Towing a trailer without brakes with a gross weight up to 1279 lb (580 kg)

Towing a trailer with brakes with a gross weight up to 2249 lb (1020 kg)

Where an oil cooler is not fitted the maximum towing weight permissible is 992 lb (450 kg)

3   An oil cooler kit is available from your Renault dealer under Part number 77 01 459 922. Specify whether you have a 14 in or 18 in radiator. This kit can be fitted to right- or left-hand drive vehicles, but not those fitted with air conditioning.

4   Once fitted, the oil cooler presents very few problems but a check should be kept in the oil inlet and outlet pipes and their connections between the cooler matrix and the transmission unit for any signs of leakage.

5   If at any time pipe sections are removed, renewed or simply disconnected, ensure when reconnecting that the respective pipe location clamps and clips are relocated and securely retained. Check that the pipes are not chafing on surrounding fittings.

6   The pipe layout and their fixings are shown in Fig. 7.9.

7   Inspection, removal and refitting of the forward section pipes necessitates the removal of the engine undertray.

8   When pipes are disconnected, watch out for a certain amount of oil spillage – especially if the oil is hot!

9   The cooler matrix is retained alongside the radiator and is secured by four bolts, two to the upper body front cross-section and the lower two to the cooler bracket support.

10   Remember when topping-up the fluid level in an automatic transmission, or models with an oil cooler, to allow for an extra $\frac{3}{4}$ pint (0.4 litre) of fluid which is consumed by the cooler and pipes.

11 Fault diagnosis – automatic transmission

1   Automatic transmission faults are almost always the result of low fluid level or incorrect adjustment of the selector linkage or governor control cable.

2   If these items are checked and found to be in order, the fault is probably internal and should be diagnosed by your Renault dealer who is specially equipped to pinpoint the problem and effect any necessary repairs.

3   Do not allow any defect in the operation of the automatic transmission to go unchecked – it could prove expensive!

4   If the starter fails to function at any time, it is possible that the starter inhibitor switch is at fault but first check that, (a) the selector control lever adjustment is correct, and (b) the transmission wiring harness plugs and socket connections are secure. Check the starter circuit wiring for continuity to the switch plug. The inhibitor switch is situated beneath the transmission governor/computer unit and within the hydraulic section of the unit. The sump plate would therefore have to be removed to gain access to the switch and this is therefore best entrusted to your Renault dealer.

Chapter 8 Driveshafts, wheels and tyres

For modifications, and information applicable to later models, see Supplement at end of manual

Contents

Specifications

Driveshafts

TL models:
Outer joint	GE 86 coupling
Inner joint	4-ball coupling

TS models:
Outer joint	6-ball coupling
Inner joint	GI 82 coupling
Outer joint housing diameter	90 mm (3·543 in)

Note: *The driveshaft on manual transmission models is longer than that for automatic transmission models (see Fig. 8.1)*

Wheels

Type:
TL models	5·50B x13
TS models	5·50J x 14
Maximum permissible rim run-out	1·2 mm (0·046 in)
Maximum permissible rim ovality	1·2 mm (0·046 in)

Tyres

Sizes:
TL models	165 x 13
TS models	165 x 14 or 175 x 14

Inflation pressures:
	front	rear
165 x 13	27·5 lbf/in² (1·9 bar)	27·5 lbf/in² (1·9 bar)
165 x 14	27·5 lbf/in² (1·9 bar)	29 lbf/in² (2 bar)
175 x 14	26 lbf/in² (1·8 bar)	29 lbf/in² (2 bar)

Note: *On automatic transmission models, add 1.5 lbf/in² (0.1 bar) to the front tyre pressures. For fully laden and/or motorway usage, add 3 lbf/in² (0·2 bar) to front and rear tyres (all models)*

Torque wrench settings

	lbf ft	Nm
Wheel hub nut (front):		
TL models	115	160
TS models	150	210
Wheel nuts	45 to 57	60 to 80
Suspension on balljoint nuts	36	50
Steering on balljoint nuts	25	35

1 General information

1 The driveshafts transmit the motion from the transmission unit to the front roadwheels. The driveshaft to each front wheel is fitted with a constant velocity joint at each end to allow for the variations of movement between the transmission and the roadwheels and hubs/suspension units.

2 The shaft is located by splines to both the transmission and front wheel hub. At the transmission end, the driveshaft is retained in position by a rollpin, whilst on the outer end the wheel hub bearing nut and special washer secure it in position.

3 Each joint assembly is covered by a rubber bellows to protect it from the ingress of dirt, which would cause rapid wear of the joint unit.

4 Whenever the driveshafts are renewed, take the old one along for exchange and compare the old and new units to ensure correct replacement. The automatic transmission models are fitted with a shorter driveshaft unit compared with its manual transmission counterpart, as shown in Fig. 8.1.

5 The driveshafts do not require servicing, being pre-lubricated during assembly. No repairs to the joint units are possible by the home mechanic; removal and refitting only.

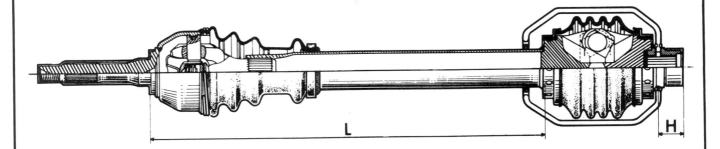

Fig. 8.1 Cutaway sectional view of the driveshaft unit – dimensions L and H differentiate the two types of shaft used

Automatic transmission models:
distance 'L' equals 444 mm (17.480 inches)
distance 'H' equals 23.5 mm (0.925 inches)

Manual transmission models:
distance 'L' equals 463 mm (18.228 inches)
distance 'H' equals 23.5 mm (0.925 inches)

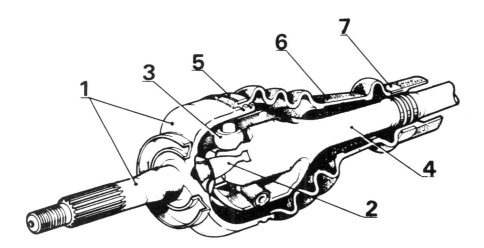

Fig. 8.2 The outer joint coupling components

1   Stub axle
2   Starplate retainer
3   Spider
4   Yoke
5   Retaining collar
6   Rubber bellows
7   Bellows retaining ring

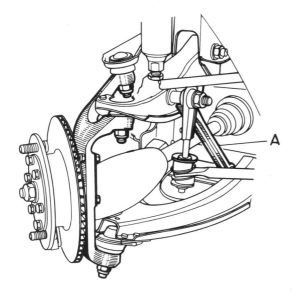

Fig. 8.3 Locate the spacer leg as shown (A)

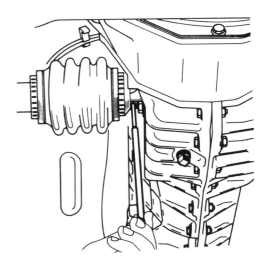

Fig. 8.4 Drift out the rollpin

2 Driveshaft – removal

1   To support the suspension during removal and refitting of the driveshaft, you will need to fabricate a spacer leg to locate between the lower suspension arm pivot pin and the upper arm-to-anti-roll bar connecting link as shown in Fig. 8.3. The details of this spacer leg are given in Chapter 11, Section 7. Renault dealers use special tool number T AV 509 (R1271) or T AV 603 (R1272) which may be available on request.

2   Having borrowed or fabricated the spacer leg, compress the suspension at the front and locate the leg securely into the position described above.

3   Raise the front of the vehicle and make secure on axle stands, then remove the roadwheel.

4   The driveshaft inner coupling (to transmission) roll pin must now be extracted. Rotate the shaft to a suitable position, and laying underneath, drive the rollpin out using a suitable punch drift as shown in Fig. 8.4.

5   Locate a lever between two wheel nut studs on the hub to prevent it turning and unscrew the stub axle nut and remove it with the washer.

6   Referring to Chapter 9, remove the brake calliper unit but do not disconnect the hydraulic hose. Support the calliper by suspending with a suitable length of wire, or place on blocks so that the weight of the calliper is not taken by the hose.

7   Unscrew the upper suspension arm and steering arm balljoint retaining nuts and, using a balljoint separator or wedges, detach the joints.

8   The driveshaft can now be withdrawn from the transmission shaft, tilting the hub unit back to suit (photo).

9   Temporarily relocate the steering arm balljoint.

10   Next, use a soft drift of suitable diameter and drive the driveshaft inwards through the hub. Once the shaft is clear of the hub, the steering arm balljoint can again be detached and the hub manoeuvred to allow the driveshaft to be removed completely.

3 Driveshaft joints – general inspection

1   As mentioned in the Section 1, very little in the way of maintenance or repair can be done by the average home mechanic.

2   Although easily dismantled, for inspection, there is no repair possible if the joint assembly is worn or defective and it must therefore be renewed as a unit. All components are match fitted during production thus preventing ready renewal of an individual component.

3   Even renewal of the rubber bellows, if damaged or defective, is beyond the scope of the home mechanic, and therefore, if on removal the joint is obviously worn or defective, take it for renewal or any possible repairs to your Renault dealer, who will have the necessary tools and equipment required to undertake any servicing operations that may be possible.

4 Driveshaft refitting

1   Clean the respective driveshaft splines thoroughly, then smear them with Molykote BR2 grease or equivalent.

2   Align the roll pin location holes between the driveshaft and transmission intake splines and slide the shaft into position. When the respective holes for the rollpin are level, check that they are in exact alignment, as the shaft only fits in one position. If the holes are not in exact alignment the shaft is 180° out and must be extracted and repositioned.

3   Always use new rollpins (photo) and drive them carefully into position using a suitable drift. Seal each end of the rollpin with a suitable sealant.

4   Relocate the driveshaft outer end into the stub axle carrier unit. As the shaft is fitted, take care not to damage the inner hub bearing oil seal. The driveshaft to stub axle assembly will be eased by using the fabricated tool shown in Fig. 8.6. If you are not able to fabricate this tool, use Renault tool number T AV 236 (R1271) or T AV 602 (R1272).

5   With the shaft in position in the hub, relocate the suspension and steering arm balljoints. Tighten the balljoint retaining nuts to the specified torque settings.

6   The stub axle nut and washer can now be refitted. Tighten the nut to the specified torque and check the hub is free to rotate without binding.

7   Refit the brake calliper unit and press the brake pedal a few times to centralize the disc pads.

8   Refit the roadwheel, lower the car and compress the suspension to remove the spacer leg.

9   Recheck the balljoint nuts for torque tightness and also check the transmission oil level and top-up if necessary.

5 Wheels – general information

Because of the design of the suspension of the car the strength and the trueness of the roadwheels is critical, particularly at the front. A great deal of excessively fast wear on the wheel bearings and universal joints can be attributed to buckled and deformed wheels. Check every 3000 miles, or when there is a sudden difference of feeling at the steering wheel, that the wheels are not buckled or dented. Check also that the front wheels are balanced. If any deformity is noticed the wheel concerned should be renewed. Do not attempt to 'repair'.

6 Tyres – general information

1   In the same way that the condition and suitability of the wheels

2.8 Withdraw the driveshaft from the transmission

4.3 Refit the driveshaft and use new rollpins (internal and external as arrowed)

fitted is critical so it is with the tyres. It is always wise to fit radial ply tyres on all wheels of these cars. Tyre wear is not great under any circumstances but the front tyres will wear faster than the rear. Do not fit oversize tyres. The wheel rims are not able to take a larger section tyre. See the Specifications for suitability of tyres. Tyre pressures are critical too.

2   Where tyres are wearing unevenly, it is indicative of either incorrect pressures or a misalignment of the front or rear suspension/steering (as applicable). It is essential, for obvious reasons, that this should not be allowed to continue unchecked.

3   Apart from the increased cost caused by rapid tyre wear, the general handling and safety of the car may well be affected when the suspension geometry and tyre inflation pressures are incorrect.

4   Many tyres now produced have minimum allowable tread wear indicators moulded into the tread base, as shown in Fig. 8.7. When the tyres have worn down to the indicated level they are due for renewal. Wherever possible, renew the tyre/s with the same make and type as fitted elsewhere on the car.

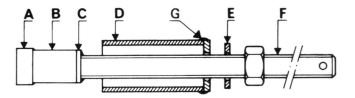

Fig. 8.6 Driveshaft-to-stub axle refitting tool

A   18 mm* driveshaft nut (150 pitch ground on o/d)
B   Sleeve (21 mm o/d x 15 mm i/d x 30 mm long)
C   Washer (20 mm o/d x 7 mm i/d x 2.5 mm thick)
D   Tube (34 mm dia x 60 mm long)
E   Washer (30 mm o/d x 16 mm i/d x 3 mm thick)
F   Threaded rod (M16 x 210 mm long)
G   Washer (34 mm o/d x 16 mm i/d x 4 mm thick)
* 20 mm driveshaft nut on some models

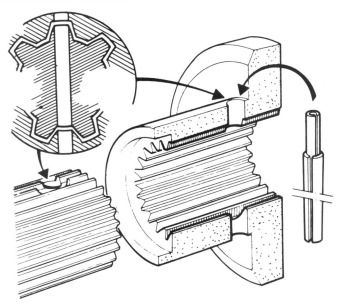

Fig. 8.5 Rollpin location

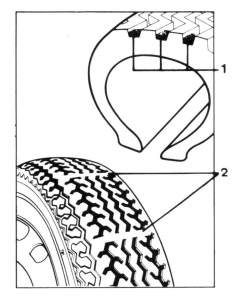

Fig. 8.7 Tyre tread minimum depth indicator strip (2), showing position in tread grooves (1)

Chapter 9 Braking system

For modifications, and information applicable to later models, see Supplement at end of manual

Contents

Specifications

System . . . .

Front disc brakes, rear drum brakes. Cable operated handbrake to rear wheels. Servo assistance. Pressure limiter on rear brakes

Hydraulic fluid specification . . . .

SAE 70RS and SAE J1703

Disc brakes

	TL	TS
Disc diameter	228 mm (8.976 in)	252 mm (9.921 in)
Disc thickness standard	20 mm (0.787 in)	24 mm (0.945 in)
Disc minimum thickness allowable	19 mm (0.748 in)	22 mm (0.866 in)
Maximum disc run-out	0.1 mm (0.004 in)	0.1 mm (0.004 in)
Pad thickness (with backing)	14 mm (0.551 in)	18.5 mm (0.728 in)
Pad thickness (minimum allowable)	7 mm (0.276 in)	9 mm (0.354 in)
Pad grade	F556	F559

Rear drum brakes

Drum diameter	228·5 mm (9 in)
Drum resurfacing diameter – maximum after resurfacing	229·5 mm (9·036 in)
Lining thickness (with shoe)	7 mm (0·276 in)
Lining – minimum thickness (riveted type)	0·5 mm (0·020 in) above rivet head
Lining width	40 mm (1·575 in)

Wheel cylinder bore diameter

Front (calliper)	54 mm (2·126 in)
Rear	22 mm (0·866 in)

Master cylinder

Bore	20·6 mm (0·811 in)
Stroke	34 mm (1·339 in)
Servo cylinder bore (TL models)	200 mm (7·874 in)
Servo unit – diameter (TS models)	225 mm (8·875 in)

Servo settings (pushrods)

'X' (servo to master cylinder)	9 mm (0·354 in)
'L' (pedal to servo)	125 mm (4·921 in)

Torque settings

	lbf ft	Nm
Bleed screw	4 to 5	5 to 7
Hydraulic hose-to-calliper union	15	20
Master cylinder unions:		
Primary circuit (2 outlets)	15	20
Secondary circuit to bypass	19	26
Secondary circuit to compensator	15	20
Brake limiter valve inlet	19	26
Limiter and bypass outlet	15	20

1 General description

1   The braking system is of four wheel hydraulic type with ventilated disc brakes on the front and drum brakes on the rear wheels.
2   A mechanically operated handbrake operates on the rear wheels only.
3   Actuation of the braking system is by means of a foot-operated pedal working through a master cylinder and combined fluid reservoir.
4   A brake pressure limiter valve is fitted in the system to prevent locking of the wheels and to adjust the braking effort between the front and rear wheels in conjunction with the weight and suspension characteristics of the vehicle.
5   The brakes are servo assisted, the servo unit receiving its vacuum from the inlet manifold.
6   The tandem type master cylinder also incorporates a pressure drop indicator switch, to give early warning should a fault occur within the hydraulic circuit.
7   An additional circuit from the master cylinder provides extra pressure to the rear brakes should a fault occur in the front brake circuit. When operated, this additional circuit overrides the brake limiter valve.

2 Front brake disc pads – removal, inspection and refitting

1   Before dismantling any parts of the brakes they should be thoroughly cleaned. The best cleaning agent is hot water and a mild detergent. Do not use petrol, paraffin or any other solvents which could cause deterioration to the friction pads or piston seals.
2   Jack up the car and remove the wheel.
3   Inspection does not necessitate the removal of the disc pads themselves. The pads abut the disc surface at all times. Therefore it is possible to put the end of a steel rule (the measure must start at the end of the rule) on the disc at a right angle to the calliper as shown in Fig. 9.2. The total pad thickness (with backing plate) must not be less than that specified. If the pads have worn down beyond this, they must be renewed as a set.
4   Extract the small spring clip (photo) from each locking key, then slide the upper and lower 'key' out of the calliper (photo). Tap the keys out with a drift if necessary.
5   Remove the calliper rear section and whilst supporting it, extract each brake pad (photo). If the pads are to be reused, they must be kept in relative order to ensure being correctly repositioned in the same place. Remove the pad springs.
6   Do not apply pressure to the brake pedal whilst the rear calliper section and pads are detached. Support the calliper whilst removed, to prevent straining the flexible hose.
7   With the pads removed, the dust covers can be detached from their housing and the end of each piston cleaned off with methylated spirit. The piston skirt can be treated to a suitable brake grease. Clean the dust covers and refit them, then push back the piston with a block of wood or similar.
8   Relocate the pad springs and insert the new pads. When fitting the

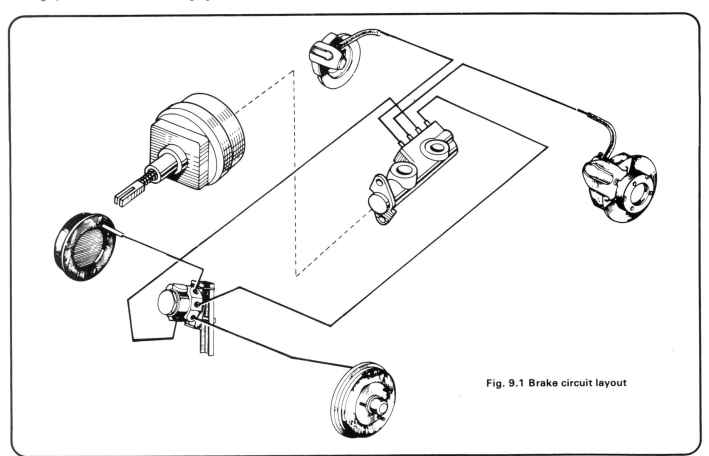

Fig. 9.1 Brake circuit layout

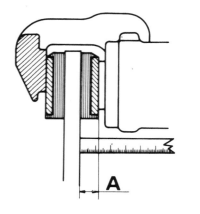

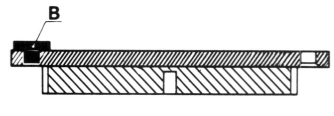

Fig. 9.3 Disc pad stop (B) to face in direction of rotation

Fig. 9.2 Check the disc pad thickness (A) as shown

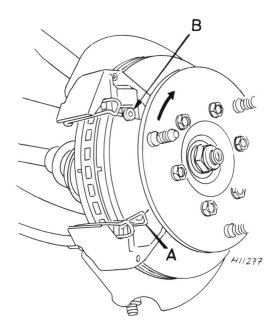

"BENT WIRE" SPRING

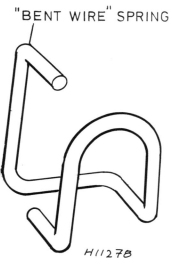

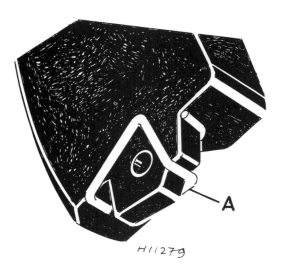

Fig. 9.4 The later type cast calliper and pad showing the 'bent wire' spring retainer and pad (A) – the stop retainer position is shown at Point 'B'

2.4a Pad retaining clip and spring

2.4b Method of removing the 'key'

2.5 Remove the pad

6.11 Unhook the handbrake cable from the lever (arrowed)

6.15 Detach the shoe retainer

6.24 Check the completed assembly before refitting the drum

pads, ensure that the retaining stop faces towards the forward rotation of the disc (ie at the top of the right-hand outer pad) as shown in Fig. 9.3.

9   Position the calliper end between the spring clip and its key location in the calliper bracket. Compress the springs, using a suitable screwdriver and fit the respective retaining keys. Once the key is in position, remove the screwdriver and tap the key fully home. Repeat this procedure for the second key.

10 New key retaining pins should always be used, and ensure they are fully located.

11 Refit the roadwheel, lower the car and pump the brake pedal to seat the piston.

12 Note that on some later models fitted with the Bendix brake unit (having a cast calliper bracket, ventilated discs and a 54 mm (2·126 in) bore calliper cylinder), a revised pad retaining spring is employed. This is shown in Fig. 9.4. The pads are recessed to take this spring, and the stop retainer must be located as shown. The blade type spring is not used on this version. Refitting is otherwise the same, and outlined above.

3   Disc brake calliper bracket – removal and refitting

1   Referring to the previous Section, follow paragraphs 1 to 6 and detach the pads and calliper unit. Do not disconnect the flexible hydraulic hose.

2   Unscrew and remove the calliper bracket retaining bolts on the inside of the stub axle, as shown in Fig. 9.5. Remove the bracket.

3   Refit the bracket and calliper unit/pads in the reverse order, but ensure the calliper and pads are cleaned prior to fitting.

4   Tighten the bracket bolts.

4   Brake discs – removal and refitting

1   Referring to Sections 2 and 3, remove the disc calliper and calliper bracket.

2   Locate a bar between two of the wheel studs, to prevent the hub from turning, and loosen the wheel hub nut. Remove the nut and washer.

3   The hub and disc unit can now be withdrawn from the stub axle unit. It should be possible to withdraw the hub/disc unit by light leverage or tapping from the rear with a soft-headed mallet. Failing this it will be necessary to use a suitable puller. The official Renault tool for this purpose is tool number T AV 235 used with attachment MS 580 as shown in Fig. 9.6.

4   The disc is held to the hub by retaining bolts with spring washers.

5   The disc cannot be resurfaced, and if badly grooved, damaged or worn beyond the specified limits, must be renewed.

6   Reassembly is a reversal of the removal procedure. All parts must be cleaned before fitting and the respective fastenings tightened to the specified torque settings, where given. Clean and grease the hub bearings before fitting. On completion, apply pressure to the brake pedal a few times to reseat the calliper pistons.

5   Callipers – servicing

1   Remove the calliper as described in Section 3, and detach the flexible pipe. Plug the end of the pipe to prevent fluid leakage.

2   Clean thoroughly the exterior of the calliper with methylated spirit prior to dismantling.

3   Detach the rubber dust cover.

4   To extract the piston, apply a regulated amount of air pressure into the hydraulic hose connection in the calliper as shown in Fig. 9.7, but position a piece of wood or rubber as shown to cushion the piston as it emerges, to prevent damaging its end face.

5   Carefully, extract the calliper seal. Avoid scoring the piston surface and calliper bore in any way. Use a new seal on reassembly.

6   Clean the piston thoroughly in methylated spirit. Then inspect it for any signs of excessive wear, scoring or possible corrosive pittings. Renew the piston if defective. Similarly clean and inspect the calliper bore.

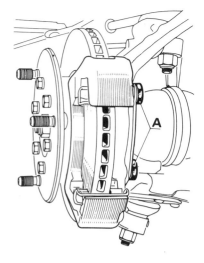

Fig. 9.5 The calliper bracket retaining bolts (A)

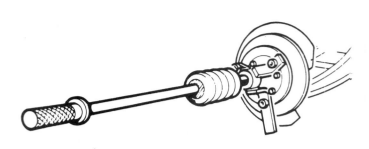

Fig. 9.6 The special Renault hub remover tool, number MS580 and T Av 235

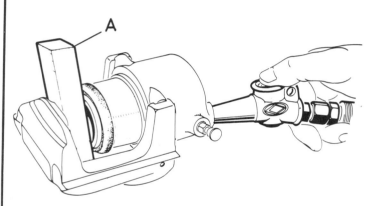

Fig. 9.7 Piston extraction method using compressed air – note wood block (A)

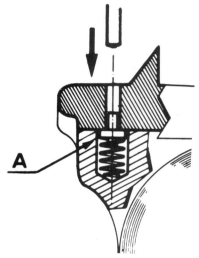

Fig. 9.8 The calliper-to-piston retaining pin and spring (A) – arrow indicates direction of depression for release

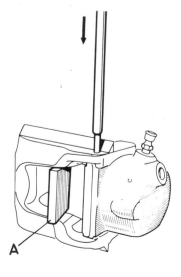

Fig. 9.9 Removing the piston – note wedge (A) in bracket

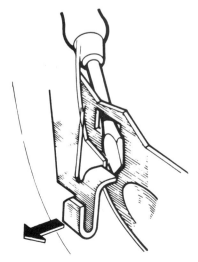

Fig. 9.10 Freeing the stop lug from the shoe

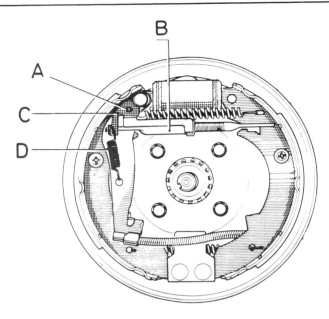

Fig. 9.11 Rear brake components

A   Pivot pin   C   Adjuster lever
B   Adjuster link   D   Tension spring

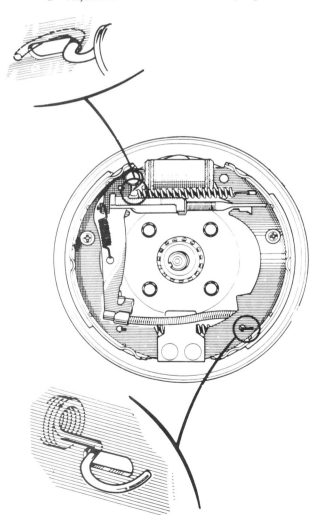

Fig. 9.12 The upper and lower spring locations

7   The calliper bracket and piston can be separated if necessary, by prising open the forked section of the bracket with a suitable wedge as shown in Fig. 9.9. Use a small diameter rod and press down the retaining peg in the cylinder to release it from the bracket, as shown in Fig. 9.8. Reassemble in the reverse order, but check the piston retaining peg is fully located in the bracket.
8   Smear the new seal in clean brake fluid and insert it into position in the calliper groove, using only finger for manipulating it to avoid scoring the groove or calliper bore.
9   Assemble the piston, pushing it carefully into position in the cylinder bore (which must also be lubricated with clean hydraulic fluid). Smear the piston with suitable brake grease.
10 Fit the new dust cover to the calliper.
11 Inject some clean brake fluid into the flexible hose locating hole. The bleed screw should be removed during this operation and, as the cylinder is filled, tilt the calliper to and fro to extract the air. Refit the bleed screw when full. This action will greatly assist bleeding the brakes later.
12 Reattach the hydraulic flexible hose (having first removed the plug) and use a new copper seal washer.
13 Refit the calliper unit and pads.
14 Refit the roadwheel and bleed the brakes as described in Section 8 to complete.

6   Rear brake linings – inspection and renewal

1   Although the rear brakes are self-adjusting, they should not be forgotten completely and must be inspected periodically for wear.
2   Raise the rear of the car and support with axle stands. Chock the front wheels and place in gear. Release the handbrake.
3   The handbrake secondary cables must now be loosened off by loosening the cable adjusters.
4   Prise the seal plug from the inside face of the brake backplate and use a suitable screwdriver to lever through the aperture. Push the handbrake actuating lever within the brake unit to free the stop lug from its shoe location as shown in Fig. 9.10. This action reduces the link thrust length, thus backing off the shoe adjustment.
5   Tap or prise free the hub grease cap, extract the split pin from the stub axle and remove the nut lockplate.
6   Unscrew and remove the hub nut and washer.
7   Withdraw the brake drum; if necessary prise carefully between the backplate and the drum at opposing points using large screwdrivers. If very tight, use the special three leg puller.
8   Clean the dust from the respective brake shoes and associate components by brushing with a dry paint brush. Do not inhale the dust as it is harmful to health. Avoid using detergents and do not get any grease or oil onto the brake linings. If the shoes are oily or greasy when the drum is removed, the cause must be rectified and the linings renewed.
9   If the linings are badly worn beyond the minimum allowable thickness (see Specifications), they must be renewed.
10 Before dismantling the shoes make a sketch of the shoe web holes in which the return springs engage so that they can be refitted in their original locations. Note carefully the 'handing' of the pairs of shoes in respect of leading and trailing edges, this is most important.
11 Unhook the handbrake cable from the lever (photo).
12 Relase the tension spring from the handbrake lever, using needle nose pliers to grip and stretch the spring hook clear of the lever.
13 Detach the adjuster lever from the pin (see Fig. 9.11).
14 Stretch the brake shoe return spring at the top and free it from the shoe at one end.
15 Using a pair of pliers, grip the shoe retaining spring cup washer and rotate it 90° to release the spring and washer from each shoe (photo). The rod can be removed through the backplate.
16 Back off the adjuster of the connecting link and remove it.
17 To loosen off the tension of the lower shoe return spring, pivot each shoe inwards at the top (having released them from the wheel cylinder) and when diagonally opposed to each other as shown in Fig. 9.12 release the spring and remove the shoes.
18 Always renew all four rear brake shoes at one and the same time. Renew shoes on an exchange basis and do not be tempted to renew the linings yourself, they are not ground to contour and seldom prove satisfactory.
19 Reassemble in the reverse order as follows. Lay the two new shoes on the bench, correctly orientated in respect of leading and trailing

edges and fit the lower return spring.

20 Fit the shoes (connected by their lower return spring) into position on the backplate.

21 The length of the top thrust link should be adjusted to give a lining diameter of about 228 mm (9 inches).

22 When the adjusting lever is relocated it must be parallel with the wheel cylinder, and the ratchet finger 7 mm (0·276 in) beneath the adjuster lever centre line. Refit the upper return spring.

23 Press the handbrake lever back against the shoe. Refit the shoe retainers and connect the handbrake cable.

24 Before refitting the brake drum, ensure all springs, shoes and associate components are correctly and securely assembled (photo).

25 Refit the brake drum and reset the hub adjustment as given in Chapter 11, Section 13.

26 Apply the footbrake a few times to centralize the shoes and take up the adjustment. If necessary, take up the handbrake adjustment (see Section 16).

---

7 Rear wheel cylinders – removal, servicing and refitting

1 Raise the car at the rear and support with axle stands. Chock the front wheels and place in gear. Release the handbrake.

2 Remove the brake drum from the side concerned as described in the previous Section.

3 Prise the brake shoe top return spring free from its location in the shoe at one end and pivot the shoes apart, away from the wheel cylinder.

4 Disconnect the hydraulic pipe union on the wheel cylinder housing and plug the pipe to prevent loss of brake fluid. Do not operate the foot pedal until reassembly is complete.

5 Unscrew and remove the two wheel cylinder securing bolts and remove the cylinder.

6 Check the shoe linings for brake fluid contamination and renew the shoes if necessary.

7 Dismantle the wheel cylinder by removing the dust covers, and ejecting the pistons by knocking the cylinder on a piece of wood or applying a tyre pump to the pipeline orifice, and removing the seals and the spring, see Fig. 9.15.

8 Wash the components in clean brake fluid or methylated spirit and examine the piston and bore surfaces for scoring or 'bright' wear marks. If these are apparent, renew the complete wheel cylinder on an exchange basis.

9 Renew the seals from the repair kit supplied and reassemble, using the fingers for manipulation and clean brake fluid for lubrication. Ensure that the components are fitted in the sequence shown and pay particular attention to the orientation of seal lips and chamfers.

10 Refit the cylinder to the backplate, reconnect the shoe upper return spring, refit the brake drum and tighten the hub nut with reference to Chapter 11.

11 Reconnect the hydraulic pipe to the cylinder housing and bleed the brakes as described in the next Section.

12 Apply the brakes a few times on completion to centralize the brake shoes.

---

8 Hydraulic system – bleeding

1 The system should need bleeding only when some part of the system has been dismantled which would allow air into the fluid circuit; or if the reservoir level has been allowed to drop so far that air has entered the master cylinder. In order to minimise fluid loss from the hydraulic system and entry of air whenever a component of the system is removed or dismantled it is helpful to remove the master cylinder reservoir cap and place a piece of polythene sheeting over the top of the reservoir and screw on the cap. This operation will have the effect of sealing the air hole in the reservoir cap and create a partial vacuum in the reservoir and prevent fluid from running out of the disconnected pipe union.

2 Ensure that a supply of clean non-aerated fluid of the correct specification is to hand in order to replenish the reservoir during the bleeding process. It is advisable, if not essential, to have someone available to help, as one person to pump the brake pedal while the other attends to each wheel. The reservoir level has also to be continuously watched and replenished. Fluid bled out should not be re-used. A clean glass jar and a 220–310 mm (9–12 in) length of 3·2 mm ($\frac{1}{8}$ inch) internal diameter rubber tube that will fit tightly over the

bleed nipples is also required (photo).

3 Bleed the front brakes first as these hold the largest quantity of fluid in the system.

4 Make sure the bleed nipple is clean and put a small quantity of fluid in the bottom of the jar. Fit the tube onto the nipple and place the other end in the jar under the surface of the liquid. Keep it under the surface throughout the bleeding operation.

5 Unscrew the bleed screw $\frac{1}{2}$ turn and get the assistant to depress and release the brake pedal in short sharp bursts when you direct him. Short sharp jabs are better than long slow ones because they will force any air bubbles along the line ahead of the fluid rather than pump the fluid past them. It is not essential to remove all the air the first time. If the whole system is being bled, attend to each wheel for three or four complete pedal strokes and then repeat the process. On the second time around operate the pedal sharply in the same way until no more bubbles are apparent. The bleed screw should be tightened and closed with the brake pedal fully depressed which ensures that no aerated fluid can get back into the system. Do not forget to keep the reservoir topped up throughout.

6 When all four wheels have been satisfactorily bled depress the foot pedal which should offer a firmer resistance with no trace of 'sponginess'. The pedal should not continue to go down under sustained pressure. If it does there is a leak or the master cylinder seals are worn out. Finally, bleed the pressure drop indicator and top-up the hydraulic fluid level.

---

9 Hydraulic pipes and hoses – inspection, removal and refitting

1 Periodically, and certainly well in advance of the DOE Test, all brakes pipes, connections and unions should be completely and carefully examined.

2 Examine first all the unions for signs of leaks. Then look at the flexible hoses for signs of fraying and chafing (as well as for leaks). This is only a preliminary inspection of the flexible hoses, as exterior condition does not necessarily indicate interior condition which will be considered later.

3 The steel pipes must be examined equally carefully. They must be thoroughly cleaned and examined for signs of dents or other percussive damage, rust and corrosion. Rust and corrosion should be scraped off, and, if the depth of pitting in the pipes is significant, they will require renewal. This is most likely in those areas underneath the chassis and along the rear suspension arms where the pipes are exposed to the full force of road and weather conditions.

4 If any section of pipe is to be removed, first take off the fluid reservoir cap, line it with a piece of polythene film to make it airtight and screw it back on. This will minimise the amount of fluid dripping out of the system when the pipes are removed.

5 Rigid pipe removal is usually quite straightforward. The unions at each end are undone and the pipe drawn out of the connection. The clips which may hold it to the car body are bent back and it is then removed. Underneath the car the exposed union can be particularly stubborn, defying the efforts of an open-ended spanner. As few people will have the special split ring spanner required, a self-griping wrench is the only answer. If the pipe is being renewed, new unions will be provided. If not, then one will have to put up with the possibility of burring over the flats on the unions and of using a self-gripping wrench for refitting also.

6 Flexible hoses are always fitted to a rigid support bracket as shown in Fig.9.14 where they join a rigid pipe, the bracket being fixed to the chassis or rear suspension arm. The rigid pipe unions must first be removed from the flexible union. Then the locknut securing the flexible pipe to the bracket must be unscrewed, releasing the end of the pipe from the bracket. As these connections are usually exposed they are, more often than not, rusted up and a penetrating fluid is virtually essential to aid removal. When undoing them, both halves must be supported as the bracket is not strong enough to support the torque required to undo the nut and can be snapped off easily.

7 Once the flexible hose is removed, examine the internal bore. If clear of fluid it should be possible to see through it. Any specks of rubber which come out, or signs of restriction in the bore, mean that the inner lining is breaking up and the hose must be renewed.

8 Rigid pipes which need renewing can usually be purchased at your local garage where they have the pipe, unions and special tools to make them up. All that they need to know is the pipe length required and the type of flare used at the ends of the pipe. These may be

Fig. 9.13 Cross shoes to remove lower spring

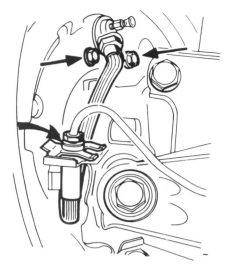

Fig. 9.14 The wheel cylinder bolts and flexible pipe mounting connection

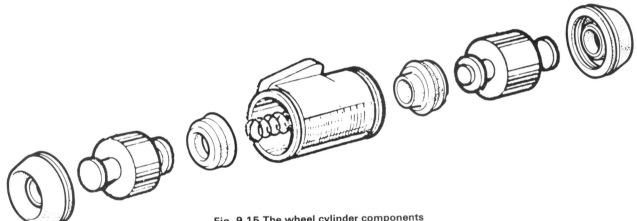

Fig. 9.15 The wheel cylinder components

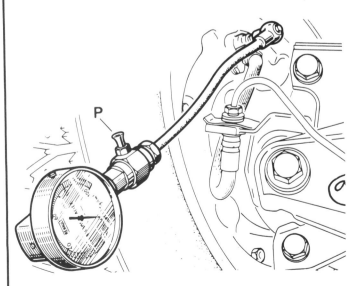

Fig. 9.16 Methods of checking brake limiter valve pressure – 'P' is the gauge unit bleeder nipple

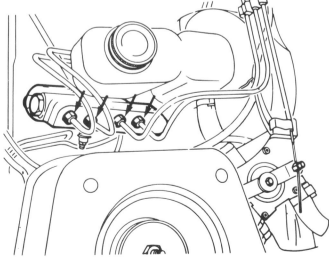

Fig. 9.17 Master cylinder pipe unions (arrowed)

different at each end of the same pipe. If possible, it is a good idea to take the old pipe along as a pattern.

9   Refitting of pipes is a straightforward reversal of the removal procedure. It is best to get all the sets (bends) made prior to fitting. Also, any acute bends should be put in by the garage on a bending machine otherwise there is the possibility of kinking them, and restricting the bore area and thus, fluid flow.

10   With the pipes refitted, remove the polythene from the reservoir cap and bleed the system as described in the previous Section.

10 Brake pressure limiter valve – inspection, adjustment and refitting

1   Correct adjustment of the brake pressure limiter valve is essential for safe and efficient braking. Before checking can be carried out, the vehicle must be placed on a level surface with a full fuel tank and a person sitting in the driver's seat.

2   A pressure gauge is essential (400 – 600 lbf/in^2 range) and must incorporate a bleed valve. A suitable instrument can be made up with a tee piece and utilising one of the proprietory type automatic brake bleeding nipples.

3   Connect the pressure gauge in place of one of the rear brake cylinder bleed nipples.

4   Bleed the system through the gauge bleed valve in a manner similar to that described previously but it will not be necessary to bleed other than from the gauge nipple.

5   Apply the footbrake pedal several times in succession and check the reading on the pressure gauge. Where necessary, loosen the nut and adjust the position of the link until the pressure reading on subsequent pedal applications lies within the range specified, (520 lbf/in^2) as shown in Fig. 9.16.

6   Remove the gauge, refit the original bleed nipple, bleed the brakes (Section 8), and top up the master cylinder reservoir.

9   The brake pressure limiter valve cannot be serviced, and in the event of failure or leakage, renew the complete unit.

8   To remove the limiter valve, detach the respective pipeline connections (photos) and plug them to prevent leakage and the ingress of dirt.

9   Unscrew and remove the four retaining bracket bolts and detach the limiter valve.

10   Refit in the reverse order, bleed the system and then adjust the cut-off pressure as described above.

11 Master cylinder – removal and refitting

1   Ideally, before removal of the master cylinder, the brake fluid should be drained from the reservoir. The fluid may be syphoned out or one of the unions disconnected and the foot brake pedal depressed until the fluid is expelled from both the master cylinder and the reservoir.

2   Disconnect all the fluid pipe unions from the master cylinder, shown in Fig. 9.17.

3   Detach the pressure drop indicator switch wire.

4   Unscrew and remove the master cylinder-to-servo unit retaining bolts and remove the master cylinder.

5   Plug the ends of the respective brake lines to prevent leakage and the ingress of dirt. The cylinder unit cannot be repaired and must therefore be renewed if defective.

6   To refit the master cylinder, engage the operating rod with the piston assembly, and bolt the master cylinder into its location. If necessary, make the adjustments in paragraphs 8 to 11 inclusive, before fitting the cylinder.

7   Reconnect the unions and the pressure drop indicator wire, refill the reservoir and bleed the system (see Section 8).

8   Check the master cylinder operating clearance. Adjustment may be necessary at one of two places – at the pushrod and master cylinder endface or the operating rod-to-pedal clevis at the rear of the servo unit.

9   The adjustment points are shown clearly in Figs. 9.18 and 9.20. The respective clearance should be as follows: X = 9 mm (0·35 in); L = 125 mm (4·92 in).

10   To adjust clearance X, turn pushrod nut P accordingly.

11   To adjust clearance L, disconnect the brake pedal (Section 17), unscrew the clevis locknut E and turn the clevis C in the desired direction, then retighten the locknut to secure.

8.2 Rear cylinder bleed nipple position (arrowed)

10.8a The limiter valve lower linkage layout

10.8b The limiter valve unit showing respective hydraulic pipe

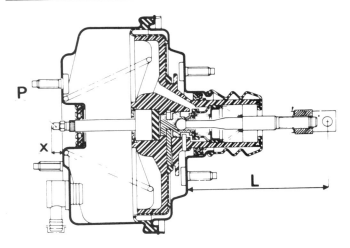

Fig. 9.18 Master cylinder operating clearance checks to be made at points 'X' 9 mm (0.35 in) and point 'L' 125 mm (4.92 in)

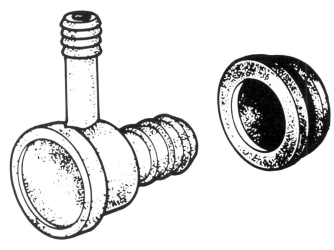

Fig. 9.19 The one-way valve unit

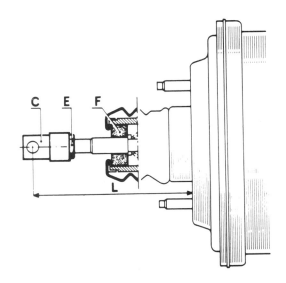

Fig. 9.20 The servo unit filter location (F) showing clevis (C) and locknut (E) – 'L' is operating clearance

12 Brake servo unit – servicing, removal and refitting

1　The brake servo unit operates from vacuum supplied from the engine manifold. It is emphasised that in the event of the unit failing then normal hydraulic braking will still be available by foot pressure, though greater effort will be required.

2　Leaks in, or failure of, the servo unit may be detected by a sudden increase in the brake pedal pressure required to retard or stop the vehicle. Uneven running or stalling of the engine may also indicate leaks in the servo system.

3　If problems do occur, check that the vacuum hose and connection from the manifold is in good condition and secure (including the one-way valve see Fig. 9.19).

4　If the problem appears to be in the vacuum unit, there is very little you can do apart from exchanging it for a new one.

5　It might, however, be an idea to have your Renault dealer give the unit a vacuum pressure check to be absolutely sure before removing it.

6　The only servicing the servo unit requires is to renew the air filter periodically. To do this, disconnect the brake pedal, unscrew the locknut on the operating rod clevis (near the pedal) and then remove the clevis.

7　Free the rubber dust boot from the rear of the unit, prise the filter retaining spring clip free and hook out the filter.

8　Insert the new filter and retain with spring clip. Check the operating clearance as described in Section 11.

9　To change the one-way valve, detach the vacuum inlet pipe to the servo unit, then pull whilst turning the one-way valve simultaneously and remove it. If in poor condition or known to be defective, renew it. Refit in the reverse procedure to removal.

10　To remove the servo unit, disconnect the battery earth lead, then remove the master cylinder unit as described in Section 11.

11　Loosen the vacuum hose clip at the servo unit end and detach the hose.

12　Working inside the vehicle, extract the brake pedal-to-operating rod clevis pin which is retained by a split-pin.

13　The servo unit retaining nuts to the bulkhead can now be unscrewed, enabling the servo unit to be removed.

14　As mentioned earlier, it cannot be repaired or adjusted in any way and must therefore be renewed if defective.

15　Refit in the reverse order, but ensure that the operating clearance is correct and in accordance with Section 11.

13 Pressure drop indicator – description and faults

1　This component is fitted in conjunction with tandem type master cylinders to indicate any difference in hydraulic pressure between the two independent braking circuits.

2　A sectional view of the pressure drop indicator is illustrated.

3　The operating principle is that where the two circuit hydraulic pressures are equal, then the pistons (3) are in balance. Any variation in pressure between one circuit and the other will cause the pistons to move and complete an electrical circuit to give a warning through an indicator lamp on the facia panel.

4　The warning lamp will illuminate for one of the following reasons; system requires bleeding, leakage (externally) from some part of the hydraulic system, operating fault within the tanden master cylinder.

5　Fault diagnosis should be made and rectified immediately.

6　When the failure is in the front brake circuit an additional circuit to the rear brakes becomes operation. This additional circuit is only used when there has been a failure in the front brake circuit, whereby the hydraulic pistons will move to the rear of the cylinder (direction of arrow in Fig. 9.21) and the additional circuit to the rear brakes becomes operational. Whilst the additional circuit is operational, the brake limiter becomes non-operation, thereby allowing additional pressure to the rear brakes.

14 Pressure drop indicator – removal and refitting

1　Drain the fluid reservoir or seal the cap (see Section 11) and disconnect the hydraulic pipe unions from the pressure indicator housing.

2　Disconnect the switch electric lead, unscrew the retaining bolt and withdraw the switch.

3　The pressure indicator switch cannot be serviced and must be renewed as an assembly.

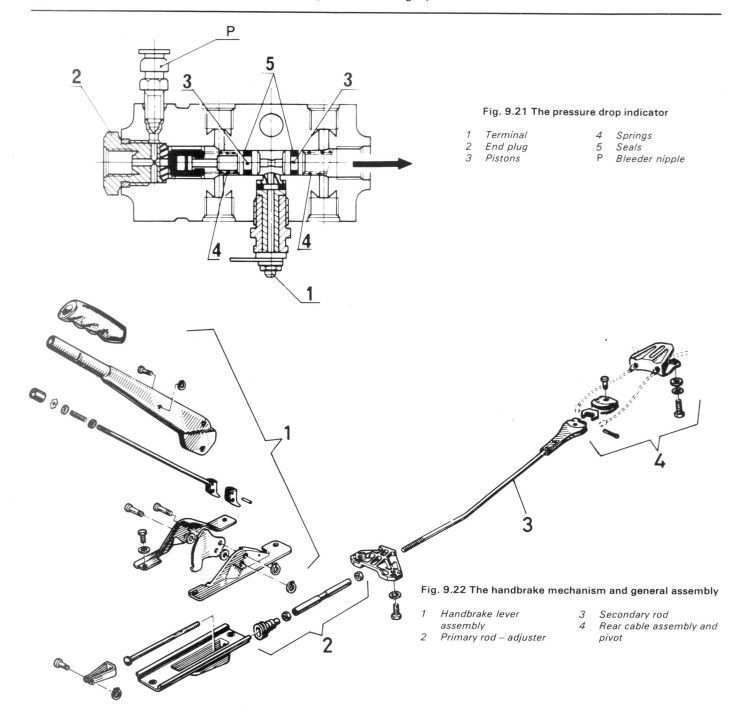

Fig. 9.21 The pressure drop indicator

1	Terminal	4	Springs
2	End plug	5	Seals
3	Pistons	P	Bleeder nipple

Fig. 9.22 The handbrake mechanism and general assembly

1	Handbrake lever assembly	3	Secondary rod
2	Primary rod – adjuster	4	Rear cable assembly and pivot

4   Refitting is a reversal of removal but bleed the system as described in Section 8. After bleeding the four wheel cylinders, bleed the pressure drop indicator at 'P' (Fig. 9.21) which is for the additional circuit.

15 Handbrake – adjustment

1   Adjustment of the handbrake should not be required unless the cable has stretched or components of the rear braking assembly have been dismantled or reassembled.
2   Jack up the rear of the vehicle and release the handbrake fully. Additionally support with axle stands. Chock the front wheels.
3   Loosen the locknuts and turn the adjuster sleeve until the shoes just make contact with the drums.
4   Turn the sleeve just sufficiently in the opposite direction to permit

the wheels to turn freely. Tighten the locknuts. As a check for correct adjustment, there should be a minimum of 12 notches felt when the handbrake is applied.

16 Handbrake mechanism – removal and refitting

Handbrake lever

1   With the vehicle parked on level ground, place it in gear and put chocks under the wheels.
2   From inside the car, release the handbrake and remove any trim from the base of the handbrake (as applicable). Unscrew and remove the two handbrake lever retaining bolts.
3   Lift the lever and detach the cable clevis pin to release it.
4   Refitting is a reversal of the removal procedure.

16.11 The handbrake cable pivot

Primary rod
5   Raise and support the vehicle with axle stands and chock the wheels.
6   Working underneath, unscrew the primary rod adjuster nuts and detach the sleeve.
7   Remove the handbrake lever (see above) and extract the clevis pin to release the rod.
8   Refitting is a reversal of the removal sequence but if necessary, adjust the handbrake as given in the previous Section.

Rear linkage
9   Unscrew the adjuster nuts and detach the sleeve. Extract the

swivel lever pivot pin which is retained by a split-pin.
10 Refit in the reverse order and adjust the handbrake as necessary.

Rear cable renewal
11 Working underneath, extract the swivel lever hingepin and withdraw the pin (photo).
12 Release the cable from its holder and tap the sleeve from its location.
13 Referring to Section 6, remove the brake drum/s at the rear to disconnect the cable from the actuating lever for the shoes. Withdraw the sleeve through the backplate.
14 Refitting is a reversal of the removal procedure. Use new split-pins; grease the swivel pin. On completion, press the brake pedal a few times to centralize the shoes and take up the adjustment. If necessary, readjust the handbrake.

17 Brake and clutch pedals – removal and refitting

1   Remove the spring clip and free the spring from the clutch pedal.
2   Remove the split pin and clevis pin from the brake master cylinder operating rod to pedal connection.
3   Withdraw the clutch pedal from the pedal cross-shaft then use a soft drift to remove the cross-shaft to the right sufficiently far so that the brake pedal can be removed.
4   Refitting is a reversal of removal, but smear the cross-shaft with grease and adjust the clutch and brake pedal clearances if necessary as described in Chapter 5 and Section 11 of this Chapter respectively.

18 Brake light switch

1   The brake light switch is mechanically rather than hydraulically operated. It is attached to the steering column support bracket just above the brake pedal and is affixed by a nut. As the pedal is depressed, the contacts close in the brake light switch.
2   If the switch fails, it must be renewed. Disconnect the feed wires and withdraw the unit. Refitting is a simple reversal of this procedure.

19 Fault diagnosis – braking system

Symptom	Reason
Pedal travels a long way before the brakes operate	Seized adjuster on rear shoes Disc pads or linings excessively worn
Stopping ability poor, even though pedal pressure is firm	Linings, pads, discs or drums badly worn or scored One or more calliper piston or rear wheel cylinder seized, resulting in some pads/shoes not pressing against discs/drums Brake pads or linings contaminated with oil Wrong type of pads or linings fitted (too hard) Brake pads or shoes incorrectly assembled Servo unit (where fitted) not functioning
Car veers to one side when brakes are applied	Brake pads on one side are contaminated with oil. Hydraulic pistons in callipers are partially or wholly seized on one side A mixture of pad materials used between sides Unequal wear between sides caused by partially seized hydraulic pistons in brake callipers
Pedal feels spongy when the brakes are applied	Air is present in the hydraulic system Rear brake linings not bedded into the drums (after fitting new ones) Master cylinder, brake calliper or drum back-plate mounting bolts loose Severe wear in rear drums causing distortion when brakes are applied
Pedal travels right down with little or no resistance and brakes are virtually non-operative	Leak in hydraulic system resulting in lack of pressure for operation of wheel cylinders If no signs of leakage are apparent the master cylinder internal seals are failing to sustain pressure
Binding, juddering, overheating	One, or a combination of causes given in the foregoing sections Reservoir air vent blocked

Chapter 10 Electrical system

For modifications, and information applicable to later models, see Supplement at end of manual

Contents

Specifications

Battery
Capacity	40 Ah
Voltage	12v
Polarity	Negative earth

Regulator
	Ducellier 8371

Starter motor
R1271 (TL models)	Paris Rhone D8E 139
R1272 (TS models)	Paris Rhone D8E 140

Alternator
TL models	Paris Rhone A13 R166
TS models	Paris Rhone A13 R189
Also available	Ducellier 7580
	SEV 712 307 12
	SEV 712 314 12
	SEV 712 311 12
	SEV 712 304 12
	Paris Rhone A13 R167
	Paris Rhone A13 R212

1 General description

1 The electrical system is of 12 volt type and comprises a battery (negative earth), an alternator and voltage regulator to keep the battery charged and supply the electrical requirements of the vehicle.
2 The alternator is driven by a V-belt from the water pump pulley and crankshaft pulley.
3 Electrical ancillary components are of conventional type and include a starter motor, distributor and ignition accessories and all necessary wiring harness.
4 On specified models, the sunroof, the windows, the screen washers and the heated rear window are all electrically operated and are described in later Sections of this Chapter.

2 Battery – removal and refitting

1 The battery is positioned within the engine compartment on a tray directly in front of the bulkhead.
2 Disconnect the earthed negative lead and then the positive lead by slackening the retaining nuts and bolts or, by unscrewing the retaining screws if these are fitted.
3 Remove the battery clamp and carefully lift the battery off its tray. Hold the battery vertical to ensure that no electrolyte is spilled.
4 Refitting is a direct reversal of this procedure. Refit the positive lead and the earth (negative) lead, smearing the terminals with petroleum jelly to prevent corrosion. NEVER use an ordinary grease as applied to other parts of the car.

5 In order to prevent damage to the alternator rectifying diodes, the following precautions must be observed whenever servicing of the electrical system or components is being undertaken. Always switch off the engine before disconnecting the battery. Never disconnect the battery terinals until the engine has been switched off and has come to rest.

Never run the engine with either the alternator leads or the vehicles own battery leads disconnected. When charging the battery from a mains charger, always remove the battery from the car. Avoid short circuits.

3 Battery – maintenance and inspection

1 The modern battery seldom requires topping up but, nevertheless, the electrolyte level should be inspected weekly as a means of providing the first indication that the alternator is overcharging or that the battery casing has developed a leak.
2 When topping up is required, use only distilled water or melted ice from a refrigerator (frosting, not ice cubes).
3 Acid should never be required if the battery has been correctly filled from new, unless spillage has occurred.
4 Inspect the battery terminals and mounting tray for corrosion. This is the white fluffy deposit which grows at these areas. If evident, clean it away and neutralise it with ammonia or baking soda. Apply petroleum jelly to the terminals and paint the battery tray with anticorrosive paint.
5 An indication of the state of charge of a battery can be obtained by checking the electrolyte in each cell using a hydrometer. The specific gravity of the electrolyte for fully charged and fully discharged conditions at the electrolyte temperature indicated, is listed below.

Fully discharged	Electrolyte temperature	Fully charged
1.098	38°C (100°F)	1.268
1.102	32°C (90°F)	1.272
1.106	27°C (80°F)	1.276
1.110	21°C (70°F)	1.280
1.114	16°C (60°F)	1.284
1.118	10°C (50°F)	1.288
1.122	4°C (40°F)	1.292
1.126	-1.5°C (30°F)	1.296

6 There should be very little variation in the readings between the different cells, but if a difference is found in excess of 0.025 then it will probably be due to an internal fault indicating impending battery failure. This assumes that electrolyte has not been spilled at some time

and the deficiency made up with water only.
7 Keep the top surface of the battery casing dry.

4 Battery – charging

1 In winter time when heavy demand is placed upon the battery, such as when starting from cold, and much electrical equipment is continually in use, it is a good idea to occasionally have the battery fully charged from an external source at the rate of 3.5 or 4 amps.
2 Continue to charge the battery at this rate until no further rise in specific gravity is noted over a four hour period.
3 Alternatively, a trickle charger at the rate of 1.5 amps can be safely used overnight.
4 Specially rapid 'boost' charges which are claimed to restore the power of the battery in 1 to 2 hours are most harmful as they can cause serious damage to the battery plates by overheating.
5 Note the precautions to be observed in order to prevent damage to the alternator – these are listed in Section 5.

5 Alternator – description and precautions

The alternator generates alternating current (AC) which is rectified by diodes to DC and is the current needed for battery storage.

The regulator is a transistorized unit which is permanently sealed and requires no attention. It will last indefinitely provided no mistakes are made in wiring connections.

Apart from the renewal of the rotor slip ring brushes and rotor shaft bearings, there are no other parts which need periodic inspection. All other items are sealed assemblies and must be renewed if indications are that they are faulty.

If there are indications that the charging system is malfunctioning in any way, care must be taken to diagnose faults properly, otherwise damage of a serious and expensive nature may occur to parts which are in fact quite serviceable. Fault diagnosis generally requires sophisticated test equipment, and should be entrusted to an auto-electrician.

The following basic requirements must be observed at all times, therefore, if damage is to be prevented:
1 ALL alternator systems use a NEGATIVE earth. Even the simple mistake of connecting a battery the wrong way round could burn out the alternator diodes in a few seconds.
2 Before disconnecting any wires in the system the engine and ignition circuits should be switched off. This will minimise accidental short circuits.

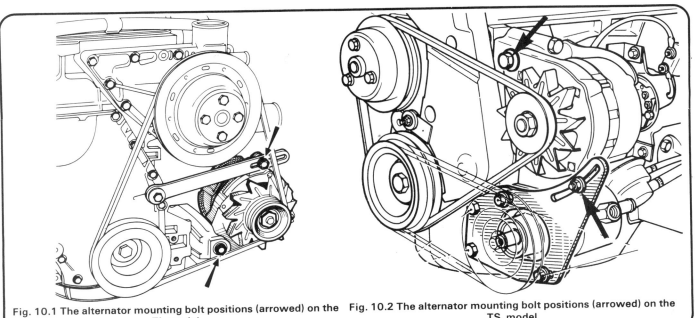

Fig. 10.1 The alternator mounting bolt positions (arrowed) on the TL model

Fig. 10.2 The alternator mounting bolt positions (arrowed) on the TS model

3   The alternator must NEVER be run with the output wire disconnected.

4   Always disconnect the battery from the car's electrical system if an outside charging source is being used.

5   Do not use test wire connections that could move accidentally and short circuit against nearby terminals. Short circuits will not blow fuses – they will blow diodes or transistors.

6   Always disconnect the battery cables and alternator output wires before any electric welding work is done on the car body.

7   Never lever on the alternator body when adjusting its fan belt drive. The casing is easily fractured.

8   No lubrication is required as the bearings are grease sealed.

9   The drivebelt tension must be maintained at all times and the adjustment procedure is given in Section 7.

6   Alternator – removal and refitting

1   Disconnect the battery earth cable from its terminal.

2   Unscrew and remove the alternator mounting bolt and adjuster strap bolt (photo).

3   Detach the drivebelt from the alternator pulley and remove the alternator from its mounting position. If the alternator is to be removed completely, take a note of the respective cables and their locations and detach them from their connecting points on the rear face of the alternator, before lifting it clear. If the alternator is being removed solely to gain access to the power steering pump (where fitted) or other associate fittings, it can be left attached to the wiring and laid aside in the nearside lower wing panel.

4   Refitting is a reversal of the removal procedure, but do not tighten fully the retaining bolts until the drivebelt is fitted and tensioned correctly (as given in the following Section). Ensure that the wires are correctly and securely located before reattaching the battery earth cable.

7   Alternator drivebelt – adjustment and refitting

1   The correct tension adjustment of the alternator drivebelt is most important, and periodic checks should be made when servicing the car to ensure that the belt is in good condition and correctly adjusted.

2   If the belt is too loose it will slip in the pulley causing premature belt wear, and the alternator will not function efficiently. Where the belt is adjusted to give too much tension, it will overload the bearings in the alternator and cause them to fail prematurely.

3   To adjust the belt tension, loosen the retaining bolts at the mounting and adjuster strap, then pivot the alternator in the desired direction to give the specified belt deflection (see Chapter 2). Move the alternator away from the engine to increase the tension, towards it to decrease it.

4   Retain the alternator in this position and retighten the mounting and adjuster strap bolts.

5   Where a belt is found to be worn or defective in any way, it must be renewed. To do this, loosen the mounting and adjuster bolts, pivot the alternator towards the engine to slacken off the tension completely, then detach the belt from the pulley. On models fitted with power steering, the hydraulic pump drivebelt must be renewed before the alternator drivebelt can be removed. This is described in Chapter 11, Section 16.

6   The new drivebelt can be fitted and tensioned in the reverse order as described above. A new belt will tend to stretch during its initial running period and its adjustment should therefore be rechecked after the engine has been run for a limited period.

8   Starter motor – general description

1   One of two types of pre-engaged starter motor may be fitted according to vehicle model and date of manufacture (See Specifications).

2   The starter motor solenoid is actuated through movement of the key in the steering column mounted multi-position switch.

9   Starter motor – testing

1   If the starter motor does not operate when the ignition key is turned, carry out the following check list before removing the motor from its location in the vehicle.

2   Check the state of charge of the battery and the security of the battery terminals.

3   Check the security of the starter motor and solenoid electrical leads.

4   In the case of automatic vehicles, check that the gear selection lever is in P. or N. If so and the starter does not operate, check that the lever and cable adjustment is correct.

5   The starter motor is of pre-engaged type and any failure of the drive gear will mean that the pinion and screwed armature shaft must be cleaned as described in Section 13 and any defective parts renewed.

6   Disconnect the lead from the distributor LT terminal in order to prevent the engine from firing, and then connect a 0-20v voltmeter between the starter terminal and earth. Operate the starter switch to crank the engine and note the voltmeter reading. A minimum reading of 7 volts indicates satisfactory cable and switch connections. Very slow cranking at this voltage indicates a fault in the starter motor.

10   Starter motor (TL models) – removal and refitting

1   Detach the battery earth lead from the terminal.

2   Loosen the dipstick tube retaining nut and withdraw the tube and dipstick.

3   Unscrew the starter motor heat shield retaining nuts and detach the shield.

4   Detach the starter motor rear support and the three retaining bolts.

5   Withdraw the starter motor from the clutch housing and detach the leads to the solenoid, noting their locations. Lift the starter motor clear.

6   Refitting is a reversal of the removal procedure, but take care when engaging the starter drive teeth with the flywheel ring gear. If the teeth are worn, chipped or otherwise defective, either or both must be renewed.

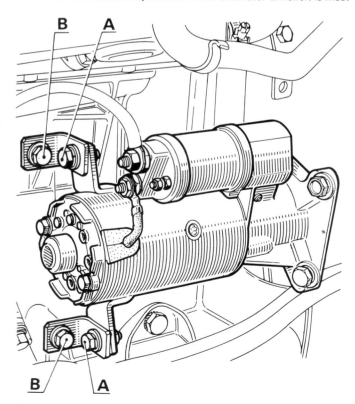

Fig. 10.3 The starter motor location on the TS model – tighten bolts A then B when refitting

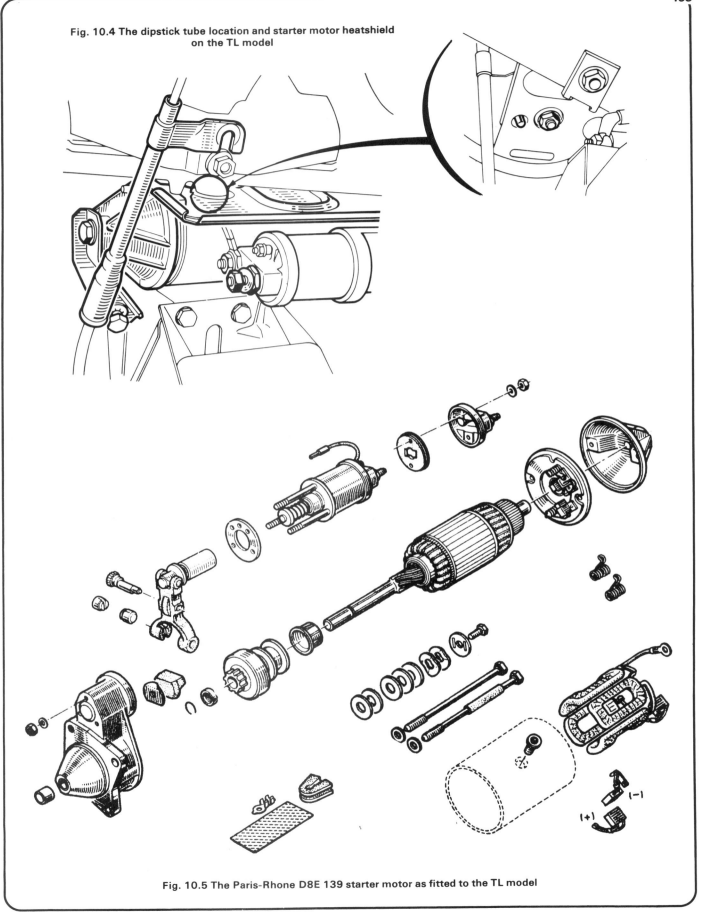

Fig. 10.4 The dipstick tube location and starter motor heatshield on the TL model

Fig. 10.5 The Paris-Rhone D8E 139 starter motor as fitted to the TL model

6.2 The alternator in position in the 20 TL

12.11 Method of undercutting the commutator segments using an old hacksaw blade shaped to suit

12.15a Using a valve spring compressor to assemble the snap-ring and collar

12.15b Relocate any thrust washers onto the shaft

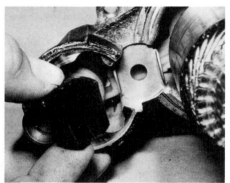

12.15c Fit the separator and special washer as shown

12.15d Align the body and cover notches/markings on assembly

11 Starter motor (TS models) – removal and refitting

1   Disconnect the battery earth lead from its terminal.
2   Detach the ignition coil from its mounting position but leave the leads connected and position it out of the way.
3   Unscrew and remove the starter motor rear mounting bolts. As the accessability to the starter motor mounting bolts is not particularly good, it may be worthwhile to consider raising the front end of the vehicle and supporting on stands, so that where necessary, you can work from underneath to remove the bolts. The engine undertray will have to be unbolted first, however.
4   Disconnect the starter motor leads, noting their respective locations for correct refitting.
5   Unscrew and remove the three starter motor location bolts at the clutch housing, then pull the unit to the front sufficiently to enable it to clear the housing and be lifted clear.
6   Refitting is a reversal of the removal procedure, but do not tighten the retaining bolts until they are all located. Ensure that the wiring is correctly connected before reattaching the battery earth lead.

12 Starter motor – dismantling and reassembly

1   Such is the inherent reliability and strength of the starter motors fitted that it is very unlikely that a motor will ever need dismantling until it is totally worn out and in need of renewal. It is not a task for the home mechanic because although the dismantling is reasonably easy to undertake, the reassembly and adjustment before refitting is beyond his scope because of the need of specialist equipment. It would under all circumstances be realistic for the work to be undertaken by the specialist auto-electrician. It is possible to renew solenoids and brushes on starter motors.
2   The starter motor components are shown in Figs. 10.5 and 10.6, as applicable to your model.
3   First remove the solenoid unit, by unscrewing the holding nuts and detaching the solenoid plunger from the operating lever. Mark the relative positions of the solenoid body to pinion housing.
4   Unscrew and remove the end cover retaining nuts and remove the

cover (type 1271), through-bolts and brush holder plate. The brushes will have to be extracted from their holders to remove the end plate completely, and therefore hook back each brush retaining spring carefully in turn and withdraw the brushes. Note the plate to housing location and make an alignment mark to ensure correct reassembly. **Note**: *The through-bolts may be tight to remove due to being treated with a thread-locking compound when assembled.*
5   The pinion housing and armature arm can now be withdrawn from the main body.
6   To dismantle and inspect the pinion/starter gear unit the special lever pivot pin must be tapped out.
7   To withdraw the pinion from the armature, tap back the special collar washer and extract the snap-ring from the groove in the shaft. The pinion assembly can then be slid from the shaft.
8   With the starter motor dismantled the various components can be cleaned and inspected for general wear and/or signs of damage. The principal components likely to need attention will be the brushes, the solenoid or possibly the drive pinion unit.
9   The brushes can be removed by unsoldering the connecting wires to the holder and to the field coil unit. Take care not to damage the latter during removal and assembly of the brushes.
10   If the starter motor has shown a tendency to jam or a possible reluctance to disengage then the starter pinion is almost certainly the culprit. Dirt around the pinion and shaft could cause this, and when cleaned check that the pinion can move freely in a spiral movement along the shaft. If the pinion tends to bind or is defective in any way renew it.
11   Undercut the separators of the commutator using an old hacksaw blade as shown (photo), to a depth of about 0.5 to 0.8 mm (0.02 to 0.03 in). The commutator may be further surface cleaned using a strip of very fine glass paper. Do not use emery cloth for this purpose as the carborundum particles will become embedded in the copper surfaces.
12   Testing of the armature is best left to an auto-electrician but if an ohmmeter is available it can be done by placing one probe on the armature shaft and the other on each of the commutator segments in turn. If there is a reading indicated at any time during the test, then the armature is defective and must be renewed.
13   The field coil can also be tested using an ohmmeter. Connect one

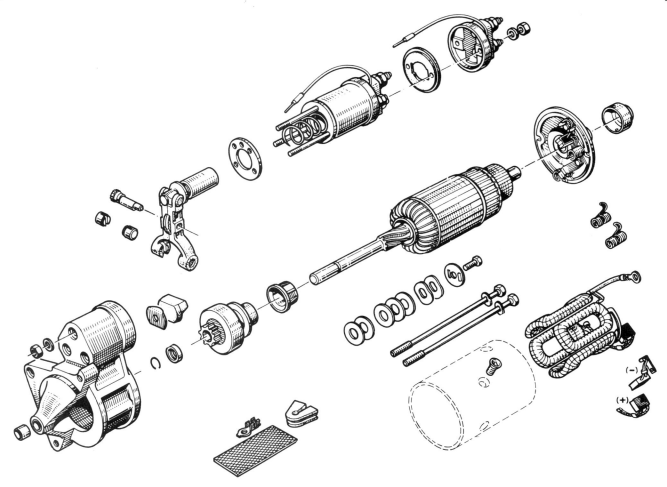

Fig. 10.6 The Paris-Rhone D8E 140 starter motor as fitted to the TS model

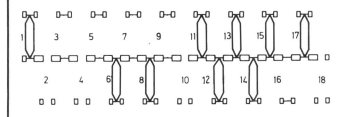

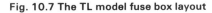

Fig. 10.7 The TL model fuse box layout

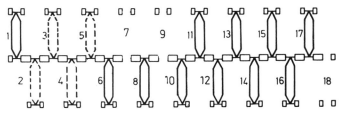

Fig. 10.8 The TS model fuse box layout

1   Auxiliary fuse (8A)
2 to 5   Not used
6   Interior light/
    map light/
    luggage
    compartment
    light/cigar lighter
    (8A)
7   Not used
8   Windscreen wiper
    motor/wiper/washer
    unit (8A)
9 and 10   Not used
11   LH window winder
     (16A)
12   Instrument panel feed
     (5A)
13   RH window winder
     (16A)
14   Automatic transmission
     feed (5A)
15   Reversing lights/rear
     screen demister
     switches (16A)
16   Not used
17   GMV heater rheostat
     (16A)
18   Not used

1   Indicators/stop light (8A)
2 to 5   Not used
6   Cigar lighter/interior
    light/clock (8A)
7   Not used
8   Wiper/washer switch (16A)
9   Not used
10   LH sidelights – front and rear
     (5A)
11   LH front window winder
     (16A)
12   RH sidelights – front and rear
     (5A)
13   RH front window winder
     (16A)
14   Panel lights (5A)
15   Reversing lights/rear screen
     demister (16A)
16   Automatic transmission
     selector feed (5A)
17   Heater rheostat (16A)
18   Not used

probe to the field coil positive terminal and the other to the positive brush holder. If there is no indication of a reading then the field coil circuit has a break in it.

14 Connect one lead of the meter to the field coil positive lead and the other one to the yoke. If there is a low resistance then the field coil is earthed due to a breakdown in the insulation. If this proves to be the case the field coils must be renewed. As field coil renewal requires special tools and equipment it is a job that should be entrusted to your auto-electrician. In fact it will probably prove more economical and beneficial to exchange the starter motor for a reconditioned unit.

15 Reassembly of the rest of the starter motor is a direct reversal of the removal procedure, but note the following:

(a) *The snap-ring and collar can be difficult to relocate and to assist in this we used a valve compressor as shown (photo)*
(b) *Reassemble the correct number of thrust washers (photo)*
(c) *Check that the brushes slide freely in their holders*
(d) *Lubricate the commutator shaft sparingly, using a medium grease*
(e) *Do not forget to install the separator and washer (photo)*
(f) *Realign the brush holder and body notches (photo)*
(g) *Realign the marks made on dismantling when assembling the solenoid, and fit the coil spring and washer as shown*

13 Starter motor drive pinion – inspection and repair

1 Persistent jamming or reluctance to disengage may mean that the starter pinion assembly needs attention. The starter motor should be removed first of all for inspection.

2 With the starter motor removed, thoroughly remove all grime and grease with a petrol soaked rag, taking care to stop any liquid running into the motor itself. If there is a lot of dirt this could be the trouble and all will now be well. The pinion should move freely in a spiral movement along the shaft against the light spring and return easily on being released. To do this the spiral splines should be completely clean and free of oil. (Oil merely collects dust and grime and gums up the splines). The spring should be intact.

3 If the preceding cleaning and check does not actually remove the fault the starter motor will need to be stripped down to its component parts and a further check made. This has been explained in the preceding Section.

14 Fuses

1 The various electrical circuits are fused. Therefore, should a fault occur within any particular circuit, check the fuse first. It may be that it is simply loose or badly connected, but if blown, a fault has occurred within the circuit concerned and must be found and rectified.

2 Check the circuit wiring and connections before assuming it is the component which is at fault.

3 The fuse box is located under the dashpanel and the cover simply unclips (photo).

4 Whenever a fuse is being renewed, refit one of the correct type and rating. If using one of the two spare fuses supplied in the fuse box, do not forget to obtain a replacement at the earliest opportunity.

5 The respective fuse circuit layouts are shown in the accompanying diagrams (Figs. 10.7 and 10.8).

6 Accessibility to the rear of the fuse box is gained by removing the thumb screw and pulling the box away from the dashpanel lower face.

15 Headlights and bulbs – adjustment, removal and refitting

Adjustment

1 Apart from the vertical beam adjustment control (from the knob on the steering column control within the car), the lights are individually adjustable for vertical and horizontal plane from within the engine compartment.

2 Adjustments other than from the column control should not normally be made unless in an emergency; as special optical beam setting equipment is needed for accurate adjustment.

3 If individual adjustment is to be made to the headlights, separate adjuster screws are provided in the rear of each unit as shown in Fig. 10.9. When making adjustment, the vehicle must be unladen and the beam height adjuster knob must be rotated fully clockwise.

4 Whenever an adjustment has been made, have it checked by your Renault dealer or local garage, using optical beam setting equipment for fine adjustments to be made.

Bulb renewal

5 The headlight bulbs can easily be removed for renewal. Raise and support the bonnet, then detach the connector from the rear of the headlight unit.

6 Unclip and pivot the bulb holder spring clips open, then extract the bulb (photo). Remove the seal washer.

7 Take care not to touch the bulb glass with your fingers. If the glass is accidentally touched, clean it at once with methylated spirit. The grease from your fingers will blacken the bulb and may cause early failure.

8 When fitting the new bulb, locate the seal washer and check that the boss on the holder ensures the correct fitting.

16 Headlight unit – removal and refitting

1 Disconnect the battery earth lead.

2 Remove the front grille panel, retained in position by two special screws. A suitable Allen key will unscrew them.

3 Working within the engine compartment, detach the wiring connector from the rear of the unit.

4 Unscrew the beam height adjuster knob and the horizontal adjuster knob.

5 Unclip the unit mounting and withdraw the unit frontwards.

6 Refit in the reverse sequence and ensure that it is correctly located. Screw in the adjuster knobs and adjust as given in the previous Section.

17 Headlight remote control adjuster unit – removal and refitting

1 The headlight remote control adjuster is hydraulic in operation, working on a similar principle to that of the brake circuit. As the control knob is turned, hydraulic fluid displacement in the sealed circuit pushes the setting screw plate on the headlight.

2 If a fault occurs in the circuit, it must be renewed as a unit – it cannot be repaired. When removing or fitting a system *never dismantle the pipe sleeves shown in Fig. 10.11* Remove the system as follows:

3 Pull the adjuster control knob free from its shaft.

4 Unscrew and detach the upper and lower steering column half casings.

5 Remove the retaining screws from the pedal assembly bracket.

6 Unclip and remove the adjuster knob shaft retaining clip and unscrew the shaft.

7 Detach the plunger unit and then unclip the control chamber/s.

8 Unclip the receiving chamber from its location at the headlight unit and carefully remove the circuit concerned.

9 Refitting is a reversal of the removal procedure. Check the headlight adjustment on completion.

18 Front combination light – bulb and unit removal and refitting

1 To check or renew the bulb, remove the two lens retaining screws and detach the lens (photo). The bulbs are removed in the normal way by pressing and twisting.

2 Refitting is a reversal of the removal procedure. Check the side/indicator light operation on completion.

3 To remove the unit, unscrew the three retaining screws (two on top and one underneath the main body) and withdraw it. Detach the wires.

4 Refitting is a reversal of the removal procedure.

19 Rear combination light – bulb and unit removal and refitting

1 Unscrew and remove the five lens retaining screws and detach the lens. Press and twist the bulbs to remove (photo).

2 Refit the bulb/s in the reverse manner.

3 To remove the light unit, disconnect the unit wires from their connectors in the corner of the boot area.

4 Insert a suitable socket with extension through the rear panel

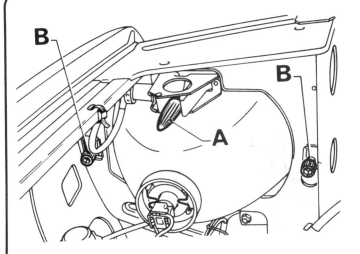

Fig. 10.9 The headlight beam alignment adjusters

A   *Beam height*   B   *Beam direction*

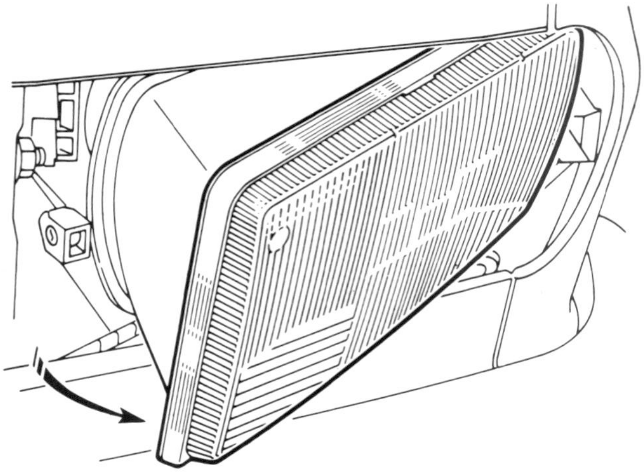

Fig. 10.10 Withdraw the headlight unit forwards

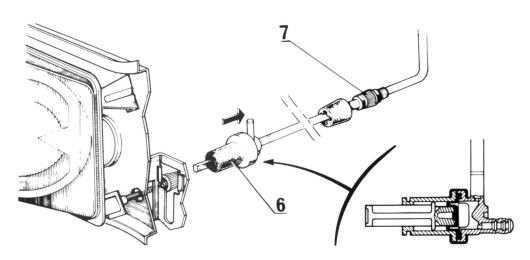

Fig. 10.11 Never detach the pipe sleeves (7) – receiving chamber (6) shown inset

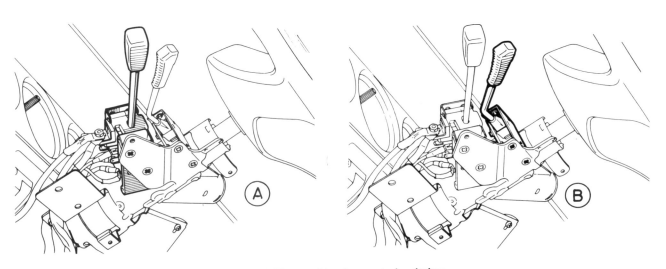

Fig. 10.12 The combination control switches

A   *Lights*   B   *Indicators*

14.3 The fuses with cover removed

15.6 Extract the bulb and holder

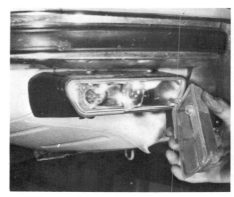
18.1 Remove the lens to change front combination light bulbs

19.1 Remove lens to change the rear combination light bulbs

22.5 Remove the side retaining bolts

23.1a Remove the lens cover retaining screws ...

23.1b ... then detach the lens and remove the bulb

24.2a The right-hand interior light removed

24.2b The left-hand interior light removed

25.1 The horn location

26.12 The inertia switch unit

26.16 The thermal cut-out switch reset button

apertures to remove the unit retaining nuts, then withdraw the unit.

5   Refitting is a direct reversal of the removal procedure, but check operation of all rear lights on completion.

20 Column control switches – removal and refitting

1   All column controlled switches (windscreen wiper/washer switch, lights/dipper/horn switch and indicator switch) are located in a similar manner on the upper steering column. To remove any or all of these switches proceed as follows.

2   Detach the battery earth lead.

3   Unscrew and remove the steering column upper and lower covers, the retaining screws being accessible from underneath. Note the respective screw lengths and positions for reassembly.

4   Detach the switch wiring concerned at the main loom connector.

5   Remove the switch retaining screws and withdraw the switch. The switches are not repairable and if defective, must therefore be renewed.

6   Refitting is a reversal of the removal procedure. Check the switch operation on completion.

21 Control panel switches and heater controls – removal and refitting

Switches

1   Pull the heater control knobs free from the controls. The knobs on our car were a tight fit, so a firm straight pull was required.

2   The panel can now be prised free to gain access to the switches and heater controls.

3   The switches are easily removed by pushing them through the panel. Detach the earth wire to the battery first however, then detach the switch wire.

4   The switches are not repairable and if defective must therefore be renewed.

Heater fan control knob

5   To change the heater fan control knob, detach the knob spindle clip as shown in Fig. 10.13. Then rotate the knob 180° to position the contact straps at right angles to the panel front (facing out). Remove the knob.

6   Refit in the reverse order.

22 Instrument panel and heater control panel – removal and refitting

1   Disconnect the battery earth cable.

2   Unscrew and remove the steering column lower cover, the retain-

ing screws being accessible from underneath.

3   Unscrew the fuse box retaining thumb screw and partially remove the box.

4   Detach the speedometer cable.

5   Prise the blanking plugs free from each endface of the dash surround and, using a socket and extension, unscrew the panel retaining bolts (photo).

6   Detach the three heater control knobs, pulling them free.

7   Detach the heater control panel.

8   Disconnect the junction blocks at the rear of the control panel.

9   Remove the three heater control panel retaining screws and the two strut securing bolts each side of the console panel as shown in Fig. 10.14. Lift and support the dash panel.

10   Detach the respective connectors at the rear of the instrument panel, noting their respective locations. Pivot the panel, allowing the dashboard to be removed.

11   The respective instrument panel layouts are shown in the accompanying illustration. Little can be done in the way of overhaul, renewal being the normal procedure.

12   Refitting is a direct reversal of the removal procedure. Ensure that the respective electrical connections are refitted correctly and securely.

23 Number plate light – bulb refitting

1   To renew the bulb, remove the two lens retaining screws (photos) and detach the lens. The bulb can now be extracted, (press and twist free) and renewed if defective.

2   Reassemble in the reverse order and check the operation.

24 Interior lights – bulb renewal, unit removal and refitting

1   Both the roof mounted interior lights simply clip into position and can be prised free using a small screwdriver. Take care not to damage the headlining however.

2   With the unit removed, the bulb can readily be renewed if necessary (photos).

3   To remove the unit completely, detach the battery earth cable, then detach the wires from the light unit concerned.

25 Horns – removal and refitting

The horns are fitted one below each headlight unit within the front panel. If either should fail, it cannot be repaired, but before renewing check the earthing, and also that it is receiving current when the horn button is pushed. If these are in order, unbolt and remove the horn/s for renewal (photo).

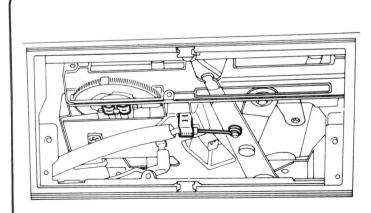

Fig. 10.13 Detach the spindle clip

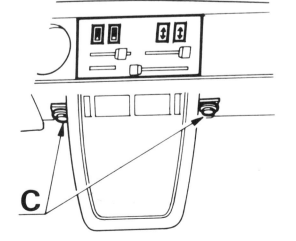

Fig. 10.14 The two strut bolts to be removed (C)

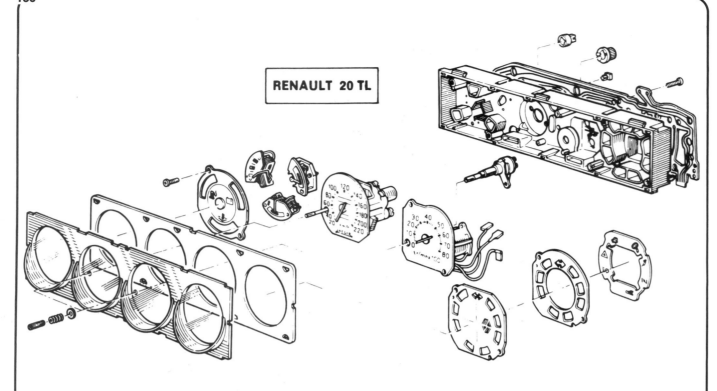

RENAULT 20 TL

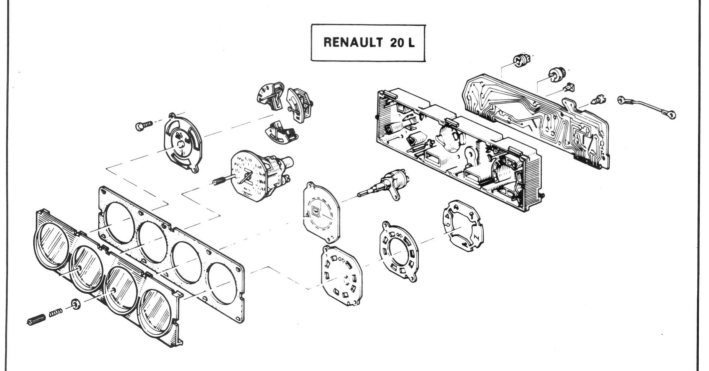

RENAULT 20 L

Fig. 10.15 The instrument panels of the TL and L models – the TS
is similar to the TL

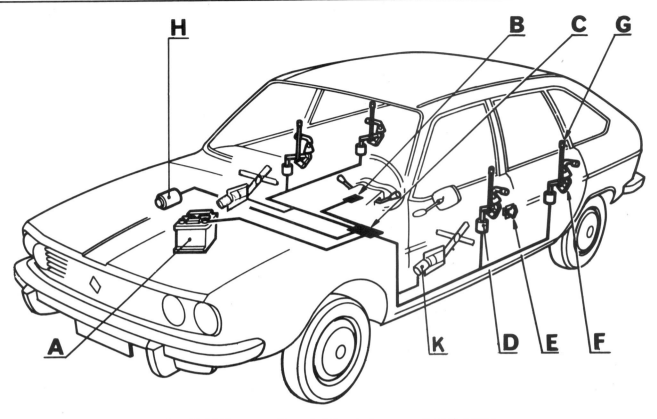

Fig. 10.16 The general layout of the electro-magnetic lock system

A	Battery	D	Actioner	F	Lock	H	Safety device
B	Main lighting switch	E	Changeover switch	G	Indicator	K	Window winder motor
C	Auxiliaries plate						

26 Electro-magnetic door locking system – general

1 The principle advantage of this system is that all four doors can be simultaneously locked from either outside (with the door lock key) or from inside (by means of the central control switch).

2 An inertia switch and thermal cut-out are incorporated into the electrical circuit of the system, and these act as safety devices which unlock all the doors automatically in the event of a collision at a speed in excess of 9 mph (15 km/h). This safety margin is necessary to safeguard against the doors being unlocked accidentally by a light impact, for example by another vehicle when parking.

3 Should an electrical fault occur, the doors can still be locked and unlocked in the normal manner, using the door lock key provided.

4 A general circuit layout is shown in Fig. 10.16 whilst the wiring diagram is shown in Fig. 10.17.

5 The mechanical door locks comprise three main interconnected components: The barrel, the changeover switch and the electro-magnetic actioner.

6 The front doors are each fitted with a barrel, the inner opening control lever pivoted eccentrically on a pin.

7 The swing lever for locking/unlocking is interconnected to the actioner by a rod. This is actuated by the front door lock barrels or the electro-magnetic actioner.

8 The changeover switch is a two-position type and one is fitted to each front door.

9 The electro-magnetic actioner (fitted to all doors) is regulated by the changeover switch location, dependent on the key position: Turn the key $\frac{1}{4}$ turn to the left to lock the doors, and a $\frac{1}{4}$ turn to the right to unlock them.

10 Each door contains a small lock position indicator capsule. When the doors are locked the red indicator should pop up into the capsule. On unlocking the doors it will drop below the capsule.

11 The electro-magnetic actioner in each door comprises two coils, between which is located a ferrite disc which slides up or down accordingly to each coil. When a coil is activated (by an electrical impulse from the switch) it causes the ferrite disc to thrust against the opposing coil. When it is against the upper coil, the system is locked. When it drops to the lower coil the system is unlocked. The control knob in each front door panel will also activate the system when rotated accordingly.

12 The inertia switch and thermal cut-out are located in front of the glovebox on the inside face of the bulkhead (photo).

13 In the event of an accident, the inertia switch is activated and automatically causes the doors to be unlocked.

14 The thermal cut-out is fitted to deactivate the electrical circuit after a given period (10 to 60 seconds) and should the inertia switch be activated when the doors are locked, the circuit is turned off automatically.

15 A reset button is provided on top of the switch to reset the system, should it be activated accidentally (photo 6.12).

16 Normally, the system is trouble free and requires no special maintenance. The following observations should be made to ensure correct usage, however.

(a) *Ensure that the doors are fully closed before locking. Slamming the door may unlock it*

(b) *Check that all of the red indicators are visible in each door when locked. Should one doorlock indicator fail to appear, check that the door is closed properly*

(c) *If the system should fail to operate at any time and the above cautional items have been adhered to, check the inertia switch reset button and the cut-out switch button (photo) and if necessary, reset them*

To reset the inertia switch, remove the front side panel trim by removing the retainer strip screws and folding back the trim to expose

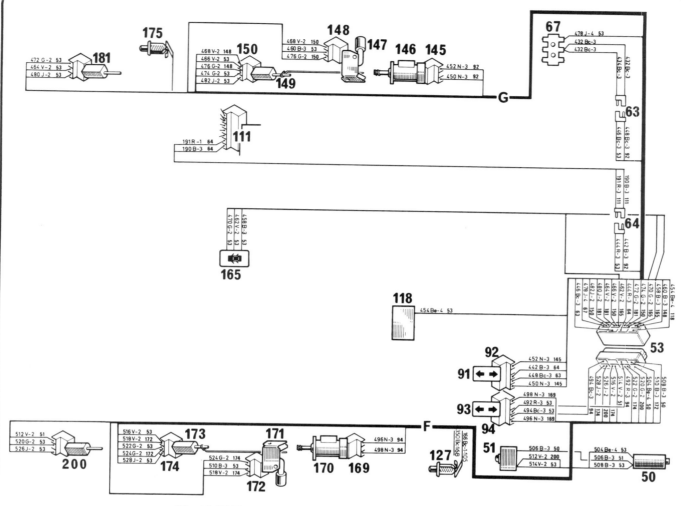

Fig. 10.17 The electro-magnetic door lock system wiring diagram

50   Inertia switch
51   Thermal cut-out
53   Electro-magnetic locks junction block
63   Earth plug and socket (LH and RH front doors changeover switch)
64   Plug and socket (LH and RH front door window winders)
67   Junction plate (earth)
91   LH front door window winder switch
92   Junction block (electro-magnetic locks harness to LH front door window winder switch)
93   RH front door window winder switch
94   Junction block (electro-magnetic locks harness to RH front door window winder switch)
111   Junction block (front harness to auxiliaries plate)
118   Junction plate (before switches)
127   RH front door pillar switch
145   Junction block (electro-magnetic door locks harness to LH front door electric window winder motor)
146   LH window winder motor

147   LH front door electro-magnetic lock changeover switch
148   Junction block (electro-magnetic locks harness to changeover switch)
149   LH front door servo lock
150   Junction block (electro-magnetic door locks harness to servo-lock)
165   Electro-magnetic door locks switch
169   Junction block (electro-magnetic door locks harness to RH front door electric window winder motor)
170   RH window winder motor
171   RH front door electro-magnetic lock changeover switch
172   Junction block (electro-magnetic door locks harness to changeover switch)
173   RH front door servo-lock
174   Junction block (electro-magnetic door locks harness to servo-lock)
175   LH rear door pillar switch
181   LH rear door servo-lock
200   RH rear door servo-lock

Wire colour code

Be	Beige	S	Pink
Bc	White	R	Red
B	Blue	V	Green
C	Clear	M	Maroon
G	Grey	Vi	Violet
J	Yellow	Or	Orange
N	Black		

Key to wire code

Example   S16V-2 53
S16   Wire code number
V   Wire colour
2   Wire gauge
53   Destination of wire

Wire gauge code

No	1	2	3	4	5	6
Wire diameter (mm)	$\frac{9}{10}$	$\frac{12}{10}$	$\frac{16}{10}$	$\frac{20}{10}$	$\frac{25}{10}$	$\frac{30}{10}$

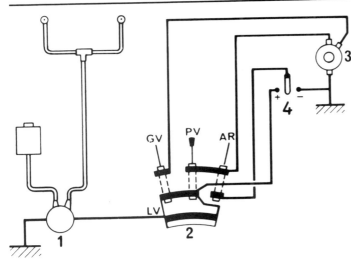

Fig. 10.18 Windscreen wiper motor/washer electrical circuit

1	Washer pump	AR Stop position
2	Switch	PV Slow speed position
3	Wiper motor	GV Fast speed position
4	Ignition controlled feed	LV Wash/wipe position

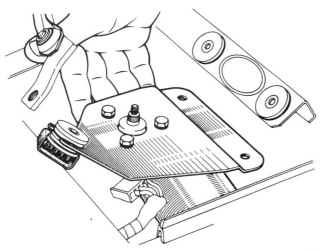

Fig. 10.19 Disconnect the motor retaining plate bolts and lift clear

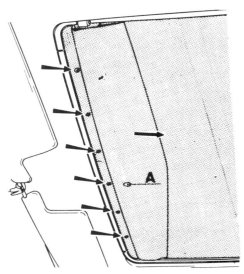

Fig. 10.20 Detach the blanking plug (A)

the inertia switch. Press the button in to reset the switch and refit the trim panel.

17 If the system fails to operate correctly, after checking the doors for full closure and resetting the appropriate switches, it is advisable to have the system checked out by your Renault dealer. Should you suspect the door locks of being defective, they can be inspected and removed if necessary, as described in Chapter 12.

27 Door lock switch – removal and refitting

The doorlock switch is clipped into the top face of the centre console and is easily removed by prising it free and disconnecting the wiring plug. Refitting is a reversal of the removal procedure, but check doorlock operation on completion.

28 Central console – removal and refitting

1 Disconnect the battery earth cable.
2 Unscrew the rearmost retaining screws on the bottom flange of the console rear face. Unscrew the retaining screw at the top forward section on each side of the console, then pull rearwards to free it.
3 To remove the console completely, disconnect the doorlock switch (see previous Section), the cigar lighter and also the radio wiring (if fitted).
4 Detach the gear lever rubber dust cover, swivel the console round and lift it clear over the lever.
5 Refitting is a reversal of the removal procedure, but check the circuits concerned for satisfactory operation on completion.

29 Windscreen wiper motor and mechanism – removal and refitting

1 Disconnect the battery earth lead.
2 Referring to Chapter 12, remove the scuttle panel.
3 Detach the wire connector to the wiper motor.
4 Unscrew and remove the three motor and mechanism plate mounting screws, and lift the assembly clear.
5 To detach the motor from the link mechanism, unscrew and remove the link retaining nut.
6 Little can be done to effect repairs on the wiper motor or linkage, renewal being the normal procedure. A competent auto-electrician may, however, be able to repair the motor. But check any repair costs against new replacements first – it may be more expensive (due to labour costs).
7 Refitting is a reversal of the removal procedure. Make sure the motor is securely retained and the respective linkage washers fitted. Lubricate the linkage pivot points during assembly.

30 Windscreen wiper arms and blades – removal and refitting

1 To remove the windscreen wiper blade, hinge the arm away from the screen, pivot the blade, and push the arm through as shown (photos) to detach.
2 The arm and blade assembly can be removed complete, by hinging back the nut cover and unscrewing the nut (photo).
3 Pull the arm from the wiper pivot shaft.
4 Refitting of the arm and blade is a reversal of the removal procedure. Fit the arm to its original position on the pivot shaft so it gives the required amount of arc over the screen when operated, and stops in the correct position when cancelled.

31 Sunroof electric motor – removal and refitting

1 Should the sunroof motor fail to operate, the roof can be opened or closed by removing the blanking plug from the point indicated in Fig. 10.20. This will expose the motor drive spindle. The spindle can then be turned as required, using a screwdriver.
2 To remove the motor, open the roof slightly to gain access to the retaining screws inside the front edge.
3 Detach the battery earth cable.

4   Unscrew and remove the motor embellisher retaining screws, move the motor to the rear and disconnect the wires at the connectors.

5   Unscrew and remove the guide bearing screws, and pull them rearwards.

6   Remove the motor retaining screws, lift the roof and withdraw the motor.

7   The motor driveshaft can be detached by drifting out the retaining pin, using a suitable punch.

8   If the motor is known to be defective, renew it, as it cannot be repaired. The drivebelt *can* be renewed, however. This is on the back of the motor as shown in Fig. 10.21.

9   Refitting is a reversal of the removal procedure, but ensure that the sunroof is located squarely with the front edge at equal distance from the front of the aperture on each side as shown in Fig. 10.23. Move the racks accordingly to adjust.

32 Heated rear window

The heating element of the rear tailgate window is integral with the glass, and as such should it become defective, cannot be repaired. Check the wiring circuit to the window for any faults using a circuit tester. If the circuit is operational, take the car to your Renault dealer or auto-electrician and have the element tested. They will be able to advise you regarding removal and renewal/refitting.

33 Heater motor – removal and refitting

1   Detach the battery earth lead.
2   Referring to Chapter 12, remove the scuttle crossmember.
3   Detach the feed wires to the fan motor.
4   Unscrew and remove the fan motor unit retaining screws and withdraw the unit.
5   Remove the clips and unseal the unit base to detach the upper and lower housing.
6   Remove the turbine retaining clip and pull the turbine from the spindle. See Fig. 10.22.
7   Unscrew and remove the motor retaining screws and extract the motor unit.
8   If defective, renew the motor and any other items in need of renewal.
9   Refitting is a reversal of the removal procedure, but be sure to locate the rubber cushion washers round the correct way and restick the aperture seal into the housing.

34 Heater control cable – removal and refitting

1   Detach the battery earth lead.
2   Remove the control panel fillet and unscrew the panel retaining screws on the dashboard.
3   Lift the panel assembly clear and detach the cable from it.
4   Loosen off the cable outer sleeve retaining clips at the panel and then at the valve end (against the bulkhead).
5   Disconnect the cable from the valve and withdraw the cable. See Fig. 10.24.
6   Refitting is a reversal of the removal procedure, but the cable must be set so that when the valve is shut, the adjuster knob at the panel is not quite at the end of the slide – see Fig. 10.25.

35 Heater valve – removal and refitting

1   To avoid draining the cooling and heater system, you will need some suitable clamps with which to compress the heater hoses as close as possible to the valve unit.
2   When the hoses are suitably clamped they can be detached from the valve unit, but allow for a small amount of spillage and wipe any antifreeze solution from the surrounding paintwork.
3   Detach the control cable.
4   Compress the valve unit retaining lugs and remove it from the bulkhead crossmember, as shown in Fig. 10.26.
5   Fit in the reverse sequence. When fitted, the cable should allow the control knob a small clearance from the end of the slide as shown

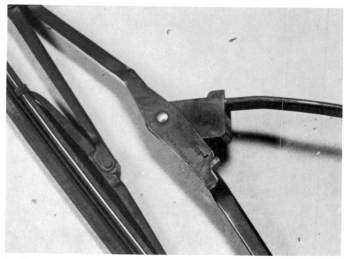
30.1a Hinge wiper arm away from screen and ...

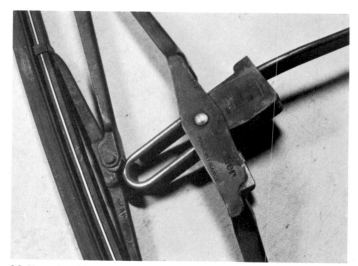
30.1b ... pivot blade and push to detach

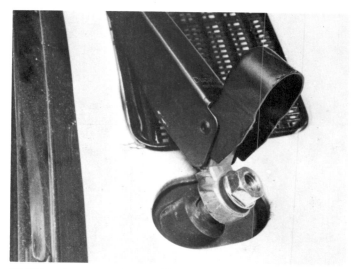
30.2 The wiper arm nut exposed for removal

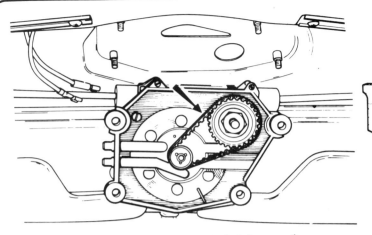

Fig. 10.21 The sunroof motor drivebelt (arrowed)

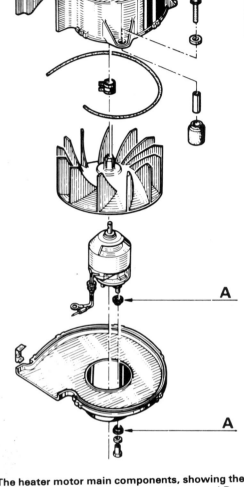

Fig. 10.22 The heater motor main components, showing the rubber cushion washer positions (A) – do not forget seal B on reassembly

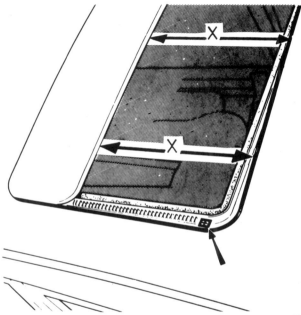

Fig. 10.23 Check distances X and adjust racks to equalise if necessary

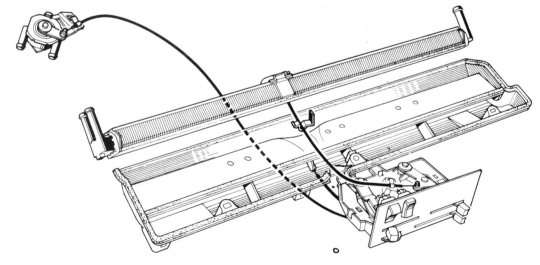

Fig. 10.24 The heater control cable assembly

in Fig. 10.25. When the hoses are reconnected and the clamps released, top-up the cooling system and bleed it as given in Chapter 2. Then check for any signs of leaks.

36 Heater matrix – removal and refitting

1   Referring to Chapter 12, remove the scuttle crossmember.
2   Close the heater hot water valve and fit suitable clamps to compress the heater return hose after the bleed screw, the matrix inlet hose and outlet hose. When the clamps are securely in position and the hoses compressed, disconnect the respective hoses from the matrix.
3   Remove the matrix bulkhead and take care when unsticking the seals.
4   Detach the air flap control cable.
5   Unscrew the retaining bolts and withdraw the matrix.
6   Refitting is a reversal of the removal procedure, but when reconnecting the cable, adjust it so that the travel of the flap and control knob are equal.
7   Top-up and bleed the cooling system as given in Chapter 2. Check for leaks around the disturbed hoses.

37 Heater ventilators – removal and refitting

Side ventilators
1   Referring to Section 22 of this Chapter, remove the dashboard. Unscrew the ventilator retaining nuts and remove it.
2   Refitting is a reverse of the removal procedure.

Centre ventilators
3   Remove the dashpanel (see Section 22 of this Chapter). Unscrew and remove the ventilator retaining nuts to remove the ventilator.
4   Refit in the reverse sequence.

38 Heater air entry flap cable – removal and refitting

1   Detach the battery earth lead.
2   Referring to Chapter 12, remove the scuttle grille panel.
3   Carefully, free the heater matrix bulkhead, taking care when unsticking the seals.
4   Loosen the air flap block cable lock screw then partially withdraw

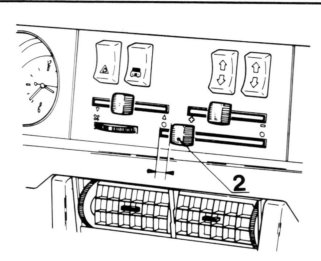

Fig. 10.25 Check when valve is shut that clearance exists between end of slide panel and knob (2)

Fig. 10.27 Cable to control rod connection

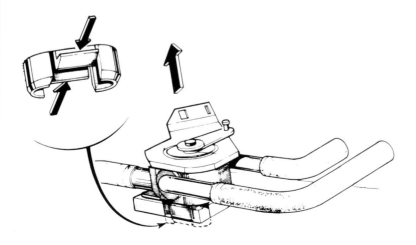

Fig. 10.26 Compress the lugs to remove unit

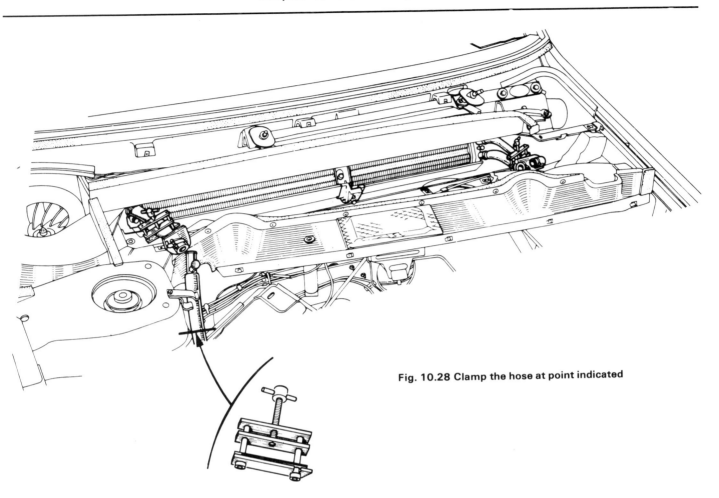

Fig. 10.28 Clamp the hose at point indicated

the heater matrix, but do not disconnect the hoses.

5   Withdraw the control panel fillet and remove the panel plastic cover.

6   Detach the cable at the control rod end as shown in Fig. 10.27. Unclip the outer sleeve retainers from the panel and scuttle upper crossmember, and remove the cable with sleeve.

7   Fit in the reverse order. Adjust the control lever in the closed position, but with a gap of 2 mm ($\frac{5}{64}$ in) relative to the slide. In this position, close the flap and tighten the cable retaining screw.

39 Heater fan control knob – removal and refitting

1   Detach the battery earth cable.

2   Detach the control panel fillet, then remove the three control panel retaining screws to the dashpanel. Lift the panel upwards for access as shown in Fig. 10.13. Detach the control knob spindle clip, then rotate the knob 180° to position the contact strips at right angles to the panel front face, pointing outwards. Detach the knob.

3   Refit in the reverse order.

40 Fault diagnosis – electrical system

Symptom	Reason/s
Starter fails to turn engine	Battery discharged
	Battery defective internally
	Battery terminal leads loose or earth lead not securely attached to body
	Loose or broken connections in starter motor circuit
	Starter motor solenoid faulty
	Starter motor pinion jammed in mesh with flywheel gear ring
	Starter brushes badly worn, sticking, or brush wires loose
	Commutator dirty, worn or burnt
	Starter motor armature faulty
	Field coils earthed
	Gear selector lever not engaged in 'P' or 'N' (automatic transmission)
Starter turns engine very slowly	Battery in discharged condition
	Starter brushes badly worn, sticking or brush wires loose
	Loose wires in starter motor circuit

Symptom	Reason/s
Starter spins but does not turn engine	Starter motor pinion fork sticking Pinion or flywheel gear teeth broken or worn Battery discharged
Starter motor noisy or excessively rough engagement	Pinion or flywheel gear teeth broken or worn Starter motor retaining bolts loose
Battery will not hold charge for more than a few days	Battery defective internally Electrolyte level too low or electrolyte too weak due to leakage Plate separators no longer fully effective Battery plates severely sulphated Drivebelt slipping Battery terminal connections loose or corroded Alternator not charging Short in lighting circuit causing continual battery drain Regulator unit nor working correctly
Ignition light fails to go out, battery runs flat in a few days	Drivebelt loose and slipping or broken Alternator brushes worn, sticking, broken or dirty Alternator brush springs weak or broken Internal fault in alternator

Failure of individual electrical equipment to function correctly is dealt with alphabetically, item-by-item, under the headings listed below

Horn/s

Horn operates all the time	Horn push either earthed or stuck down Horn cable to horn push earthed
Horn fails to operate	Cable or cable connection loose, broken or disconnected Horn has an internal fault
Horn emits intermittent or unsatisfactory noise	Cable connections loose

Lights

Lights do not come on	If engine not running, battery discharged Wire connections loose, disconnected or broken Light switch shorting or otherwise faulty
Lights come on but fade out	If engine not running battery discharged Light bulb filament burnt out or bulbs broken Wire connections loose, disconnected or broken Light switch shorting or otherwise faulty
Lights work erratically — flashing on and off, especially over bumps	Battery terminals or earth connection loose Lights not earthing properly Contacts in light switch faulty

Wipers

Wiper motor fails to work	Blown fuse Wire connections loose, disconnected or broken Brushes badly worn Armature worn or faulty Field coils faulty
Wiper motor works very slowly and takes excessive current	Commutator dirty, grease or burnt Armature bearings dirty or unaligned Armature badly worn or faulty
Wiper motor works slowly and takes little current	Brushes badly worn Commutator dirty, greasy or burnt Armature badly worn or faulty
Wiper motor works but wiper blades remain static	Wiper motor gearbox parts badly worn Faulty linkage

Fig. 10.29 Key to wiring diagram – TL models

1 LH sidelight/front indicator
2 LH headlight
3 LH headlight connector
4 LH horn
5 RH horn
6 RH headlight
8 RH sidelight/front indicator
9 Windscreen washer electric pump
10 Ignition coil
12 Distributor
13 Windscreen washer pump earth (ground)
14 RH headlight earth (ground)
21 Oil pressure switch
22 Water temperature switch
24 Engine earth (ground)
25 Starter motor
26 Alternator
27 LH headlight earth (ground)
29 Alternator earth (ground)
30 Regulator
33 LH front brake
34 Plug and socket (air conditioning magnetic clutch)
35 Reversing lights switch
39 Battery
41 Junction block (front harness to engine)
42 Plug and socket (air conditioning magnetic clutch)
44 RH front brake
45 Brake pad wear warning light plug and socket
50 Inertia switch
51 Thermal cut-out
53 Junction block – electro-magnetic lock harness
55 GMV heater fan motor
56 Windscreen wiper motor/cigar lighter earth (ground)
58 Brake pressure drop indicator
60 Windscreen wiper plate
61 Junction block (engine front harness to windscreen wiper)
63 Changeover switch earth (ground) plug and socket for LH and RH front doors
64 Plug and socket (LH and RH front door window winder)
67 Earth (ground) junction plate
69 Plug and socket lighting switch
74 Instrument panel
75 Instrument panel – connector 1
76 Instrument panel – connector 2
77 Instrument panel – connector 3
78 Instrument panel – connector 4
81 Hazard warning lights system switch
82 Junction block (front harness to Hazard warning lights switch)
85 Rear screen demister switch
86 Junction block (front harness to rear screen demister switch)
90 Heater fan rheostat
91 LH front door window winder switch
92 Junction block – electro-magnetic locks harness to LH front door window winder switch
93 RH front door window winder switch
94 Junction block – electro-magnetic locks harness to RH front door window winder switch
97 Air conditioning harness plug and socket
99 Heater rheostat light
100 Plug and socket heater rheostat light
105 LH front door pillar switch
106 Auxiliaries plate
107 Feed to auxiliaries plate
108 Junction block (front harness to auxiliaries plate)
110 Junction block (front harness to auxiliaries plate)
111 Junction block (front harness to auxiliaries plate)
112 Junction block (front harness to auxiliaries plate)
113 Junction block (front harness to auxiliaries plate)
117 Stoplight switch
118 Junction plate before ignition switch
119 Junction block (front harness to ignition/starter switch)
120 Ignition/starter switch
123 Plug and socket for glove compartment light
124 Glove compartment light
125 Plug and socket for sunroof
127 RH front door pillar switch
130 Junction block (front harness to indicators switch)
131 Direction indicators switch
132 Junction block (front harness to windscreen wiper switch)
133 Windscreen wiper switch
135 Plug and socket for interior light
137 Junction block (front harness to bridge harness)
138 Plug and socket rear interior light and map reading light
139 Cigar lighter
140 Plug and socket for cigar lighter light
141 Plug and socket for cigar lighter light
142 Ashtray illumination
145 Junction block – electro-magnetic door lock harness to LH front door electric window
146 LH window winder motor
147 LH front door electro-magnetic door lock changeover switch
148 Junction block – electro-magnetic lock harness to changeover switch
149 LH front door servo lock
150 Junction block – electro-magnetic door servo lock harness to servo lock
155 Junction block – front harness to indicator harness
156 Direction indicators switch
157 Plug and socket – fuel gauge tank unit to brake pressure drop indicator (ICP)
161 Junction block – front harness to rear harness
162 Handbrake
165 Electro-magnetic door locks switch
168 Map reading light
169 Junction block – electro-magnetic door lock harness to RH door window winder motor
170 RH window winder motor
171 RH front door electro-magnetic door lock changeover switch
172 Junction block – electro-magnetic lock harness to changeover switch
173 RH front door servo lock
174 Junction block – electro-magnetic door servo lock harness to servo lock
175 LH rear door pillar switch (not connected)
177 Rear interior light (not connected)
179 RH rear door pillar switch (not connected)
181 LH rear door servo lock
183 Junction block – rear harness to LH rear light assembly
184 Plug and socket – RH rear indicator
185 Plug and socket – (fuel gauge tank unit)
191 Luggage compartment light
192 Earth (ground)
193 Rear screen demister switch
194 Rear screen demister
196 Fuel gauge (tank)
198 Junction block – rear harness to RH rear light assembly
200 RH rear door servo lock
201 LH rear light assemblies
202 Number plate light
203 RH rear light assemblies
204 LH rear lights earth (ground)
205 RH rear lights earth (ground)

Not all components are fitted to all models

Key to wire code

Example   S16V-2 53
S16   Wire code number
V   Wire colour
2   Wire gauge
53   Destination of wire

Colour code

Be Beige	J Yellow	V Green
Bc White	N Black	M Maroon
C Blue	S Pink	Vi Violet
C Clear	R Red	Or Orange
G Grey		

Wire gauge code

No	1	2	3	4	5	6
Wire diameter (mm)	9/10	12/10 10/10	19/10 10/10	20/10 10/10	25/10 10/10	30/10 10/10

Harness identification

A Engine front
B Rear
C Engine (manual anual transmission)
D Rear interior light
E Bridge
F Electro-magnetic door lock
G Electro-magnetic door lock
H Lighting switch
P Starter negative
Q Starter positive
M Indicators
N Charge

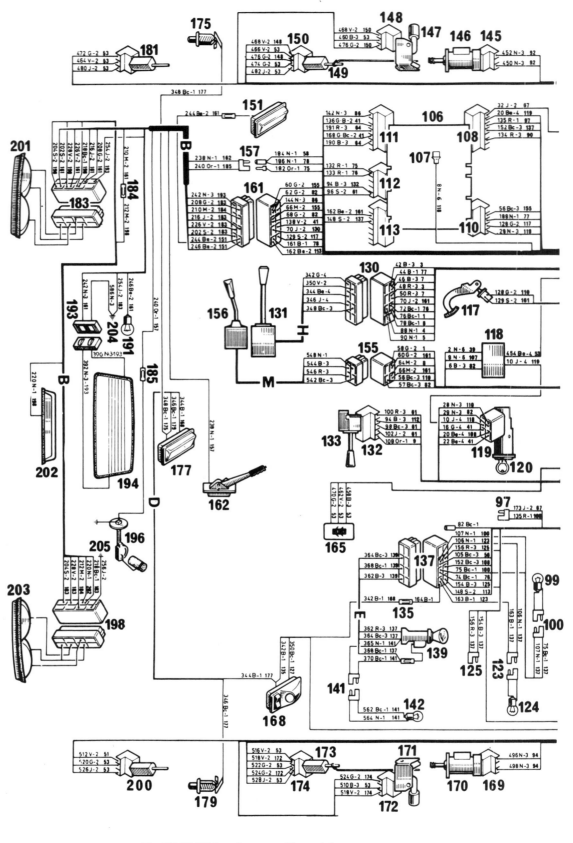

Fig. 10.29 Wiring diagram – TL models

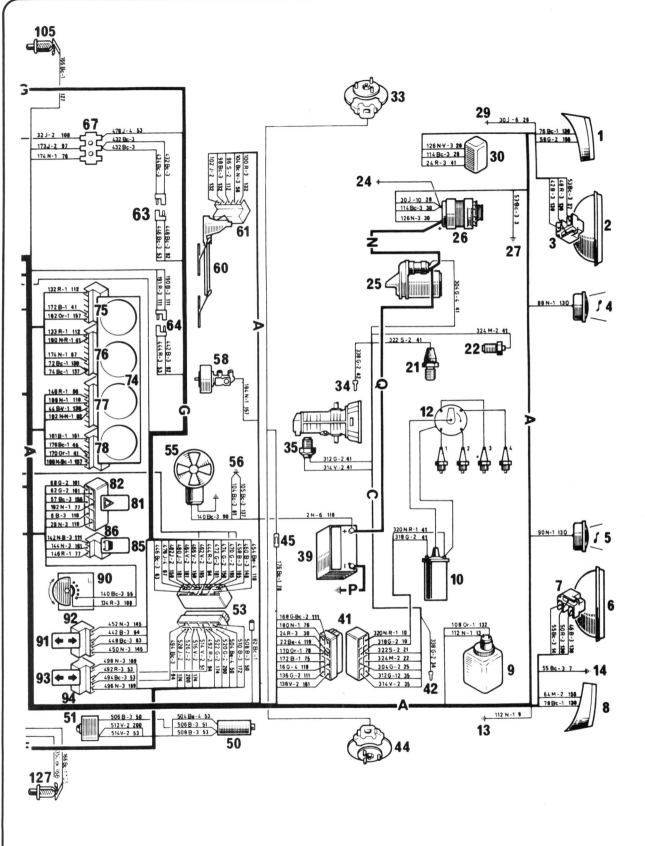

Fig. 10.29 Wiring diagram – TL models continued

Fig. 10.30 Key to wiring diagram – TS models

1   LH front sidelight/direction indicator
2   RH front sidelight/direction indicator
7   LH headlight main/dipped beam
8   RH headlight main/dipped beam
9   LH horn
10 RH horn
11 Regulator
12 Alternator
13 Earth LH
14 Earth RH
15 Starter motor
16 Battery
17 Cooling fan motor
18 Ignition coil
19 Distributor
20 Electric windscreen washer pump
21 Oil pressure switch
22 Radiator thermal switch
24 LH front brake
25 RH front brake
26 Windscreen wiper plate
27 Brake master cylinder
28 Heating/ventilating fan motor
30 Connector No 1 – instrument panel
31 Connector No 2 – instrument panel
32 Connector No 3 – instrument panel
33 Connector No 4 – instrument panel
34 Hazard warning lights switch
35 Rear screen demister switch
36 Heating/ventilating fan motor rheostat
37 LH front window winder switch
38 RH front window winder switch
40 LH front door pillar switch
41 RH front door pillar switch
42 LH front window winder
43 RH front window winder
44 Accessories plate (fusebox)
45 Junction block (front harness and accessories plate)
46 Junction block (front harness and accessories plate)
47 Junction block (front harness and accessories plate)
48 Junction block (front harness and accessories plate)
49 Junction block (front harness and accessories plate)
52 Stoplights switch
53 Anti-theft ignition/starter switch
54 Heater controls illumination
55 Glove compartment light
56 Cigar lighter
58 Windscreen wiper/washer switch
59 Lighting switch
60 Direction indicators switch
61 Feed wire junction before switch
62 LH interior light
63 RH interior light
64 Handbrake 'ON' warning light switch
65 Tank unit fuel gauge
66 Rear screen demister
67 Luggage compartment light
68 LH rear light
69 RH rear light
70 Number plate light
72 Reversing lights switch
77 Wire junction – diagnostic socket
80 Junction block (front harness and engine harness)
81 Junction block (front and rear harnesses)
82 Junction block (front harness and console harness)
86 Junction block (time relay harness)
91 Wire junction (brake pad wear warning light)
92 Wire junction (optional air conditioning)
97 Body earth
99 Dashboard earth
106 Rear foglights switch
110 Engine cooling fan motor relay
114 Windscreen wiper time switch
116 Junction with rear foglights harness
131 Electro-magnetic locks cut-out
132 Electro-magnetic locks inertia switch
133 LH front door lock changeover switch
134 RH front door lock changeover switch
135 LH front door electro-magnetic lock solenoid
136 RH front door electro-magnetic lock solenoid
137 LH rear door electro-magnetic lock solenoid
138 RH rear door electro-magnetic lock solenoid
140 Junction block – electro-magnetic locks
142 Wire junction – window winder harness
144 Wire junction – interior light harness
146 Thermal switch
148 Tailgate fixed contact
150 LH front door loudspeaker
151 RH front door loudspeaker
152 Electro-magnetic door locks switch
153 Car radio loudspeaker wires
158 Automatic transmission selector illumination
194 Junction block (cooling system harness)
195 Idle cut-out

Not all components are fitted to all models

Harness identification

A   Engine front
B   Rear
K   Starter
L   Interior light – door pillar switches
P   Electro-magnetic door locks
R   Engine
T   Console

Colour code

Be	Beige	S	Pink
Bc	White	R	Red
B	Blue	V	Green
C	Clear	M	Maroon
G	Grey	Vi	Violet
J	Yellow	Or	Orange
N	Black		

Key to wire code

Example   S16V-2 53
S16   Wire code number
V   Wire colour
2   Wire gauge
53   Destination of wire

Wire gauge code

No	1	2	3	4	5	6
Wire diameter (mm)	$\frac{9}{10}$	$\frac{12}{10}$	$\frac{16}{10}$	$\frac{20}{10}$	$\frac{25}{10}$	$\frac{30}{10}$

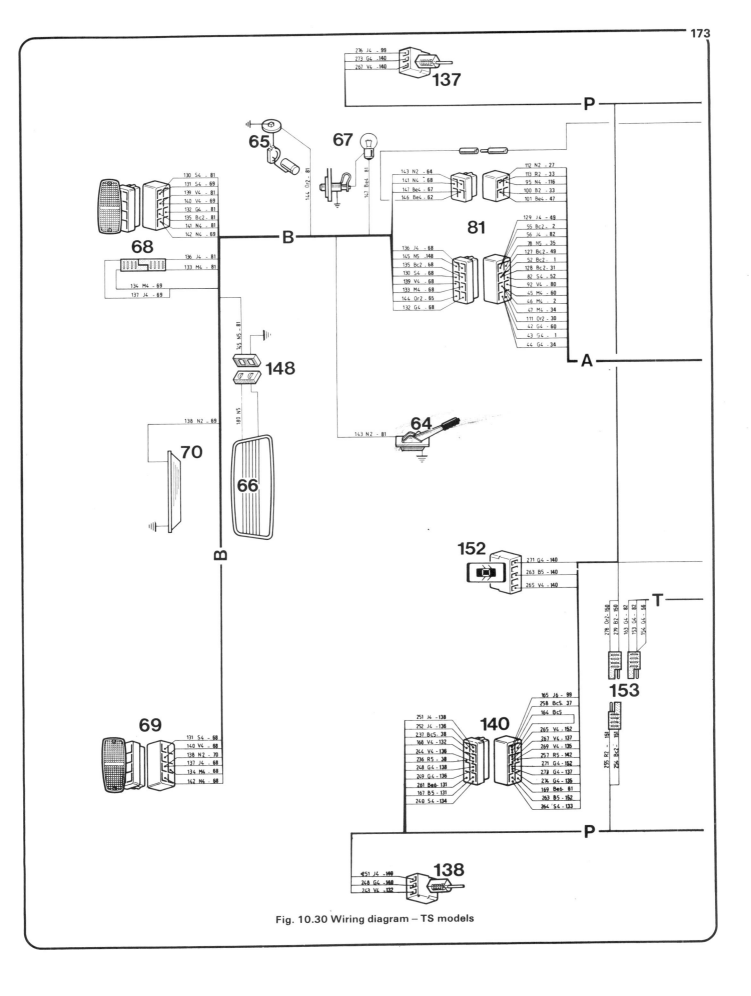

Fig. 10.30 Wiring diagram – TS models

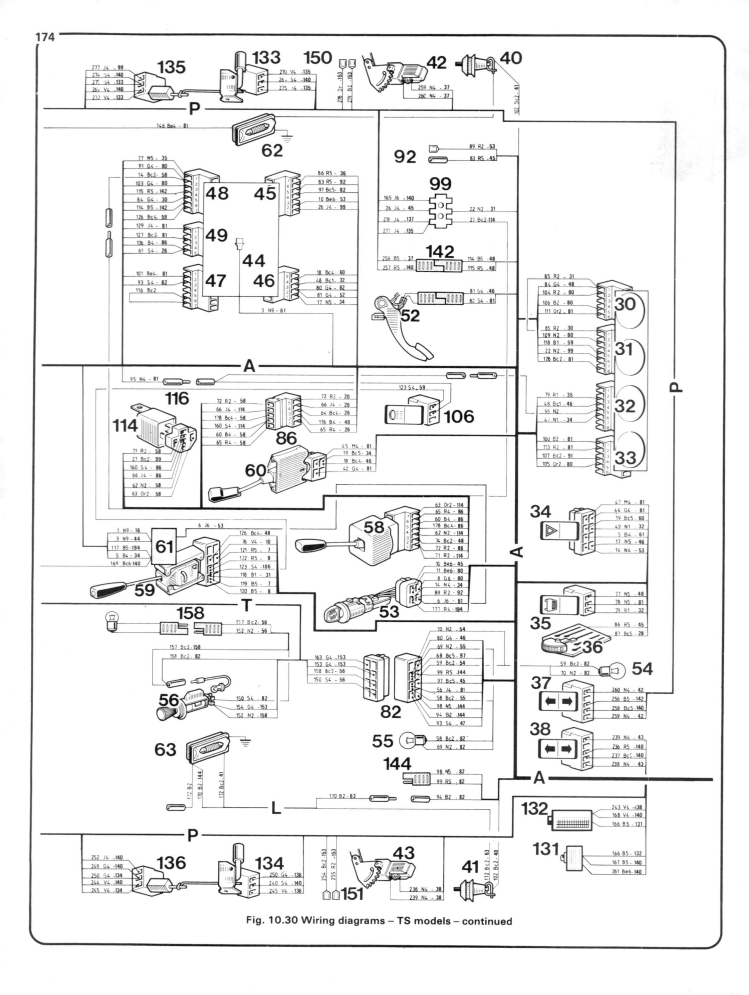

Fig. 10.30 Wiring diagrams – TS models – continued

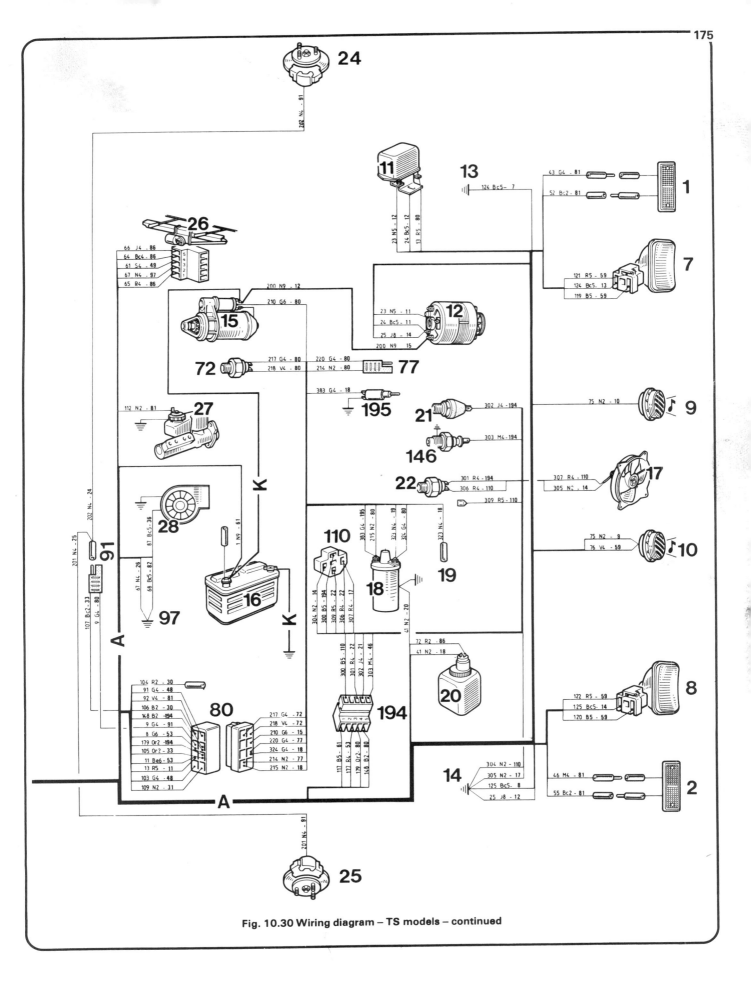

Fig. 10.30 Wiring diagram – TS models – continued

Chapter 11 Suspension and steering

For modifications, and information applicable to later models, see Supplement at end of manual

Contents

Specifications

Suspension type

.... Independent, front and rear. Double wishbone at the front, three element system at the rear. Anti-roll bar at the front and rear. Double acting shock absorbers

Anti-roll bar diameters
Front:
    TL models .... 20·5 mm (0·807 in)
    TS models .... 22·5 mm (0·885 in)
Rear:
    TL models .... 14·0 mm (0·551 in)
    TS models .... 19·0 mm (0·748 in)

Steering type

.... Rack and pinion (power assisted on TS models and on certain TL models)

Front axle and steering geometry
Camber angle .... 0° ± 30′

	Laden	Unladen
Castor angle:		
Standard steering	2° 30′ ± 30′	2° ± 30′
Power steering	5° ± 30′	4° 30′ ± 30′

Kingpin inclination .... Equal within 1°
Toe-out .... 0 to + 3 mm (0 to + 0·125 in)
Steering reduction ratio:
    TL models .... 22·2 : 1
    TS models .... 17·8 : 1

Rear axle
Camber angle .... 0° ± 1°
Parallelism – rear wheels .... 0 ± 1 mm (0 ± 0·039 in)

Lubricants
Power steering capacity .... 1·9 pints (1·1 litre)
Steering box .... Molykote BR2 or equivalent

Torque wrench settings
Front suspension

	lbf ft	Nm
Front shock absorber:		
Top nut	11	15
Bottom nut	45	60

	lbf ft	Nm
Upper suspension arm:		
Pivot bolt	70	95
Balljoint nut	36	50
Lower suspension arm:		
Pivot bolt	94	130
Balljoint nut	36	50
Castor tie-rod nut to upper wishbone	25	35
Shock absorber:		
Lower pivot pin	57	80
Lower locknut	45	60
Anti-roll bar	11	15
Stub axle nut:		
TL models	120	163
TS models	158	214
Wheel nuts	45 to 57	60 to 80
Rear suspension		
Lateral arm pivot pin nuts	25	35
Rear wheel stub axle nut	25	35
Shock absorber:		
Upper nut	55	70
Lower nut	75	100
Lower mounting bolts	75	100
Transverse arm:		
Outer pivot bolt	65	90
Inner pivot bolt	55	70
Anti-roll bar retaining bolts	15	20
Steering		
Steering arm:		
Pivot bolt	25	35
Balljoint nut	25	35
Adjuster locknut	29	40
Steering rack to crossmember bolts	20 to 30	30 to 40
Hub bearing closure plate bolts	15 to 20	20 to 25

1 General description and maintenance

1 .The suspension system on all four wheels is independent having double wishbones at the front with coil springs and a 'three element' type layout at the rear. This comprises one transverse and one, lateral swing arm to each side, together with a vertical coil spring and shock absorber.

2 An anti-roll bar is fitted front and rear; the shock absorbers are of the telescopic double-acting type.

3 Rack and pinion steering gear is employed and is located at the rear of the engine above the transmission housing. In this position it is unlikely to sustain any damage in the event of front end collision (although should you be unlucky enough to be so involved it should be checked before using the car).

4 A jointed type of steering column is used and an anti-theft steering lock incorporated into the ignition switch. Power assisted steering is available as an optional extra and this comprises of three main components: the hydraulic pump (belt driven from the crankshaft), the rotary valve unit (attached to the steering box at the lower end of the column) and the double-acting ram, mounted in line with the box.

5 Some steering and suspension tasks require the use of special tools and it is therefore suggested that you read through the relevant Section concerned, prior to undertaking any jobs. For the same reason, steering and suspension adjustments should be entrusted to your Renault dealer who has the necessary specialised tools and knowledge required to achieve the necessary accuracy.

6 For maximum safety combined with vehicle efficiency, the steering and suspension systems should be checked regularly during the normal maintenance procedures. Although there are no grease nipples to the steering and suspension joints, it does not mean they can be completely ignored. The following items should be checked occasionally, and definitely prior to having your annual government vehicle test.

7 Inspect the outside of the shock absorbers for leakage and check their operation by pressing down the front end of the car and releasing it. It should return to normal position without any repeated 'bouncing' action.

8 With the car parked on level ground, check that it sits level from left to right, and does not appear to be drooping at one end, particularly down at the back.

9 Examine all the rubber bushes of the suspension arms. The rubber should be firm, not softened by oil or cracked by weathering. The pin pivotted in the bush should be held central, and not able to make metal to metal contact (photo).

10 Check the outside of the springs. If rusting, they should be sprayed with oil.

11 Check the tightness of all nuts, particularly those holding the front suspension balljoints and the shock absorbers to their fixings.

12 Grip the top of each wheel in turn and rock vigorously. Any looseness in the bearings or the suspension can be felt, as can failed rubber bushes giving metal to metal contact sound.

13 Freewheel slowly with the engine switched off, and 'listen for unusual noises.

14 The rubber boots of the balljoints that exclude dirt and water should be inspected to ensure they are properly in position and not torn. If dirt or water gets into such a joint, it is ruined within a few hundred miles. The joint should be removed and a new boot fitted without delay.

15 Check the steering for wear. An assistant should wiggle the steering to and fro, just hard enough to make the front wheels move. Watch the balljoints. There should be no visible free movement. Then grasp a front wheel with the hands at three and nine o'clock on the wheel. Work at the wheel hard to twist it. The rocking should shift the steering wheel but no lost motion should be felt.

16 Where power assisted steering is fitted, check the hoses and associate fittings for any signs of leakage.

17 Check the steering rack to tie-rod gaiters are in good condition and securely located.

2 Front shock absorbers and coil springs – removal and refitting

1 Raise the front of the vehicle and support with axle stands or blocks. Remove the front roadwheel/s.

2 You will now need a suitable coil spring compressor similar to that shown in Fig. 11.3. The tool shown is the official Renault tool number Sus 596, which should be used if available. **Do not** use makeshift methods – serious injury could result.

3 Compress the spring sufficiently to permit the spring to be lifted clear of the shock absorber cup.

4 Detach the shock absorber at its top mounting position in the

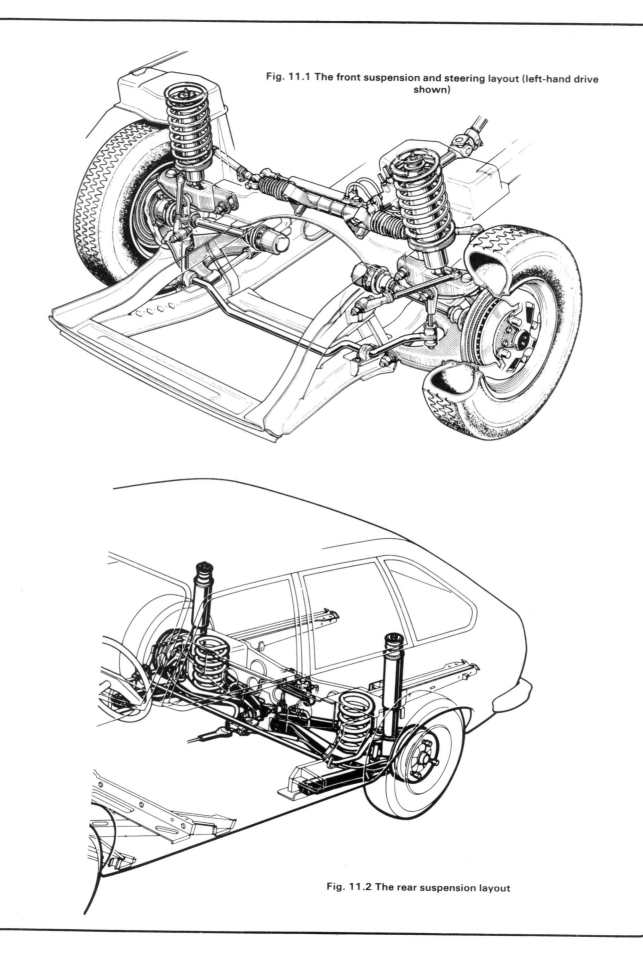

Fig. 11.1 The front suspension and steering layout (left-hand drive shown)

Fig. 11.2 The rear suspension layout

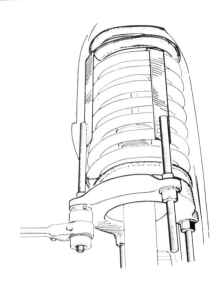

Fig. 11.3 Coil spring compressor (typical) in position

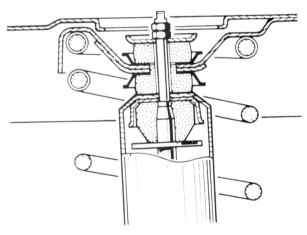

Fig. 11.4 The front shock absorber upper mounting

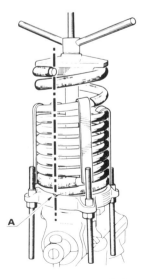

Fig. 11.5 Locate the spring with small diameter in cup and align end of top coil with the notch in the cup (A)

engine compartment inner wing panel. Loosen and remove the top locking nut and then the retaining nut; see Fig. 11.4.

5   At the bottom of the shock absorber, hold firm with a suitable wrench and unscrew and remove the lower retaining nut.

6   Unscrew the shock absorber to detach it complete with the compressed spring assembly.

7   Unscrew the spring compressor bolts in a cautious and progressive manner so the spring is not allowed suddenly to become released when under compression.

8   It is not possible to repair the shock absorber or coil spring if either are worn or defective and they must therefore be renewed. If the shock absorber shows any signs of fluid leakage and/or is easy to compress, then it must be renewed. Both items are best checked by comparing them with new ones if possible.

9   Refitting is a reversal of the removal procedure. When inserting the spring into position, locate its upper end into the top thrust plate and ensure that the cups are fitted in the correct manner as shown in Fig. 11.5.

10   When the shock absorber and spring assembly are reinstalled, tighten the locknut to the specified torque whilst retaining the shock absorber with a wrench at the bottom.

3   Front suspension upper arm – removal and refitting

1   Raise the front of the vehicle so that both front wheels are clear of the ground and support with axle stands or blocks to make secure. Remove the roadwheel from the side to be worked on.

2   Loosen the shock absorber lower mounting locknut.

3   Remove the castor tie-rod retaining nut from the suspension arm and detach the rod.

4   Unscrew and remove the shock absorber lower mounting pivot bolt.

5   Unscrew and remove the upper arm balljoint retaining nut and use a balljoint separator to detach the joint (photo).

6   Unscrew and remove the suspension arm pivot bolt, lifting it sufficiently clear to allow the shock absorber lower mounting to be unscrewed and detached.

7   Remove the suspension arm. Refer to Section 6 for bush renewal.

8   Refitting is a reversal of the removal procedure, but do not tighten the respective retaining nuts and bolts fully until the fitting is complete. Then lower the car and tighten the respective fastenings to their specified torque settings.

4   Suspension balljoints – removal and refitting

1   The suspension balljoints are sealed for life and therefore need renewal rather than servicing if defective. However, it may be possible to purchase a new rubber bellows kit if one should fail but the ball remains in good condition. Follow the preceding paragraphs for balljoint removal but go only so far as to enable the old bellows to be cut off and the new one fitted. Repack the balljoint with high melting point grease and take care fitting the circlip. Your own conclusions must be drawn as to its efficiency once everything is dismantled!

2   *Top balljoints:* Jack up the car and place on axle stands. Fit the spacer leg described in Section 7. Turn the steering to left lock when working on a right-hand balljoint and vice versa. Unscrew the balljoint nut.

3   Using a patent balljoint remover, split the top balljoint. If necessary, to free the balljoint from the upright finally, obtain a small wooden wedge. With a tyre lever or strong screwdriver, lever on the wedge under the upper suspension arm on top of the driveshaft outer joint. The balljoint should then be free.

4   The original balljoints are rivetted onto the wishbones, as shown in Fig. 11.7. These rivets will have to be drilled out. Clean up the rivet heads with a wire brush and file a good flat onto their heads. Use an electric drill if possible. Be patient and very careful. It is not a 'rush' job. Do not attempt to drill from below and try not to drill into the wishbone itself. If done carefully it is not necessary to remove the wishbone from the vehicle.

5   When puchasing new balljoints make sure that the correct fixing setscrews and nuts, to replace the rivets, are supplied. This is important.

6   Refit the new balljoint into its correct seating and place the setscrews from below up through the balljoint and then wishbone. Tighten

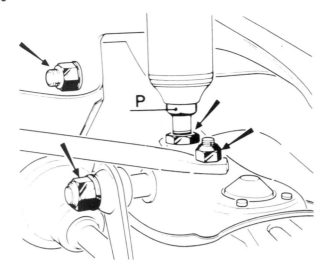

Fig. 11.6 Upper suspension arm removal – detach items arrowed; support shock absorber at P when unscrewing locknut

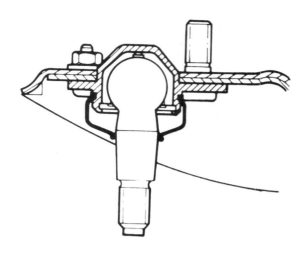

Fig. 11.7 The balljoint location showing rivet and retaining nut positions

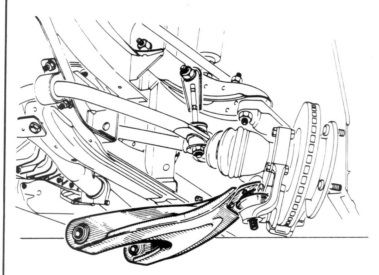

Fig. 11.8 Remove the lower suspension arm

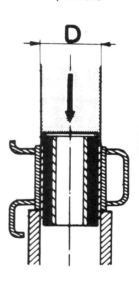

Fig. 11.9 Press the bush out using a tube of the correct diameter (D)

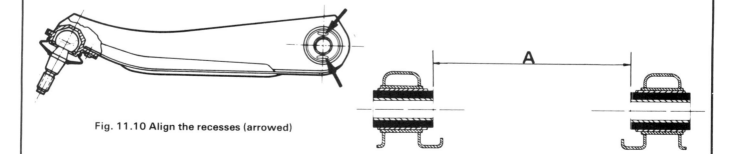

Fig. 11.10 Align the recesses (arrowed)

Fig. 11.11 Check the clearance between the lower wishbone bushes

A = 187 mm (7.362 in) – R1271 or 151 mm (5.945 in) – R1272

the nyloc nuts firmly.

7 Refit all the parts in an opposite procedure to their removal. Be sure that the balljoints are finally tight onto the upright when the car is resting on all four wheels.

8 It is advisable to have the car re-tracked if a balljoint is refitted. Have this done by a Renault agent.

9 *Lower balljoints:* The suspension arm must be removed for renewal. This is described in Section 5. The balljoint refitting procedure is otherwise the same as that for the upper joint as described in paragraphs 4 to 7.

---

5 Front suspension lower arm – removal and refitting

1 Before proceding to remove either or both of the front suspension lower arms, the following should be noted:

   (a) *The right-hand arm differs from that of the left and should therefore be kept separate if both are removed*

   (b) *Do not remove the chassis crossmember located between the front side-members*

2 Raise the front of the vehicle and make secure with axle stands or blocks. Remove the roadwheel on the side concerned.

3 Unscrew the suspension arm lower balljoint retaining nut and detach the joint using a suitable separator.

4 Unscrew and remove the lower arm pivot bolt and remove the lower suspension arm as shown in Fig. 11.8. Refer to Section 6 for bush renewal.

5 When refitting, locate the balljoint and screw the nut hand tight to retain.

6 Smear the pivot bolt with grease and reassemble. Do not tighten fully at this stage.

7 Lower the vehicle, then tighten the pivot bolt and balljoint nut to their specified torque wrench settings.

---

6 Front suspension arm bushes – renewal

1 The removal and refitting of the suspension arm bushes necessitates removal of the upper and/or lower wishbone arm as applicable (refer to Section 3 or 5 accordingly).

The resilient (rebound) bush – lower wishbone

2 With the arm removed, each bush must be removed and a new one fitted, one at a time. This is necessary to enable the symmetrical bush spacing and alignment with the pivot pin to be kept.

3 To press a bush out you should support the arm in a vice.

4 Using a piece of suitable tube with an outside diameter of 40 mm ($1\frac{17}{64}$ in) press or drive the old bush out of its housing. Where the old bush is difficult to remove, use a hacksaw blade and cut through the old bush to section it. Take care not to cut beyond the bush!

5 Clean out the housing and press the new bush into position, so that the two recesses are in alignment as shown in Fig. 11.10. When fitted, check that the clearance between the bushes is 187 mm (7.362 in) for R1271 models or 151 mm (5.945 in) for R.1272 models, as shown in Fig. 11.11. Do not mix the honeycomb type bush with the solid rubber type found on the same axle on R1271 models.

6 Repeat the procedure with the opposing bush and recheck the clearance.

Flexible bush – upper wishbone

7 The flexible suspension bushes are removed in a similar manner to that described above. The press tube diameter must be 30.5 mm (1.20 in) overall for R1271 models or 31.5 mm (1.24 in) for R1272 models. Refer to Fig. 11.12 for the correct fitted position of each bush.

---

7 Stub axle (Front) – removal and refitting

1 Raise the side of the car to be worked on and support with axle stands or blocks to secure. Remove the roadwheel.

2 A spacer leg will have to be positioned between the lower mounting pin of the shock absorber and the suspension lower arm hinge pin as shown in Fig. 11.13. Spacer leg/s can be manufactured quite easily, using some 1 in square section tubing out to length, which is approximately 185 mm (7·25 inches). The end sections must be 'V'-shaped as shown (photo), to locate on the hinge pin and mounting pin. The official Renault spacer legs are designated tool number T AV 509.

1.9 Check bushes and joints (arrowed) for wear

3.5 The upper suspension arm joint to stub axle unit

7.2a Spacer legs manufactured in square section tube to ...

7.2b ... locate as shown

9.3 Remove rubber cup to gain access to the rear shock absorber upper mounting nut

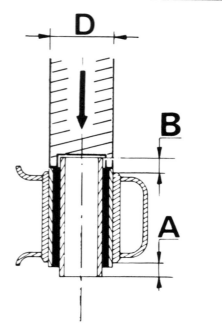

Fig. 11.12 Fitted position of upper wishbone bushes – press out with tube (D)

R1271 model:　A = 5.7 mm (0.22 in)
　　　　　　　B = 13.5 mm (0.53 in)
R1272 model:　A = B

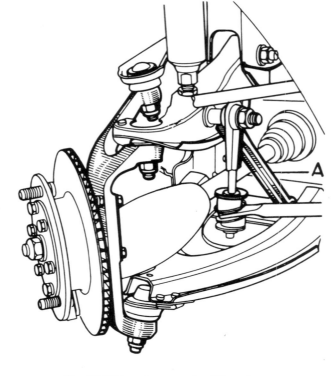

Fig. 11.13 Locate spacer leg (A) as shown

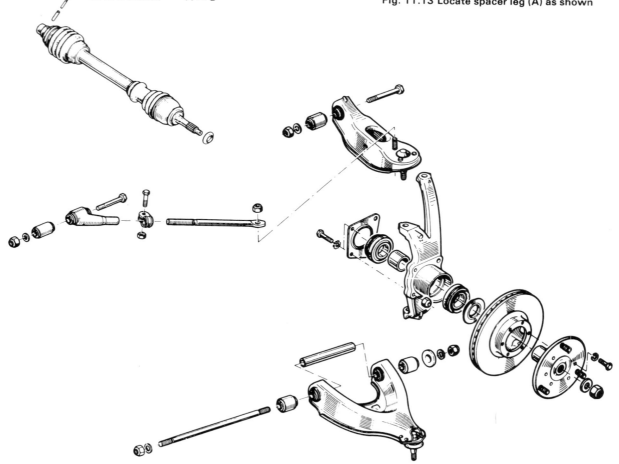

Fig. 11.14 Front stub axle and associate parts

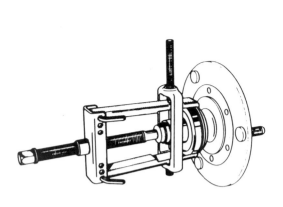

Fig. 11.15 Use puller to remove bearings from hub

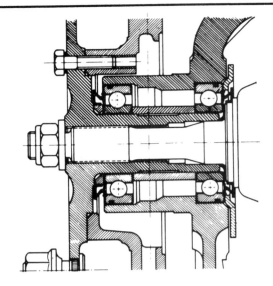

Fig. 11.16 Cross-sectional view of assembled stub axle and hub
unit

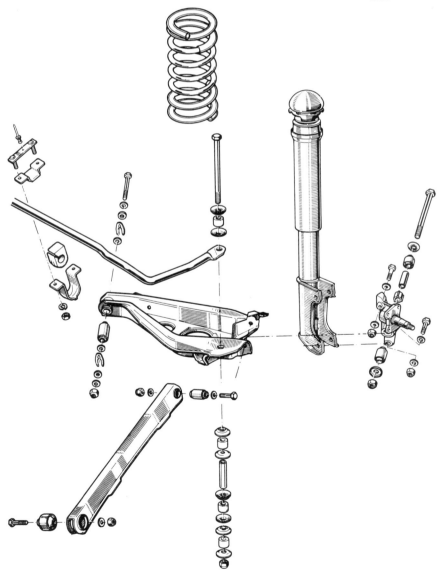

Fig. 11.17 The principal rear suspension components

It is worth making up or obtaining a pair of these spacer legs as several operations require the use of them.

3   With a spacer leg firmly in position as described, refer to Chapter 9 and remove the disc calliper unit from the front axle. Do not detach the hydraulic pipe, nor allow the calliper unit to hang suspended by the pipe – support its weight.

4   Remove the front hub and disc assembly (see Chapter 9).

5   Unscrew and remove the respective balljoint retaining nuts, using a balljoint separator to detach each joint in turn.

6   Carefully, withdraw and remove the stub axle unit, disengaging it from the driveshaft.

7   To remove the inner stub axle bearing, remove the inner closure plate and then pull or drive out the inner bearing for inspection.

8   The outer stub axle bearing can be removed from the wheel hub in a similar manner, using a suitable puller. Take care not to damage the seal, although it is advisable to renew it anyway.

9   Check the stub axle for signs of damage or excessive wear and renew if necessary.

10   Before reassembly, check that all fittings are perfectly clean and the protective coatings washed from new parts.

11   Lubricate all items with wheel bearing grease prior to assembly.

12   Press the new bearings into position, ensuring the sealed face of the inner bearing faces toward the closure plate (which must be smeared with sealant). Press the bearing fully home in its housing using a suitable tube of 68 mm ($2\frac{11}{16}$ in) outside diameter.

13   Smear some wheel bearing grease into the cavity of the stub axle.

14   Locate the oil seal into the wheel hub (together with the distance collar), then carefully press or drive the new bearing into position using a tube drift of suitable diameter.

15   Relocate the stub axle unit and reconnect to the respective ball-joints. Do not tighten the joint nuts fully at this stage.

16   Reassemble the wheel hub/disc unit over the driveshaft splines and, using a suitable tube drift, drive the unit into position in the inner hub bearing.

17   Refit the stub axle nut and washer, tightening to the specified torque setting.

18   Check the hub for ease of rotation then refit the brake calliper assembly (see Chapter 9).

19   Refit the roadwheel and lower the car. When the vehicle is free standing, tighten the balljoint nuts to the specified torque settings.

Note: *If the balljoints have also been renewed, it is advisable to have the steering geometry checked and, if necessary, adjusted*

8   Anti-roll bar (front and rear) – removal and refitting

1   The anti-roll bar is normally only removed to renew its rubber bushings, if damaged (due to an accident) or possibly to give access to surrounding components. Whatever the reason, always check the condition of the bushes and renew if they are suspect. If the bar is defective, renew it.

2   It is easiest if the vehicle is over a pit when removing the anti-roll bar to refit the bushes or other suspension parts, although it matters little. Make sure the vehicle is properly secure on stands (if available) or on the ground with the handbrake on. It is not always necessary to remove the front wheels.

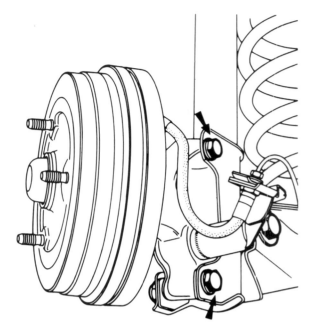

Fig. 11.18 The rear shock absorber lower mounting bolts (arrowed)

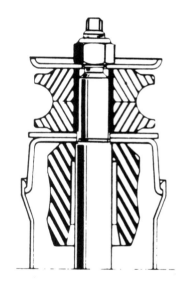

Fig. 11.19 The rear shock absorber upper mounting

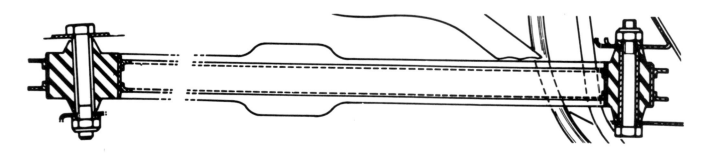

Fig. 11.20 The lateral arm assembly

Front anti-roll bar

3   Unscrew and remove the roll bar-to-connecting link retaining nut on each side.
4   Unscrew and remove the roll bar-to-chassis mounting nuts and remove the bar complete with bushes and clamps.
5   To remove the connecting link, unscrew the retaining nut to the suspension arm pivot and withdraw it forwards.
6   Refit in the reverse sequence, ensuring the bushes and cups are correctly located.

Rear and anti-roll bar

7   The rear anti-roll bar is attached at each end to the respective transverse arm at each end and centrally on the body underside by two rubber cushioned brackets.
8   To remove the bar, unscrew and withdraw the retaining bolt on each side, removing simultaneously the respective cup washers, rubber bushes and distance piece, keeping them in order.
9   Unscrew and remove the two retaining bracket nuts and brackets, rubber distance pieces and anti-roll bar.
10   Check the bar for alignment and renew if necessary. Inspect the various rubber distance pieces and bushes and renew any that have perished or are badly worn.
11   Refitting is a reversal of the removal procedure. Do not tighten the fastenings until the reassembly is complete. Ensure that the respective bushes, cup washers and distance pieces are correctly located as shown in Fig. 11.17.

---

9   Rear shock absorber – removal and refitting

1   Raise the vehicle at the rear and make secure on axle stands or blocks. Remove the wheel/s.
2   Position a pillar jack under the suspension arm on the side to be worked on and raise it to just support the arm.
3   From inside the vehicle, unfasten and remove the rear shelf to gain access to the upper mounting of the shock absorber which is covered by rubber. Prise the cover free and unscrew the retaining nut (photo).
4   Unscrew and remove the shock absorber lower mounting bolts as shown in Fig. 11.18.
5   Compress the shock absorber downwards to detach it from its upper location and when clear, tilt it outwards and remove it.
6   The shock absorber is not repairable and if worn (weak compression) or showing signs of fluid leakage, must be renewed. Compare it with a new shock absorber if possible to evaluate its compression valve.
7   Refitting is a reversal of the removal process. Grease the bottom mounting bolts before fitting and tighten them to the specified torque setting.
8   To relocate the upper threaded portion of the unit into its location, align it and raise the upper section into position sufficiently to enable the retaining nut to be fitted. You will probably require an assistant to achieve this unless you fabricate a suitable tool with which to draw the threaded section upwards into position from within the car. Ensure that the bushes and cups are correctly located before tightening the nut to the specified torque, as shown in Fig. 11.19.

---

10   Rear suspension coil spring – removal and refitting

1   Remove the rear shock absorber on the side concerned as described in the previous Section.
2   You will need a suitable coil spring compressor, which when located onto the spring should be progressively tightened sufficiently to enable the spring to be removed rearward from its location. Take great care during this operation as the spring will be under considerable tension. Make sure that the spring compressor is of a suitable type and is fully located.
3   Unwind the spring compressor in a progressive manner.
4   Refitting is a reversal of the removal procedure, but note the following:

   (a)   *The spring must be fitted with its small diameter end located in the lower 'dish retainer' and with the colour code marking at the end of the second coil from the bottom*
   (b)   *When the spring is relocated, unwind the compressor carefully, ensuring the spring is seated correctly into the top*

and bottom location 'cups'
   (c)   *Once the spring is in position and the compressor removed, refit the shock absorber as described in the previous Section and tighten the retaining bolts/nut to the specified torque*

---

11   Lateral arm – removal and refitting

1   Raise the rear of the vehicle and support on axle stands or blocks to secure.
2   Unscrew the pivot bolt retaining nuts and extract the bolts.
3   Pull the transverse arm rearward and separate the lateral arm.
4   Refitting is a reversal of the removal procedure. Smear the pivot pins with grease prior to fitting and use new Nylstop type nuts when assembling. Tighten the nuts to the specified torque only when the vehicle is lowered to its free standing position.

---

12   Transverse arm – removal and refitting

1   Raise the car at the rear and support on axle stands or blocks to make secure. Remove the wheel at the rear from the side to be worked on.
2   Referring to Sections 9 and 10, remove the rear shock absorber and suspension coil spring. Disconnect the anti-roll bar link.
3   Unscrew the lateral arm pivot bolt retaining nut and remove the bolt.
4   Referring to Chapter 9, disconnect the brake hoses and limiter control unit from the arm.
5   Detach the handbrake cable from its retaining clip.
6   Unscrew the inner pivot bolt retaining nut and extract the bolt.
7   Make a note of the adjuster shim positions and remove them. Keep them safe for correct reassembly when the time comes.
8   The transverse arm can now be removed.
9   Refitting of the transverse arm is a direct reversal of the removal process, but note the following:

   (a)   *Be sure to refit the exact number of shims to their relative locations*
   (b)   *Use new Nylstop type nuts to retain the pivot pin bolts and tighten to the specified torque once the vehicle is fully reassembled and free standing*
   (c)   *Referring to Chapter 9, reconnect the brake lines and limiter unit. Bleed the brakes and, if necessary, adjust the limiter*
   (d)   *If the shims have been renewed (and even if they have not) have the rear axle parallelism checked by your Renault dealer*

---

13   Rear wheel bearings – removal and refitting

1   Raise the car at the rear on the side concerned and support with axle stands or blocks to make secure. Remove the roadwheel.
2   Referring to Chapter 9, remove the brake drum.
3   Place the outer bearing inner track ring to one side and extract the seal from the brake drum.
4   Withdraw the bearing outer tracks from the drum, either using a suitable puller or by driving out using a soft drift.
5   The inner bearing track ring can be removed from the hub using a suitable puller as shown (photo).
6   Clean and inspect the respective bearing assemblies and also the stub axle. Where signs of damage or excessive wear are apparent, renew the defective components concerned. Where the bearings are being renewed, it is important that the new bearing inner and outer tracks and rings are renewed as a pair. Do not fit a new bearing cone (inner track) to a used bearing cup (outer track).
7   If a new stub axle thrust washer is being fitted, it can be heated to ease assembly or drifted into location together with the bearing using a suitable tube drift.
8   Smear the bearings and tracks with grease prior to fitting.
9   Carefully, press or drift the new bearing outer tracks (cups) into position in the brake drum using a tube drift of suitable diameter.
10   Fit a new oil seal using a suitable tube drift.
11   Smear about 20 g (0·75 oz) of wheel bearing grease between the bearings in the drum and relocate the drum to the stub axle (photo).
12   Locate the outer bearing inner track (cone) and retain the drum assembly with the thrust washer and nut (photo).

13.5 Removing the inner wheel bearing track ring using a puller

13.11 Smear grease between the bearings in the drum

13.12 Locate the outer bearing cone and special washer

13.16 Fit the locking cap and make secure with new split-pin

16.3 Topping-up the power steering fluid reservoir

16.5 The power steering pump unit and drivebelt viewed from underneath

13 The nut when tightened adjusts the wheel bearings so be sure to tighten it to the specified torque whilst rotating the brake drum.

14 Unscrew the nut by about 1/6th of a turn and tap around the hub and drum using a soft-headed hammer to seat the bearings. Next, check the endfloat of the drum assembly using a clock gauge. The correct endplay should be between 0·01 and 0·05 mm (0·001 and 0·002 in). Tighten or loosen the hub nut accordingly to make any necessary adjustment.

15 Check the drum is free to rotate. There may be a slight binding due to the possibility of the brake linings being in contact with the drum.

16 Fit the special locking cap over the nut and retain with a new split-pin (photo).

17 Smear about 10g (0·33 oz) of bearing grease into the grease cap and tap it carefully back into position on the hub.

14 Rear axle geometry and body height – checking and adjustment

1 The rear axle assembly settings and body height will rarely need adjustment; only after an accident or possibly when new rear suspension components are fitted.

2 It is generally recommended that any checking and adjustments of the rear suspension and body height be entrusted to your Renault dealer who is equipped to tackle this task.

3 Before assuming that the suspension is in need of adjustment, first check the following points are correct as there are several basic factors that contribute towards the accuracy of the rear axle geometry:

    (a) Tyre inflation pressures
    (b) Shock absorbers must be in good operational condition
    (c) The suspension pivot points must be in good order and their fastenings correctly tightened
    (d) The wheel bearing/hub endplay must be correct
    (e) The roadwheel run-out and balance must be correct

4 If these items are known to be in order, arrange for your Renault dealer to make further checks and adjustments (if required).

15 Steering assembly – general information

1 The rack and pinion steering system fitted to all models is a maintenance-free design, although an occasional check should be made to ensure that it is securely located and the steering arm protective bellows are in good condition.

2 The steering rack unit is located directly to the rear of the engine above the clutch housing, and mounted to the body crossmember.

3 The steering column shaft is interconnected with the steering box by a universal joint on models with power assisted steering, and a flexible coupling on models with standard steering.

4 On models equipped with power assisted steering, the column shaft is connected via a rotary valve unit which regulates the direction of flow to the double acting ram unit, attached to the steering gear, and actuates the steering arm accordingly. A belt driven pump provides the hydraulic pressure.

5 The maintenance procedures for the power steering unit are given in Section 16.

6 Apart from removing and refitting the steering gear and/or power steering component units, there is little that a home mechanic can do to repair or overhaul them; specialised tools and fitting techniques are required. Therefore if damage or excessive wear exist in any of the major units of the steering system, remove the offending item and let your Renault dealer effect any repairs that are possible.

16 Power steering – servicing and problem diagnosis

Oil level – check and top-up

1 Where power steering is fitted it is essential that the oil level in the system is kept to the correct level and also that the specified grade of oil is used.

2 Check the level every 3000 miles (5000 km).

3 To check the oil level, remove the reservoir filler cap, start the engine and then rotate the steering to its full extent on each lock in turn. Next, check the oil level in the reservoir which should be just

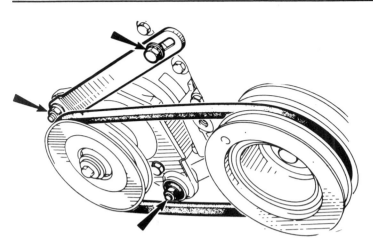

Fig. 11.21a Power steering pump mounting/adjusting bolts and strap (TL models)

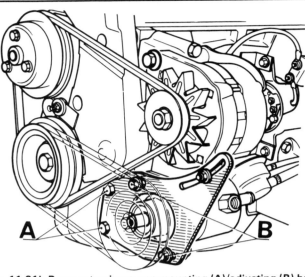

Fig. 11.21b Power steering pump mounting (A)/adjusting (B) bolts and mounting plate (TS models)

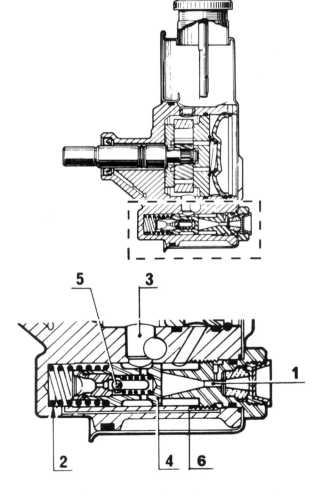

Fig. 11.22 The pump unit regulator components

1 *Pressure release bore*	5 *Ball valve (pressure*
2 *Plunger spring*	*release)*
3 *Bypass hole*	6 *Regulator pressure channel*
4 *Flow regulator plunger*	

visible above the gauze filter. Top-up with the correct grade of lubricant (see Specifications) as necessary (photo).

4   A continuous need to top up indicates a leak in the system and a check should be made around the pump and the interconnecting hoses to the ram on the steering box for obvious signs of leakage. It may be that a hose joint simply needs tightening, but if it is otherwise defective renew it.

Pump drivebelt – tension adjustment and renewal

5   The power steering drivebelt must be in good condition and correctly adjusted or the pump will not function effectively (photo).

6   The belt tension is correct when there is a deflection of 6·5 mm (0·25 in) in the middle of its run between the crankshaft and pump pulleys. To adjust the tension, slacken the pump mounting and adjustment strap bolt just sufficiently to allow the pump to be pivoted accordingly for the correct tension. Do not overtension the belt or the pump drive bearings will suffer.

7   If the belt is in need of renewal loosen the mounting bolts right off, pivot the pump fully inward and remove the old belt. Fit and retension the new belt, run the engine for about ten minutes then recheck the tension. New belts tend to stretch a fraction initially and will probably require further slight adjustment.

Note: *Where the vehicle is fitted with air conditioning, the compressor drivebelt should first be removed. This is achieved in a similar manner to that of the power steering pump drivebelt.*

Power steering – problem diagnosis

8   Should the steering develop problems or become abnormally stiff in action, do not assume that it is necessarily the power steering system which is at fault.

9   Make some initial checks of the steering and front suspension components as described in Section 1. If these are in order, check the oil level in the steering hydraulic circuit is up to normal level and the pump drivebelt is tensioned correctly as described earlier.

10 Check the power steering pump unit and ram unit on the steering box are secure.

11 If these items are in order, the problem can be diagnosed according to its symptoms. If the steering is stiff and heavier than normal, the problem is most likely to be within the steering pump or hydraulic ram on the steering box. If the steering requires normal pressure at the steering wheel but is defective in other aspects, the problem is unlikely to be associated with the power steering. Where power assistance is felt to be intermittent in action, a check can be made to ensure that the regulator valve in the pump unit is in order by removing the valve assembly and checking the ball and seat are perfectly clean. The regulator valve unit is located in the base of the pump unit, the components of which are shown in Fig. 11.22. If the above checks do not solve the problem, get your Renault dealer to inspect the system. In particular, he will be able to conduct a pressure check of the hydraulic

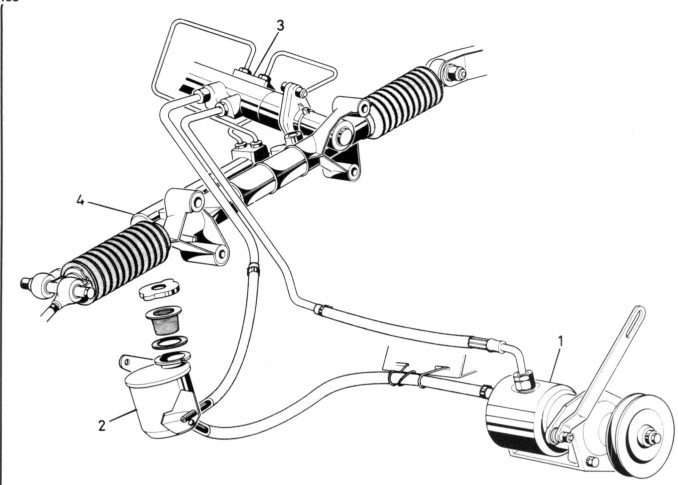

Fig. 11.23 Power steering layout showing pump (1), oil reservoir filler (2), rotary valve unit (3) and hydraulic ram (4)

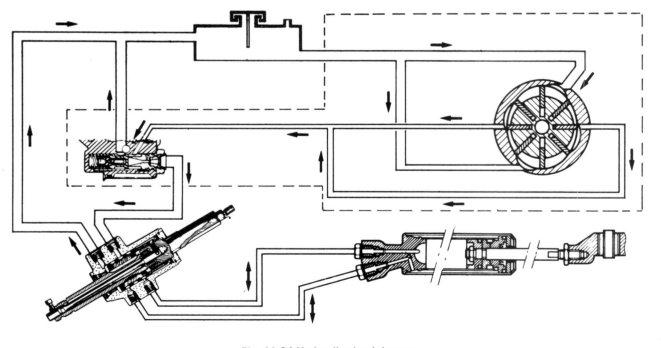

Fig. 11.24 Hydraulic circuit layout

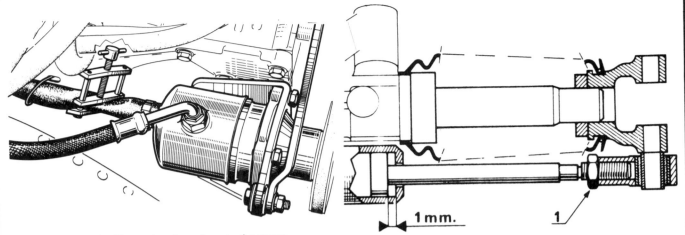

Fig. 11.25 Clamp the pipes close to the pump

Fig. 11.26 Loosen locknut (1) and adjust ram
to give 1 mm (0.040 in) clearance as indicated

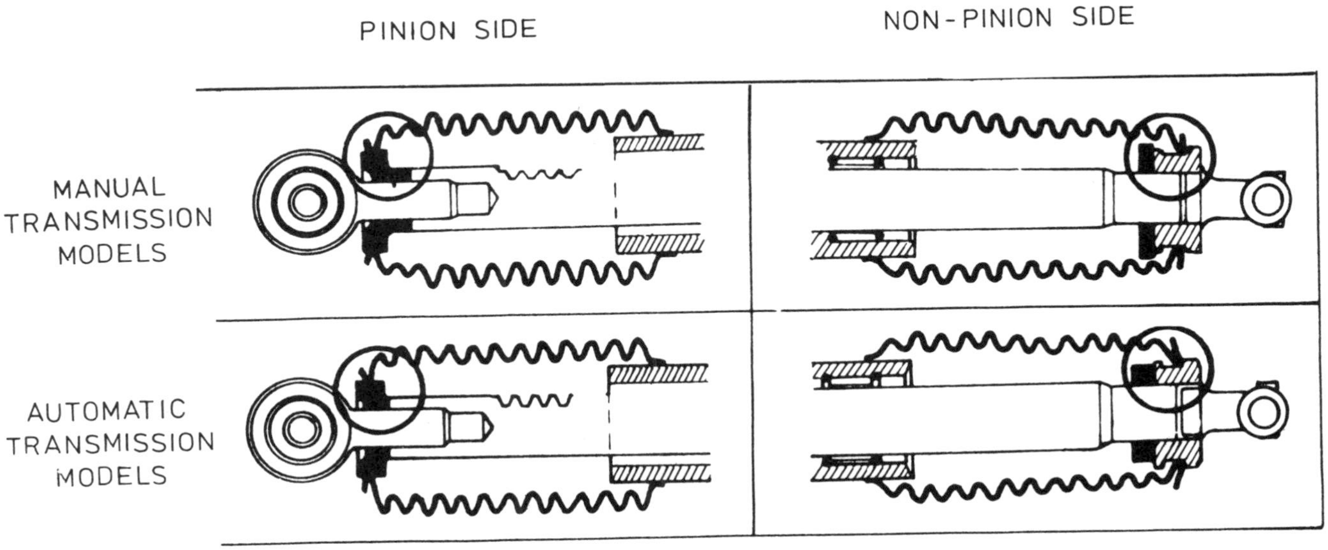

PINION SIDE   NON-PINION SIDE

MANUAL
TRANSMISSION
MODELS

AUTOMATIC
TRANSMISSION
MODELS

Fig. 11.27 Locknut fitting positions at the rack ends

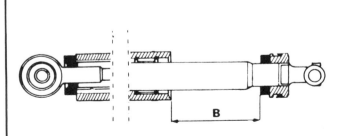

Fig. 11.28 Check clearance B on completion

On manual transmission models B = 183 mm (7.203 in)
On automatic transmission models B = 179 mm (7.046 in)

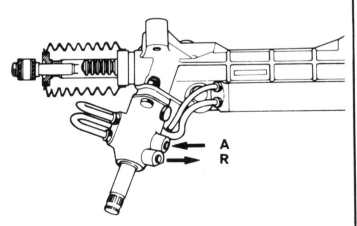

Fig. 11.29 Rotary valve with inlet (A)
and return to reservoir (R) pipe positions

circuit in the power steering system. It is essential to diagnose this whether the problem is within the pump or ram unit.

12 Both the power steering pump and hydraulic ram unit are easily removed, but repairs should be entrusted to your Renault dealer.

17 Power steering pump – removal and refitting

1   On TS models, remove the engine undertray.

2   The first things to be disconnected are the pump inlet and outlet hoses. To minimise the spillage of hydraulic oil, clamp the respective hoses as near to the pump as possible as shown in Fig. 11.25. Unscrew the pipe to pump unions and detach the hoses.

3   Loosen the pump mounting and adjuster strap bolts and detach the drivebelt.

4   Remove the mounting and adjuster bolts and remove the pump. On TS models, it is also necessary to unscrew the pulley retaining bolt and withdraw the pulley from the pump shaft so the unit can be withdrawn rearwards through the mounting plate (photo).

5   Refitting is a reversal of the removal procedure. When in position, reconnect and retension the drivebelt. Ensure that the hoses are securely connected and top-up the system as necessary (see Section 16).

18 Power steering hydraulic ram – removal and refitting

1   Disconnect the battery earth and positive cables from the terminals. Remove the battery retaining clamps, lift the battery from its tray and place safely out of the way.

2   Disconnect and remove the battery support tray.

3   To minimise oil spillage, clamp the hydraulic supply and return pipes as close as possible to their connections to the hydraulic ram.

4   Detach the steering arm connecting pin bolt (to the rack unit).

5   Note the respective hydraulic pipe connections and detach them carefully from the unions to the ram unit.

6   Unscrew and remove the ram pivot bolt.

7   Withdraw the ram unit.

8   Refitting is a reversal of the removal procedure but note the following:

(a) *The car must be free standing when tightening the flexible bushes and steering arm pin. Tighten to the specified torque (where given)*

(b) *Ram adjustment is possible once it is fitted into position (if necessary)). Turn the steering to full lock position, enabling the rack to be extended fully on the non-pinion side. In this position, the rack end fitting nut should be in contact with the steering box at the pinion end. If it is not adjust as follows.*

(c) *Referring to Fig. 11.26, loosen the locknut (1) and unscrew the piston rod a few revolutions to adjust so the rack end fitting nut is in contact with the steering box. With the steering held in this position, the ram piston is then screwed back until it contacts its bearing at which point unscrew it about $\frac{3}{4}$ turn to give a clearance of 1 mm (0.040 in) between the piston and its bearing. Tighten the locknut in this position*

19 Steering box (power steering) – removal and refitting

1   Disconnect the battery earth and positive leads, remove the battery retaining clamp and lift the battery clear.

2   Remove the battery support tray.

3   Clamp the hydraulic hoses at the steering box end to minimize oil loss when disconnected.

4   Unscrew and remove the steering shaft lower universal joint connecting bolt, then lift the steering tube as much as possible to disconnect the universal joint.

5   Unscrew the steering arm balljoint nuts and, using a balljoint separator, disconnect the arms (photo).

6   Note their relative positions, then disconnect the hoses to the rotary valve unit at the base of the column.

7   Unscrew and remove the steering box retaining bolts and carefully, withdraw the steering box unit (photo).

8   Refitting is a reversal of the removal procedure, but note the following.

9   The steering arm balljoint stems must be smeared with a general purpose grease prior to assembly.

10 Whenever the steering rack or steering box unit is renewed, the steering rack travel must be readjusted as follows:

(a) *Locate the pinion and nut, also the nut at the yoke at the jack retaining end as shown for your particular model type – see Fig. 11.27*

(b) *Position the rack against the pinion end stop, then tighten the nut and yoke (jack end) to give the dimension given in Fig. 11.28 (as applicable). The steering arm pins must be horizontal when locating the final yoke positions (once the steering box is fitted)*

11 In reconnecting the hydraulic pipes, locate them beneath the rotary valve as shown in Fig. 11.29 and locate the hose in its clip as shown underneath the engine mounting (photo).

12 The tie-rod balljoint and hinge pin bolts must be tightened to the specified torque only with the car free standing.

13 Reconnect the steering column and universal joint with the steering wheel spokes horizontal.

14 Top-up the power steering circuit as given in Section 16 and check for leaks around the pipe joints.

15 Arrange to have the steering box height and parallelism checked by your Renault dealer at the earliest opportunity.

20 Steering box (standard steering) – removal and refitting

1   Disconnect the battery earth and positive cables, remove the battery retaining clamp and lift the battery clear.

2   Remove the battery tray.

3   Unscrew and remove the steering arm/tie-rod connecting bolts at the rack end.

4   Disconnect the steering column-to-steering box flexible coupling.

5   Unscrew and remove the four bolts retaining the steering box to the body crossmember and carefully, lift the steering box clear.

6   Refitting is a reversal of the removal sequence but note the following:

(a) *The steering rack rubber bellows must be in good condition and held securely by the retaining clips before fitting*

(b) *The steering arm-to-tie-rod bolts must be smeared with a general purpose grease before fitting, and when fitted, ensure that the bolts are in the horizontal position*

(c) *Tighten the retaining nuts and bolts*

(d) *If necessary, implement the instructions given in paragraph 10 of the previous Section*

21 Steering tie-rods – removal, refitting and adjustment

Standard steering models

1   Removal of either or both of the steering tie-rods (track rods) does not necessitate rack removal. The unit is not reparable although the end fittings can be renewed when necessary.

2   Use a suitable balljoint separator to detach the outer joint at the stub axle connection.

3   Remove the inner connecting bolt to the steering arm connection and withdraw the rod assembly.

4   If the rod unit is bent or damaged in any way, it must be renewed. To renew either of the end pieces, clean any dirt from the threads using a wire brush. Referring to Fig. 11.31, measure between points A and B and make a note of the distance. Also note the relative set angles of each end piece.

5   Loosen the clamp bolt, grip the rod and unscrew the end piece.

6   Refit in the reverse order but check the end piece is positioned to give the original distance measured (point A to point B), then tighten the clamp bolt. This will provide a guide for the track setting.

7   Grease the connecting pin before refitting to the steering arm. The car must be free-standing when tightening the respective fastenings to the specified torque settings.

8   Arrange to have your Renault dealer check the track and steering angles after renewal as they are most important to the general handling and safety of the car.

9   If you have an accurate means of checking the toe-out, then the respective rods can be adjusted when in place by loosening the clamp bolts and rotating the rod using suitable grips. Set the steering in the

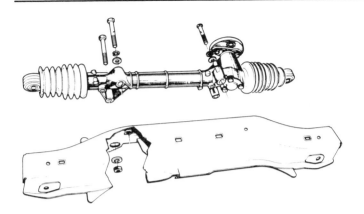

Fig. 11.30 Steering box and location bolts

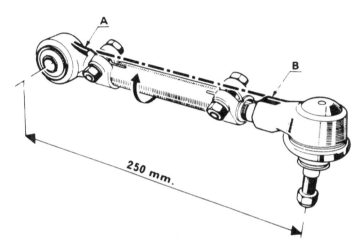

Fig. 11.31 Note relative settings before removal

250 mm.

A

B

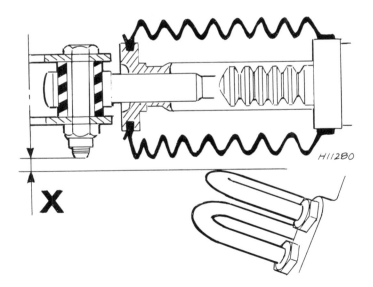

Fig. 11.32 Check clearance between hydraulic pipe and end of bolt (X)

straight-ahead position when checking and adjusting the track setting.

10 When an adjustment has been made, check on completion that the steering arm connecting bolt has sufficient clearance to pass the power steering hydraulic pipes (where fitted). Cut or grind down the end of the bolt if necessary, to give sufficient clearance as shown in Fig. 11.32.

Power steering models

11 On earlier models (up to July 1976) equipped with power steering the tie-rod arm on each side differs, the rack pinion side rod being non-adjustable, see Fig. 11.33.

12 Where adjustment is needed to the pinion side on such models (in order to correct the track setting), set the wheels in the straight-ahead position then loosen the locknut on the steering rack end fitting. The end fitting is then rotated in the required direction to adjust the track as necessary. Screw it in to give toe-out, screw it out for toe-in. A half turn of the end fitting is equal to 1.5 mm (0.0625 in) of adjustment. Retighten the locknut to secure and ensure the end fitting bolt is in the horizontal position on completion.

13 The opposing tie-rod is adjusted (and removed) in the same manner as that for the standard steering system, but note that a complete turn of the rod when adjusting is equal to 4 mm (0.156 in) of adjustment.

14 On later power assisted steering equipped models, the adjustable type steering rod is fitted on each side. As with the other types mentioned the wheels must be set in the straight-ahead position when checking or making adjustments. A complete rotation of the adjustable rod on each side is equal to about 8 mm (0.312 in). The direction of the arrow shown in Fig. 11.31 increases the toe-out.

22 Steering column – removal and refitting

1 Disconnect the battery earth lead from its terminal.

2 Unscrew and remove the lower column housing retaining screws. Unclip the housing from the top half to remove, then detach the upper half to expose the switches.

3 Disconnect the bonnet release catch lever from the column.

4 Unscrew and release the respective switches from their column locations (photo) or take a note of their respective positions and detach the various switch wires-to-harness connectors.

5 To remove the steering wheel, prise the central embellisher free and mark the relative alignment positions of the steering wheel and shaft. Unscrew the retaining nut and withdraw the wheel. A special steering wheel pulley may be required here to avoid damaging the wheel, should it prove tight to withdraw from the shaft (photo).

6 Disconnect the clutch and brake pedal pushrods from the pedals, then unscrew and withdraw the lower shaft universal joint through-bolt (photo).

7 Pull the plastic retaining bungs from the carpet surround section around the clutch and brake pedal support bracket, where it is mounted to the bulkhead. Pull the carpet away and then unscrew the four bracket retaining bolts.

8 Disconnect the brake light switch wire.

9 Unscrew the retaining bolt and disconnect the column from its mounting to the upper bulkhead at the point just to the right of the speedometer (viewed from the driving position).

10 Check that all column connections and fittings are disconnected, then withdraw the column assembly from the car through the interior.

11 Refitting the column is a reversal of the removal procedure but the following points must be observed:

(a) *Do not tighten the respective column and bracket bolts fully until the assembly is complete*

(b) *Tighten the bolts to the specified torque settings*

(c) *The following instruction in this sub paragraph does not apply to models fitted with power steering; these models have a universal joint which incorporates needle roller bearings. When connecting the universal joint unit, set the steering to its centre point position, and tighten bolt 'A' as shown in Fig. 11.34. Then rotate the steering one quarter turn to the right and tighten bolt 'B'. The bolts must be greased when fitted*

(d) *When assembly is complete, check the clutch and brake pedal free play and adjust if necessary. Also check the various switch circuit operations when the battery is reconnected*

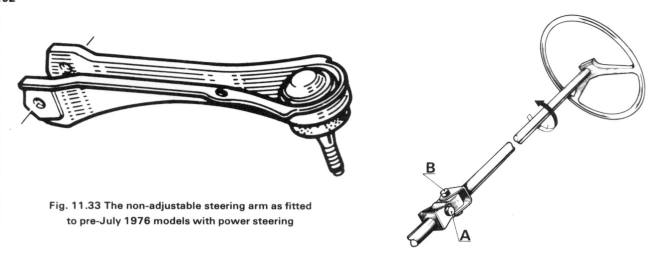

Fig. 11.33 The non-adjustable steering arm as fitted
to pre–July 1976 models with power steering

Fig. 11.34 Tighten bolt A, turn steering 90° and tighten bolt B

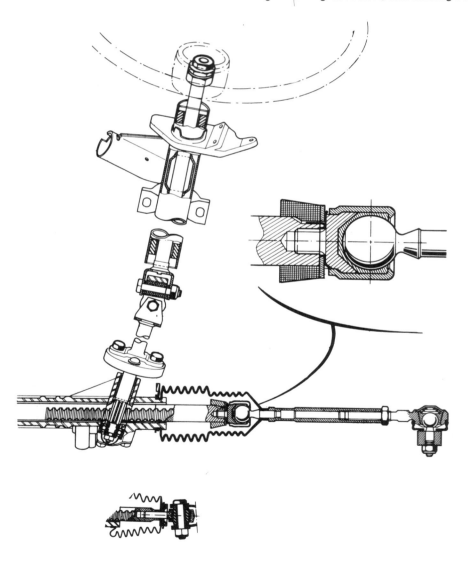

Fig. 11.35 The steering column and rack assemblies

17.4 On TS models, remove the pulley from the pump shaft

19.5 Detach the steering arm balljoints

19.7 The steering box unit and power assistance ram

19.11 Power steering hose and clip location viewed from underneath (engine removed)

22.4 The column switches and retaining brackets and screws (lower cover removed)

22.5 The steering wheel retaining nut (embellisher removed)

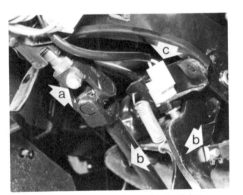

22.6 Disconnect the universal joint (a) the pushrods (b) and the brake light wire (c)

23 Steering column bushes – renewal

1 Where play in the steering column shaft is evident, the problem is almost certainly caused by worn upper and lower column bushes, and they must therefore be renewed.
2 To do this, first remove the steering column as described in the previous Section.
3 To extract the lower bush, tap the splined end of the shaft at the top (steering wheel end). Protect the end of the shaft against hammer blows with a plastic or hardwood block.
4 The lower bush should be ejected with its split collar.
5 Before withdrawing the shaft downward, turn the ignition key to unlock the column anti-theft lock.
6 At the top end, remove the retaining circlip from the sleeve and then drive the top bush out using a length of suitable tubing, inserted from the lower end of the column.
7 Refitting of the new bushes is a reversal of the removal procedure, but note the following:

   (a) Ensure that the upper bush is hard up against the depression in the column when fitted
   (b) Locate the bottom bush onto the shaft and also the collar halves. Drive them carefully into position, using a suitable angled drift working evenly round until fully fitted. Apply grease to the bushes (upper and lower) before fitting

24 Fault diagnosis – suspension and steering

Symptom	Reason/s

Front suspension and steering

Symptom	Reason/s
Heavy steering	Corroded or seized balljoints Incorrect suspension geometry and track Power steering unit defective
Lost motion (steering)	Worn flexible coupling bolt holes Worn steering column universal joint Loose steering wheel Worn balljoints Worn rack and pinion mechanism
Wheel wobble and vibration	Worn hub bearings Loose wheel bolts Worn suspension arm bushes Driveshafts bent or out of balance Driveshafts couplings worn Front roadwheels out of balance Wear in rack and pinion and balljoints Incorrect steering geometry
Poor roadholding and cornering	Dampers unserviceable
Sensitive to road camber	Wear in upper or lower suspension arm balljoints Wear in hub bearings

Rear suspension

Symptom	Reason/s
Wheel wobble and vibration	Damper rubber bushes worn Loose damper mounting Suspension arm bushes worn
Uneven tyre wear	Rear stub axles twisted or out of alignment Hubs incorrectly adjusted for endfloat
Poor roadholding and cornering	Dampers unserviceable

Chapter 12 Bodywork and fittings

Contents

1 General description

The bodywork is of all-steel monocoque construction, the integral components being spot welded together. In addition to the normal hinged body panels, the front wings are removable, being bolted into position.

Apart from the normal cleaning, maintenance and minor body repairs, there is little that the DIY owner can do in the event of structural defects caused by collision damage or possibly rust. This Chapter is therefore devoted to the normal maintenance, removal and refitting of those parts of the vehicle body and associate components that are readily dismantled.

Although the underbody is given a protective coating when new, it is still likely to suffer from corrosion in certain exposed areas or where road dirt deposits can congeal. Light corrosion can be treated as described in Section 4 but severe rusting of a structural area in the underbody must be repaired by your Renault dealer or competent vehicle body repair shop.

2 Maintenance – bodywork and underframe

The general condition of a vehicle's bodywork is the one thing that significantly affects its value. Maintenance is easy but needs to be regular. Neglect, particularly after minor damage, can lead quickly to further deterioration and costly repair bills. It is important also to keep watch on those parts of the vehicle not immediately visible, for instance the underside, inside all the wheel arches and the lower part of the engine compartment.

The basic maintenance routine for the bodywork is washing – preferably with a lot of water, from a hose. This will remove all the loose solids which may have stuck to the vehicle. It is important to flush these off in such a way as to prevent grit from scratching the finish. The wheel arches and underframe need washing in the same way to remove any accumulated mud which will retain moisture and tend to encourage rust. Paradoxically enough, the best time to clean the underframe and wheel arches is in wet weather when the mud is thoroughly wet and soft. In very wet weather the underframe is usually

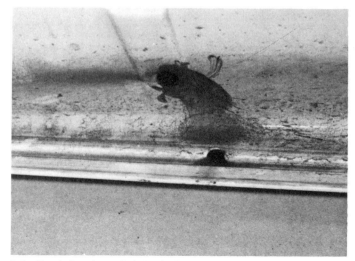

2.4a Check that the drain holes in the doors and lower body are clear ...

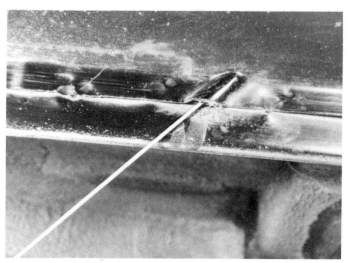

2.4b ... and poke them through with a piece of wire to remove dirt

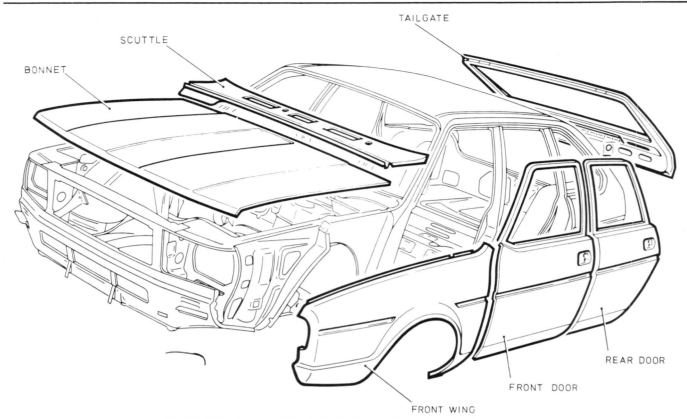

Fig. 12.1 The Renault 20 bodyshell, showing the detachable body panels

cleaned of large accumulations automatically and this is a good time for inspection.

Periodically, except on vehicles with a wax-based underbody protective coat, it is a good idea to have the whole of the underframe of the vehicle steam cleaned, engine compartment included, so that a thorough inspection can be carried out to see what minor repairs and renovations are necessary. Steam cleaning is available at many garages and is necessary for removal of the accumulation of oily grime which sometimes is allowed to become thick in certain areas. If steam cleaning facilities are not available, there are one or two excellent grease solvents available which can be brush applied. The dirt can then be simply hosed off. Note that these methods should not be used on vehicles with wax-based underbody protective coating or the coating will be removed. Such vehicles should be inspected annually, preferably just prior to winter, when the underbody should be washed down and any damage to the wax coating repaired. Ideally, a completely fresh coat should be applied. It would also be worth considering the use of such wax-based protection for injection into door panels, sills, box sections etc, as an additional safeguard against rust damage.

After washing paintwork, wipe off with a chamois leather to give an unspotted clear finish. A coat of clear protective wax polish will give added protection against chemical pollutants in the air. If the paintwork sheen has dulled or oxidised, use a cleaner/polisher combination to restore the brilliance of the shine. This requires a little effort, but such dulling is usually caused because regular washing has been neglected. Care needs to be taken with metallic paintwork, as special non-abrasive cleaner/polisher is required to avoid damage to the finish. Always check that the door and ventilator opening drain holes and pipes are completely clear so that water can be drained out. Bright work should be treated in the same way as paintwork. Windscreens and windows can be kept clear of the smeary film which often appears by the use of a proprietary glass cleaner. Never use any form of wax or other body or chromium polish on glass.

3 Maintenance – upholstery and carpets

Mats and carpets should be brushed or vacuum cleaned regularly

to keep them free of grit. If they are badly stained remove them from the vehicle for scrubbing or sponging and make quite sure they are dry before refitting. Seats and interior trim panels can be kept clean by wiping with a damp cloth. If they do become stained (which can be more apparent on light coloured upholstery) use a little liquid detergent and a soft nail brush to scour the grime out of the grain of the material. Do not forget to keep the headlining clean in the same way as the upholstery. When using liquid cleaners inside the vehicle do not over-wet the surfaces being cleaned. Excessive damp could get into the seams and padded interior causing stains, offensive odours or even rot. If the inside of the vehicle gets wet accidentally it is worthwhile taking some trouble to dry it out properly, particularly where carpets are involved. *Do not leave oil or electric heaters inside the vehicle for this purpose.*

4 Minor body damage – repair

The photographic sequences on pages 198 and 199 illustrate the operations detailed in the following sub-sections.

Repair of minor scratches in bodywork

If the scratch is very superficial, and does not penetrate to the metal of the bodywork, repair is very simple. Lightly rub the area of the scratch with a paintwork renovator, or a very fine cutting paste, to remove loose paint from the scratch and to clear the surrounding bodywork of wax polish. Rinse the area with clean water.

Apply touch-up paint to the scratch using a fine paint brush; continue to apply fine layers of paint until the surface of the paint in the scratch is level with the surrounding paintwork. Allow the new paint at least two weeks to harden: then blend it into the surrounding paintwork by rubbing the scratch area with a paintwork renovator or a very fine cutting paste. Finally, apply wax polish.

Where the scratch has penetrated right through to the metal of the bodywork, causing the metal to rust, a different repair technique is required. Remove any loose rust from the bottom of the scratch with a penknife, then apply rust inhibiting paint to prevent the formation of rust in the future. Using a rubber or nylon applicator fill the scratch with bodystopper paste. If required, this paste can be mixed with cellulose thinners to provide a very thin paste which is ideal for filling narrow scratches. Before the stopper-paste in the scratch hardens, wrap a piece of smooth cotton rag around the top of a finger. Dip the finger in cellulose thinners and then quickly sweep it across the surface of the stopper-paste in the scratch; this will ensure that the surface of the stopper-paste is slightly hollowed. The scratch can now be painted over as described earlier in this Section.

Repair of dents in bodywork

When deep denting of the vehicle's bodywork has taken place, the first task is to pull the dent out, until the affected bodywork almost attains its original shape. There is little point in trying to restore the original shape completely, as the metal in the damaged area will have stretched on impact and cannot be reshaped fully to its original contour. It is better to bring the level of the dent up to a point which is about $\frac{1}{8}$ in (3 mm) below the level of the surrounding bodywork. In cases where the dent is very shallow anyway, it is not worth trying to pull it out at all. If the underside of the dent is accessible, it can be hammered out gently from behind, using a mallet with a wooden or plastic head. Whilst doing this, hold a suitable block of wood firmly against the outside of the panel to absorb the impact from the hammer blows and thus prevent a large area of the bodywork from being 'belled-out'.

Should the dent be in a section of the bodywork which has a double skin or some other factor making it inaccessible from behind, a different technique is called for. Drill several small holes through the metal inside the area – particularly in the deeper section. Then screw long self-tapping screws into the holes just sufficiently for them to gain a good purchase in the metal. Now the dent can be pulled out by pulling on the protruding heads of the screws with a pair of pliers.

The next stage of the repair is the removal of the paint from the damaged area, and from an inch or so of the surrounding 'sound' bodywork. This is accomplished most easily by using a wire brush or abrasive pad on a power drill, although it can be done just as effectively by hand using sheets of abrasive paper. To complete the preparation for filling, score the surface of the bare metal with a screwdriver or the tang of a file, or alternatively, drill small holes in the affected area. This will provide a really good 'key' for the filler paste.

To complete the repair see the Section on filling and re-spraying.

Repair of rust holes or gashes in bodywork

Remove all paint from the affected area and from an inch or so of the surrounding 'sound' bodywork, using an abrasive pad or a wire brush on a power drill. If these are not available a few sheets of abrasive paper will do the job just as effectively. With the paint removed you will be able to gauge the severity of the corrosion and therefore decide whether to renew the whole panel (if this is possible) or to repair the affected area. New body panels are not as expensive as most people think and it is often quicker and more satisfactory to fit a new panel than to attempt to repair large areas of corrosion.

Remove all fittings from the affected area except those which will act as a guide to the original shape of the damaged bodywork (eg headlamp shells etc). Then, using tin snips or a hacksaw blade, remove all loose metal and any other metal badly affected by corrosion. Hammer the edges of the hole inwards in order to create a slight depression for the filler paste.

Wire brush the affected area to remove the powdery rust from the surface of the remaining metal. Paint the affected area with rust inhibiting paint; if the back of the rusted area is accessible treat this also.

Before filling can take place it will be necessary to block the hole in some way. This can be achieved by the use of aluminium or plastic mesh, or aluminium tape.

Aluminium or plastic mesh is probably the best material to use for a large hole. Cut a piece to the approximate size and shape of the hole to be filled, then position it in the hole so that its edges are below the level of the surrounding bodywork. It can be retained in position by several blobs of filler paste around its periphery.

Aluminium tape should be used for small or very narrow holes. Pull a piece off the roll and trim it to the approximate size and shape required, then pull off the backing paper (if used) and stick the tape over the hole; it can be overlapped if the thickness of one piece is insufficient. Burnish down the edges of the tape with the handle of a screwdriver or similar, to ensure that the tape is securely attached to the metal underneath.

Bodywork repairs – filling and re-spraying

Before using this Section, see the Sections on dent, deep scratch, rust holes and gash repairs.

Many types of bodyfiller are available, but generally speaking those proprietary kits which contain a tin of filler paste and a tube of resin hardener are best for this type of repair. A wide, flexible plastic or nylon applicator will be found invaluable for imparting a smooth and well contoured finish to the surface of the filler.

Mix up a little filler on a clean piece of card or board – measure the hardener carefully (follow the maker's instructions on the pack) otherwise the filler will set too rapidly or too slowly.

Using the applicator apply the filler paste to the prepared area; draw the applicator across the surface of the filler to achieve the correct contour and to level the filler surface. As soon as a contour that approximates to the correct one is achieved, stop working the paste – if you carry on too long the paste will become sticky and begin to 'pick up' on the applicator. Continue to add thin layers of filler paste at twenty-minute intervals until the level of the filler is just proud of the surrounding bodywork.

Once the filler has hardened, excess can be removed using a metal plane or file. From then on, progressively finer grades of abrasive paper should be used, starting with a 40 grade production paper and finishing with 400 grade wet-and-dry paper. Always wrap the abrasive paper around a flat rubber, cork, or wooden block – otherwise the surface of the filler will not be completely flat. During the smoothing of the filler surface the wet-and-dry paper should be periodically rinsed in water. This will ensure that a very smooth finish is imparted to the filler at the final stage.

At this stage the 'dent' should be surrounded by a ring of bare metal, which in turn should be encircled by the finely 'feathered' edge of the good paintwork. Rinse the repair area with clean water, until all of the dust produced by the rubbing-down operation has gone.

Spray the whole repair area with a light coat of primer – this will show up any imperfections in the surface of the filler. Repair these imperfections with fresh filler paste or bodystopper, and once more smooth the surface with abrasive paper. If bodystopper is used, it can be mixed with cellulose thinners to form a really thin paste which is ideal for filling small holes. Repeat this spray and repair procedure until you are satisfied that the surface of the filler, and the feathered edge of the paintwork are perfect. Clean the repair area with clean water and allow to dry fully.

The repair area is now ready for final spraying. Paint spraying must be carried out in a warm, dry, windless and dust free atmosphere. This condition can be created artificially if you have access to a large indoor working area, but if you are forced to work in the open, you will have to pick your day very carefully. If you are working indoors, dousing the floor in the work area with water will help to settle the dust which would otherwise be in the atmosphere. If the repair area is confined to one body panel, mask the surrounding panels; this will help to minimise the effects of a slight mis-match in paint colours. Bodywork fittings (eg chrome strips, door handles etc) will also need to be masked off. Use genuine masking tape and several thicknesses of newspaper for the masking operations.

Before commencing to spray, agitate the aerosol can thoroughly, then spray a test area (an old tin, or similar) until the technique is mastered. Cover the repair area with a thick coat of primer; the thickness should be built up using several thin layers of paint rather than one thick one. Using 400 grade wet-and-dry paper, rub down the surface of the primer until it is really smooth. While doing this, the work area should be thoroughly doused with water, and the wet-and-dry paper periodically rinsed in water. Allow to dry before spraying on more paint.

Spray on the top coat, again building up the thickness by using several thin layers of paint. Start spraying in the centre of the repair area and then, using a circular motion, work outwards until the whole repair area and about 2 inches of the surrounding original paintwork is covered. Remove all masking material 10 to 15 minutes after spraying on the final coat of paint.

Allow the new paint at least two weeks to harden, then, using a paintwork renovator or a very fine cutting paste, blend the edges of the paint into the existing paintwork. Finally, apply wax polish.

5 Major body damage – repair

Because the body is built on the monocoque principle and is

This sequence of photographs deals with the repair of the dent and paintwork damage shown in this photo. The procedure will be similar for the repair of a hole. It should be noted that the procedures given here are simplified — more explicit instructions will be found in the text

In the case of a dent the first job — after removing surrounding trim — is to hammer out the dent where access is possible. This will minimise filling. Here, the large dent having been hammered out, the damaged area is being made slightly concave

Now all paint must be removed from the damaged area, by rubbing with coarse abrasive paper. Alternatively, a wire brush or abrasive pad can be used in a power drill. Where the repair area meets good paintwork, the edge of the paintwork should be 'feathered', using a finer grade of abrasive paper

In the case of a hole caused by rusting, all damaged sheet-metal should be cut away before proceeding to this stage. Here, the damaged area is being treated with rust remover and inhibitor before being filled

Mix the body filler according to its manufacturer's instructions. In the case of corrosion damage, it will be necessary to block off any large holes before filling — this can be done with aluminium or plastic mesh, or aluminium tape. Make sure the area is absolutely clean before ...

... applying the filler. Filler should be applied with a flexible applicator, as shown, for best results; the wooden spatula being used for confined areas. Apply thin layers of filler at 20-minute intervals, until the surface of the filler is slightly proud of the surrounding bodywork

Initial shaping can be done with a Surform plane or Dreadnought file. Then, using progressively finer grades of wet-and-dry paper, wrapped around a sanding block, and copious amounts of clean water, rub down the filler until really smooth and flat. Again, feather the edges of adjoining paintwork

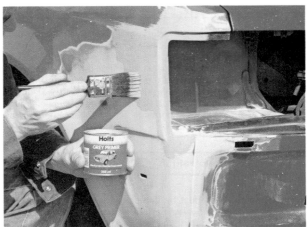

The whole repair area can now be sprayed or brush-painted with primer. If spraying, ensure adjoining areas are protected from over-spray. Note that at least one inch of the surrounding sound paintwork should be coated with primer. Primer has a 'thick' consistency, so will find small imperfections

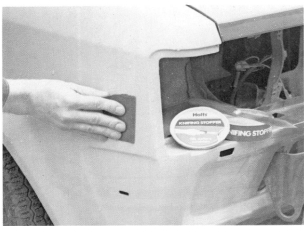

Again, using plenty of water, rub down the primer with a fine grade wet-and-dry paper (400 grade is probably best) until it is really smooth and well blended into the surrounding paintwork. Any remaining imperfections can now be filled by carefully applied knifing stopper paste

When the stopper has hardened, rub down the repair area again before applying the final coat of primer. Before rubbing down this last coat of primer, ensure the repair area is blemish-free — use more stopper if necessary. To ensure that the surface of the primer is really smooth use some finishing compound

The top coat can now be applied. When working out of doors, pick a dry, warm and wind-free day. Ensure surrounding areas are protected from over-spray. Agitate the aerosol thoroughly, then spray the centre of the repair area, working outwards with a circular motion. Apply the paint as several thin coats

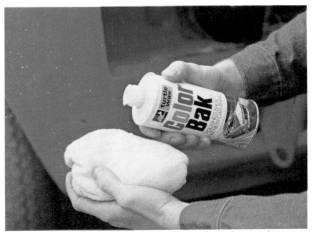

After a period of about two weeks, which the paint needs to harden fully, the surface of the repaired area can be 'cut' with a mild cutting compound prior to wax polishing. When carrying out bodywork repairs, remember that the quality of the finished job is proportional to the time and effort expended

integral with the underframe, major damage must be repaired by competent mechanics with the necessary welding and hydraulic straightening equipment.

If the damage has been serious it is vital that the body is checked for correct alignment, as otherwise the handling of the car will suffer and many other faults such as excessive tyre wear and wear in the transmission and steering may occur. Renault produce a special alignment jig and to ensure that all is correct a repaired car should always be checked on this jig.

6 Bumpers – removal and refitting

Front bumper

1   The front bumper unit must be detached together with the outer retaining brackets. The main brackets are mounted to the front body panel and the retaining nuts removed from within the engine compartment. The cardboard grille section will have to be removed on one side for access.

2   Detach the corner sections from the brackets inside the wing panel on each side, within the engine compartment.
3   Remove the bumper with brackets.
4   Refitting is a reversal of the removal procedure.

Rear bumper

5   Unscrew and remove the bumper corner fixing bolts to the brackets on each side. If the brackets are to also be removed, remove the luggage compartment side trim to gain access to the bracket bolts through the panel box sections.
6   Unscrew the overrider bolts.
7   Detach the number plate wires at the connector and withdraw the bumper assembly.
8   Refitting is a reversal of the removal process.

7 Front grille and headlight panels – removal and refitting

1   The front grille panel is retained by just two special screws and

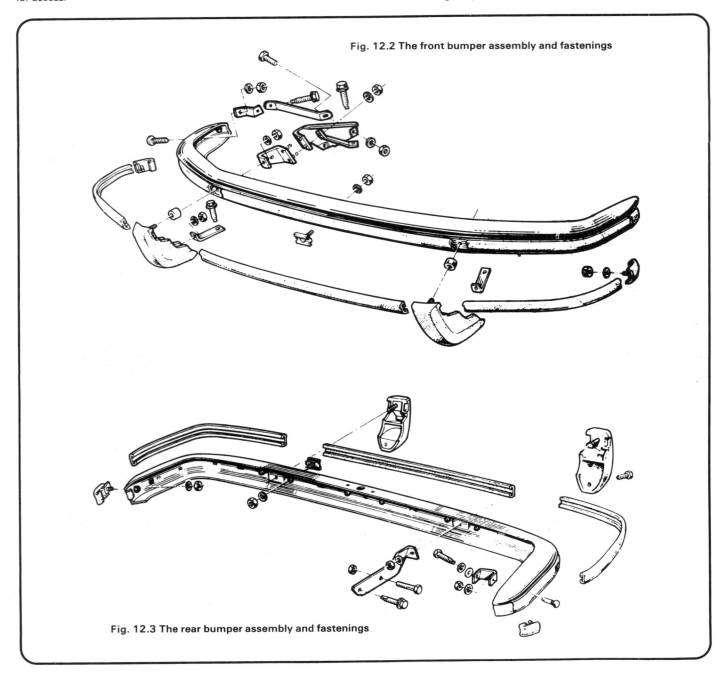

Fig. 12.2 The front bumper assembly and fastenings

Fig. 12.3 The rear bumper assembly and fastenings

Fig. 12.4 The front grille and headlight surround panels showing the fixing point locations

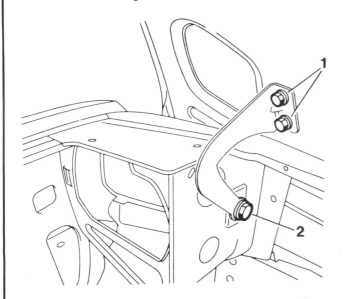

Fig. 12.5 The bonnet hinge showing retaining bolts (1) and pivot bolt (2)

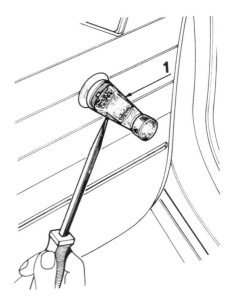

Fig. 12.6 Prise back the winder cover (1)

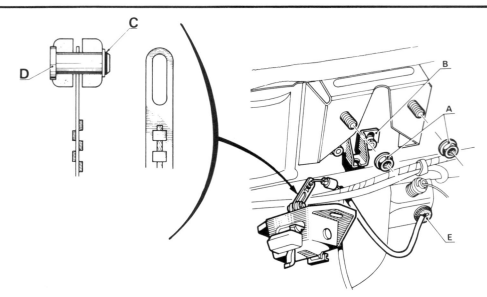

Fig. 12.7 Release catch assembly showing retaining nuts (A), cable sleeve stop (B), cable catch pin and retaining clip (C and D), and grommet (E)

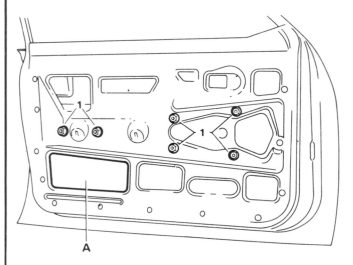

Fig. 12.8 Inner door showing the retaining plate nut positions (1) – withdraw counterbalance through aperture A

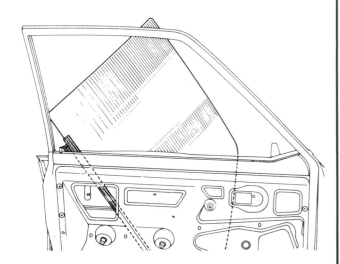

Fig. 12.9 Method of removing window

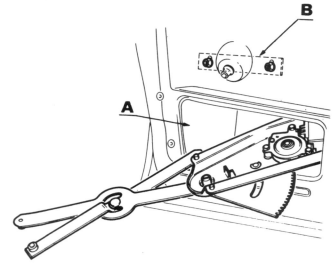

Fig. 12.10 Insert the winder mechanism through aperture A and locate fixed slide B

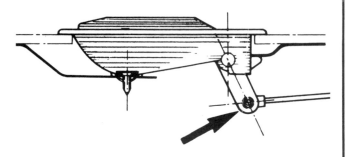

Fig. 12.11 Detach the control rod

7.1 Front grille retaining screw and Allen key for removal

9.2 Press catch lever at point indicated to release

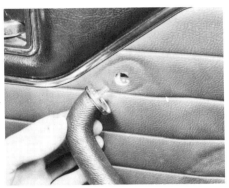

10.1 Arm rest/door pull retainer

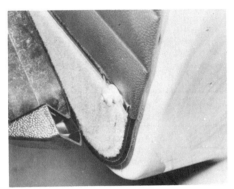

10.2 Slide the pocket from the retainers

10.4 Remove the door catch escutcheon

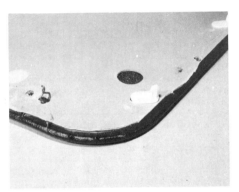

10.6 Door panel retaining clips

these can be undone using a suitable Allen key as shown in the photo. The grille can then be extracted from the car, lifting it clear of the location peg.

2   Refitting is a reversal of the removal procedure.

3   To remove the light panels, remove the grille, then unscrew the panel retaining screws. Withdraw the panel/s.

4   Refit in the reverse sequence.

8   Bonnet – removal and refitting

1   Raise the bonnet and get an assistant to support whilst you unscrew the two retaining bolts of each swan neck bracket. Mark around the bracket prior to removal, using a pencil to act as a guide for correct alignment when refitting. Alternatively, the hinge bolt can be removed if desired, but it will be necessary to remove the front grille and headlight panels as given in the previous Section for the method. Remove the bonnet.

2   Refitting is a reversal of the removal procedure, but check the bonnet for correct fitting adjustment on completion.

3   To adjust the bonnet for alignment, loosen the two hinge bracket retaining bolts and move the bonnet to adjust as necessary. Then retighten the bolts.

9   Bonnet lock release cable assembly – removal and refitting

1   If the release catch cable has broken, the bonnet can be raised and the catch released in the following manner.

2   Remove the front grille and headlight panels (see Section 7), and withdraw the inboard light unit each side. Unscrew and remove the bonnet hinge pivot bolt each side and raise and support the bonnet at the front sufficiently to pass a thin rod through to press onto the release catch at the point indicated (photo). Simultaneously, raise the bonnet at its rear edge and lift clear.

3   To renew the cable, unscrew and remove the catch retaining nuts and detach the cable.

4   Disconnect the cable from its sleeve stop on the bulkhead.

5   Prise the cable catch retaining pin C-clip free and extract the pin.

6   From within the car, pull the cable through the bulkhead.

7   Unscrew the lower steering column surround, then unscrew the steering column catch release fixing screws. Remove the cable assembly.

8   Refitting is a reversal of the removal procedure, but check the bonnet for adjustment and security when closed and, if necessary, make further adjustment (see Section 8).

10   Door trim – removal and refitting

1   Unscrew and remove the door pull/arm rest retaining screws, after prising the caps free as necessary. Rotate the arm rest and remove it (photo).

2   Slide the front door pocket up and detach it from the retainers. Remove the retainer screws (photo).

3   Prise the rubber free from around the lock indicator capsule.

4   Unscrew the door catch escutcheon retaining screw (photo).

5   On the rear doors use a screwdriver blade to prise back the window winder handle plastic cover, as shown in Fig. 12.7. Unscrew the retaining nut to remove the handle. On models manufactured after 1978 (fitted with a remote control door mirror) unscrew the control sleeve (just forward of the arm rest).

6   The trim panel can now be removed by prising it free from the various retaining clips around the door panel (photo). Start at the door lower edge and take care not to damage the panel or clips. When all the panel clips are released, lift the panel clear of the lock indicator capsule and remove it.

7   Access to the door panel inner mechanisms can be gained by peeling back the plastic dirt seal sheet.

8   Refitting is a reversal of the removal procedure.

11 Front door window and electric winder mechanism – removal and refitting

1 Lower the window about halfway. Disconnect the battery earth lead.
2 Remove the front door trim panel (see Section 10).
3 Disconnect the window winder motor wiring.
4 Remove the six winder assembly retaining nuts as shown in Fig. 12.8.
5 Support the window in the half way position, then push the plate in to free it, and the counterbalance, from the lower window channel, and detach the rollers.
6 Pivot the counterbalance and extract it through the lower rear door inner panel aperture.
7 The window can now be lowered, tilted and then lifted out as shown in Fig. 12.9.
8 To refit, locate the outer rubber seal strip into position, engaging into the clips with a wooden dowel.
9 Insert the window into the door frame, locating it into the frame side channels.
10 Locate the winder mechanism and engage the slide and roller.
11 With the roller engaged, locate the fixed plate but do not tighten the retaining nuts fully before checking the window mechanism for correct engagement.
12 Reconnect the battery and motor feed wires, then test the window operation fully in both directions before refitting the trim panel.

12 Electro-magnetic door lock – removal and refitting

A description of the electro-magnetic locks system is given in Chapter 10.
1 Refer to Section 10, remove the door trim panel.
2 Close the door window completely.
3 Unscrew and remove the three lock retaining screws (photo) and the lower actioner securing bolt.
4 Detach the remote control rod, as shown in Fig. 12.11.
5 Refeferring to Fig. 12.12, remove the remote control rod bearing by rotating it 90°.
6 Pull the retaining clip from the lock barrel, then disconnect the junction block from the change-over switch. The lock barrel can now be extracted from the door.
7 Detach the pushbutton and, holding it in the vertical position, pass the lock round the window channel and extract the lock unit through the door frame aperture.
8 To remove the door lock indicator, prise the capsule retaining flange tab free, then turn the capsule 90° to release the lug and detach.
9 Refittting of the door lock mechanism components is a reversal of the removal procedure.
10 When checking the locks for operation, note that the childproof locks operate in the same manner as normal, being actuated when the lever is in the 'up' position.

13 Front door lock barrel – removal and refitting

1 Open the door and lock it, then remove the handle retaining screw from the rear edge, tilt the handle downwards and remove it.
2 Working through the aperture in the door, withdraw the barrel sleeve retaining clip. It is slotted and can be prised from the sleeve, but try not to drop it down into the door or you will have to remove the trim panel to retrieve it.
3 Withdraw the lock barrel assembly and disconnect the change-over block where an electro-magnetic door lock is fitted.
4 Extract the pin to remove the barrel from the sleeve.
5 Refittting is a reversal of the removal procedure. Ensure that the retaining clip is firmly in position over the sleeve, when fitted, and use a new clip if the old one has become defective or lost its tension on the sleeve. When finally assembled, test the lock mechanism for operation to ensure that it is satisfactory.

14 Doors – removal and refitting

1 Referring to Section 10, remove the door trim.

2 Disconnect the battery earth lead.
3 Take a note of the respective positions and detach the leads to the door lock switch unit and the window winder motor unit (where fitted).
4 Position a jack or support under the door. Use a suitable punch drift and drive out the hinge pins from the top and bottom door hinges. An assistant would be helpful here, to hold the door and support it once the pins are removed.
5 Refitting is a reversal of the removal procedure. Always use new hinge pins and ensure that the respective wires are correctly reconnected. Lubricate the hinges with engine oil. Use the same number of shims on assembly to each hinge to adjust the door initially.
6 The door adjustment is made (if needed) by inserting or removing hinge shims (as applicable) to align the door to the front pillar. Height adjustment is gained by loosening the hinges and moving accordingly in the slotted holes.

15 External door handle – removal and refitting

1 Remove the inner trim panel (see Section 10).
2 Unscrew and remove the handle retaining nut on the inner panel face, as shown in Fig. 12.13.
3 Prise the forked retainer clip free and remove the handle.
4 Refit in the reverse order, but use a new retainer clip if the old one was damaged or defective on removal.

16 Window and window winder mechanism (manual type) – removal and refitting

1 Referring to Section 10, remove the door trim panel.
2 Open the window half way, then unscrew and remove the three winder plate retaining screws. Press the plate inwards to detach it as shown in Fig. 12.14.
3 Remove the counterbalance from the lower channel, disengaging the rollers.
4 Pivot the counterbalance unit and extract it through the aperture in the lower door frame, as shown.
5 The window can now be lowered, tilted and pulled upwards to remove it from the door.
6 If a new glass is being fitted to the runner, ensure that when fitted, it is located as shown in Fig. 12.15, 75mm (3 in) from the edge.
7 Fit in the reverse order. When the glass is located into the window slide at the bottom edge, insert the plate retaining bolts (hand tight). Lift the window fully, then tighten the three retainer nuts. Smear some light grease into the slide and check the operation of the winder before refitting the panel.

17 Tailgate – removal and refitting

1 The tailgate is hinged along its top edge at two points, and when opened, is retained by a counterbalance arm each side. Remove as follows.
2 Disconnect the heated rear window wire at the counter joint.
3 Get an assistant to support the tailgate in the open position whilst you unscrew the counterbalance arm retaining screws each side.
4 Unscrew the respective hinge nuts (photo) and lift the tailgate clear. Note the respective adjuster shims with each hinge.
5 Refitting is a reversal of the above procedure. If, when refitted, the tailgate needs adjustment to allow correct positioning, add or remove more shims at the hinges as applicable for height setting. To adjust the tailgate aperture frame alignment loosen the hinge nuts and slide the tailgate in the desired direction. Retighten the nuts.

18 Tailgate counterbalance arm – removal and refitting

1 It is not necessary to remove the tailgate when a counterbalance arm has to be detached.
2 Remove the main parcel shelf and the secondary parcel shelf.
3 Unscrew the tailgate arm retaining screws (photo).
4 Prise the hinge pin retaining clip free (photo) and remove the counterbalance arm.
5 Refitting is a reversal of the removal procedure.

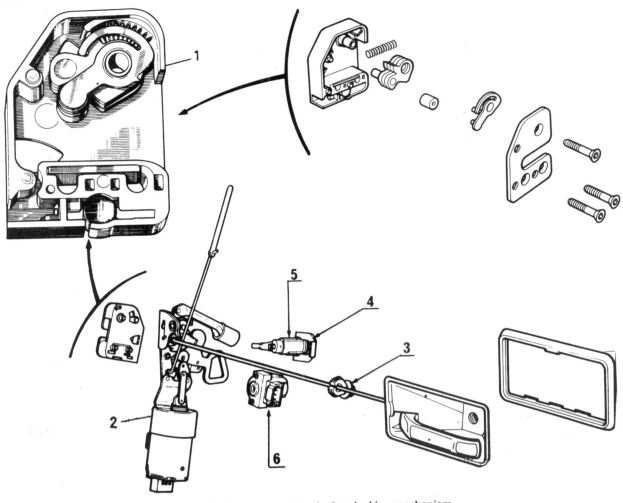

Fig. 12.12 Electro-magnetic door locking mechanism

1 Door catch and components	2 Electro-magnetic actioner	4 Lock barrel retaining clip	6 Changeover switch
	3 Control rod bearing	5 Lock barrel	

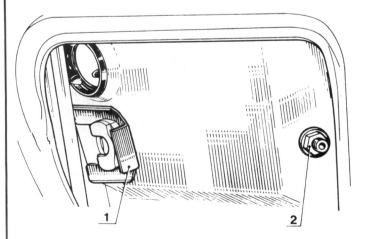

Fig. 12.13 External door handle retaining nut (2) and clip (1)

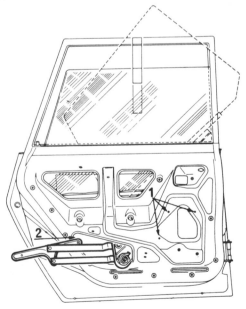

Fig. 12.14 The inner panel showing the three plate retaining screws (1) and counterbalance removal aperture (2) — note angle of window for removal

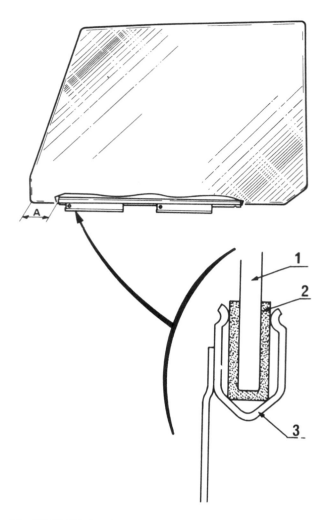

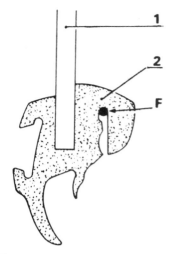

Fig. 12.16 The windscreen (1) and seal rubber (2) showing location for string (F)

Fig. 12.15 Window bottom channel to be located as shown, distance A to equal 75 mm (3 in) — inset shows glass (1), seal (2) and channel (3)

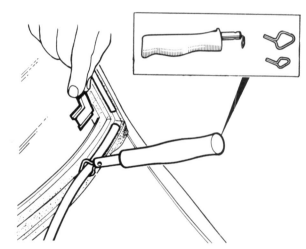

Fig. 12.17 Fitting the embellisher strip and corner pieces using special Renault tool no 438

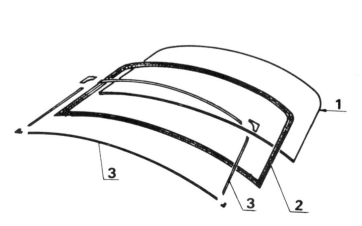

Fig. 12.18 Windscreen fittings, showing glass (1) seal (2) and embellishers (3)

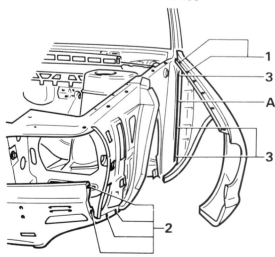

Fig. 12.19 Front wing panel fixing points — see text

19 Scuttle grille – removal and refitting

1   The scuttle grille is the body panel directly in front of the windscreen lower edge which must be removed to gain access to the windscreen wiper motor, heater matrix and associate components.
2   Remove the windscreen wiper arm and blade assembly each side.
3   Prise the three ventilation grilles free, but take care as they are made of plastic.
4   Unscrew the three screws retaining the scuttle to the bulkhead and the two to the windscreen moulding.
5   Detach the windscreen washer tubes to the jets and lift the grille clear.
6   Refitting is a reversal of the removal procedure. The self-adhesive sealing strips should be renewed if defective or badly worn. Engage all the screws before tightening them. Align the windscreen wiper arms on the pivots and check alignment when operating and parked.

20 Windscreen and rear window – removal and refitting

1   Removal of either the windscreen or rear window will be required for one of two reasons; the glass shattering or deterioration of the rubber surround causing water leaks into the interior of the vehicle. Remove the wiper arms.

2   Where the glass has shattered, the easiest way to remove the screen is to stick a sheet of self-adhesive paper or plastic sheeting to each side and push it from the inside outwards. Seal the air intake grille on the scuttle and air ducts and radio speaker slots on the facia panel to prevent glass crystals from falling into them during the removal operation. Protect the surface of the bonnet with a blanket to prevent scratching. On the rear screen disconnect the heater element wire.
3   Where the glass is to be removed in order to renew the rubber surround, make up two pads of cloth and with the aid of an assistant press the two top corners of the screen from the inside outwards and at the same time pulling the rubber surround from the upper corners. Remove the rubber surround as soon as the screen is withdrawn and clean the edges of both the glass and the body screen frame.
4   Commence refitting by positioning the rubber surround round the edge of the windscreen glass. Place the assembly flat down on a bench or table.
5   Lay a length of string or thin cord (F) in the channel in the inner side of the rubber surround as shown in Fig. 12.17.
6   The string should be about 3 mm (0.125 in) diameter and the ends should overlap at the bottom edge by 100 mm (4 in) and leave a few inches to grip with the hands.
7   Place a bead of sealing mastic in the lower two corners of the screen frame.
8   Locate the lower edge of the screen surround in the body frame so that the two ends of the string hang inside the car, then pull both ends

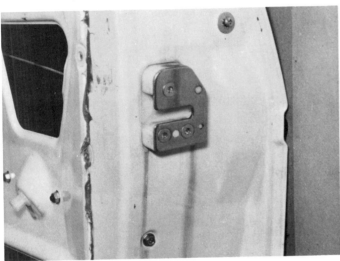
12.3 Door lock showing three retaining screws

17.4 Tailgate hinge nuts

18.3 Counterbalance arm retaining screws – note slots in bracket for adjustment

18.4 Counterbalance arm top pivot pin and retaining clip

208

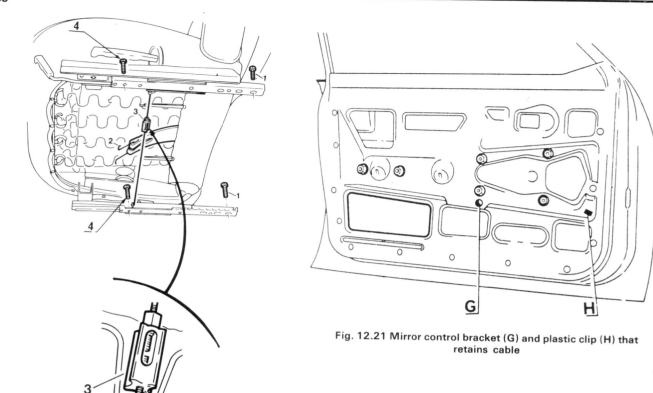

Fig. 12.21 Mirror control bracket (G) and plastic clip (H) that retains cable

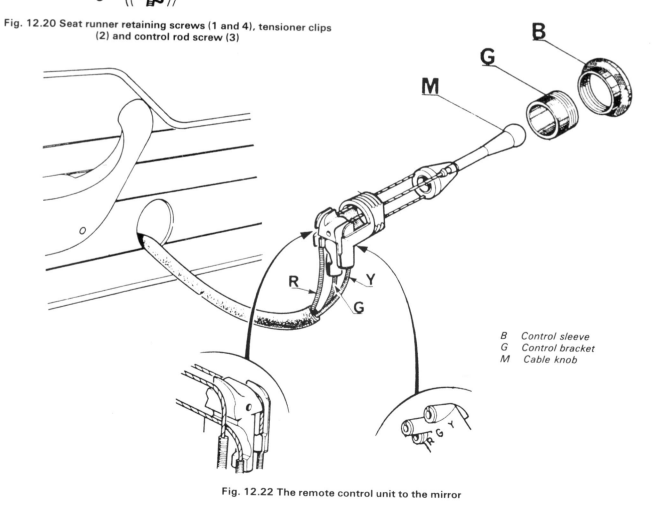

Fig. 12.20 Seat runner retaining screws (1 and 4), tensioner clips (2) and control rod screw (3)

B Control sleeve
G Control bracket
M Cable knob

Fig. 12.22 The remote control unit to the mirror

of the string while an assistant presses the glass and surround into position as the operation progresses.

9   The string will finally emerge from the top centre of the rubber surround and the screen and rubber surround lip should be in correct engagement with the screen frame.

10   Using either a sealing mastic gun or tube, insert the nozzle between the rubber surround lip and the outer surface of the screen frame and insert a thin even bead of sealer. Press the rubber surround hard to spread the sealer and to ensure correct location. Wipe away any excess sealer with a paraffin moistened cloth.

11   The embillisher should be located round the seal before it is fitted. You will need to improvise here and fabricate a suitable tool to insert the embillisher strips. The official Renault tool for the job (No 438) is shown in Fig. 12.18. When the strips are fitted, locate the corner piece to complete.

21   Front wing panel – removal and refitting

1   Disconnect the battery earth lead.

2   Referring to Section 19, remove the scuttle grille.

3   Referring to Section 6, remove the front bumper.

4   Unscrew and remove the wing retaining screws at the points shown in Fig. 12.19. Unscrew them from the top edge (1), the wing to lower front and panel (2) and the rear vertical edge (3). Remove the wing panel.

5   Refitting the wing panel is a reversal of the removal instructions. Apply sealer to the rear edge joint (A) when fitting. Before tightening the fasteners fully, check the wing for alignment. When in position and secured, apply underseal to the wing underside. Apply sealer to the area around the front panel to wing joint.

22   Front seats – removal and refitting

1   Slide the seat forward to gain access to the runner rear retaining bolts. Unscrew and remove the bolt from each runner.

2   Slide the seat rearwards and repeat the procedure with the front runner bolts.

3   Use a screwdriver and prise the two tensioner clips free underneath as shown in Fig. 12.20. Lift the seat out.

4   Refit in the reverse order and, if necessary, adjust the slide control by tensioning the control rod screw accordingly.

23   Remote control rear view mirror – removal and refitting

1   Remove the door trim panel as detailed in Section 10.

2   Lower the window so that its top edge is 100 mm (4 in) from the seal edge.

3   Remove the mirror control bracket and the plastic seal sheet as shown in Fig. 12.21.

4   Prise the mirror control cable retaining clip free within the door.

5   Remove the mirror retaining screws, then pull the mirror free from the outside and guide the control cable through the window channel.

6   To refit the mirror, pass the control and cable through from the outer door panel and guide the control and cable past the channel of the window and through the inner panel aperture as shown in Fig. 12.22.

7   Insert the mirror retaining screws and refit the control bracket. Locate the plastic clip to retain the cable and check the window and mirror operate satisfactorily. Refit the inner trim panel and adjust the mirror to complete.

Chapter 13 Supplement:
Revisions and information on later models

Contents

1 Introduction

This Chapter contains information which has become available since this manual was first written. Most of the information, therefore, relates to the Renaults 20 TS annd 20 LS (R1277) and the Renault 20 TX (R1279), all of which were introduced into the UK after 1980.

The Sections in this Chapter follow the same order as the first twelve Chapters of the book. The Specifications are all grouped together for convenience, but they too are arranged in Chapter order.

It is suggested that before undertaking a particular job, reference be made first to this Supplement for the latest information, then to the appropriate Chapter earlier in the book. In this way any revisions can be noted before the job begins.

2 Specifications

The following Specifications are supplementary to, or revisions of, those at the beginning of the preceding Chapters

OHC engine (R1277 20 TS and 20 LS models)
Except for the following information, Specifications are as for R1272 models

Engine (general)
Type	829 – for identification see table in text
Compression ratio	See identification table
Static ignition advance	10° ± 1°

Valve assemblies
Valve seat width:	
Inlet	1.80 mm (0.071 in)
Exhaust	1.60 mm (0.063 in)
Valve spring free length (inlet and exhaust):	
J5R type	47.2 mm (1.858 in)
J6R type	46.0 mm (1.811 in)

Camshaft
Valve timing:	
J5R (suffix E7 20) and J6R (suffix A7 00, B7 01, C7 00,	
D7 01, G7 02, H7 03, N7 02, P7 03 and P7 14)	As R1272 models
J5R (suffix A7 30 and B7 31) and J6R (suffix L7 16, J7 10	
and K7 11):	
Inlet opens	17° BTDC
Inlet closes	63° ABDC
Exhaust opens	63° BBDC
Exhaust closes	17° ATDC

Crankshaft
Crankshaft endfloat	0.07 to 0.25 mm (0.003 to 0.010 in)

OHC engine (R1279 20 TX models)
Except for the following information, Specifications are as for R1272 models

Engine (general)

Type:	
With manual transmission	851 (or J6T) A7 00
With automatic transmission	851 (or J6T) B7 01
Stroke	89 mm (3.504 in)
Cubic capacity	2165 cm³
Maximum power	115 bhp (DIN) at 5500 rpm
Maximum torque	133 lbf ft at 3000 rpm
Static ignition advance	10° ± 1°
Valve clearances (cold):	
Inlet	0.10 mm (0.004 in)
Exhaust	0.25 mm (0.010 in)

Valve assemblies

Valve seat width:	
Inlet	1.80 mm (0.071 in)
Exhaust	1.60 mm (0.063 in)
Valve spring free length:	
Inlet and exhaust	46.0 mm (1.811 in)

Camshaft

Endfloat	0.07 to 0.15 mm (0.003 to 0.006 in)
Valve timing:	
Inlet opens	17° BTDC
Inlet closes	63° ABDC
Exhaust opens	63° BBDC
Exhaust closes	17° ATDC

Crankshaft

Crankshaft endfloat	0.13 to 0.30 mm (0.005 to 0.012 in)

Torque wrench settings

	Nm	lbf ft
Crankshaft pulley bolt	120 to 135	88.5 to 99.5
Connecting rod cap bolts	60 to 65	44 to 48

Cooling system
Specifications for the cooling system fitted to 20 LS and 20 TX models are as given for the 20 TS model in Chapter 2

Fuel and exhaust systems
Carburettors (model fitment)

Vehicle	Carburettor type	Carburettor mark/suffix
R1271 (20 TL - 1980)	Weber 32 DARA 50	099 or 100
R1277 (20 TS and 20 LS - 1981 on):		
Manual transmission	Weber 32 DARA 42	101
Automatic transmission	Weber 32 DARA 43	101
Automatic transmission with air conditioning	Weber 32 DARA 43	104
R1279 (20 TX):		
Manual transmission	Weber 32 DARA 6	—
Automatic transmission	Weber 32 DARA 7	104
Automatic transmission with air conditioning	Weber 32 DARA 7c	104

Weber 32 DARA 50

	1st barrel	2nd barrel
Choke tube	24	26
Main jet	132	150
Idle jet	50	45
Air compensation jet	180	145
Emulsifier	F53	F6
Mixture centraliser	3.5	4.5
Accelerator pump jet	60	
Needle valve	1.75	
Float level	7 mm (0.275 in)	
Float travel	8 mm (0.315 in)	
Initial throttle butterfly opening (extreme cold)	1.30 mm (0.051 in)	
Pneumatic part-open setting:		
Compensator depressed	5 mm (0.197 in)	
Compensator released	7 mm (0.275 in)	
Deflooding	10 mm (0.394 in)	

Weber 32 DARA 42 and 43

	1st barrel	2nd barrel
Choke tube	26	26
Main jet:		
DARA 42 - 1981 model year	132	132

	1st barrel	2nd barrel
DARA 42 - 1982 model year	135	130
DARA 43 - 1981 model year	132	135
DARA 43 - 1982 model year	135	135
Idle jet:		
DARA 42	52	45
DARA 43	57	42
Air compensation jet:		
DARA 42 - 1981 model year	160	145
DARA 42 - 1982 model year	155	155
DARA 43 - 1981 model year	160	140
DARA 43 - 1982 model year	155	140
Emulsifier	F58	F6
Mixture centraliser	3.5	4
Accelerator pump jet	60	
Needle valve	2.25	
Fuel level	7 mm (0.275 in)	
Float travel	8 mm (0.315 in)	
Initial throttle butterfly opening:		
Extreme cold:		
DARA 42 - 1981 model year	1.30 mm (0.051 in)	
DARA 43 - 1981 model year	1.45 mm (0.057 in)	
Medium cold:		
DARA 42 and 43 - 1982 model year	0.95 mm (0.037 in)	
Pneumatic part-open setting:		
Compensator depressed	5.5 mm (0.216 in)	
Compensator released	10 mm (0.394 in)	
Deflooding	9 mm (0.354 in)	
Throttle butterfly angle:		
DARA 42	5.39 mm (0.212 in) − 12° 40'	
DARA 43	5.83 mm (0.229 in) − 13° 40'	
Throttle opener:		
DARA 43 suffix 104	0.45 mm (0.018 in)	
Exhaust gas CO content at idle:		
DARA 42 and 6	1 to 2%	
DARA 43, 7 and 7c:		
1981 model year	1 to 2%	
1982 model year	0.5 to 1.5%	

Weber 32 DARA 6, 7 and 7c

	1st barrel	2nd barrel
Choke tube	26	28
Main jet:		
DARA 6	127	145
DARA 7 and 7c - 1981 model year	130	160
DARA 7 and 7c - 1982 model year	132	160
Idle jet:		
DARA 6	62	42
DARA 7 and 7c	60	42
Air compensation jet:		
DARA 6	155	155
DARA 7 and 7c - 1981 model year	170	170
DARA 7 and 7c - 1982 model year	160	170
Emulsifier	F58	F6
Mixture centraliser	3.5	4
Accelerator pump jet	60	
Needle valve	2.25	
Fuel level	7 mm (0.275 in)	
Float travel	8 mm (0.315 in)	
Initial throttle butterfly opening (medium cold):		
DARA 6	1.0 mm (0.039 in)	
DARA 7 and 7c - 1981 model year	1.2 mm (0.047 in)	
DARA 7 and 7c - 1982 model year	1.05 mm (0.041 in)	
Pneumatic part-open setting:		
Compensator depressed	5.5 mm (0.216 in)	
Compensator released	10 mm (0.394 in)	
Deflooding:		
DARA 6	9 mm (0.354 in)	
DARA 7 and 7c - 1981 model year	10 mm (0.394 in)	
DARA 7 and 7c - 1982 model year	9 mm (0.354 in)	
Throttle butterfly angle:		
DARA 6	5.46 mm (0.215 in) − 12° 50'	
DARA 7 and 7c - 1981 model year	5.54 mm (0.218 in) − 13°	
DARA 7 and 7c - 1982 model year	5.83 mm (0.229 in) − 13° 40'	
Throttle opener (automatic transmission with air conditioning)	0.45 mm (0.018 in))	
Exhaust gas CO content at idle:		
DARA 7 and 7c - 1982 model year	0.5 to 1.5%	

Idle speeds
Weber 32 DARA 50, 42 and 6 .... 800 rpm
Weber 32 DARA 43, 7 and 7c:
    1981 model year .... 675 rpm
    1982 model year .... 900 rpm

Fuel tank capacity
TS, LS and TX models .... 64 litres (14.0 gallons)

Ignition system
The following Specifications are for R1277 (20 TS and 20 LS – 1981 on) and R1279 (20 TX) models only

Ignition system type .... Electronic ignition (no contact breaker points). Non-adjustable – computer controlled

Spark plugs
Type .... Marchal SCGT 34 5H or Champion BN7Y
Electrode gap .... 0.55 to 0.65 mm (0.022 to 0.026 in)

Clutch
The clutch fitted to the R1277 (20 TS and 20 LS) and R1279 (20 TX) is similar to that fitted to R1272 (20 TS) models – see Chapter 5

Manual gearbox
Renault type number
R1272 (20 TS and 20 LS):
    1980 model year 369 000
    1981 model year NG2 000
R1277 (20 TS and 20 LS):
    1981 model year .... NG2 000 or NG3 005
    1982 on .... As 1981 or 369 000
R1279 (20 TX) 369 000

Gearbox lubrication
Oil capacity:
    369 .... 6.0 pints (3.4 litres)
    NG2 and NG3 .... 3.5 pints (2.0 litres)
Oil type .... SAE 80W hypoid gear oil to API GL5

Gear ratios
NG2 and NG3:
    1st .... 3.82 : 1 (42/11)
    2nd .... 2.17 : 1 (37/17)
    3rd .... 1.41 : 1 (31/22)
    4th .... 1.03 : 1 (34/33)
    5th (NG3 only) .... 0.86 : 1 (31/36)
    Reverse .... 3.08 : 1 (37/12)
    Final drive .... 9 x 34
369:
    1st to reverse .... As Chapter 6
    Final drive .... 9 x 37 (1980 on)

Primary shaft endfloat
NG2 only .... 0.02 to 0.12 mm (0.0008 to 0.0047 in)

Differential bearings pre-load
NG2 and NG3:
    New bearings .... 9 to 13 lbf (4 to 6 da N)
    Re-used bearings .... Free turning, no play

Torque wrench settings	lbf ft	Nm
Crownwheel bolt:		
NG2 and NG3	92	125
Primary shaft nut:		
369	88 to 110	120 to 150
NG3	96	130
Secondary shaft nut:		
NG2 and NG3	110	150
Reverse selector securing bolt:		
369	25	34
NG2 and NG3	18	25

Automatic transmission
Renault type number
R1277 (20 TS and 20 LS):
    1981 model year 4141-29
    1982 on .... MJ3 suffix 100, 102 and 500
R1279 (20 TX):
    1981 model year 4141-53
    1982 on .... MJ3 suffix 000 and 002

Transmission lubrication (MJ3)
Oil capacity:
    From dry .... 10.5 pints (6.0 litres)
    Drain and refill .... 4.4 pints (2.5 litres)

Drive ratios
Step-down:
    MJ3 500 .... 23 x 25
    All other MJ3 types .... 26 x 25
Final drive .... 9 x 32
Speedometer drive:
    MJ3 500 .... 6 x 19
    MJ3 100 and 102 .... 6 x 18
    MJ3 000 and 002 .... 7 x 20

Torque wrench settings	lbf ft	Nm
Sunwheel cover plate bolts	14.5	20

Driveshafts, wheels and tyres
Wheels

	R1272 and R1277 (20 TS and 20 LS)	R1279 (20 TX)
Size	5½B13	5½J14

Tyres

	R1272 and R1277 (20 TS and 20 LS)	R1279 (20 TX)
Size	165 SR 13 or 165 HR 13	165 SR 14 or 190/65 HR 390
Inflation pressures:		
Normal running:		
Front	32 lbf/in² (2.2 bar)	27.5 lbf/in² (1.9 bar)
Rear	29 lbf/in² (2.0 bar)	29 lbf/in² (2.0 bar)
Fully laden or motorway use:		
Front	33.5 lbf/in² (2.3 bar)	30.5 lbf/in² (2.1 bar)
Rear	30.5 lbf/in² (2.1 bar)	32 lbf/in² (2.2 bar)

Note: *On automatic transmission models, add 1.5 lbf/in² (0.1 bar) to the front tyre pressures*

Braking system
The front and rear brake assemblies fitted to the R1277 (20 TS and 20 LS) and R1279 (20 TX) are similar to those specified for the R1272 (20 TS) models in Chapter 9

Electrical system
Starter motor
R1279 (20 TX) .... Paris Rhone D8E 140,
Paris Rhone D10E 74 or
Ducellier 532 004

Alternator
R1279 (20 TX) .... Paris Rhone A13 R228

Suspension and steering
Front axle and steering geometry

	R1277 (20 TS and 20 LS)	R1279 (20 TX)
Camber angle:		
Unladen	0° 20' ± 30'	0° ± 30'
Maximum difference between left and right-hand sides	1°	1°
Kingpin inclination:		
Unladen	13° ± 30'	6° 30' ± 30'
Maximum difference between left and right-hand sides	1°	1°
Castor angle (all models):	**Standard steering**	**Power steering**
Nominal value – vehicle floor level:		
H5 - H2 = 5 mm (0.20 in)	2° ± 30'	5° ± 30'
H5 - H2 = 30 mm (1.20 in)	1° 30'	4° 30'
H5 - H2 = 50 mm (2.0 in)	1°	4°
H5 - H2 = 75 mm (3.0 in)	0° 30'	3° 30'
H5 - H2 = 100 mm (4.0 in)	0°	3°
Adjustment by tie-rod rotation	0° 15' = 1 turn	

Parallelism:
Toe-out (unladen) .... 0° 10' ± 10' (1 mm ± 1 mm/0.04 in ± 0.04 in)
Adjustment by steering arm rotation .... 0° 30' (3 mm/0.12 in) = 1 turn

Rear axle
Camber angle (unladen) .... −1° ± 30'
Parallelism (unladen) .... 0° ± 10' (0 ± 1 mm/0 ± 0.04 in)

Torque wrench settings – lbf ft (Nm)

Front suspension

	R1277	R1279
Front shock absorber:		
Top nut	11 (15)	11 (15)
Bottom nut	59 (80)	59 (80)
Bottom locknut	29.5 (40)	44 (60)
Upper suspension arm:		
Pivot bolt	66.5 (90)	37 (50)
Balljoint nut	48 (65)	26 (35)
Lower suspension arm:		
Pivot bolt	66.5 (90)	96 (130)
Balljoint nut	48 (65)	37 (50)

Fig. 13.1 The engine identification plate location on TS (1981 on), LS and TX models

A	Engine type	D	Engine suffix
B	Homologation letter	E	Engine number (preceded by
C	RNUR identity		suffix)

3 Engine identification – TS (1981 on), LS and TX models

1   When buying spare parts for an engine, it is necessary to clearly identify the engine type. The engine identification plate is attached to the cylinder block, as shown in the accompanying figure (Fig. 13.1).
2   The following table is provided as a means of clarifying engine adaptation:

829 or J5R (1995 cm³)

Suffix	Compression ratio	Vehicle type
A7 00	9.2:1	1272 (manual)
B7 01	9.2:1	1272 (automatic)
C7 00	8.0:1	1272 (manual)
D7 01	8.0:1	1272 (automatic)
G7 02	9.2:1	1277 (manual)
H7 03	9.2:1	1277 (automatic)
N7 02	8.0:1	1277 (manual)
P7 03	8.0:1	1277 (automatic)
P7 14	8.6:1	1277 (manual)

851 or J6T (2165 cm³)

Suffix	Compression ratio	Vehicle type
A7 00	9.2:1	1279 (manual)
B7 01	9.2:1	1279 (automatic)

4 Engine – ohc types 829 and 851

Connecting rods – fitting (type 851)
1   Each connecting rod is drilled to ensure that oil is sprayed onto the underside of the piston. During fitting, check that the drilling in each rod faces the oil filter.
2   The big-end bearing shells must be fitted so that the plain half is in the cap and the drilled half in the rod. Renault recommend that the cap bolts be changed each time the caps are removed.
3   Apart from the above information, the procedure given in Section 85, Chapter 1, holds good. Note the torque wrench settings given in the Specifications Section of this Chapter.

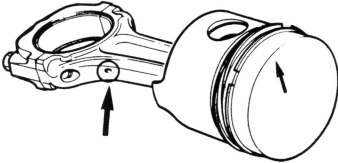

Fig. 13.2 Type 851 engines have each connecting rod drilled
Arrow on piston faces flywheel

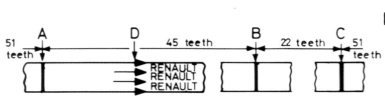

Fig. 13.3 The timing belt markings

A, B and C Setting marks
D   Direction of fitting (engine rotation)

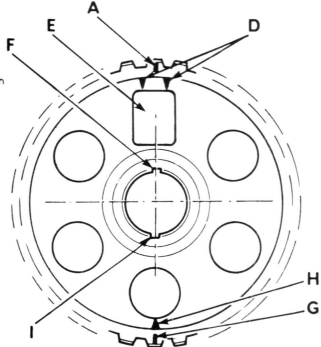

Fig. 13.4 The camshaft sprocket markings

Type 851 engine	Type 829 engine (post 1981)
A Timing mark	*G Timing mark*
D Bosses	*H Boss*
E Inspection hole	*I Keyway*
F Keyway	

Timing sprockets, tensioner and belt — fitting and adjustment (types 829 and 851)

4   The timing belt is marked to indicate which way it should be fitted and as an aid to setting the timing. The belt for the 829 engine has 116 teeth whereas the belt for the 851 engine has 118 teeth.
5   The camshaft sprocket shown in the accompanying figure (Fig. 13.4) will be found fitted to all 851 engines but only to post 1981 829 engines. The timing marks and keyways are clearly indicated; choose the correct keyway for your engine type before fitting and position the camshaft with the keyway vertical.
6   The procedure for timing belt removal is similar to that given for ohc engines in Chapter 1, but ensure the timing mark on the camshaft sprocket is aligned with the fixed pointer on the timing belt cover before commencing the operation.
7   To obtain the correct valve timing, refer to the accompanying figure (Fig. 13.5) and turn the crankshaft so that its keyway is positioned as shown. Positioning the crankshaft thus will place the pistons halfway down their bores, thereby obviating the risk of the valves touching the piston crowns as the camshaft is turned.
8   Now turn the camshaft so that its sprocket timing mark is 45° to the left of a vertical taken through the camshaft centreline.
9   Position the intermediate shaft so that its sprocket timing mark is 70° to the right of a downwards vertical taken through the shaft centre.
10 Using a 0.1 mm (0.004 in) thick feeler gauge, check the clearance between the tensioner plate and the body of the intermediate shaft. The gauge should be a light, sliding fit. If necessary, adjust the clearance by releasing the adjuster screw locknut and turning the screw. Tighten the locknut on completion and recheck the clearance.
11 Fit the timing belt. Each mark on the belt should be aligned with the respective sprocket timing mark. Viewed from the front of the engine, the arrows on the belt should appear on the right-hand side of the belt run.
12 To tension the belt, release the two nuts securing the tensioner $\frac{1}{4}$ of a turn each. The tensioner will automatically move to tension the belt and it must be confirmed that this movement has taken place before the securing nuts are retightened.

Flywheel — fitting (types 829 and 851)

13 The flywheel fitted to vehicles with electronic ignition has holes machined in its periphery which enable the ignition sensor to determine the crankshaft position.
14 Before fitting the flywheel, clean and degrease the crankshaft and flywheel mating surfaces before coating one of them with Loctite Autoform or an equivalent locking compound. The threads of the flywheel securing bolts must also be degreased and coated with a thread locking compound.

Oil leakage (types 829 and 851)

15 Instances of camshaft oil seal failure have resulted in oil appearing around the cylinder head-to-block just at the timing gear end of the engine. Due to movement of the engine whilst running, oil tends to find its way along the joint towards the alternator.
16 Where seal failure is suspected, remove the timing cover and thoroughly clean the area around the seal and joint. Generously cover the cleaned area in talc and run the engine for 10 minutes. Oil discolouring the talc will show the source of leakage.

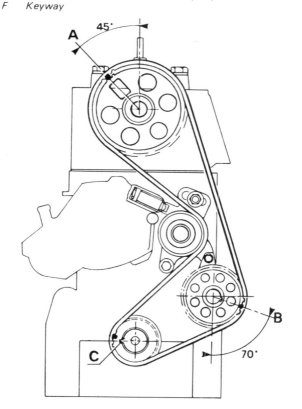

Fig. 13.5 Setting the valve timing

A   Camshaft sprocket position   *C   Crankshaft keyway position*
B   Intermediate sprocket position

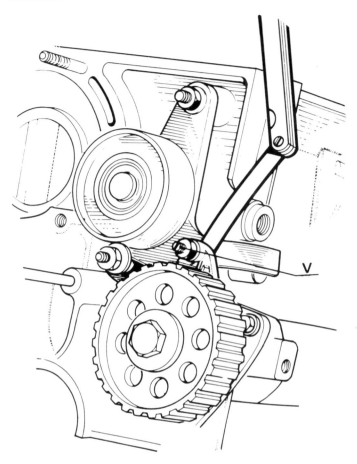

Fig. 13.6 Checking the timing belt tensioner plate clearance

V   *Adjuster screw and locknut*

5   Fuel and exhaust systems

Weber 32 carburettor – modifications and adjustment

1   Apart from the following modifications, the Weber 32 carburettor has changed very little from those fitted to earlier vehicles; therefore the service information given in Chapter 3 still holds good if used in conjunction with the Specifications at the beginning of this Chapter.

Constant CO idling circuit

2   Carburettors fitted to vehicles manufactured for 1981 on are equipped with a constant CO idling circuit. Although similar to the idling circuit of previous carburettors, another adjustment screw and circuit have been added.

3   Reference to the accompanying figure (Fig. 13.7) will show that the additional circuit comprises a channel which connects the flange of the second barrel to the heating flange before progressing to a point downstream of the first barrel butterfly. This channel also joins the progression circuit of the second barrel.

4   With the first barrel butterfly set to a specified angle, the second barrel butterfly should be set to close without jamming. It will be seen that the stop screw of the first barrel butterfly is fitted with a tamperproof cap, the object of this cap being to discourage (and to detect) adjustment by unqualified or unskilled operators.

5   Should you think it necessary to remove the tamperproof cap in order to adjust the butterfly angle, satisfy yourself that you are not breaking any local or national anti-pollution laws by doing so. If the vehicle is still under warranty, be aware that you may be in breach of warranty conditions. Fit a new seal on completion where this is required by law.

6   In order to measure accurately the position of the first barrel butterfly, one of two special tools is required. The first tool (Renault tool no Mot 522) is a dial test indicator coupled to a special adaptor and will measure the butterfly position in millimetres. The second tool (a Solex instrument) will measure the butterfly position in degrees. Before using either tool, it is necessary to remove the carburettor, detach its heating flange and disconnect its fast idle linkage.

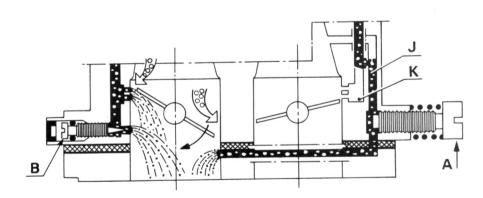

Fig. 13.7 Weber 32 carburettor constant CO idling circuit

A   *Idle speed adjusting screw*
B   *Fuel screw*
J   *Additional circuit*
K   *Second barrel progression circuit*

7   The accompanying figure (Fig. 13.8) shows the method of fixing tool Mot 522. Check that the washer is correctly located in the first barrel opening when fitting the tool. Initially, the tool must be fitted with its setscrew in position A and the gauge then zeroed. Rotate the knurled section of the tool 180 degrees to bring the setscrew to position B and note the gauge reading, which should be as specified at the beginning of this Chapter.

8   Before using the Solex instrument, it is necessary to stand it upright on a surface plate and, with both stems of the tool aligned, check that their needles are in line with the black and red triangles on the gauge. If necessary, alignment can be effected by loosening the lockscrew which passes through the knurled section of the tool and moving the gauge before retightening the screw.

9   Setting the counterweight as near horizontal as possible, position the instrument with its fixed screw in contact with the highest side of the butterfly. Check the base of the instrument is in proper contact with the first barrel flange and is as near centre as possible. Align the red triangles on the gauge with the throttle spindle centreline. The gauge reading should be as specified at the beginning of this Chapter.

10   Whichever tool is used, any necessary adjustment should be made by turning the screw shown in the accompanying figure (Fig. 13.9).

Idling enrichment – manual gearbox

11   Reference to the accompanying figure (Fig. 13.10) will show the operation of the idling enrichment system fitted to vehicles equipped with a manual gearbox from 1981 on.

12   A temperature sensitive valve fitted to the air filter cover is set to close when the temperature inside the cover drops below 15°C (59°F). Directly the valve closes, the fuel/air mixture is enriched by the shut-off of air to the choke tube. As the temperature inside the filter cover rises above 15°C (59°F), the valve opens and enrichment ceases.

13   **Warning:** This system must not be allowed to function during adjustment of the idle speed. Isolate the system by disconnecting the pipe at the carburettor end.

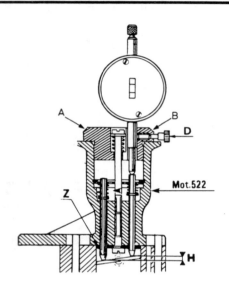

Fig. 13.8 Setting the first barrel butterfly position (tool Mot 522)

A   Initial setscrew location for zeroing the gauge
B   Final setscrew location for measuring the butterfly setting
D   Setscrew
H   Butterfly setting mm (in)
Z   Washer

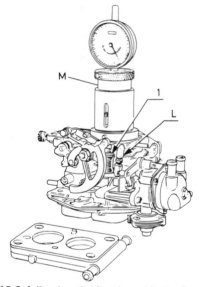

Fig. 13.9 Adjusting the first barrel butterfly position

1   Adjuster screw   M   Solex instrument
L   Fast idle link

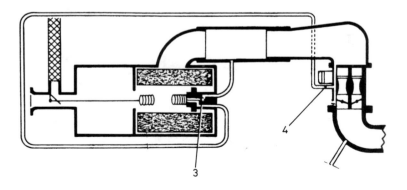

Fig. 13.10 Idling enrichment system (manual gearbox)

3   Temperature sensitive valve
4   Disconnection point (before idle adjustment)

Idling enrichment – automatic transmission

14 The earlier form of enrichment system, fitted to vehicles equipped with automatic transmission for 1981, functions thus. The second barrel idling jet of the carburettor is replaced by a solenoid which is controlled by a vacuum-operated switch at the inlet manifold linked to a temperature sensitive switch on the cylinder head.

15 Enrichment is set to occur when the vacuum in the inlet manifold is in excess of 440 millibars and the coolant temperature below 15°C (59°F). A delay valve holds vacuum pressure constant at the switch for a few seconds after it has dropped in the manifold, thereby retaining enrichment for this time. **Note**: The delay valve must be fitted with its yellow side facing the inlet manifold.

16 The latest form of enrichment system is shown in the accompanying figure (Fig. 13.12). In place of the second barrel idling jet, there is now fitted a jet which incorporates a diaphragm valve. A temperature sensitive valve in the choke coolant circuit is connected to the diaphragm valve and to the inlet manifold. With the coolant temperature below 15°C (59°F), the temperature sensitive valve opens and allows vacuum pressure to act on the diaphragm valve, thereby enriching the fuel/air mixture. As the coolant temperature rises above 15°C (59°F), the temperature sensitive valve closes, cuts off the vacuum circuit and enrichment ceases. A delay valve holds pressure constant for a few seconds after the temperature sensitive valve closes, retaining enrichment for this time. **Note**: The delay valve must be fitted with its blue side facing the temperature sensitive valve.

Idle speed adjustment

17 Refer to the Specifications Section of this Chapter and note the figures relating to exhaust gas CO content at idle and to engine idle speed for the appropriate carburettor type. Run the engine until it reaches normal operating speed before attempting any adjustment. Ensure no electrical accessory is switched on during adjustment. Connect an exhaust gas analyser in accordance with the maker's instructions.

18 The adjustment screws are identified in the accompanying figure (Fig. 13.13). Slowly turn screw A to obtain the correct idle speed. Now turn screw B to obtain the correct reading on the gas analyser. If necessary, repeat the operation until both idle speed and gas content are correct. Any failure to bring the CO content within limitations will indicate a system fault or a well worn engine. It is possible that very fine adjustment will be necessary to obtain exact readings.

19 **Note**: It is necessary to isolate the idling enrichment system fitted

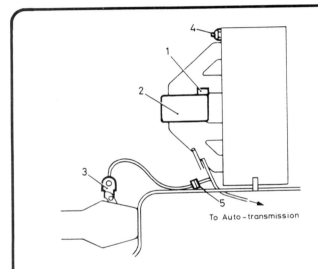

Fig. 13.11 Idling enrichment system (early type – automatic transmission)

1 Solenoid	4 Temperature sensitive switch
2 Carburettor	5 Delay valve
3 Vacuum-operated switch	

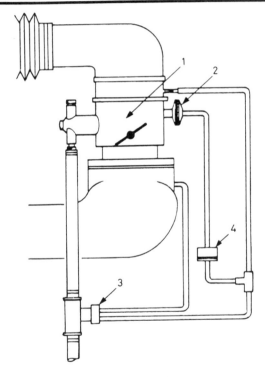

Fig. 13.12 Idling enrichment system (latest type – automatic transmission)

1 Carburettor second barrel	3 Temperature sensitive valve
2 Diaphragm valve	4 Delay valve

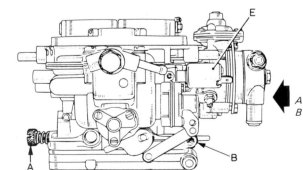

Fig. 13.13 Idle speed adjustment screws

A Idle speed adjusting screw	E Idle cut-out
B Fuel screw	

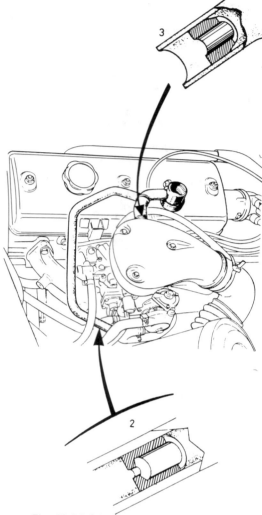

Fig. 13.14 Oil fume recirculation system

2   1.7 mm (0.067 in) bore diameter jet
3   6.5 mm (0.256 in) bore diameter jet

to vehicles equipped with manual gearboxes before adjustment takes place, see paragraph 13 of this Section.

Idle cut-out

20 The purpose of the idle cut-out is to shut off the idling circuit directly the ignition is switched off. The cut-out takes the form of an electrically-operated valve mounted on the carburettor.

21 If the engine 'runs on' after the ignition is switched off, then suspect the valve. To check valve operation, run the engine at idle speed and pull the electrical wire off the valve terminal, whereby the engine should stop. To remove a defective valve, remove the grub screw securing it to the carburettor and pull the valve from its housing.

Emission control

22 Like previous models, Renault 20 models from 1981 on are fitted with a device which recirculates crankcase oil fumes from the rocker cover into the inlet manifold.

23 The accompanying figure (Fig. 13.14) shows the fitted position and size of the two jets which control the direction of fume flow in the system hoses.

Exhaust system

24 Renault 20 TX models have a balljoint type connection between the exhaust downpipe and the expansion box inlet pipe. When fitting this connection, tighten the two securing nuts evenly, a little at a time, until both springs are compressed to a length of 20 mm (0.80 in). Ensure each nut has retained its self-locking qualities before running the engine and checking for exhaust leaks.

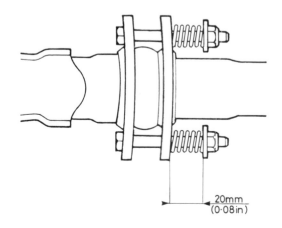

Fig. 13.15 Exhaust system balljoint fitting

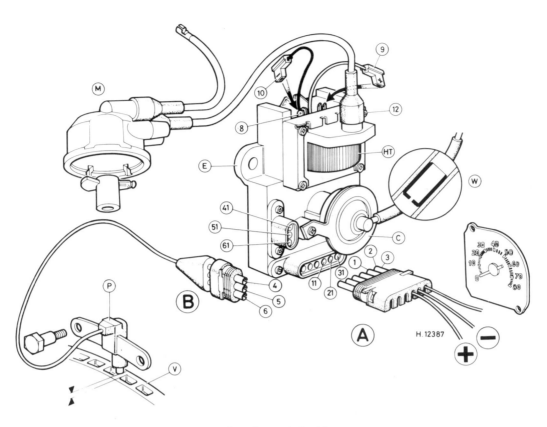

Fig. 13.16 The electronic ignition system

A	Connector	C	Vacuum capsule	HT	HT coil	P	Angular position sensor	W	Vacuum jet
B	Connector	E	Module	M	Distributor	V	Flywheel		All numbers relate to test connections

A   Connector C   Vacuum capsule   HT HT coil   P   Angular position sensor   W   Vacuum jet
B   Connector E   Module   M   Distributor   V   Flywheel   All numbers relate to test connections

6   Ignition system

Electronic ignition system
Operation
1   The centre of the system is an electronic module which receives information sent by a one-piece vacuum capsule attached to it, and by an angular position sensor which is mounted on the clutch housing and which picks up information relating to engine speed and crankshaft positon from cut-outs on the flywheel edge.
2   The module translates engine speed and vacuum into a timing curve and transmits low tension current pulses to the primary windings of the HT coil. Each low tension pulse induces a high tension pulse in the secondary windings of the coil which is then fed onto the distributor and transmitted to the spark plugs in the correct firing order.
3   Ignition timing is effectively fixed, the sensor being attached to the clutch housing by two special shouldered bolts which allow no adjustment of position.

Testing
4   The system does not require maintenance in the generally accepted sense. There are no mechanical parts, therefore wear does not take place and the need for compensation by adjustment does not arise. Problems in the system can be diagnosed as follows:

    (a)   Loose, broken or corroded connections
    (b)   Damaged or broken wiring
    (c)   Faulty or inoperative system components

    The above are arranged in the order in which they are most likely to be found and with the exception of (c), should provide no undue problem in the event of fault finding or rectification.
5   Where a system component fails, unless the fault is obviously mechanical, diagnosis can prove difficult. The following paragraphs provide details of the necessary test procedures most of which can be

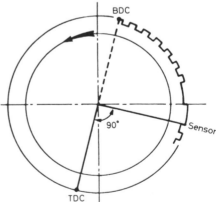

Fig. 13.17 The flywheel cut-out positions

carried out by using an inexpensive pocket multimeter.
6   Before carrying out tests on any electronic ignition system, bear in mind that wrong connections can easily damage a system component. **Note**: Do not earth the LT and HT leads to and from the HT coil. Do not allow the HT lead to contact the module body and do not attempt to detach the vacuum capsule from the module. Beware of shocks from HT connections.
7   If time is not to be wasted, fault finding must be tackled in a methodical fashion. The test procedures which follow show the correct sequence for investigating a complete failure of the system. Each numbered contact is clearly shown on the accompanying figure (Fig. 13.16). Carry out a preliminary check by ensuring the voltage measured between terminal 7 (HT coil +) and a good earth point with the ignition switched on is 9.5 volts.

8   With connector A unplugged, the ignition switched on and the starter spinning the voltage between the module + feed (1) and vehicle earth must be at least 9.5 volts. If not, check the battery current (recharge if necessary) and check the feed wire to the module, otherwise continue to the next test.

9   With connector A unplugged and the ignition off, connect an ohmmeter between terminal 2 and vehicle earth; the reading should be zero. If not, check the module earth wire, otherwise continue to the next test.

10 With connector A unplugged and the ignition switched off connect an ohmmeter between the coil terminals 9 and 11; the reading should be zero. If not, change the module, otherwise continue to the next test.

11 With connector A plugged in and the ignition switched on the voltage between terminal 1 and vehicle earth should be at least 9.5 V. If not, move connector A in and out; if the voltage reading is still incorrect change connector A. If the voltage reading is correct, continue to the next test.

12 With connector B unplugged and the ignition switched off connect an ohmmeter between terminals 4 and 5. The sensor resistance should be 150 ± 50 ohm; if not, change the sensor, otherwise continue to the next test.

13 With connector B unplugged check the sensor insulation by connecting an ohmmeter between terminals 5 and 6. The reading should be infinity; if not, change the sensor assembly, otherwise continue to the next test.

14 With connector B unplugged and the ignition switched off connect an ohmmeter between terminals 4 and 6. The reading should be infinity; if not, change the sensor assembly, otherwise continue to the next test.

15 Check the distance between the sensor and the flywheel, this should be 1 ± 0.5 mm (0.04 ± 0.02 in). If not, change the sensor assembly, otherwise continue to the next test.

16 With connectors A and B plugged in and the engine turning on the starter a test bulb connected between terminals 9 and 10 (with their wires disconnected) should flash at the starter motor speed. If not, change the module, otherwise continue to the next test. **Warning**: Do not transpose leads 9 and 10 when reconnecting the HT coil.

17 With the coil HT lead disconnected and the ignition switched off connect an ohmmeter between terminals 7 and 12. The resistance should be 4000 to 5500 ohm; if not, change the HT coil, otherwise continue to the next test. **Note**: If the meter reads infinity, check that the meter probe is pushed fully into terminal 12.

18 With wires 9 and 10 disconnected and the ignition switched off connect an ohmmeter between terminals 7 and 8. The reading should be less than 10 ohm; if not, change the HT coil, otherwise continue to the next test. **Warning**: Do not transpose leads 9 and 10 when reconnecting the HT coil.

19 Check for the presence of HT current at the distributor. If there is no HT current, change the module.

20 If difficulty in starting is experienced but the engine runs evenly once started, then carry out the following checks:

21 Refer to Chapter 4, Section 13 and check the component parts of the HT system. If the system is found to work perfectly, then suspect a fault in carburation, mechanical condition or initial ignition advance. If the HT spark appears weak or erratic, proceed as follows:

22 Check the feed voltage to the module; this should be at least 9.5 volts. If not, check the battery current (recharge if necessary) otherwise continue to the next test.

23 Measure the sensor resistance between terminals 4 and 5; the ohmmeter reading should be 150 ± 50 ohm. If not, change the sensor, otherwise continue to the next test.

24 Check the sensor distance from the flywheel; this should be 1 ± 0.5 mm (0.04 ± 0.02 in). If not, change the sensor, otherwise continue to the next test.

25 Clean the sensor sensitive face; if the fault remains, renew the sensor.

26 To check the condition of the vacuum capsule, start the engine and allow it to run at a steady 3000 rpm. The capsule is serviceable if, directly the vacuum pipe is pulled from it, the engine speed drops. If the engine speed does not drop, then remove the pipe and examine it closely for splits or deterioration. Ensure the 0.5 mm (0.02 in) diameter jet is correctly located in the vacuum pipe.

27 The vacuum capsule is effectively part of the module, to which it is attached by a very fine wire which will break if the capsule is moved. This means that in the event of capsule failure, the module must be renewed.

7   Manual gearbox

Type 369 gearbox

1   Full information on servicing this type of gearbox is given in Chapter 6, but before commencing any operation, note the Specifications at the beginning of this Chapter.

Type NG2 and NG3 gearboxes

2   The principle operations of removal, refitting and examination of these 'new generation' gearboxes are similar to those given in Chapter 6. When dismantling and reassembling these gearboxes, however, work in a clean and orderly manner whilst noting the following information and the accompanying figures.

3   Before commencing work on the NG3 gearbox, select 3rd or 4th gear. Doing this will prevent the 5th speed interlocking ball from dropping into the gearbox directly the casing is disturbed.

4   On both gearboxes, whilst separating the rear casing, take care to retain the spacer together with the preload adjusting shims for the primary shaft bearing.

5   Upon separation of the casings and removal of the primary and secondary shafts, punch out the roll pin which passes through the primary and clutch shafts and pull the shafts apart. Doing this will allow examination of the shaft splines and, if necessary, dismantling of the primary shaft.

Primary shaft

6   On the NG3 gearbox, difficulty may be experienced when attempting to remove the 5th gear pinion. If necessary, position the shaft vertically between the protected jaws of a vice and use a good strong

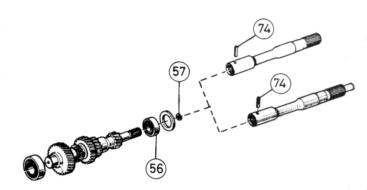

Fig. 13.18 Primary shaft – NG2 gearbox

56   Roller bearing   74   Roll pin
57   Washer

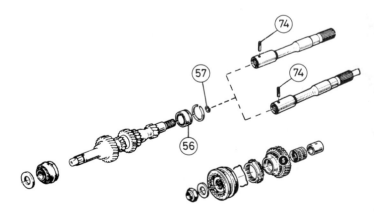

Fig. 13.19 Primary shaft – NG3 gearbox

56   Roller bearing   74   Roll pin
57   Washer

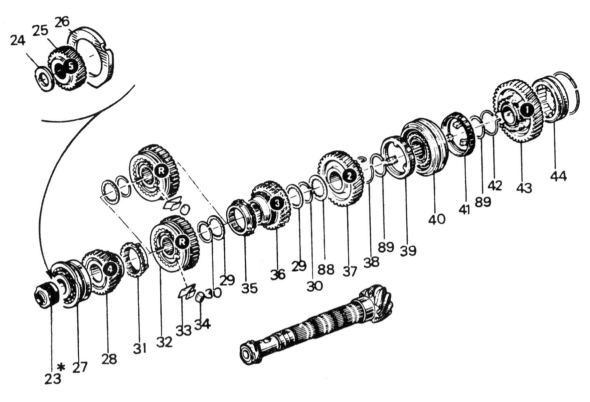

Fig. 13.20 Secondary shaft – NG2 and NG3 gearbox

23 End nut	30 Circlip	37 2nd gear idler pinion	42 1st gear synchro spring
24 Washer	31 4th gear synchro	38 2nd gear synchro spring	43 1st gear idler pinion
25 5th gear pinion	32 3rd/4th gear hub sliding pinion	39 2nd gear synchro	44 Roller bearing
26 Spacer	33 Spring	40 1st/2nd gear sliding hub	88 Splined washer
27 Double taper roller bearing	34 Roller cage	sliding pinion	89 Circlip
28 4th gear idler pinion	35 3rd gear synchro	41 1st gear synchro	* Apply thread locking compound
29 Splined washer	36 3rd gear idler pinion		

puller, with its legs or plates locked under the pinion, to pull the pinion from the shaft.

7   Once removed, check the 5th gear pinion hub for traces of locking compound. If traces are found, clean and degrease the hub-to-shaft mating surfaces before assembly and apply three drops only of Loctite Scelbloc or equivalent before pressing the hub into position. If no traces are found, then simply press the hub into position whilst using a force of 100 to 1500 kg (221 to 3307 lb).

8   On the NG3 gearbox, apply thread locking compound to the shaft end nut before fitting and tightening to the specified torque.

Secondary shaft

9   Position the shaft vertically between the protected jaws of a vice, holding it by the 1st gear pinion. Use a C-spanner to remove the worm nut from the shaft end after having selected 1st gear, see accompanying figure (Fig. 13.21).

10 On the NG3 gearbox, use a puller to remove the 5th gear pinion.

11 Remove the circlips, thrust washers and pinions from the shaft. Remove the shaft from the vice before removing the 1st gear pinion retaining circlip and take care to avoid loss of bearing rollers as the pinion is removed. Renew all circlips before reassembly.

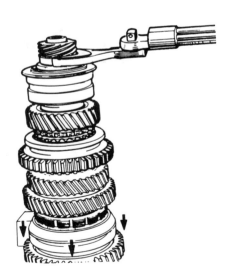

Fig. 13.21 Removing the secondary shaft worm nut

Arrows indicate selection of 1st gear

12 When fitting the 1st/2nd and 3rd/4th pinion hubs, ensure they slide easily on the shaft. Note the accompanying figures (Figs. 13.22 and 13.23).

13 If traces of locking compound are found on the 5th gear pinion centre splines, clean and degrease the splines of both pinion and shaft before applying three drops only of Loctite Scelbloc to the pinion splines prior to refitting.

14 Where the 5th gear pinion is not secured by locking compound, it is free turning by up to three quarters of the number of splines on the shaft. Site the shaft assembly in a press so force is applied only to the 5th gear pinion. Refer to the accompanying figure (Fig. 13.24) and wrap a length of cord around the outer track of the double taper roller bearing. Connect the cord to a spring balance and measure the bearing preload which must be between 15 to 40 N (3.4 to 9.0 lb). Press the 5th gear pinion onto the shaft until the preload is correct. Use a force of 100 to 1500 kg (221 to 3307 lb) on the pinion.

15 Degrease the threads of the worm nut and apply a thread locking compound to them before fitting the nut and tightening it to the specified torque loading.

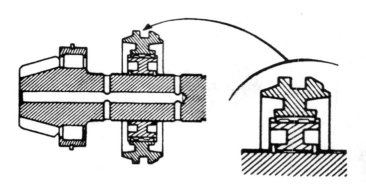

Fig. 13.22 Fitting the 1st/2nd gear pinion hub

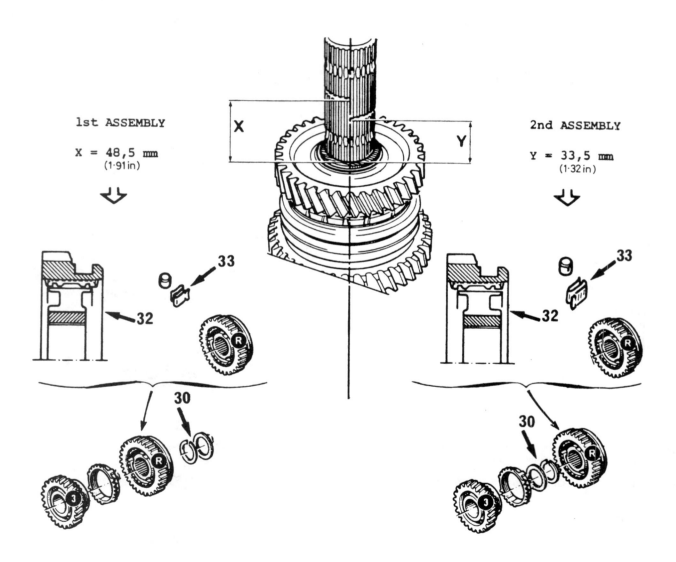

1st ASSEMBLY

X = 48,5 mm
(1·91 in)

X

Y

2nd ASSEMBLY

Y = 33,5 mm
(1·32 in)

Fig. 13.23 Fitting the 3rd/4th gear pinion hub

30 Circlip   32 3rd/4th gear hub sliding pinion   33 Spring

All the parts are identical, but the two assemblies differ – depending on the dimension X or Y of the secondary shaft

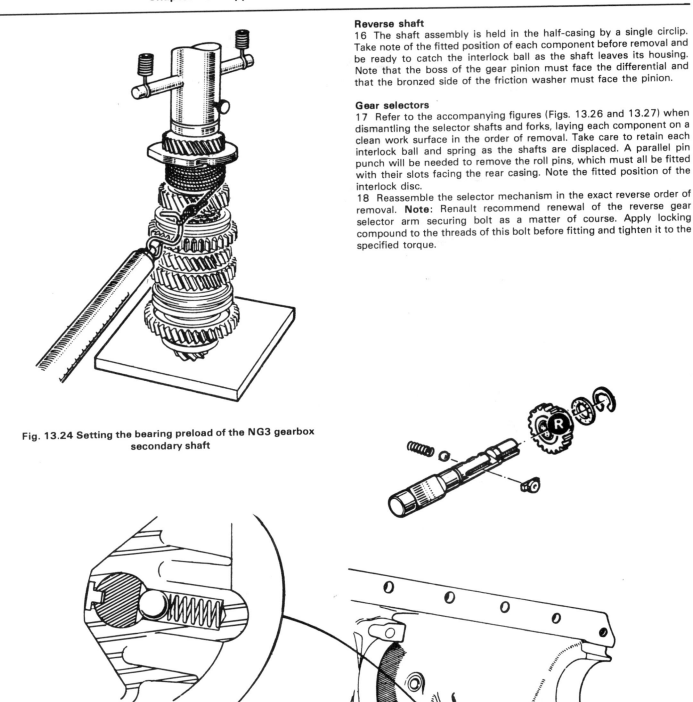

Reverse shaft

16 The shaft assembly is held in the half-casing by a single circlip. Take note of the fitted position of each component before removal and be ready to catch the interlock ball as the shaft leaves its housing. Note that the boss of the gear pinion must face the differential and that the bronzed side of the friction washer must face the pinion.

Gear selectors

17 Refer to the accompanying figures (Figs. 13.26 and 13.27) when dismantling the selector shafts and forks, laying each component on a clean work surface in the order of removal. Take care to retain each interlock ball and spring as the shafts are displaced. A parallel pin punch will be needed to remove the roll pins, which must all be fitted with their slots facing the rear casing. Note the fitted position of the interlock disc.

18 Reassemble the selector mechanism in the exact reverse order of removal. **Note:** Renault recommend renewal of the reverse gear selector arm securing bolt as a matter of course. Apply locking compound to the threads of this bolt before fitting and tighten it to the specified torque.

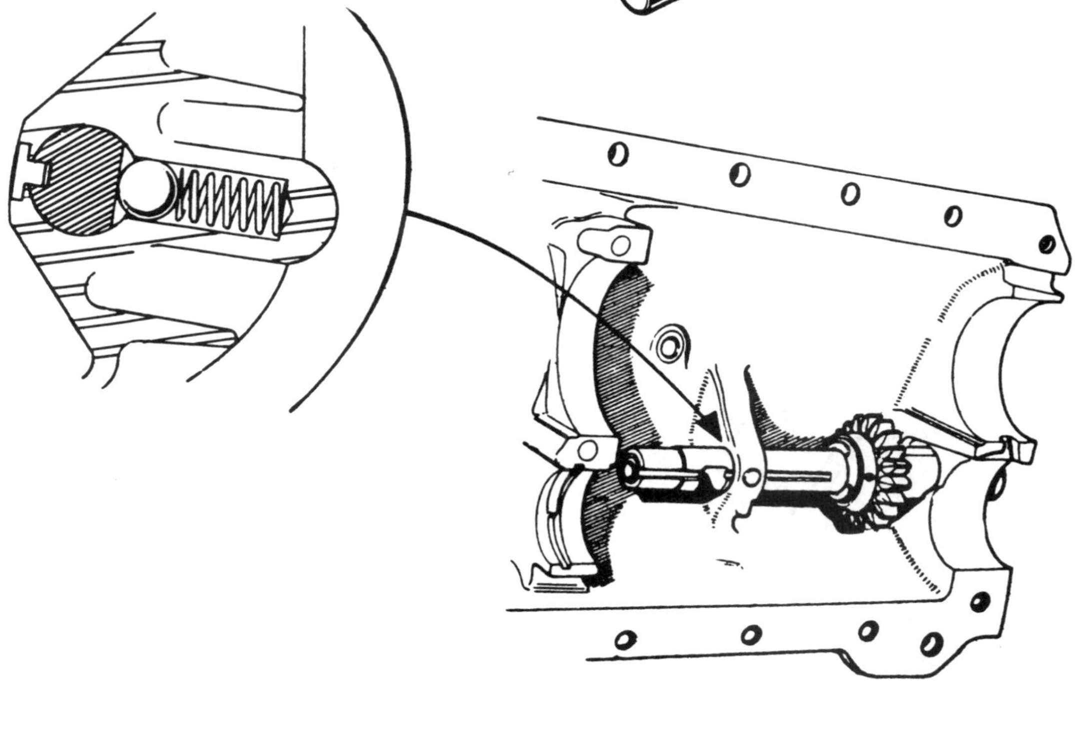

Fig. 13.24 Setting the bearing preload of the NG3 gearbox secondary shaft

Fig. 13.25 The reverse shaft assembly

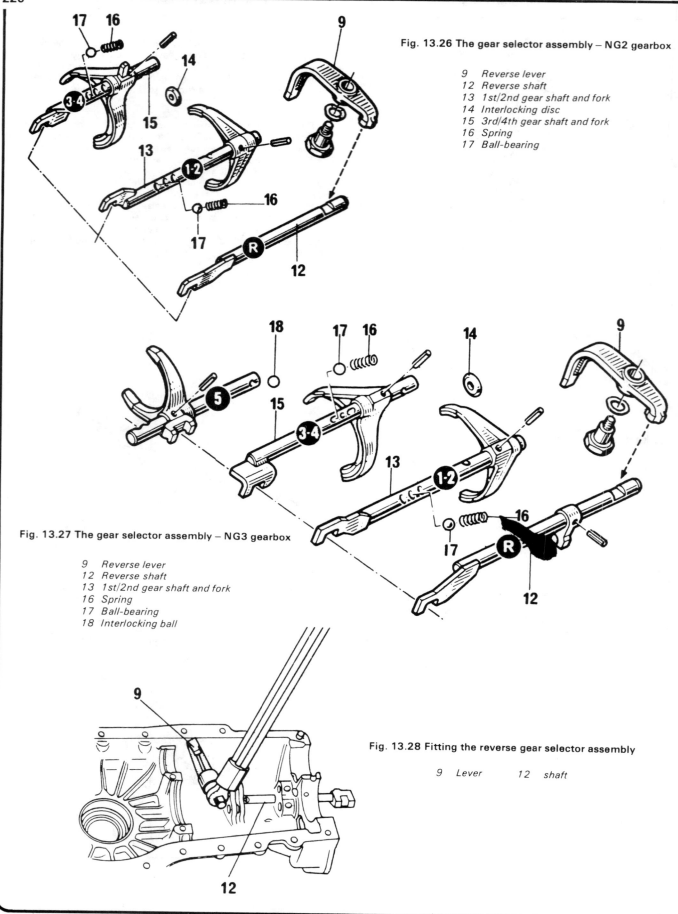

Fig. 13.26 The gear selector assembly – NG2 gearbox

9   Reverse lever
12   Reverse shaft
13   1st/2nd gear shaft and fork
14   Interlocking disc
15   3rd/4th gear shaft and fork
16   Spring
17   Ball-bearing

Fig. 13.27 The gear selector assembly – NG3 gearbox

9   Reverse lever
12   Reverse shaft
13   1st/2nd gear shaft and fork
16   Spring
17   Ball-bearing
18   Interlocking ball

Fig. 13.28 Fitting the reverse gear selector assembly

9   Lever   12   shaft

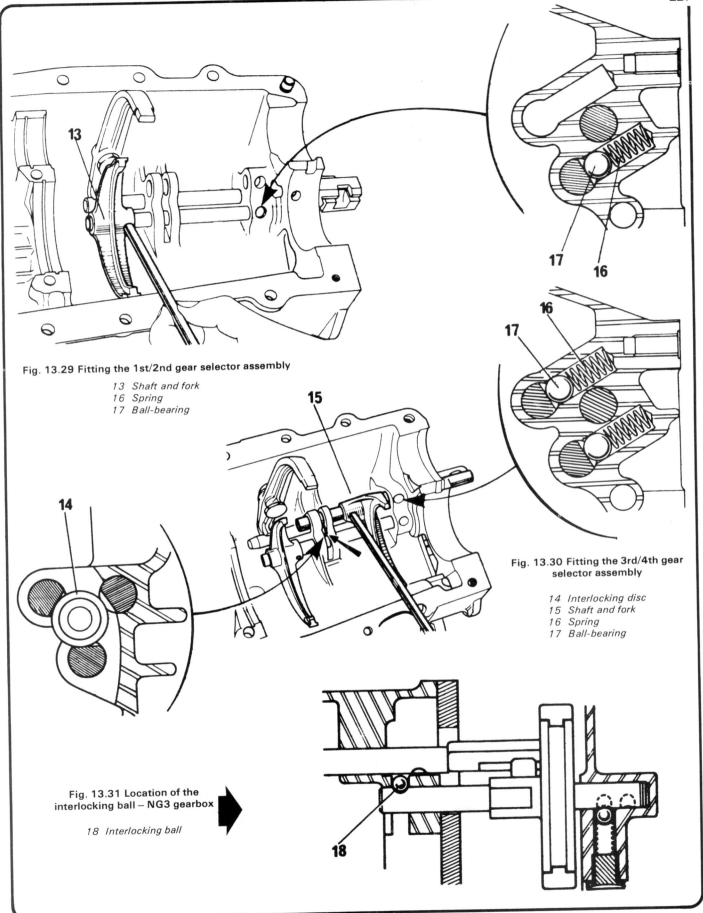

Fig. 13.29 Fitting the 1st/2nd gear selector assembly

13 *Shaft and fork*
16 *Spring*
17 *Ball-bearing*

Fig. 13.30 Fitting the 3rd/4th gear selector assembly

14 *Interlocking disc*
15 *Shaft and fork*
16 *Spring*
17 *Ball-bearing*

Fig. 13.31 Location of the interlocking ball – NG3 gearbox

18 *Interlocking ball*

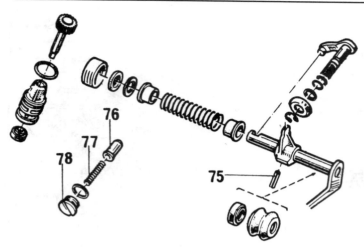

Fig. 13.32 Rear casing shaft assembly – NG2 gearbox

75 Input shaft selector finger roll pin   77 Spring
76 Reverse stop plunger   78 Retaining screw

Rear casing

19 A parallel pin punch will be needed to remove the casing shaft assembly roll pins. Lay each component out in the order of removal. Any defective seals can be removed by careful use of a screwdriver.

20 When examining the shafts, deburr the end which passes through the oil seal with fine emery cloth and then lightly smear it with grease. Doing this will obviate any risk of damage to the seal lip as the shaft is pushed through it. Renew O-rings as a matter of course. Reassemble in the exact reverse order of removal.

21 On the NG3 casing, smear the threads of the spring and pin retaining screw with CAF Thixo compound or an equivalent before fitting. To remove the speedometer drive nut from this type of casing, it is necessary to spread the nut retaining tabs, thereby rendering it unfit for further use. Do not attempt to refit a used speedometer drive nut. When renewing the speedometer drive oil seal, use a shouldered drift to push the new item into its housing. Ensure the drift is a firm fit through the centre of the seal to avoid any risk of it collapsing.

Final assembly

22 The basic procedure for assembly is as given for the types 367 and 369 in Chapter 6, but take careful note of the Specifications and figures in this Chapter and modify your approach accordingly.

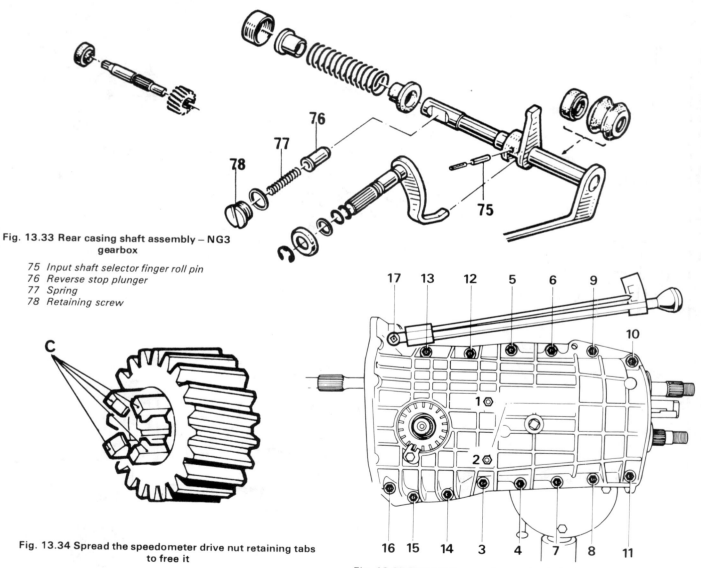

Fig. 13.33 Rear casing shaft assembly – NG3 gearbox

75 Input shaft selector finger roll pin
76 Reverse stop plunger
77 Spring
78 Retaining screw

Fig. 13.34 Spread the speedometer drive nut retaining tabs to free it

C   Retaining tabs

Fig. 13.35 Tighten the gearbox casing bolts in the sequence shown – NG2 and NG3

229

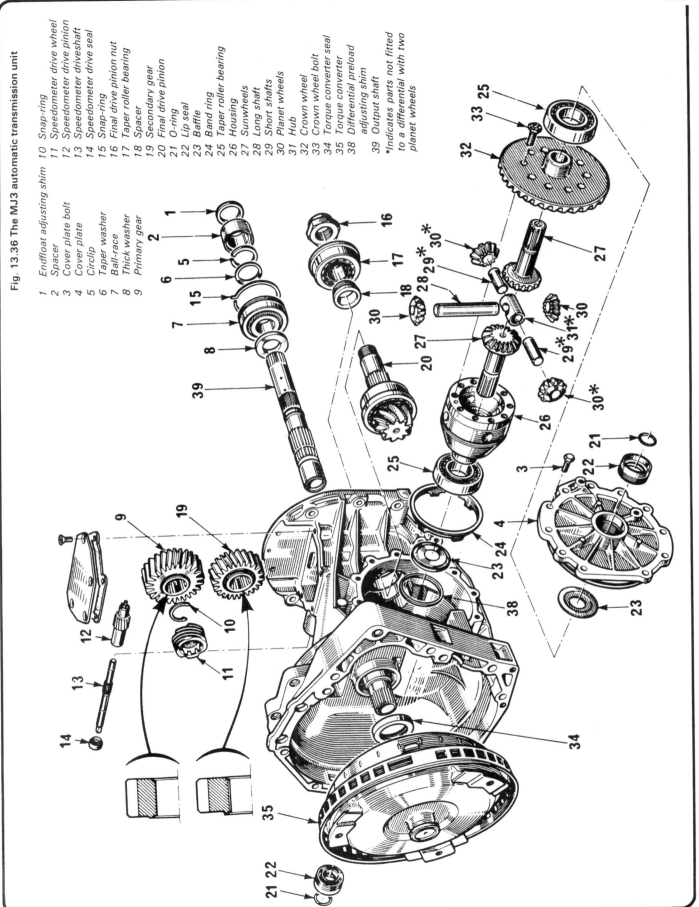

Fig. 13.36 The MJ3 automatic transmission unit

1 Endfloat adjusting shim
2 Spacer
3 Cover plate bolt
4 Cover plate
5 Circlip
6 Taper washer
7 Ball-race
8 Thick washer
9 Primary gear
10 Snap-ring
11 Speedometer drive wheel
12 Speedometer drive pinion
13 Speedometer driveshaft
14 Speedometer drive seal
15 Snap-ring
16 Final drive pinion nut
17 Taper roller bearing
18 Spacer
19 Secondary gear
20 Final drive pinion
21 O-ring
22 Lip seal
23 Baffle
24 Band ring
25 Taper roller bearing
26 Housing
27 Sunwheels
28 Long shaft
29 Short shafts
30 Planet wheels
31 Hub
32 Crown wheel
33 Crown wheel bolt
34 Torque converter seal
35 Torque converter
38 Differential preload adjusting shim
39 Output shaft

*Indicates parts not fitted to a differential with two planet wheels

8   Automatic transmission – type MJ3

General information

1   As with the 4141 series transmission covered in Chapter 7, the amount of repair and reconditioning which can be done by the home mechanic on the MJ3 unit is very limited. Given that the unit is regularly maintained and not abused, it should last for some considerable mileage before serious attention is required.

2   The following table can be used as a guide to unit operation, but note that tolerances built into the unit computer, the speedometer and tyres may cause readings to vary.

Unit type	Accelerator position	Gearchange speeds (mph)			
		1 to 2	2 to 1	2 to 3	3 to 2
MJ3-000	PL	15.5	9.0	31.0	15.5
and	PF	40.0	28.0	71.5	53.0
MJ3-100	RC	43.5	37.0	77.5	65.0
MJ3-500	PL	12.5	9.0	28.0	15.5
	PF	37.0	25.0	68.0	49.5
	RC	40.0	34.0	71.5	59.0

PL is accelerator pedal raised (light throttle)
PF is accelerator pedal fully depressed but without kick-down activated (full throttle)
RC is accelerator pedal depressed to stop with kick-down activated (kick-down)

Maintenance

3   Before commencing with the following operation, check if the transmission dipstick handle is colour coded. If the coding is any other colour than green (that is, grey or yellow) then query this with your Renault dealer.

4   There is only one filler point and one drain plug for the complete transmission unit. The oil type and quantities are given in the Specifications Section of this Chapter.

Oil level check

5   Carry out this check every 1000 miles (1600 km). With the vehicle unladen, park it on an area of flat, horizontal ground. Move the selector lever to park 'P'. Start the engine and run it for two minutes to allow the torque converter and cooler to fill with oil.

6   If the engine has been started from cold, refer to the accompanying figure (Fig. 13.38) and check that the level is between the 'cold' limits on the dipstick. **Warning**: Too much oil will cause the unit to overheat and leak, whereas not enough oil will lead to permanent damage through lack of lubrication.

7   If the vehicle has been driven for approximately half an hour before checking (minimum time) then the oil level should be between the 'hot' limits on the dipstick. Note the preceding warning.

Oil change

8   Carry out this operation every 40 000 miles (60 000 km) with the unit cold.

9   Position a suitable container beneath the unit and remove the drain plug. Remove the dipstick. Whilst waiting for the oil to drain,

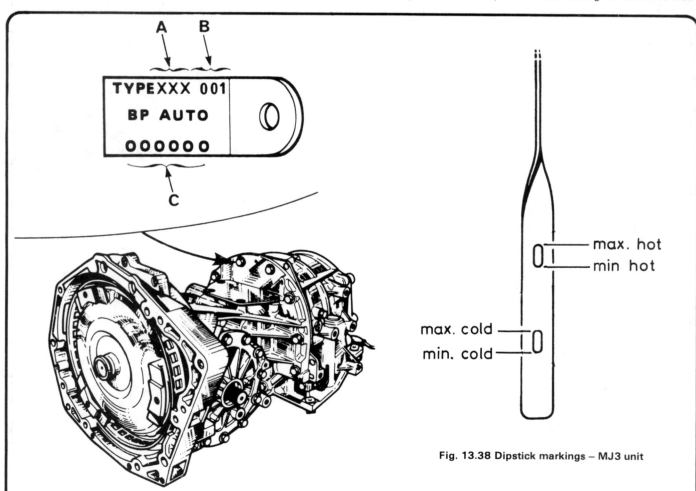

max. hot
min hot

max. cold
min. cold

Fig. 13.38 Dipstick markings – MJ3 unit

Fig. 13.37 The MJ3 automatic transmission identification plate location

A   Transmission type   C   Fabrication number
B   Type suffix

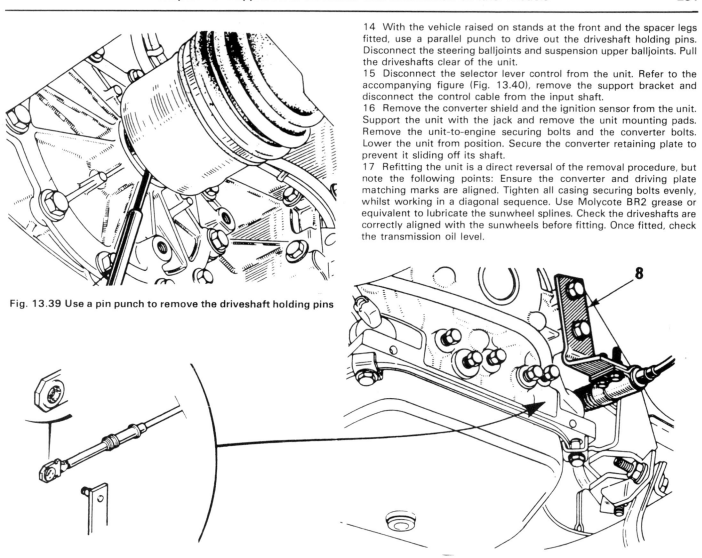

Fig. 13.39 Use a pin punch to remove the driveshaft holding pins

14 With the vehicle raised on stands at the front and the spacer legs fitted, use a parallel punch to drive out the driveshaft holding pins. Disconnect the steering balljoints and suspension upper balljoints. Pull the driveshafts clear of the unit.

15 Disconnect the selector lever control from the unit. Refer to the accompanying figure (Fig. 13.40), remove the support bracket and disconnect the control cable from the input shaft.

16 Remove the converter shield and the ignition sensor from the unit. Support the unit with the jack and remove the unit mounting pads. Remove the unit-to-engine securing bolts and the converter bolts. Lower the unit from position. Secure the converter retaining plate to prevent it sliding off its shaft.

17 Refitting the unit is a direct reversal of the removal procedure, but note the following points: Ensure the converter and driving plate matching marks are aligned. Tighten all casing securing bolts evenly, whilst working in a diagonal sequence. Use Molycote BR2 grease or equivalent to lubricate the sunwheel splines. Check the driveshafts are correctly aligned with the sunwheels before fitting. Once fitted, check the transmission oil level.

Fig. 13.40 Disconnect the selector lever control from the unit

8   Support bracket

renew the drain plug seal and carefully clean around the dipstick housing.

10 Upon completion of draining, refit and tighten the drain plug. Replenish the unit with oil through the dipstick hole, taking care not to allow contamination into the unit. Carry out a 'cold' level check and check around the drain plug for leaks.

Unit removal and refitting

11 Before attempting removal of the unit, carefully read Section 7, Chapter 7 and note the equipment required for the task. Decide upon the method of unit removal and prepare the vehicle accordingly.

12 The MJ3 unit need not be drained of oil before removal. The battery must be disconnected before disturbing any of the electronic ignition connections.

13 The following procedure is that recommended by Renault for removing the unit from beneath the vehicle. Clear all wiring and pipe connections from the unit.

Fig. 13.41 Secure the converter retaining plate

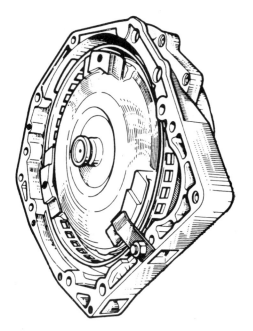

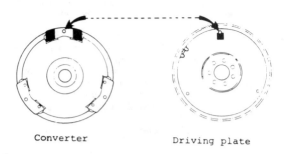

Fig. 13.42 Check alignment of the converter and driving plate alignment marks

Converter   Driving plate

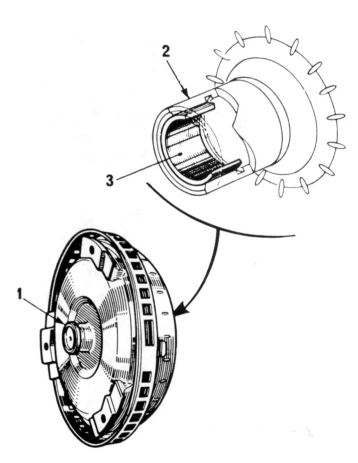

Fig. 13.43 Examine the converter for damage

1   Locating boss   3   White metal bush
2   Sealing area

Fig. 13.44 Free the speedometer driven gear

A   Gear lugs

Converter removal and refitting

18 With the transmission unit removed from the vehicle and the converter retaining plate released, pull the converter off its splined shaft.

19 Blackened oil drained from the converter, especially where traces of clutch and brake disc surfaces are found, will give an indication of internal damage. Any external damage should be obvious. Pay particular attention to the locating boss on the crankshaft side, to the white metal centre bush and to its surrounding sealing area. The converter must be renewed if damaged.

20 If defective, the converter oil seal can be levered from its housing with a screwdriver. Before fitting the new seal, wipe clean its housing and lightly grease the seal lip. Use a hammer and a length of tube of the appropriate diameter to tap the seal home.

21 Refitting the converter is a reversal of the removal procedure. Take care to keep the unit clean and protected at all times.

Differential oil seal renewal

22 Renewal of the differential oil seals will necessitate removal of the sunwheel cover plates. Each plate should be unbolted and its casing lightly tapped around the periphery with a soft-faced hammer to help free the joint. Take care when easing each plate clear to retain the baffles and to prevent the differential shaft from dropping.

23 Note the fitted position of each seal before removal. Carefully lever each seal from position with a screwdriver. Clean each seal housing before drifting each new seal home with a hammer and length of tube of the appropriate diameter. Ensure each seal is placed in the previously noted position.

24 Renew all O-rings and, if necessary, the baffles. Refit the baffles and cover plates. Tighten the plate retaining bolts, a little at a time and in a diagonal sequence to the specified torque.

Speedometer drivegear renewal

25 The speedometer drive assembly is contained in a housing on top of the transmission unit. To allow removal of the housing cover plate, it is first necessary to either free or remove the steering box (depending on the type of vehicle).

26 Disconnect the speedometer cable and remove the cover plate. Take care when lifting the plate from position to prevent its spacers from dropping into the housing.

27 Check the plate gasket is in good condition and renew if necessary. Closely examine the drive assembly *in situ*.

28 If only the driven gear and its spindle is worn or damaged, then free the gear by using a 0.05 mm (0.002 in) feeler gauge and a screwdriver. Fit the gauge beneath the gear lugs whilst freeing them with the screwdriver, see accompanying figure (Fig. 13.44). Use flat-nosed pliers to pull the spindle free.

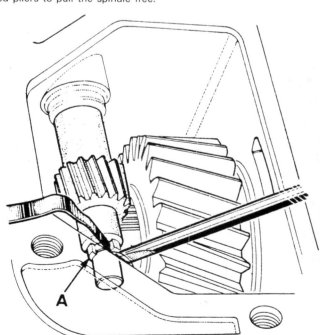

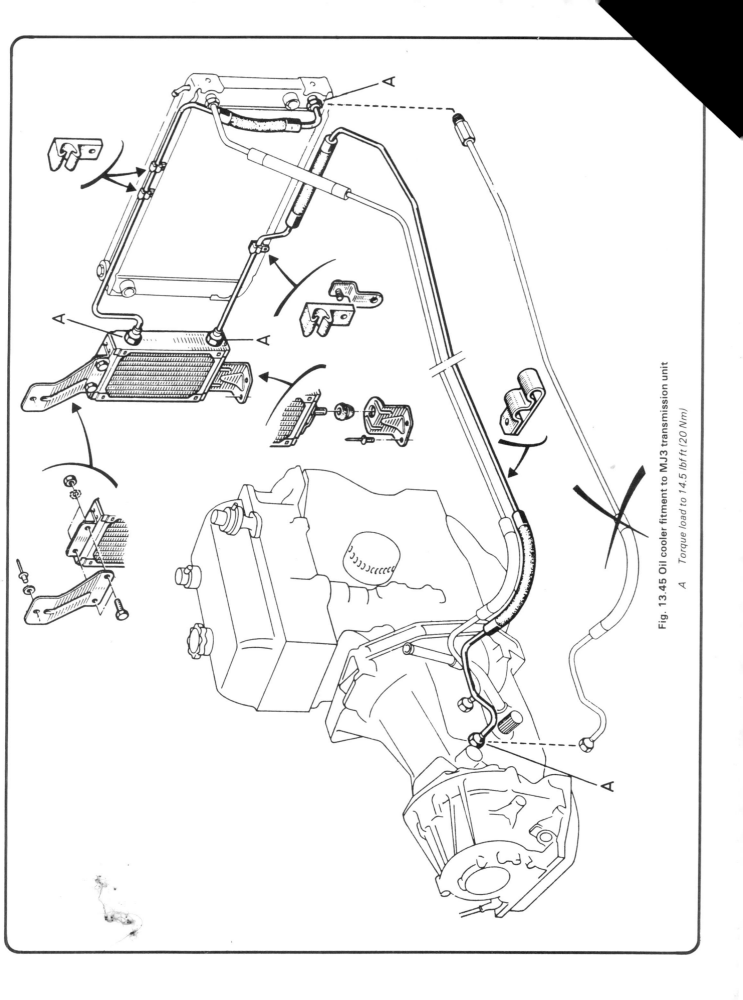

Fig. 13.45 Oil cooler fitment to MJ3 transmission unit

A   Torque load to 14.5 lbf ft (20 Nm)

worm gear is worn or damaged, then the
[ ] be removed from the vehicle and dismantled.
[ ]mission oil if any wear or damage is found. The
[ ] be changed. Particles of polyamide material from
[ ]serious oil contamination.
[ ]icate each component before reassembly.
[ ]eanliness and, on completion, check the transmission oil level.

Oil cooler fitment

32 As stated in Chapter 7, Section 10, an oil cooler can be particularly
useful where the vehicle is used for towing. The accompanying figure
(Fig. 13.45) shows the method of fitting a cooler to the MJ3
transmission unit. Renault specify the following towing maximums:

Vehicle type	Unbraked trailer	Braked trailer
R1277:		
No cooler	992 lb (450 kg)	992 lb (450 kg)
Cooler	1345 lb (610 kg)	2866 lb (1300 kg)
R1279:		
No cooler	992 lb (450 kg)	992 lb (450 kg)
Cooler	1422 lb (645 kg)	2866 lb (1300 kg)

Note: With a cooler fitted, the oil capacity of the transmission unit
is increased by 0.35 pint (0.2 litre).

Control adjustments

33 The controls for the MJ3 transmission are all electrical and
therefore any fault diagnosis and adjustment should be entrusted to
your Renault dealer.

9 Braking system

Brake pressure limiter values

1 When adjusting the cut-off pressure for the limiter valve, see
Chapter 9, Section 10, refer to the following values:

Vehicle type	Fuel tank level	Cut-off pressure (lbf/in²)
R1277	Full	406.0
	Half-full	362.5
	Empty	333.5
R1279	Full	522.0
	Half-full	478.5
	Empty	449.5

No luggage being carried and driver in position.

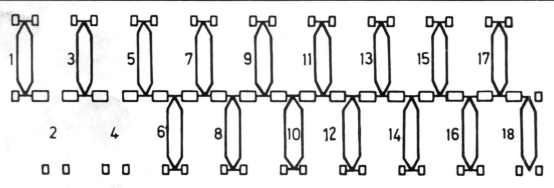

Fig. 13.46 Fusebox layout – 1981 models

1	Flasher unit (8A)	12	Right-hand sidelight and rearlight/glove compartment illumination (5A)
3	Stop light switch (5A)	13	Right-hand front door window (10A)
5	Clock and radio supply (5A)	14	Instrument panel supply (5A)
6	Cigar lighter/interior light/map light/windscreen wiper motor (8A)	15	Reversing light switch/windscreen wiper and wash time switch (16A)
7	Left-hand headlight dip beam (5A)	16	Automatic transmission (1.5A)
8	Combination lighting and windscreen wiper/wash switch (16A)	17	Heating fan motor rheostat/air conditioning (16A)
9	Right-hand headlight dip beam (5A)	18	Rear screen wash/wipe and demister switch (16A)
10	Left-hand sidelight and rearlight/dashboard illumination (5A)		
11	Left-hand front door window (10A)		

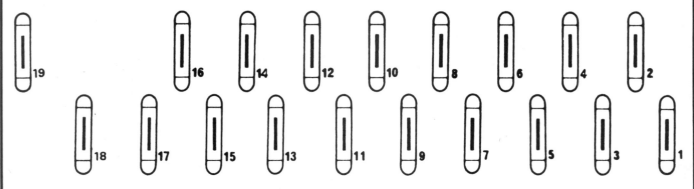

Fig. 13.47 Fusebox layout – 1982 models

Fuse functions as for 1981 apart from:
3   Stoplight switch and 'Normalur' cruise control (5A)
5   Clock, radio and 'Driving aid' supply (5A)

17   Rear screen demister switch and wash/wipe switch (16A)
18   Heating fan motor rheostat/air conditioning (16A)
19   Rear foglight switch

Fuses 2 and 4 are not used

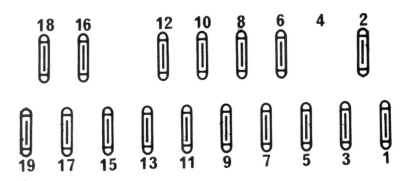

Fig. 13.48 Fusebox layout – 1983 models

1   Flasher unit (8A)
2   Left-hand side and rear lights/instrument illumination (5A)
3   Right-hand side and rear lights (5A)
5   Cigar lighter (8A)
6   Interior lights (8A)
7   Windscreen wiper park (5A)
8   Air conditioning (25A)
9   Window motor (16A)
10 Window motor (16A)

11 Rear screen demister/wiper (16A)
12 Automatic transmission (1.5A)
13 Reversing lights/Heating fan motor (8A)
15 Windscreen wiper motor (16A)
16 Starter lever/instrument illumination (5A)
17 Accessories/radio (5A)
18 Rear foglight (5A)
19 Stop light switch (5A)

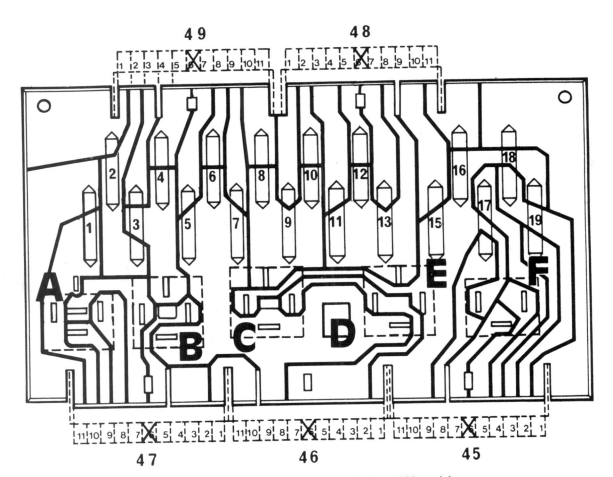

Fig. 13.49 Accessories plate printed circuit – 1983 models

Key overleaf

Fig. 13.49 Key to accessories plate printed circuit – 1983 models

Connector 45
1 Rear foglight switch (+)
2 Rear foglight fuse (+)
3 Stop-lights switch (+)
4 Accessories fuse (+)
5 Lighting 'On' buzzer
6 Safety notch
7 Lighting 'On' buzzer earth
8 Clock (+)/Radio (+)/Driving aid
9 (+) After ignition switch
10 Heater plugs (+)/Ignition coil (+)
11 (+) After ignition switch

Connector 46
1 (+) After ignition switch
2 Glove compartment illumination earth/Accessories plate earth
3 Driving Aid earth/Cruise Control earth
4 Heater controls illumination earth
5 Rear screen demister switch illumination earth/Clock earth
6 Safety notch
7 Not used
8 (+) Before ignition switch
9 Not used
10 Lighting 'On' buzzer (+)
11 Instrument lighting rheostat (+)

Connector 47
1 Sunroof switch illumination (+)
2 Clock illumination (+)
3 Cigar lighter illumination (+)
4 Cruise Control switch illumination (+)
5 Headlight dipped beams relay energizing
6 Safety notch
7 Flasher unit earth/Headlight dipped beams relay earth
8 Direction indicators switch (+)
9 Direction indicators tell-tale
10 Not used
11 Flasher unit (+)

Connector 48
1 LH window switch (+)
2 RH window switch (+)
3 Rear screen demister switch (+)
4 Rear screen demister switch (+)/Rear screen wiper switch (+)
5 Automatic transmission (+)
6 Safety notch
7 Reversing lights switch (+)/Heating-ventilating fan motor c+)
8 Not used
9 Windscreen wiper (+)
10 Sunroof switch (+)
11 Instrument panel (+)

Connector 49
1 LH side and rear lights/Instrument panel lighting
2 Side and rear lights (+)
3 RH side and rear lights
4 Headlight dipped beams
5 Not used
6 Safety notch
7 Cigar lighter (+)
8 Interior lights (+)
9 Windscreen wiper 'Park' (+)
10 Air conditioning (+)
11 Air conditioning (+)

Units
A Flasher unit
B Not used
C Windows relay
D Accessories plate feed
E Relay after ignition-starter switch
F Lighting 'on' buzzer

Example:

Or as shown in the diagram on the right:
Unit 40 (L.H. door pillar switch) with wire 133 - N - 2 - 41 connected to Unit 41.

Wire 133 is seen again connected to Unit 41 (R.H. door pillar switch) but this time it is numbered:
133 - N - 2 - 40.

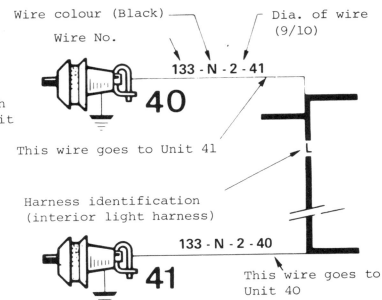

Wire colour (Black)   Dia. of wire (9/10)
Wire No.

133 - N - 2 - 41

40

This wire goes to Unit 41

Harness identification (interior light harness)

133 - N - 2 - 40

41

This wire goes to Unit 40

Fig. 13.50 Wire identification

Each wire is identified by its number followed by a letter(s) indicating its colour, a number giving its diameter and finally a number giving the unit destination

Colour code		Wire diameters	
B	Blue	No	mm
Bc	White	1	0.7
Be	Beige	2	0.9
C	Clear	3	1.0
G	Grey	4	1.2
J	Yellow	5	1.6
M	Maroon	6	2.1
N	Black	7	2.5
Or	Orange	8	3.0
R	Red	9	4.5
S	Pink	10	5.0
V	Green	11	7.0
Vi	Violet	12	8.0

238

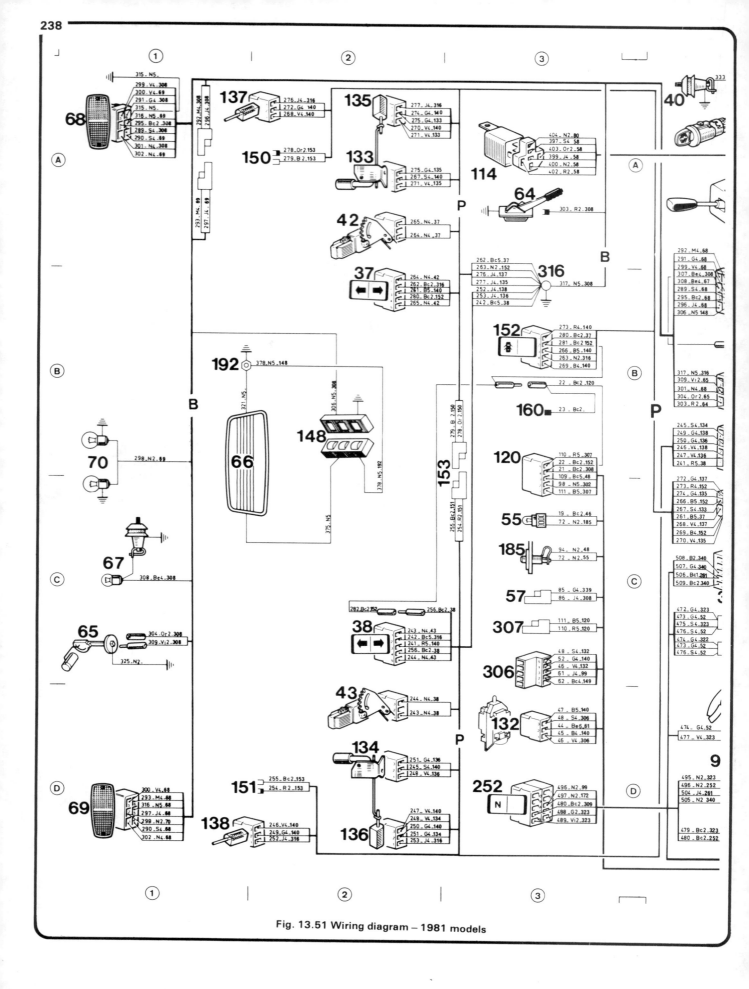

Fig. 13.51 Wiring diagram – 1981 models

Fig. 13.51 Wiring diagram – 1981 models (continued)

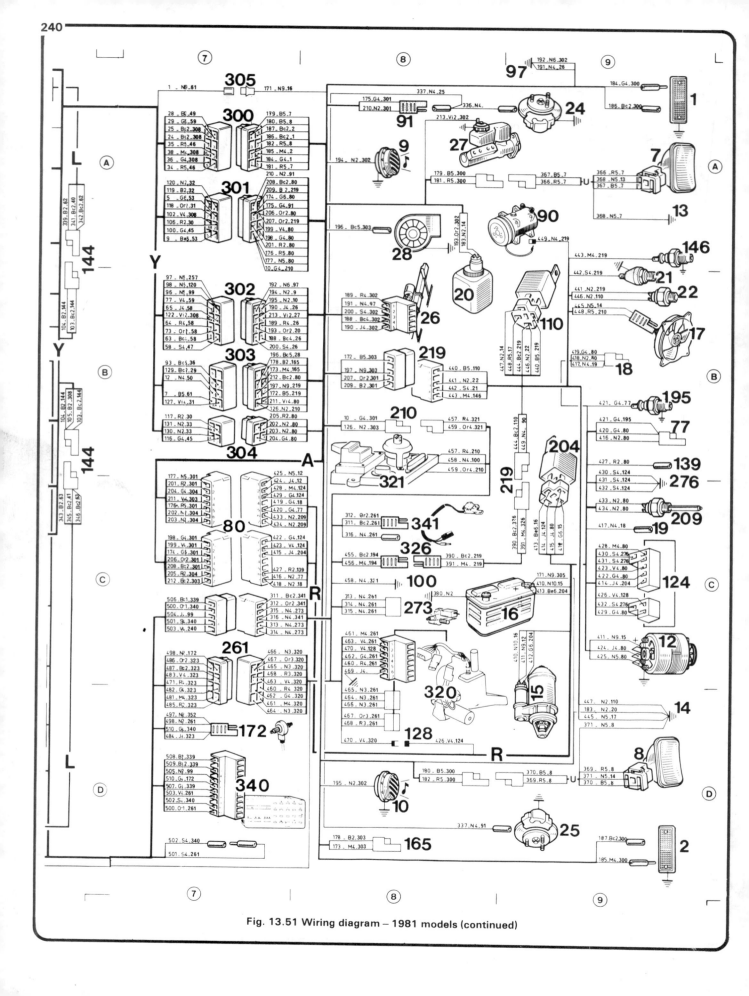

Fig. 13.51 Wiring diagram – 1981 models (continued)

Key to wiring diagram for 1981 models

1	LH sidelight and direction indicator	A-9
2	RH sidelight and direction indicator	D-9
7	LH headlight	A-9
8	RH headlight	D-9
9	LH horn	A-8
10	RH horn	D-8
12	Alternator	C-9
13	LH earth	A-9
14	RH earth	D-9
15	Starter	D-9
16	Battery	C-9
17	Engine cooling fan motor	B-9
18	Ignition coil	B-9
20	Windscreen washer pump	B-8
21	Oil pressure switch	B-9
22	Thermal switch on radiator	B-9
24	LH front brake	A-9
25	RH front brake	D-9
26	Windscreen wiper plate	B-8
27	Master cylinder	A-8
28	Heating-ventilating fan motor	A-8
29	Instrument panel	A-6
30	Connector No 1 - Instrument panel	A-6
31	Connector No 2 - Instrument panel	A-6
32	Connector No 3 - Instrument panel	B-6
33	Connector No 4 - Instrument panel	B-6
34	"Hazard" warning light switch	B-6
35	Rear screen demister switch	C-6
36	Heating-ventilating fan resistance	B-5
37	LH front door window switch	B-2
38	RH front door window switch	C-2
40	LH front door pillar switch	A-4
41	RH front door pillar switch	D-5
42	LH window winder	A-2
43	RH window winder	D-2
44	Accessories plate	C-5
45	Junction block - front harness and accessories plate	C-5
46	Junction block - front harness and accessories plate	C-5
47	Junction block - front harness and accessories plate	D-5
48	Junction block - front harness and accessories plate	C-5
49	Junction block - front harness and accessories plate	C-5
50	Junction block - front harness and accessories plate	D-5
52	Stop-lights switch	D-4
53	Ignition - starter-anti-theft switch	A-4
54	Heater controls illumination	B-5
55	Glove compartment light	C-3
56	Cigar lighter	B-5
57	Feed to car radio	C-3
58	Windscreen wiper-washer switch	A-5 & A-4
59	Lighting switch	B-5
61	Junction - + feed before ignition	D-5
62	LH interior light	A-6
63	RH interior light	D-6
64	Handbrake "On" warning light switch	A-3
65	Fuel gauge tank unit	C-1
66	Rear screen demister	B-1
67	Luggage compartment light	C-1
68	LH rear light assembly	A-1
69	RH rear light assembly	D-1
70	Number plate light	B-1
76	Instrument panel lighting rheostat	B-5
77	Wire junction - diagnostic socket	B-9
80	Junction block - front and engine harnesses	C-7
86	Junction block - time switch relay harness	A-5
90	Wire junction - air conditioning el.mag. clutch	A-9
91	Wire junction - brake pad wear warning light	A-8

97	Bodyshell earth	A-9
99	Dashboard earth	D-4
100	Scuttle panel gusset earth	C-8
103	Feed to accessories plate	C-5
104	Wire junction - steering wheel switch	D-6
106	Rear foglight switch	C-6
110	Engine cooling fan motor relay	B-9
114	Windscreen wiper time switch	A-3
120	Sunroof switch	D-3
138	Kick-down switch	D-8
132	Inertia switch	D-3
133	LH front door lock switch	A-2
134	RH front door lock switch	D-2
135	LH front door el.mag. switch	A-2
136	RH front door el.mag. switch	D-2
137	LH rear door el.mag. switch	A-1
138	RH rear door el.mag. switch	D-1
139	Automatic transmission oil temperature switch	B-9
140	Junction block - el.mag. lock harness	B-4
146	Thermal switch	A-9
148	Tailgate fixed contact	B-2
149	Headlight switch illumination	C-5
150	LH front door loudspeaker	A-2
151	RH front door loudspeaker	D-1
152	El.mag. door locks switch	B-3
153	Car radio loudspeaker wires	B-2
158	Auto-transmission selector illumination	D-5
160	Rear cigar lighter	B-3
165	Wire junction - fuel injection harness	D-8
172	Impulse generator	D-7
185	Glove compartment switch	C-3
192	Tailgate earth	B-1
194	Junction block - engine cooling fan motor	D-5
195	Idle cut-out	B-9
204	Starter relay	B-9
209	Engine oil level indicator sensor	C-9
210	Junction block - engine front harness to integral electronic ignition harness	B-8
219	Junction block - engine cooling fan feed relay	B-8
252	Normalur "Cruise" Control switch	D-3
257	Cool air fan motor	D-5
261	Wire junction - rpm control	C-7
273	Flowmeter	C-8
300	Junction block No 1 - dashboard and engine front harnesses	A-7
301	Junction block No 2 - dashboard and engine front harnesses	A-7
302	Junction block No 3 - dashboard and engine front harnesses	B-7
303	Junction block No 4 - dashboard and engine front harnesses	B-7
304	Junction block No 5 - dashboard and engine front harnesses	B-7
305	Junction block No 6 - dashboard and engine front harnesses	A-7
306	Remote unlocking control	C-3
307	Wire junction - sunroof motor	C-3
308	Wire junction - dashboard and rear harnesses	B-4
309	Junction plate - sidelights	D-4
316	Console earth	B-3
320	Normalur servo motor	D-8
321	Junction - electronic ignition module	C-8
322	Clutch pedal switch	D-4
323	Normalur electronic box	C-6
326	Junction - Normalur with air conditioning	C-8
336	Connector No 5 - instrument panel	B-6
339	Junction with driving aid harness	C-4
340	Driving aid control box	D-7
341	Temperature sensor	C-8

Letter-number reference relates to unit identification grid

Wiring harness identification

A	Engine front
B	Rear
L	Interior lights - door pillar switches
P	Electro-magnetic door locks
R	Engine
U	Headlights
Y	Dashboard

See Fig. 13.50 for colour code

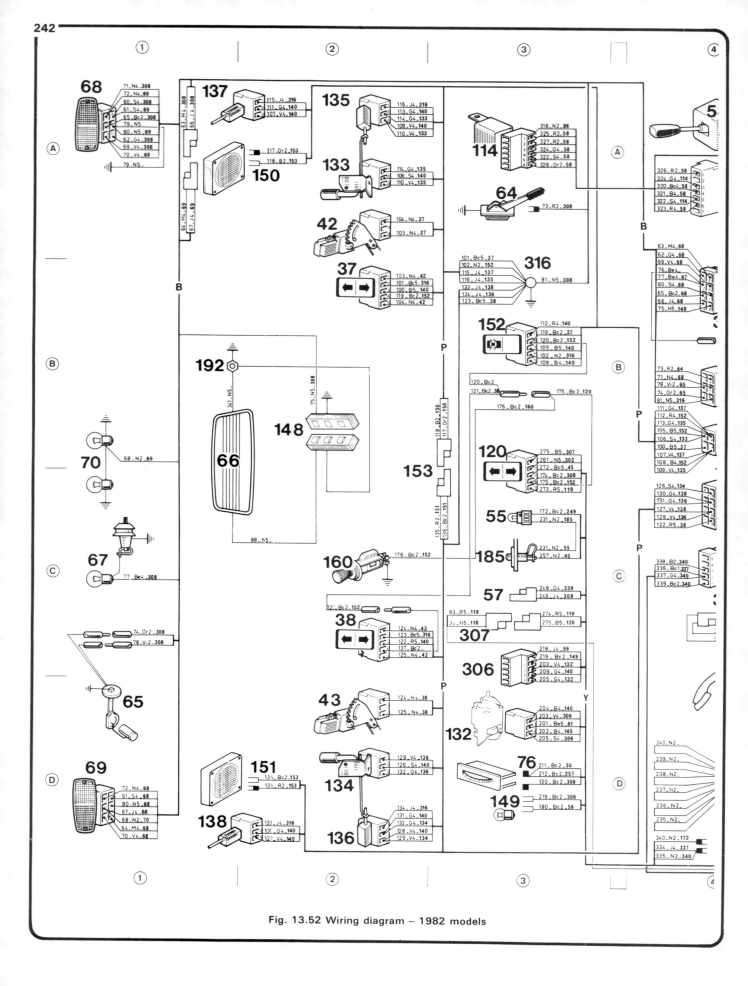

242

Fig. 13.52 Wiring diagram – 1982 models

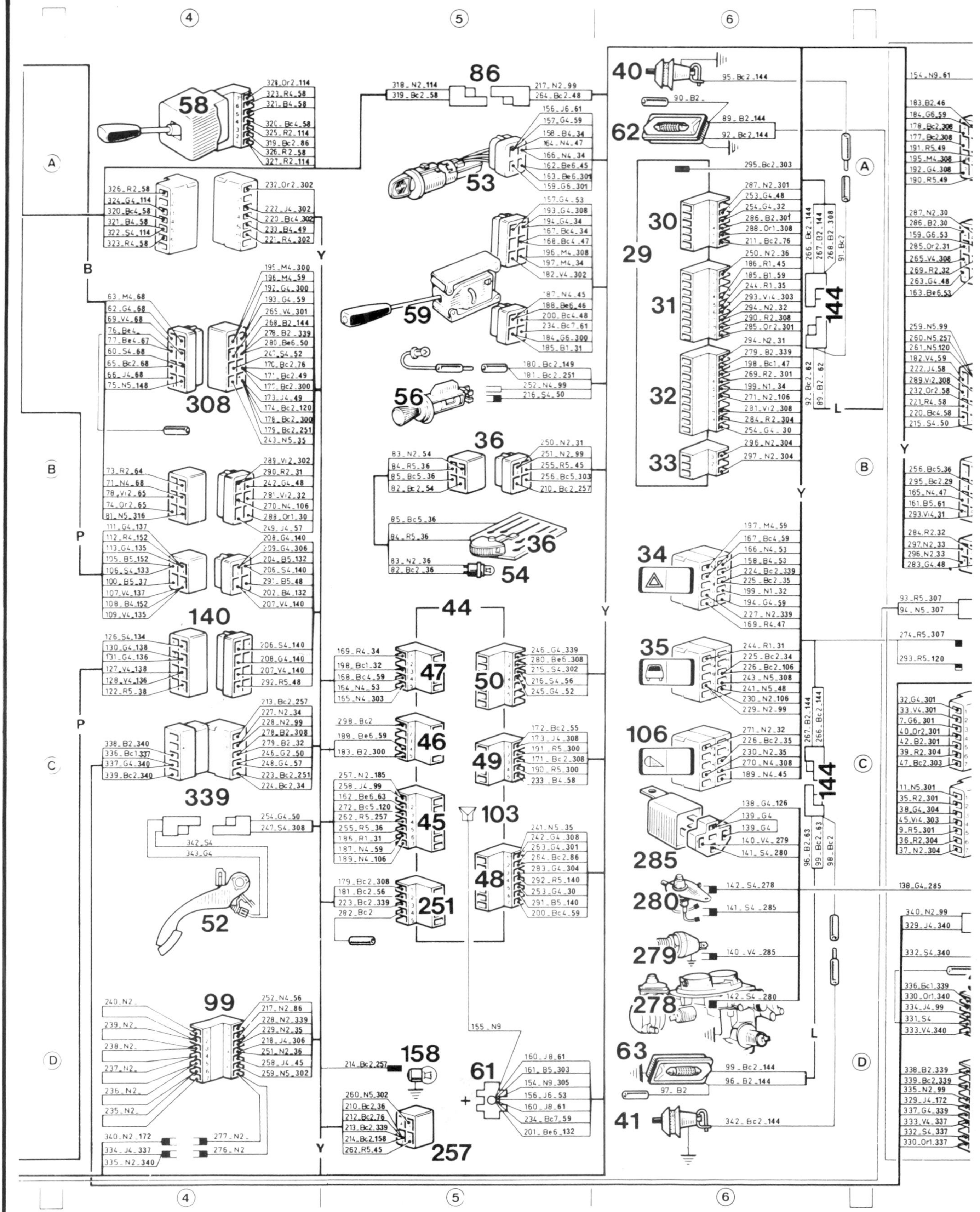

Fig. 13.52 Wiring diagram – 1982 models (continued)

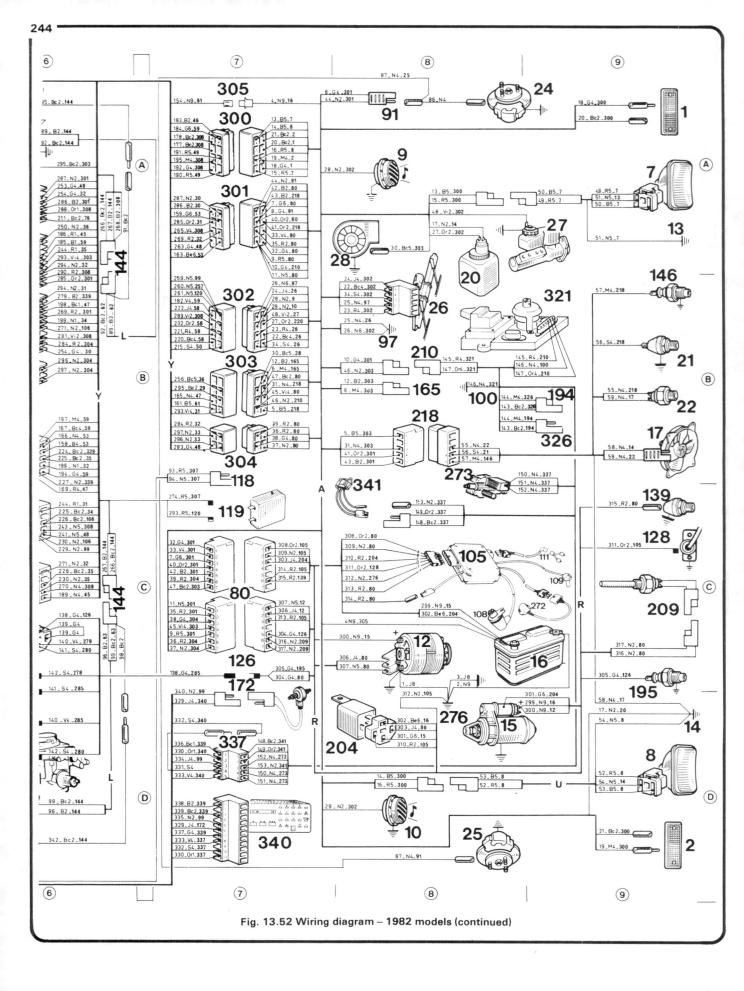

Fig. 13.52 Wiring diagram – 1982 models (continued)

Key to wiring diagram for 1982 models

1	LH sidelight and direction indicator	A9
2	RH sidelight and direction indicator	D9
7	LH headlight	A9
8	RH headlight	D9
9	LH horn	A8
10	RH horn	D8
12	Alternator	C8
13	LH earth	A9
14	RH earth	D9
15	Starter	D8
16	Battery	C9
17	Engine cooling fan motor	B9
20	Windscreen washer pump	A8
21	Oil pressure switch	B9
22	Thermal switch on radiator	B9
24	LH front brake	A9
25	RH front brake	D8
26	Windscreen wiper motor	B8
27	Nivocode or ICP (pressure drop indicator)	A9
28	Heating-ventilating fan motor	A8
29	Instrument panel	A6
30	Connector No 1 - instrument panel	A6
31	Connector No 2 - instrument panel	B6
32	Connector No 3 - instrument panel	B6
33	Connector No 4 - instrument panel	B6
34	"Hazard" warning lights switch	B6
35	Rear screen demister switch	C6
36	Heating-ventilating fan motor rheostat or resistance	B5
37	LH window switch	B2
38	RH window switch	C2
40	LH front door pillar switch	A6
41	RH front door pillar switch	D6
42	LH window motor	A2
43	RH window motor	D2
44	Accessories plate or fusebox	C5
45	Junction block - front harness accessories plate	C5
46	Junction block- front harness and "accessories" plate	C5
47	Junction block - front harness and "accessories" plate	C5
48	Junction block - front harness and "accessories" plate	C5
49	Junction block - front harness and "accessories" plate	C5
50	Junction block - front harness and "accessories" plate	C5
52	Stop-lights switch	C4
53	Ignition-starter-anti-theft switch	A5
54	Heater controls illumination	B5
55	Glove compartment illumination	C3
56	Cigar lighter	B5
57	Feed to car radio	C3
58	Windscreen wiper/washer switch	A4
59	Lighting switch	B5
61	Feed terminal before ignition-starter switch	D5
62	LH or front interior light	A6
63	RH interior light	D6
64	Handbrake "On" warning light switch	A3
65	Fuel gauge tank unit	D1
66	Rear screen demister	B2
67	Luggage compartment light	C1
68	LH rear light assembly	A1
69	RH rear light assembly	D1
70	Number plate lights	B1
76	Instrument panel and warning light rheostat	D3
80	Junction block - front and engine harnesses	C7
86	Junction block - windscreen wiper time switch relay	A5
91	Wire junction - brake pad wear warning light	A8
97	Bodyshell earth	B8
99	Dashboard earth	D4
100	Side panel gusset earth	B8
103	Feed to "accessories" plate	C5
105	Automatic transmission computer	C8
106	Rear foglight switch	C6

108	Multi-function switch	C8
109	Speed sensor	C9
111	Solenoid valves 1 and 2	C9
114	Windscreen wiper time switch relay	A3
118	Sunroof motor	C7
119	Sunroof cut-out	C7
120	Sunroof switch	B3
126	Junction block - engine harness and cold start device wiring	C7
128	Kick-down switch	C9
132	Inertia switch	D3
133	LH front door switch	A2
134	RH rear door solenoid	D2
135	LH front door solenoid	A2
136	RH front door solenoid	D2
137	LH rear door solenoid	A1
138	RH rear door solenoid	D1
139	Automatic transmission oil temperature switch	C9
140	Junction block - electro-magnetic lock harness	B4
144	Wire junction - interior light	A6
148	Tailgate or luggage compartment fixed contact	B2
149	Main lighting or headlights switch	D3
150	LH front door loudspeaker	A2
151	RH front door loudspeaker	D2
152	Electro-magnetic locks centre switch	B3
158	Automatic transmission selector illumination	D5
160	Rear cigar lighter	C2
165	Wire junction - fuel injection harness	B8
172	Impulse generator	C7
185	Glove compartment light switch	C3
192	Tailgate earth	B2
194	Connector No 1 - cooled air blower	B9
195	Idling cut-out	D9
204	Starter relay	D8
209	Engine oil level indicator sensor	C9
210	Wire junction - AEI wiring	B8
218	Wire junction - feed to engine cooling fans	B8
251	Junction block - front harness and accessories plate	C5
257	Junction No 2 - cooled air blower	D5
272	Throttle butterfly spindle switch	C9
273	Fuel flowmeter	C8
276	Engine earth	D8
278	Carburettor	D6
279	Oil temperature switch 15°C (59°F)	D6
280	Vacuum switch	C6
285	Cold start enrichment relay	C6
300	Connector No 1 - dashboard and front harnesses	A7
301	Connector No 2 - dashboard and front harnesses	A7
302	Connector No 3 - dashboard and front harnesses	B7
303	Connector No 4 - dashboard and front harnesses	B7
304	Connector No 5 - dashboard and front harnesses	B7
305	Connector No 6 - dashboard and front harnesses	A7
306	Remote control door unlocking device	C3
307	Wiring junction - sunroof wiring	C3
308	Junction block - dashboard and rear harnesses	B4
316	Console earth	B3
321	AEI module	B9
326	Junction block - "Normalur" Cruise Control - air conditioning harness	B9
337	Junction block - "Driving Aid" harness - engine compartment to passenger compartment	D7
339	Junction block - "Driving Aid" wiring	C4
340	"Driving Aid" computer	D7
341	Temperature sensor	C8

Letter-number reference relates to unit identification grid

Wiring harness identification

A	Engine front
B	Rear
L	Interior light
P	Door locks
R	Engine
Y	Dashboard

For colour code see Fig. 13.50.

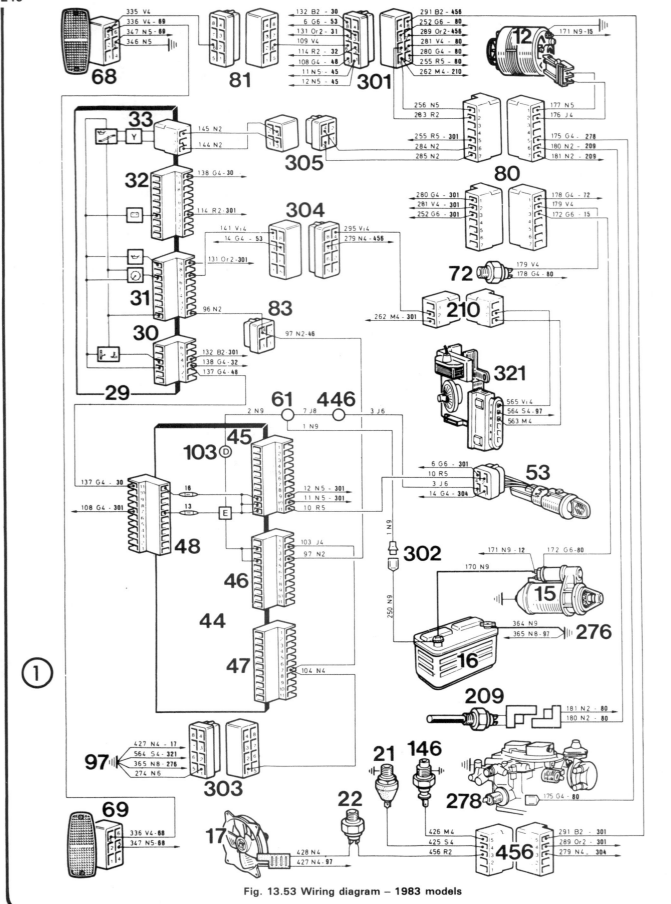

Fig. 13.53 Wiring diagram – 1983 models

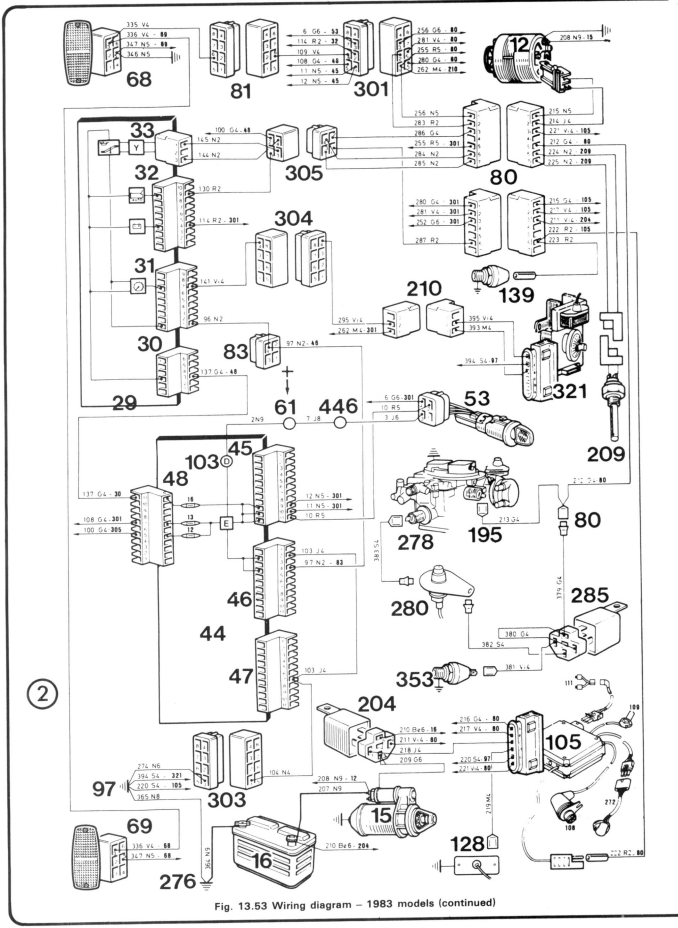

Fig. 13.53 Wiring diagram – 1983 models (continued)

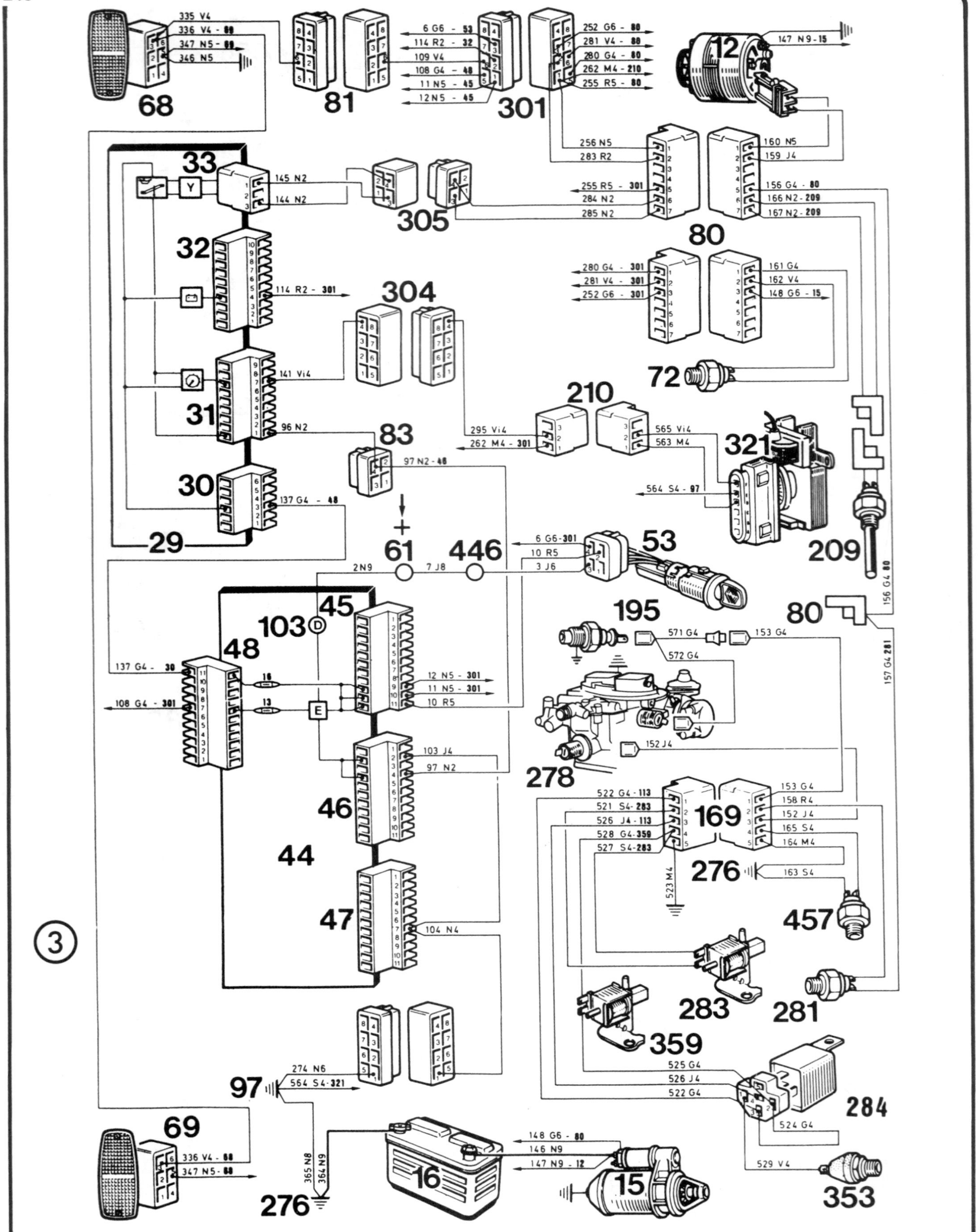

Fig. 13.53 Wiring diagram – 1983 models (continued)

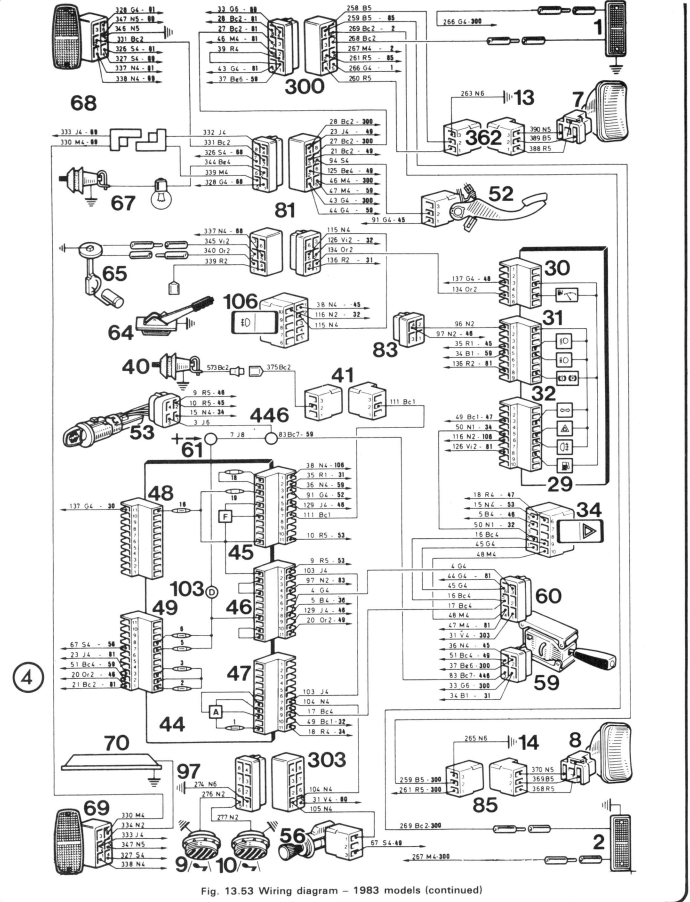

Fig. 13.53 Wiring diagram – 1983 models (continued)

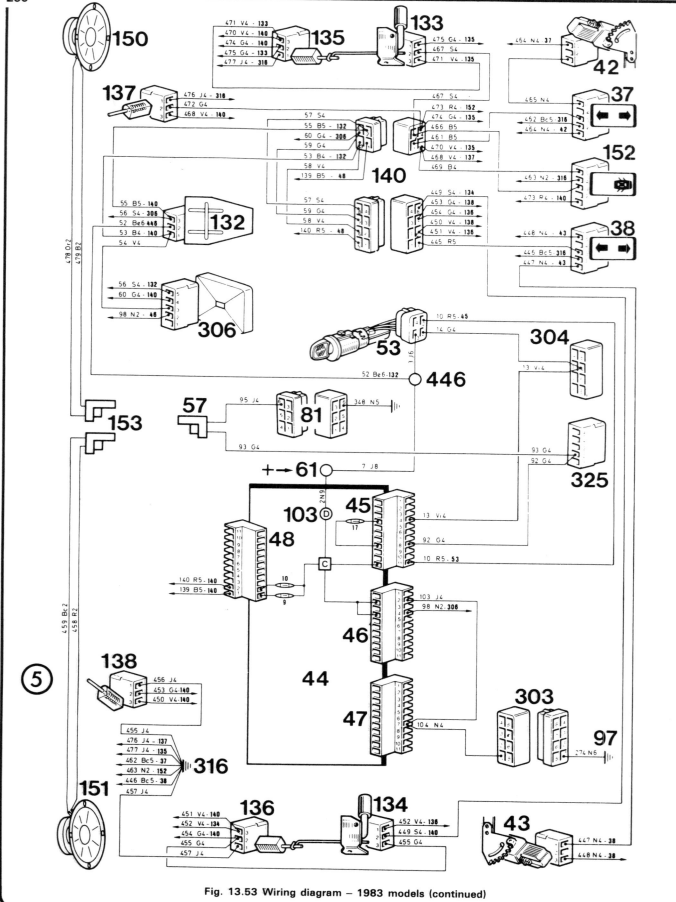

Fig. 13.53 Wiring diagram – 1983 models (continued)

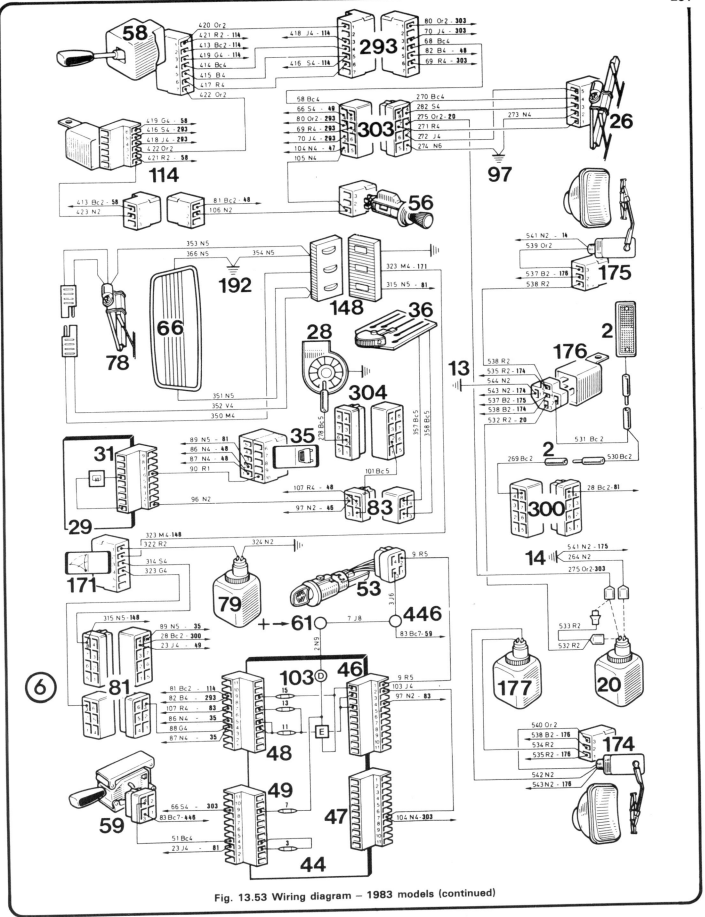

Fig. 13.53 Wiring diagram – 1983 models (continued)

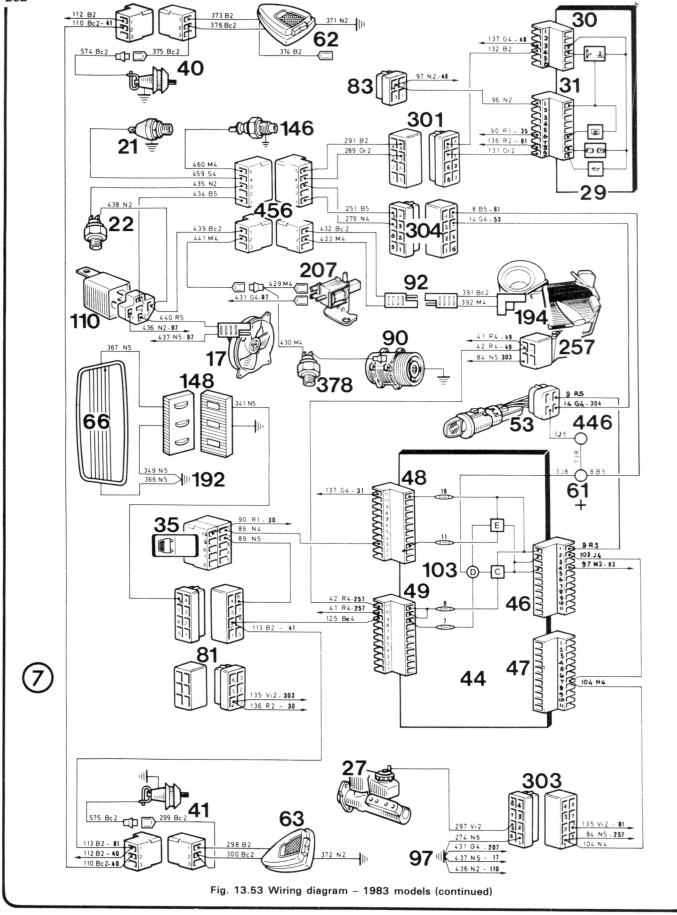

Fig. 13.53 Wiring diagram – 1983 models (continued)

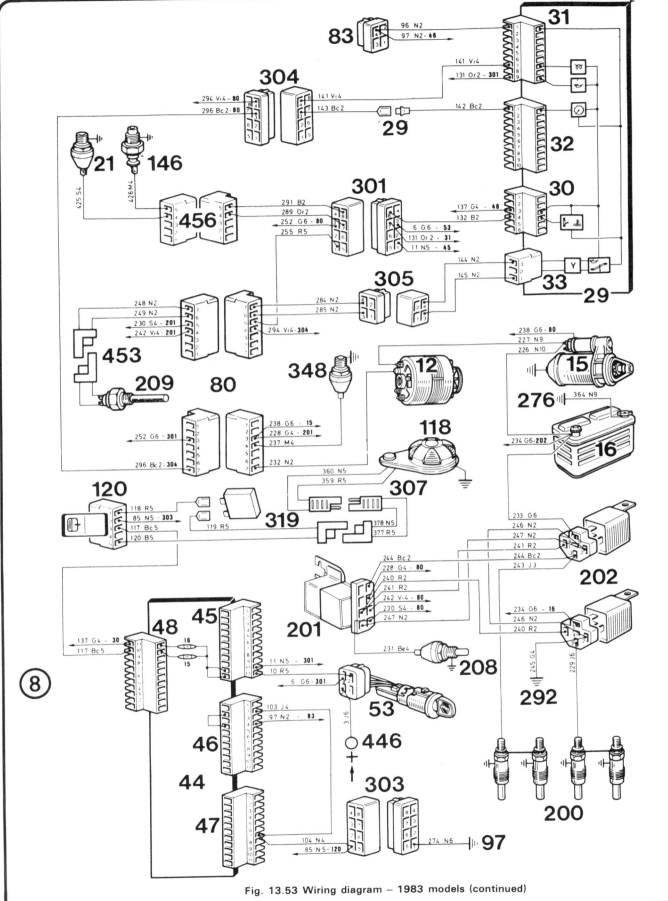

Fig. 13.53 Wiring diagram – 1983 models (continued)

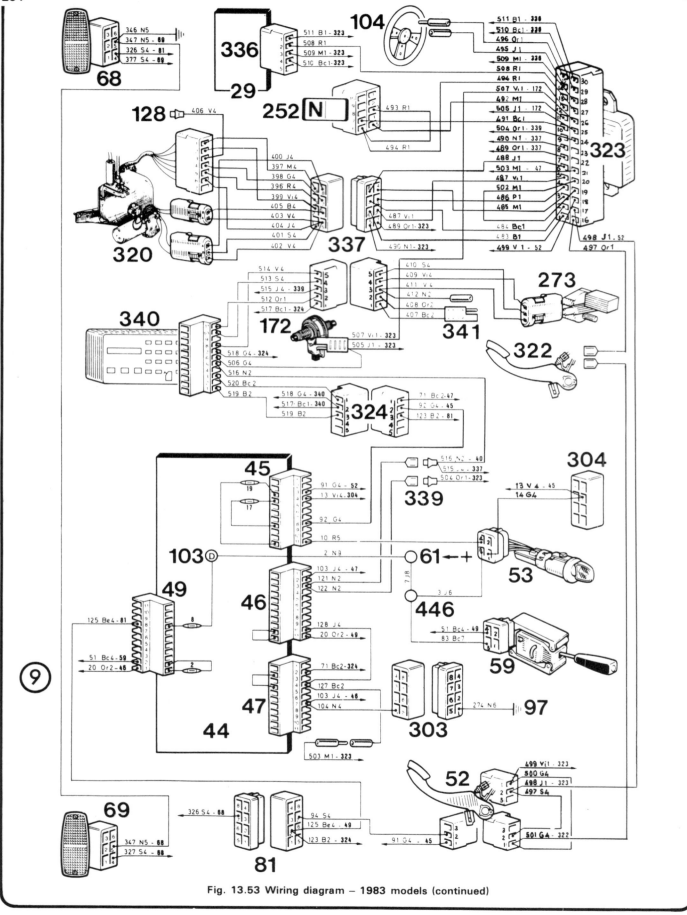

Fig. 13.53 Wiring diagram – 1983 models (continued)

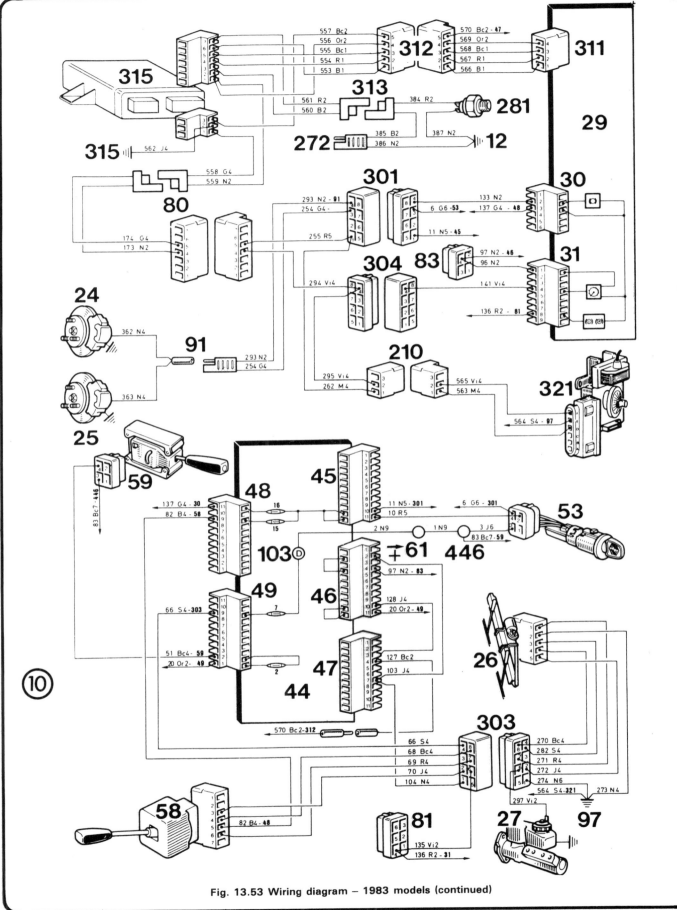

Fig. 13.53 Wiring diagram – 1983 models (continued)

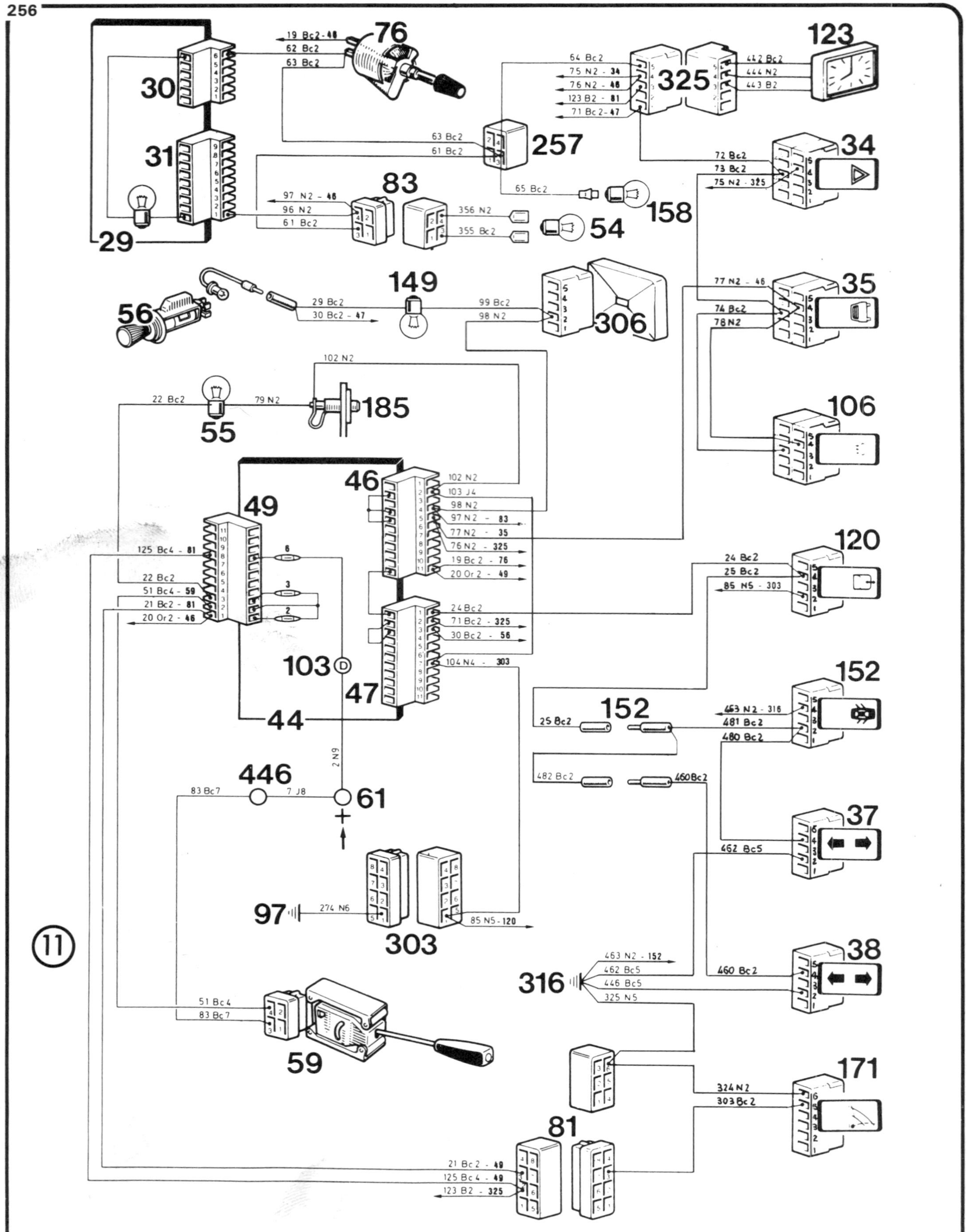

30

76
19 Bc2 - 48
62 Bc2
63 Bc2

64 Bc2
75 N2 - 34
76 N2 - 48
123 B2 - 81
71 Bc2 - 47
325

442 Bc2
444 N2
443 B2
123

31

63 Bc2
61 Bc2
257

72 Bc2
73 Bc2
75 N2 - 325
34

65 Bc2

97 N2 - 48
96 N2
61 Bc2
83

356 N2
355 Bc2
158

54

29

77 N2 - 48
74 Bc2
78 N2
35

56

29 Bc2
30 Bc2 - 47
149

99 Bc2
98 N2
306

106

102 N2

22 Bc2
79 N2
55
185

46
102 N2
103 J4
98 N2
97 N2 - 83
77 N2 - 35
76 N2 - 325
19 Bc2 - 76
20 Or2 - 49

49
125 Bc4 - 81
22 Bc2
51 Bc4 - 59
21 Bc2 - 81
20 Or2 - 46

6
3
2

24 Bc2
25 Bc2
85 N5 - 303
120

24 Bc2
71 Bc2 - 325
30 Bc2 - 56
104 N4 - 303
47

103 Ⓓ

44

2 N9

152
25 Bc2

463 N2 - 318
481 Bc2
480 Bc2
152

482 Bc2
460 Bc2

446
83 Bc7
7 J8
61

462 Bc5
37

97 ꓲ
274 N6
303
85 N5 - 120

463 N2 - 152
462 Bc5
446 Bc5
325 N5
316
460 Bc2
38

59
51 Bc4
83 Bc7

81

324 N2
303 Bc2
171

21 Bc2 - 49
125 Bc4 - 49
123 B2 - 325

⑪

Fig. 13.53 Wiring diagram – 1983 models (continued)

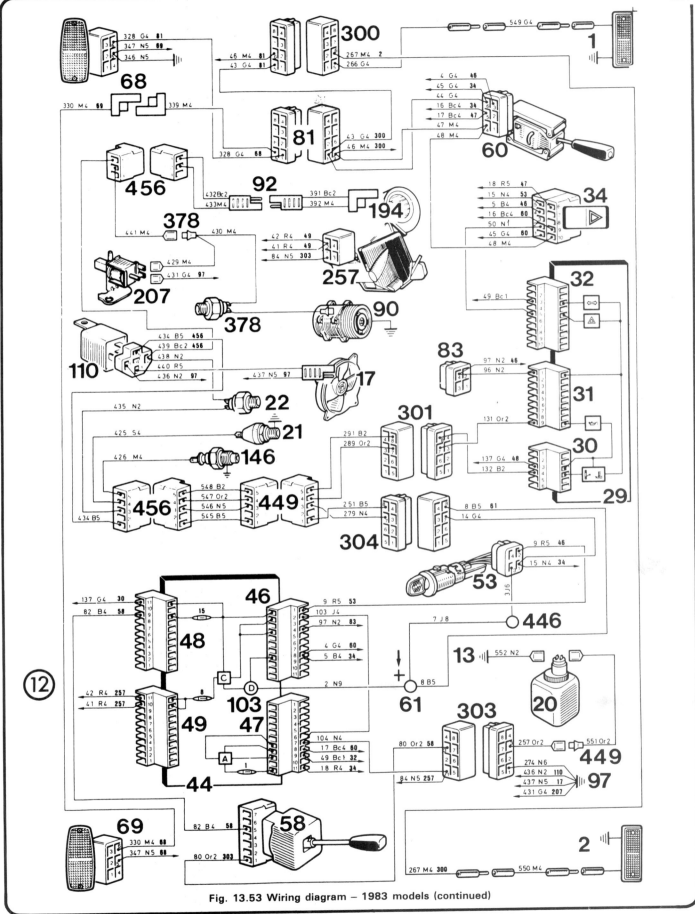

Fig. 13.53 Wiring diagram – 1983 models (continued)

Key to wiring diagrams for 1983 models

Depending on the function required the wiring diagram number is given below

	All models	LHD	RHD	Auto trans	Manual trans
Air conditioning	–	7	12	–	–
Anti-pollution	–	–	–	–	–
Automatic transmission	–	–	–	2	–
Brake pad wear warning light	10	–	–	–	–
Charging circuit	7	–	–	2	1
Cigar lighter	4	–	–	–	–
Clock	11	–	–	–	–
Cold start enrichment device	–	–	–	2	1
Coolant temperature switch	–	1	12	–	–
Cooling fan motor	1	–	–	–	–
Direction indicators	–	4	12	–	–
Door locking	5	–	–	–	–
Driving Aid	9	–	–	–	–
Econometer	10	–	–	–	–
Fuel gauge	7	–	–	–	–
Handbrake	7	–	–	–	–
Headlight dipped beams	4	–	–	–	–
Headlight main beams	4	–	–	–	–
Headlight wipers/washers	6	–	–	–	–
Heating/ventilating	6	–	–	–	–
Horn	4	–	–	–	–
Identification plates illumination	12	–	–	–	–
Idle cut-out	–	–	–	2	1
Ignition	–	–	–	2	1
Interior lights	7	–	–	–	–
Luggage compartment light	7	–	–	–	–
Nivocode	10	–	–	–	–
Normalur Cruis Control	9	–	–	–	–
Oil filter pressure switch	8	–	–	–	–
Oil level indicator	–	–	–	2	7
Oil pressure switch	–	1	12	–	–
Radio feed	5	–	–	–	–
Rear foglight	4	–	–	–	–
Rear screen	7	–	–	–	–
Rear screen wiper/washer +/demister	6	–	–	–	–
Rev. counter	–	–	–	4	5
Reversing lights	–	–	–	2	1
Selector lever illumination	–	–	–	–	–
Sidelights	4	–	–	–	–
Speakers	1	–	–	–	–
Starter	–	–	–	2	1
Stop-lights	4	–	–	–	–
Sunroof	8	–	–	–	–
Switches and identification plate illumination	11	–	–	–	–
Window winders	5	–	–	–	–
Windscreen washer	–	3	10	–	–
Windscreen washer/headlight washers pump	3	–	–	–	–
Windscreen wiper/washer	10	–	–	–	–
Windscreen wiper/washer with timer	6	–	–	–	–

Key to wiring diagrams for 1983 models (continued)

1	LH sidelight and/or direction indicator
2	RH sidelight and/or direction indicator
7	LH headlight
8	RH headlight
9	LH horn
10	RH horn
12	Alternator
13	LH earth
14	RH earth
15	Starter
16	Battery
17	Engine cooling fan motor
20	Windscreen washer pump
21	Oil pressure switch
22	Thermal switch on radiator
24	LH front brake
25	RH front brake
26	Windscreen wiper motor
27	Nivocode or ICP (pressure drop indicator)
28	Heating-ventilating fan motor
29	Instrument panel
30	Connector No 1 – instrument panel
31	Connector No 2 – instrument panel
32	Connector No 3 – Instrument panel
33	Connector No 4 – instrument panel
34	"Hazard" warning lights switch
35	Rear screen demister switch
36	Heating-ventilating fan motor rheostat or resistance
37	LH window switch
38	RH window switch
40	LH front door pillar switch
41	RH front door pillar switch
42	LH window motor
43	RH window motor
44	Accessories plate or fusebox
45	Junction block – front harness – accessories plate
46	Junction block – front harness – accessories plate
47	Junction block – front harness – accessories plate
48	Junction block – front harness – accessories plate
49	Junction block – front harness – accessories plate
52	Stop-lights switch
53	Ignition-starter-anti-theft switch
54	Heater controls illumination
55	Glove compartment light
56	Cigar lighter
57	Feed to car radio
58	Windscreen wiper/washer switch
59	Lighting and direction indicators switch
60	Direction indicator switch or connector
61	Feed terminal before ignition-starter switch
62	LH or front centre interior light
63	RH interior light
64	Handbrake 'On' warning light switch
65	Fuel gauge tank unit
66	Rear screen demister
67	Luggage compartment light
68	LH rear light assembly
69	RH rear light assembly
70	Number plate lights
71	Choke "On" warning light
72	Reversing lights switch
76	Instrument panel and warning lights rheostat
78	Rear screen wiper motor
79	Rear screen washer pump
80	Junction block – engine harness
81	Junction block – front and rear harnesses
83	Junction block – front and heater harnesses
85	Junction block – RH headlight harness
90	Air conditioning compressor
92	Wire junction – air conditioning harness (engine end)
97	Bodyshell earth
104	Wire junction – steering wheel tracks
105	Automatic transmission computer
106	Rear foglight switch
108	Multi-function switch
109	Speed sensor
110	Engine cooling fan motor relay
111	Solenoid valves 1 and 2
114	Windscreen wiper timer relay
118	Sunroof motor
120	Sunroof switch
123	Clock
128	Kick-down switch
132	Inertia switch

133	LH front door lock switch
134	RH front door lock switch
135	LH front door solenoid
136	RH front door solenoid
137	LH rear door solenoid
138	RH rear door solenoid
139	Automatic transmission oil temperature switch
140	Junction block – electro-magnetic locks harness
146	Temperature or thermal switch
148	Tailgate or luggage compartment fixed contact
149	Headlight beam adjuster illumination
150	LH front door speaker
151	RH front door speaker
152	Electro-magnetic locks central switch
152	Radio speaker wires
158	Automatic transmission selector illumination
169	Junction – solenoid valves harness
171	Rear screen wiper/washer switch
172	Impulse generator
175	LH headlight wiper motor
176	Headlight wipers timer relay
177	Headlight washers pump
185	Glove compartment light switch
192	Tailgate earth
194	Junction No 1 – cold air blower
195	Idling cut-out
200	Heater plugs
201	Air pre-heating box
202	Heater plugs relay
204	Starter relay
207	Anti-stall solenoid valve
208	Diesel fuel cut-off solenoid
209	Oil level indicator sensor
210	Junction – AEI harness
252	Normalur switch
257	Junction No 2 – cold air blower
272	Throttle spindle switch
273	Flowmeter
276	Engine earth
278	Carburettor
280	Vacuum switch
281	Gearbox highest ratio switch
283	Advance solenoid valve
284	Cold start relay
285	Cold start enrichment relay
292	Steering column bracket earth
293	Junction – windscreen wiper wiring
300	Connector No 1 – dashboard and front harnesses
301	Connector No 2 – dashboard and front harnesses
302	Connector No 3 – dashboard and front harnesses
303	Connector No 4 – dashboard and front harnesses
304	Connector No 5 – dashboard and front harnesses
305	Connector No 6 – dashboard and front harnesses
306	Remote control door unlocking device – "Plip"
307	Wire junction – sunroof harness
311	Connector – Econometer in instrument panel
312	Junction – Econometer and engine Econometer harnesses
313	Junction block – additional harness for Econometer – engine end
315	Econometer computer
316	Console earth
319	Ignition cut-out relay
321	AEI module
322	Declutching switch
323	Normalur computer
325	Junction – clock wiring
336	Connection No 5 – instrument panel
337	Junction block – "Driving Aid" harness – engine compartment to passenger compartment
339	Junction block – "Driving Aid" wiring
340	Car-borne computer for "Driving Aid"
341	Temperature sensor
348	Clogged oil filter pressure switch
353	Thermal switch 15°C (59°F)
359	Recycling valve solenoid valve
362	Junction – LH headlight harness
378	Air conditioning high pressure sensor
446	Junction terminal No 2 before ignition-starter switch
453	Junction – oil level indicator harness
456	Junction – engine cooling fan harness
457	Thermal switch – 60°C (140°F)

Letter Y corresponds to the engine oil level indicator electronic box

For colour code see Fig. 13.50

10 Suspension and steering

Steering box removal and fitting
1   It should be noted that from 1979, the steering box securing bolts were changed from 8 mm to 10 mm shank diameter. On no account fit a steering box with 10 mm holes using the old 8 mm bolts.

2   When renewing the box, it is possible to order bolts with a 10 mm diameter shank and 8 mm threads so that a new box can be fitted to an older body unit.
3   Renault supply a fixing kit formed of special studs, nuts and shouldered washers, so that an older steering box can be fitted to a new body mounting.

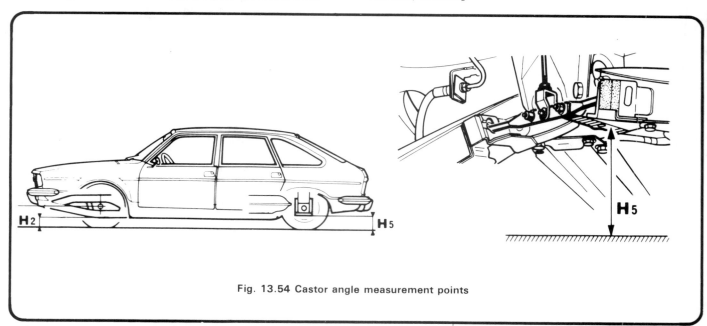

Fig. 13.54 Castor angle measurement points

General repair procedures

Whenever servicing, repair or overhaul work is carried out on the car or its components, it is necessary to observe the following procedures and instructions. This will assist in carrying out the operation efficiently and to a professional standard of workmanship.

Joint mating faces and gaskets

Where a gasket is used between the mating faces of two components, ensure that it is renewed on reassembly, and fit it dry unless otherwise stated in the repair procedure. Make sure that the mating faces are clean and dry with all traces of old gasket removed. When cleaning a joint face, use a tool which is not likely to score or damage the face, and remove any burrs or nicks with an oilstone or fine file.

Make sure that tapped holes are cleaned with a pipe cleaner, and keep them free of jointing compound if this is being used unless specifically instructed otherwise.

Ensure that all orifices, channels or pipes are clear and blow through them, preferably using compressed air.

Oil seals

Whenever an oil seal is removed from its working location, either individually or as part of an assembly, it should be renewed.

The very fine sealing lip of the seal is easily damaged and will not seal if the surface it contacts is not completely clean and free from scratches, nicks or grooves. If the original sealing surface of the component cannot be restored, the component should be renewed.

Protect the lips of the seal from any surface which may damage them in the course of fitting. Use tape or a conical sleeve where possible. Lubricate the seal lips with oil before fitting and, on dual lipped seals, fill the space between the lips with grease.

Unless otherwise stated, oil seals must be fitted with their sealing lips toward the lubricant to be sealed.

Use a tubular drift or block of wood of the appropriate size to install the seal and, if the seal housing is shouldered, drive the seal down to the shoulder. If the seal housing is unshouldered, the seal should be fitted with its face flush with the housing top face.

Screw threads and fastenings

Always ensure that a blind tapped hole is completely free from oil, grease, water or other fluid before installing the bolt or stud. Failure to do this could cause the housing to crack due to the hydraulic action of the bolt or stud as it is screwed in.

When tightening a castellated nut to accept a split pin, tighten the nut to the specified torque, where applicable, and then tighten further to the next split pin hole. Never slacken the nut to align a split pin hole unless stated in the repair procedure.

When checking or retightening a nut or bolt to a specified torque setting, slacken the nut or bolt by a quarter of a turn, and then retighten to the specified setting.

Locknuts, locktabs and washers

Any fastening which will rotate against a component or housing in the course of tightening should always have a washer between it and the relevant component or housing.

Spring or split washers should always be renewed when they are used to lock a critical component such as a big-end bearing retaining nut or bolt.

Locktabs which are folded over to retain a nut or bolt should always be renewed.

Self-locking nuts can be reused in non-critical areas, providing resistance can be felt when the locking portion passes over the bolt or stud thread.

Split pins must always be replaced with new ones of the correct size for the hole.

Special tools

Some repair procedures in this manual entail the use of special tools such as a press, two or three-legged pullers, spring compressors etc. Wherever possible, suitable readily available alternatives to the manufacturer's special tools are described, and are shown in use. In some instances, where no alternative is possible, it has been necessary to resort to the use of a manufacturer's tool and this has been done for reasons of safety as well as the efficient completion of the repair operation. Unless you are highly skilled and have a thorough understanding of the procedure described, never attempt to bypass the use of any special tool when the procedure described specifies its use. Not only is there a very great risk of personal injury, but expensive damage could be caused to the components involved.

Fault diagnosis

Introduction

The vehicle owner who does his or her own maintenance according to the recommended schedules should not have to use this section of the manual very often. Modern component reliability is such that, provided those items subject to wear or deterioration are inspected or renewed at the specified intervals, sudden failure is comparatively rare. Faults do not usually just happen as a result of sudden failure, but develop over a period of time. Major mechanical failures in particular are usually preceded by characteristic symptoms over hundreds or even thousands of miles. Those components which do occasionally fail without warning are often small and easily carried in the vehicle.

With any fault finding, the first step is to decide where to begin investigations. Sometimes this is obvious, but on other occasions a little detective work will be necessary. The owner who makes half a dozen haphazard adjustments or replacements may be successful in curing a fault (or its symptoms), but he will be none the wiser if the fault recurs and he may well have spent more time and money than was necessary. A calm and logical approach will be found to be more satisfactory in the long run. Always take into account any warning signs or abnormalities that may have been noticed in the period preceding the fault – power loss, high or low gauge readings, unusual noises or smells, etc – and remember that failure of components such as fuses or spark plugs may only be pointers to some underlying fault.

The pages which follow here are intended to help in cases of failure to start or breakdown on the road. There is also a Fault Diagnosis Section at the end of each Chapter which should be consulted if the preliminary checks prove unfruitful. Whatever the fault, certain basic principles apply. These are as follows:

Verify the fault. This is simply a matter of being sure that you know what the symptoms are before starting work. This is particularly important if you are investigating a fault for someone else who may not have described it very accurately.

Don't overlook the obvious. For example, if the vehicle won't start, is there petrol in the tank? (Don't take anyone else's word on this particular point, and don't trust the fuel gauge either!) If an electrical fault is indicated, look for loose or broken wires before digging out the test gear.

Cure the disease, not the symptom. Substituting a flat battery with a fully charged one will get you off the hard shoulder, but if the underlying cause is not attended to, the new battery will go the same way. Similarly, changing oil-fouled spark plugs for a new set will get you moving again, but remember that the reason for the fouling (if it wasn't simply an incorrect grade of plug) will have to be established and corrected.

Don't take anything for granted. Particularly, don't forget that a 'new' component may itself be defective (especially if it's been rattling round in the boot for months), and don't leave components out of a fault diagnosis sequence just because they are new or recently fitted. When you do finally diagnose a difficult fault, you'll probably realise that all the evidence was there from the start.

Electrical faults

Electrical faults can be more puzzling than straightforward mechanical failures, but they are no less susceptible to logical analysis if the basic principles of operation are understood. Vehicle electrical wiring exists in extremely unfavourable conditions – heat, vibration and chemical attack – and the first things to look for are loose or corroded connections and broken or chafed wires, especially where the wires pass through holes in the bodywork or are subject to vibration.

All metal-bodied vehicles in current production have one pole of the battery 'earthed', ie connected to the vehicle bodywork, and in nearly all modern vehicles it is the negative (–) terminal. The various electrical components – motors, bulb holders etc – are also connected to earth, either by means of a lead or directly by their mountings. Electric current flows through the component and then back to the battery via the bodywork. If the component mounting is loose or corroded, or if a good path back to the battery is not available, the circuit will be incomplete and malfunction will result. The engine and/or gearbox are also earthed by means of flexible metal straps to the body or subframe; if these straps are loose or missing, starter motor, generator and ignition trouble may result.

Assuming the earth return to be satisfactory, electrical faults will be due either to component malfunction or to defects in the current supply. Individual components are dealt with in Chapter 10. If supply wires are broken or cracked internally this results in an open-circuit,

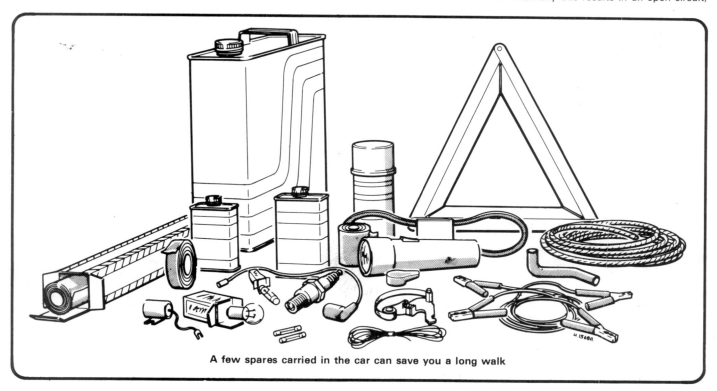

A few spares carried in the car can save you a long walk

and the easiest way to check for this is to bypass the suspect wire temporarily with a length of wire having a crocodile clip or suitable connector at each end. Alternatively, a 12V test lamp can be used to verify the presence of supply voltage at various points along the wire and the break can be thus isolated.

If a bare portion of a live wire touches the bodywork or other earthed metal part, the electricity will take the low-resistance path thus formed back to the battery: this is known as a short-circuit. Hopefully a short-circuit will blow a fuse, but otherwise it may cause burning of the insulation (and possibly further short-circuits) or even a fire. This is why it is inadvisable to bypass persistently blowing fuses with silver foil or wire.

Spares and tool kit

Most vehicles are supplied only with sufficient tools for wheel changing; the *Maintenance and minor repair* tool kit detailed in *Tools and working facilities,* with the addition of a hammer, is probably sufficient for those repairs that most motorists would consider attempting at the roadside. In addition a few items which can be fitted without too much trouble in the event of a breakdown should be carried. Experience and available space will modify the list below, but the following may save having to call on professional assistance:

> *Spark plugs, clean and correctly gapped*
> *HT lead and plug cap — long enough to reach the plug furthest from the distributor*
> *Distributor rotor, condenser and contact breaker points*
> *Drivebelt(s) — emergency type may suffice*
> *Spare fuses*
> *Set of principal light bulbs*
> *Tin of radiator sealer and hose bandage*
> *Exhaust bandage*
> *Roll of insulating tape*
> *Length of soft iron wire*
> *Length of electrical flex*
> *Torch or inspection lamp (can double as test lamp)*
> *Battery jump leads*
> *Tow-rope*
> *Ignition waterproofing aerosol*
> *Litre of engine oil*
> *Sealed can of hydraulic fluid*
> *Emergency windscreen*
> *Worm drive clips*
> *Tube of filler paste*

If spare fuel is carried, a can designed for the purpose should be used to minimise risks of leakage and collision damage. A first aid kit and a warning triangle, whilst not at present compulsory in the UK, are obviously sensible items to carry in addition to the above.

When touring abroad it may be advisable to carry additional spares which, even if you cannot fit them yourself, could save having to wait while parts are obtained. The items below may be worth considering:

> *Clutch and throttle cables*
> *Cylinder head gasket*
> *Alternator brushes*
> *Fuel pump repair kit*
> *Tyre valve core*

One of the motoring organisations will be able to advise on availability of fuel etc in foreign countries.

Engine will not start

Engine fails to turn when starter operated

Flat battery (recharge, use jump leads, or push start)
Battery terminals loose or corroded
Battery earth to body defective
Engine earth strap loose or broken
Starter motor (or solenoid) wiring loose or broken
Automatic transmission selector in wrong position, or inhibitor switch faulty
Ignition/starter switch faulty
Major mechanical failure (seizure)
Starter or solenoid internal fault (see Chapter 10)

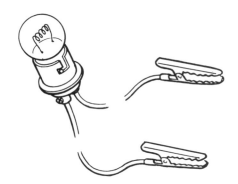

A simple test lamp is useful for tracing electrical faults

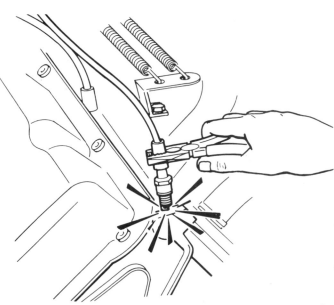

Crank engine and check for spark. Use an insulated tool, especially where electronic ignition is fitted

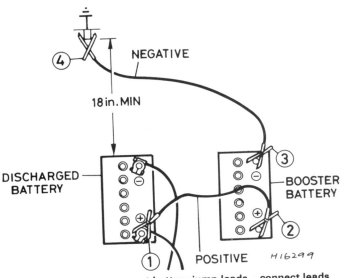

The correct way to connect battery jump leads — connect leads in the order shown

Starter motor turns engine slowly
Partially discharged battery (recharge, use jump leads, or push start)
Battery terminals loose or corroded
Battery earth to body defective
Engine earth strap loose
Starter motor (or solenoid) wiring loose
Starter motor internal fault (see Chapter 10)

Starter motor spins without turning engine
Flat battery
Starter motor pinion sticking on sleeve
Flywheel gear teeth damaged or worn
Starter motor mounting bolts loose

Engine turns normally but fails to start
Damp or dirty HT leads and distributor cap (crank engine and check for spark)
Dirty or incorrectly gapped distributor points (if applicable)
No fuel in tank (check for delivery at carburettor)
Excessive choke (hot engine) or insufficient choke (cold engine)
Fouled or incorrectly gapped spark plugs (remove, clean and regap)
Other ignition system fault (see Chapter 4)
Other fuel system fault (see Chapter 3)
Poor compression (see Chapter 1)
Major mechanical failure (eg camshaft drive)

Engine fires but will not run
Insufficient choke (cold engine)
Air leaks at carburettor or inlet manifold
Fuel starvation (see Chapter 3)
Ballast resistor defective, or other ignition fault (see Chapter 4)

Engine cuts out and will not restart

Engine cuts out suddenly – ignition fault
Loose or disconnected LT wires
Wet HT leads or distributor cap (after traversing water splash)
Coil or condenser failure (check for spark)
Other ignition fault (see Chapter 4)

Engine misfires before cutting out – fuel fault
Fuel tank empty
Fuel pump defective or filter blocked (check for delivery)
Fuel tank filler vent blocked (suction will be evident on releasing cap)
Carburettor needle valve sticking
Carburettor jets blocked (fuel contaminated)
Other fuel system fault (see Chapter 3)

Engine cuts out – other causes
Serious overheating
Major mechanical failure (eg camshaft drive)

Engine overheats

Ignition (no-charge) warning light illuminated
Slack or broken drivebelt – retension or renew (Chapter 10)

Ignition warning light not illuminated
Coolant loss due to internal or external leakage (see Chapter 2)
Thermostat defective
Low oil level
Brakes binding
Radiator clogged externally or internally
Electric cooling fan not operating correctly
Engine waterways clogged
Ignition timing incorrect or automatic advance malfunctioning
Mixture too weak

Note: *Do not add cold water to an overheated engine or damage may result*

Low engine oil pressure

Gauge reads low or warning light illuminated with engine running
Oil level low or incorrect grade
Defective gauge or sender unit
Wire to sender unit earthed
Engine overheating
Oil filter clogged or bypass valve defective
Oil pressure relief valve defective
Oil pick-up strainer clogged
Oil pump worn or mountings loose
Worn main or big-end bearings

Note: *Low oil pressure in a high-mileage engine at tickover is not necessarily a cause for concern. Sudden pressure loss at speed is far more significant. In any event, check the gauge or warning light sender before condemning the engine.*

Engine noises

Pre-ignition (pinking) on acceleration
Incorrect grade of fuel
Ignition timing incorrect
Distributor faulty or worn
Worn or maladjusted carburettor
Excessive carbon build-up in engine

Whistling or wheezing noises
Leaking vacuum hose
Leaking carburettor or manifold gasket
Blowing head gasket

Tapping or rattling
Incorrect valve clearances
Worn valve gear
Worn timing chain or belt
Broken piston ring (ticking noise)

Knocking or thumping
Unintentional mechanical contact (eg fan blades)
Worn fanbelt
Peripheral component fault (generator, water pump etc)
Worn big-end bearings (regular heavy knocking, perhaps less under load)
Worn main bearings (rumbling and knocking, perhaps worsening under load)
Piston slap (most noticeable when cold)

Index

Conversion factors

Length (distance)

Inches (in)	X	25.4	= Millimetres (mm)	X 0.0394	= Inches (in)
Feet (ft)	X	0.305	= Metres (m)	X 3.281	= Feet (ft)
Miles	X	1.609	= Kilometres (km)	X 0.621	= Miles

Volume (capacity)

Cubic inches (cu in; in^3)	X	16.387	= Cubic centimetres (cc; cm^3)	X 0.061	= Cubic inches (cu in; in^3)
Imperial pints (Imp pt)	X	0.568	= Litres (l)	X 1.76	= Imperial pints (Imp pt)
Imperial quarts (Imp qt)	X	1.137	= Litres (l)	X 0.88	= Imperial quarts (Imp qt)
Imperial quarts (Imp qt)	X	1.201	= US quarts (US qt)	X 0.833	= Imperial quarts (Imp qt)
US quarts (US qt)	X	0.946	= Litres (l)	X 1.057	= US quarts (US qt)
Imperial gallons (Imp gal)	X	4.546	= Litres (l)	X 0.22	= Imperial gallons (Imp gal)
Imperial gallons (Imp gal)	X	1.201	= US gallons (US gal)	X 0.833	= Imperial gallons (Imp gal)
US gallons (US gal)	X	3.785	= Litres (l)	X 0.264	= US gallons (US gal)

Mass (weight)

Ounces (oz)	X	28.35	= Grams (g)	X 0.035	= Ounces (oz)
Pounds (lb)	X	0.454	= Kilograms (kg)	X 2.205	= Pounds (lb)

Force

Ounces-force (ozf; oz)	X	0.278	= Newtons (N)	X 3.6	= Ounces-force (ozf; oz)
Pounds-force (lbf; lb)	X	4.448	= Newtons (N)	X 0.225	= Pounds-force (lbf; lb)
Newtons (N)	X	0.1	= Kilograms-force (kgf; kg)	X 9.81	= Newtons (N)

Pressure

Pounds-force per square inch (psi; lbf/in^2; lb/in^2)	X	0.070	= Kilograms-force per square centimetre (kgf/cm^2; kg/cm^2)	X 14.223	= Pounds-force per square inch (psi; lbf/in^2; lb/in^2)
Pounds-force per square inch (psi; lbf/in^2; lb/in^2)	X	0.068	= Atmospheres (atm)	X 14.696	= Pounds-force per square inch (psi; lbf/in^2; lb/in^2)
Pounds-force per square inch (psi; lbf/in^2; lb/in^2)	X	0.069	= Bars	X 14.5	= Pounds-force per square inch (psi; lbf/in^2; lb/in^2)
Pounds-force per square inch (psi; lbf/in^2; lb/in^2)	X	6.895	= Kilopascals (kPa)	X 0.145	= Pounds-force per square inch (psi; lbf/in^2; lb/in^2)
Kilopascals (kPa)	X	0.01	= Kilograms-force per square centimetre (kgf/cm^2; kg/cm^2)	X 98.1	= Kilopascals (kPa)

Torque (moment of force)

Pounds-force inches (lbf in; lb in)	X	1.152	= Kilograms-force centimetre (kgf cm; kg cm)	X 0.868	= Pounds-force inches (lbf in; lb in)
Pounds-force inches (lbf in; lb in)	X	0.113	= Newton metres (Nm)	X 8.85	= Pounds-force inches (lbf in; lb in)
Pounds-force inches (lbf in; lb in)	X	0.083	= Pounds-force feet (lbf ft; lb ft)	X 12	= Pounds-force inches (lbf in; lb in)
Pounds-force feet (lbf ft; lb ft)	X	0.138	= Kilograms-force metres (kgf m; kg m)	X 7.233	= Pounds-force feet (lbf ft; lb ft)
Pounds-force feet (lbf ft; lb ft)	X	1.356	= Newton metres (Nm)	X 0.738	= Pounds-force feet (lbf ft; lb ft)
Newton metres (Nm)	X	0.102	= Kilograms-force metres (kgf m; kg m)	X 9.804	= Newton metres (Nm)

Power

Horsepower (hp)	X	745.7	= Watts (W)	X 0.0013	= Horsepower (hp)

Velocity (speed)

Miles per hour (miles/hr; mph)	X	1.609	= Kilometres per hour (km/hr; kph)	X 0.621	= Miles per hour (miles/hr; mph)

Fuel consumption*

Miles per gallon, Imperial (mpg)	X	0.354	= Kilometres per litre (km/l)	X 2.825	= Miles per gallon, Imperial (mpg)
Miles per gallon, US (mpg)	X	0.425	= Kilometres per litre (km/l)	X 2.352	= Miles per gallon, US (mpg)

Temperature

Degrees Fahrenheit = (°C x 1.8) + 32

Degrees Celsius (Degrees Centigrade; °C) = (°F - 32) x 0.56

*It is common practice to convert from miles per gallon (mpg) to litres/100 kilometres (l/100km), where mpg (Imperial) x l/100 km = 282 and mpg (US) x l/100 km = 235

**Printed by
Haynes Publishing Group
Sparkford Yeovil Somerset
England**